Cryptography and Security Services:

Mechanisms and Applications

Manuel Mogollon
University of Dallas, USA

Cybertech Publishing

Hershey • New York

Acquisition Editor:	Kristin Klinger
Senior Managing Editor:	Jennifer Neidig
Managing Editor:	Sara Reed
Development Editor:	Kristin M. Roth
Assistant Development Editor:	Meg Stocking
Editorial Assistant:	Deborah Yahnke
Copy Editor:	Erin Meyer
Typesetter:	Jeff Ash
Cover Design:	Lisa Tosheff
Printed at:	Yurchak Printing Inc.

Published in the United States of America by
    CyberTech Publishing (an imprint of IGI Global)
    701 E. Chocolate Avenue
    Hershey PA 17033
    Tel: 717-533-8845
    Fax: 717-533-8661
    E-mail: cust@igi-pub.com
    Web site: http://www.cybertech-pub.com

and in the United Kingdom by
    CyberTech Publishing (an imprint of IGI Global)
    3 Henrietta Street
    Covent Garden
    London WC2E 8LU
    Tel: 44 20 7240 0856
    Fax: 44 20 7379 0609
    Web site: http://www.eurospanonline.com

Library of Congress Cataloging-in-Publication Data

Mogollon, Manuel.
  Cryptography and security services : mechanisms and applications / Manuel Mogollon.
    p. cm.
  Summary: "This book addresses cryptography from the perspective of security services and mechanisms available to implement them: discussing issues such as e-mail security, public-key architecture, virtual private networks, Web services security, wireless security, and confidentiality and integrity. It provides scholars and practitioners working knowledge of fundamental encryption algorithms and systems supported in information technology and secure communication networks"--Provided by publisher.
  Includes bibliographical references and index.
  ISBN 978-1-59904-837-6 (hardcover) -- ISBN 978-1-59904-839-0 (ebook)
  1. Computers--Access control. 2. Data encryption (Computer science) I. Title.

  QA76.9.A25M663 2007
  005.8--dc22

British Cataloguing in Publication Data
A Cataloguing in Publication record for this book is available from the British Library.

Cryptography and Security Sevices:

Mechanisms and Applications

Table of Contents

Foreword

Having spent most of my adult life working with the design, development, production, and deployment of secure communications equipment and networks used by over 90 countries and many multinationals, it is an honor and pleasure to write this foreword.

It is quite striking that as I draft this piece, TJX Companies, Inc. revealed some 45.6 million credit and debit card numbers were stolen from two of its systems over the better part of two years. This happening in fact is just one in a long series of information compromises—albeit a big one—that could have been mitigated via the application of cryptographic tools, policies, and procedures.

Because we live in a world today where we basically have a ONE to ALL relationship via the interconnectivity of the Internet, the two fundamentals of good security—BORDERS AND TRUST—take on new meaning. This new dynamic in security requires the application of cryptographic tools and practices regarding information, and the access, use, storage, transmission, and destruction of that information over its life cycle. In fact this problem will only grow as: (1) assets move from the physical to the virtual realm (bits and bytes), (2) information grows at a rate of 2+ exabytes a year—a "target rich" environment, and (3) more and more of the world's population becomes "connected."

As most professionals know, comprehensive, understandable, and easy to read treatises on complex, mathematically based subject matter are usually few and far between. So too with cryptography. However, with this volume professor Mogollon not only addresses the historical foundations of cryptographic tools and methods, but delivers a very clear and understandable picture of the breadth and depth of secure communications today. And he does this while providing very clear graphics on how historical and modern approaches and systems work. The clarity of these examples and the understanding they impart is unparalleled in technical literature.

This book is a must read for all professionals as the application of the tools and methods discussed herein are a required "best practice" today. And it will serve as a useful reference for years to come.

Dr. John H. Nugent, CPA, CFE, CISM, FCPA
Director of the Center of Information Assurance, University of Dallas

Preface

Information assurance, the body of knowledge, policies, processes, practices, and tools that provide reasonable assurance that one's information and communications are used only as intended and only by authorized parties, has become a complex discipline. Today, because of Internet interconnectivity, we live in a world where one may reach all. Such interconnectivity and attendant vulnerabilities require that IT managers and end-users have an understanding of the risks and solutions available to better protect their information and operations. This volume was written to address these issues.

When network security is mentioned, the general public is more often aware of security failures than of the technology available for secure communications. Viruses, worms, Trojan horses, denial-of-service attacks, and phishing are well known occurrences. Access controls, authentication, confidentiality, integrity, and non-repudiation, which are measures to safeguard security, are neither well known nor appreciated. However, when these security mechanisms are in place, users can have a degree of confidence that their communications will be sent and received as intended.

The basic principles of secure communications have not changed with technology and communication advances. Today, communications companies are working to provide security services and to implement security mechanisms in email correspondence, virtual private networks, ecommerce, Web services, and wireless products. However, the tremendous increase in the use of technology has made it challenging to keep up with the need for security.

Fortunately, security today is an open research field in which there are thousands of experts looking for weak security implementations. When a weakness is found, for example, in the case of Wi-Fi (Wireless Fidelity Standard—IEEE 802.11a, b, g) in 2004, the crypto community immediately acts and changes are proposed to correct the weakness, which is what happened after this case. By using open standards, it is possible to have security applications reviewed by the world crypto community.

This book started as a collection of lecture notes on cryptography written by the author over many years. It was initially intended as a way to describe the security levels of certain crypto products. This material was later expanded with the addition of other lectures notes written for the Cryptography and Network Security course the author teaches at the University of Dallas in the Graduate School of Management's MBA and Master of Science in Information Assurance programs.

Intended Audience

This book is intended to provide those in the information assurance field with a basic technical reference that provides the language, knowledge, and tools to understand and implement security services, mechanisms, and applications in today's secure communications networks. This book could also be used as a text in a one-semester information assurance course, especially in Master of Business Administration and Master of Science programs.

Readers with backgrounds in telecommunications and information technology will probably be somewhat familiar with certain parts of the material covered in this book. Other readers, for example, those in the Master of Business Administration in Information Assurance program may find that this book has too much technical information for their future needs. In those situations, professors may decide not to emphasize the technical parts of the material and focus on those principles that are essential to information assurance.

The crypto, security services, and security mechanisms topics presented in this book map the training requirements in CNSS 4011, the National Training Standard for Information Systems Security (INFOSEC) Professionals, and CNSS 4012, the National Information Assurance Training Standard for senior systems managers.

Standards and Requests for Change

This book's approach to information assurance is from the point of view of security services, security mechanisms, and the standards that define their implementation. In this way, it is easier for the reader to associate the standard with a certain security service or security mechanism.

The word "standard" implies a set of guidelines for interoperability. Networks would not be able to operate unless they voluntarily adhered to open protocols and procedures defined by some type of standards. When talking about the Internet and IP networks, the word "standard" is associated with Request For Change (RFC), even though not every RFC is a standard. The need for standards applies not only to interconnecting IP networks, but also to the implementation of security services and mechanisms.

RFCs have been created since the days of the ARPANET, and, later on, for the Internet through the Internet Engineering Task Group (IETG). According to the RFC Index on the IETG.org Web page, RFC 001 was published in April 1969. The first RFC related to security was RFC 644, "On the Problem of Signature Authentication for Network Mail," written by Bob Thomas, BBN-TENEX, and published in July 1974. The network mail message that Bob Thomas was referring to was the ARPANET. It is interesting to note that e-mail security has been a major concern since the days of the ARPANET; however, there are still very few companies that encipher or authenticate their e-mails.

It is the author's opinion that when security services and mechanisms are reviewed, their related RFCs should be studied. RFCs as standards define how to implement key exchanges, encryption algorithms, integrity, hash and digital signatures, as well as authentication algorithms. Therefore, in this book, those RFCs that are related to information assurance are explained along with security applications. Understanding security-related RFCs provides excellent knowledge, not only about security mechanisms, but also on secure applications such as email security, VPNs, IPsec, TLS, Web services, and wireless security.

Organization of the Book

This book is organized into three sections. In the first two sections, crypto systems, security mechanisms, and security services are discussed and reviewed. The third section discusses how those crypto services and mechanisms are used in applications such as e-mail security, VPNs, IPsec, TLS, Web services, and wireless security.

The following is a brief description of each chapter:

Chapter I, "Classic Cryptography," provides a historical perspective of cryptography and code breaking, including some of the techniques employed over the centuries to attempt to encode information. Some early crypto machines and the Vernam Cipher, developed by Gilbert Vernam in 1917, are discussed in this chapter.

Chapter II, "Information Assurance," discusses the TCP/IP protocol. When data communications security is discussed in this book, it refers to communications security for the TCP/IP protocol and to the security mechanisms implemented at the different layers of the TCP/IP stack protocol.

Chapter III, "Number Theory and Finite Fields," describes certain basic concepts of number theory such as modular arithmetic and congruence, which are necessary for an understanding of Public-Key crypto systems.

Chapter IV, "Confidentiality: Symmetric Encryption," covers confidentiality using the different types of symmetric encryption stream ciphers and block ciphers. The theory for using shift registers as stream ciphers is also covered in this chapter, as well as DES and Advanced Encryption Standard (AES) block encryption algorithms.

Chapter V, "Confidentiality: Asymmetric Encryption (public key)," covers confidentiality using asymmetric encryption (public key). The most used public-key ciphers, including the Pohlig-Hellman algorithm, RSA algorithm, ElGamal algorithm, and Diffie-Hellman are discussed in this chapter.

Chapter VI, "Integrity and Authentication," discusses methods that are used to check if a message was modified using hash functions and ways to verify a sender's identity by using digital signatures.

Chapter VII, "Access Authentication," describes authentication mechanisms such as (1) IEEE 802.1X access control protocol; (2) extensible authentication protocol (EAP) and EAP methods; (3) traditional passwords; (4) remote authentication dial-in-service (RADIUS); (5) Kerberos authentication service; and (6) X.509 authentication.

Chapter VIII, "Elliptic Curve Cryptography," covers ECC public-key crypto systems, which offer the same level of security as other public-key crypto systems, but with smaller key sizes. This chapter is written for those with some knowledge of cryptography and public-key systems who want a quick understanding of the basic concepts and definitions of elliptic curve cryptography.

Chapter IX, "Certificates and Public-Key Architecture," discusses how the authenticity of a public-key is guaranteed by using certificates signed by a certificate authority. When public-key is used, it is necessary to have a comprehensive system that provides public-key encryption and digital signature services to ensure confidentiality, access control, data integrity, authentication, and non-repudiation. That system, called *public-key infrastructure* or PKI, is also discussed in this chapter.

Chapter X, "Electronic Mail Security," covers two ways of securing electronic mail, secure MIME and Pretty Good Privacy (PGP).

Chapter XI, "VPNs and IPsec," covers virtual private networks (VPNs), which emulate a private wide area network (WAN) facility using IP networks, such as the public Internet, or private IP backbones. IPsec, also covered in this chapter, provides security services at the IP network layer such as data origin authentication, access control, confidentiality (encryption), connectionless integrity, rejection of replayed packets (a form of partial sequence integrity), and limited traffic flow confidentiality.

Chapter XII, "TLS, SSL, Secure Electronic Transactions (SET)," describes how transport layer security (TLS) or secure socket layer (SSL) protocols are used to secure an Internet transaction between a secure Web server and a client's computer that is using a Web browser. Secure electronic transaction (SET), a secure payment process that was proposed by VISA and MasterCard, is also described.

Chapter XIII, "Web Services," explains Web services and open standards such as extensible markup language (XML), and simple object access protocol (SOAP). The following Web services mechanisms are also discussed in this chapter: (1) XML Encryption, XML signature, and XML key management specification (XKMS); (2) security association markup language (SAML), and Web services security (WS-Security).

Chapter XIV, "Wireless Security," discusses the three primary categories of wireless networks: wireless local area network (WLAN), wireless metropolitan-area network (WMAN), and wireless personal area network (WPAN), as well as the security services and mechanisms for each of them.

Acknowledgment

We cannot educate others unless we ourselves value education and have benefited from it. My parents, Manuel and Hilda Mogollon, made education a priority in our family and sacrificed to provide us with the best educational opportunities that they could. I will always be grateful for their encouragement and support.

Dr. Diana Natalicio, President of the University of Texas at El Paso, said at a recent conference at Nortel in Richardson, TX, "Talent is everywhere," and we as learners only need guidance and encouragement from teachers, family, and/or friends to trust in our abilities, work hard, and accept the challenges and opportunities in being lifelong learners. Many teachers gave me that guidance. In the field of mathematics, professor Jacques Bardonet at the Colegio Americano in Barranquilla, Colombia, and professor Luis Polo-Mercado at the Colombian Naval Academy in Cartagena, Colombia, made mathematics easy to learn and to like; thus began my lifelong love of math. Also, my thanks to Barrie Morgan, at Datotek, Inc., who got me into the field of cryptography and was generous in sharing his knowledge with me. With regard to communications security, we talked about trusted and untrusted systems. The same could be applied to friends, and Barry was a trusted friend and mentor.

Thanks also to my students at the University of Dallas, who by arguing a concept or asking for more explanation, make me realize that the material needs to be explained in a different way for better and easier understanding.

My ultimate and biggest thanks goes to my wife, Sandra. Editing a book is not an easy task, and editing a technical book about cryptography is even more difficult. This book is dedicated to my wife, Sandra, who not only gave me the moral support to write it, but who also took on the tremendous task of editing it. Without knowing that I could count on her help, comments, proofreading, and editing, I would not have ventured to write this book.

Manuel Mogollon

Chapter I

Classic Cryptography

Classic Cryptography

Chapters 1 and 2 cover information on classic cryptography and the aspects of information security related to security services and mechanisms. The history of cryptography and code-breaking is very interesting and, in this chapter, some of the types of implementation employed over the centuries to attempt to code information are covered. These implementations are not very sophisticated by today's standards and are considered too weak for serious applications. Some early crypto machines and the Vernam Cipher developed by Gilbert Vernam in 1917 are discussed in this chapter.

Objectives

- Gain an historical perspective of cryptography
- Become familiar with terms used in cryptography and network security

Introduction

The purpose of cryptography is to render information unintelligible to all but the intended receiver. The sender enciphers a message into unintelligible form, and the receiver deciphers it into intelligible form. The word "cryptology" is derived from the Greek *kryptos* (hidden) and *logos* (word) (*The American Heritage College Dictionary*, 1987).

- **Cryptology:** The scientific study of cryptography and cryptanalysis
- **Cryptography:** The enciphering and deciphering of messages into secret codes by means of various transformations of the plaintext
- **Cryptanalysis:** The process of deriving the plaintext from the ciphertext (breaking a code) without being in possession of the key or the system (code breaking)

The history of codes and ciphers goes back almost 4,000 years to a time during the early Egyptian civilization when scribes told the story of their masters' lives using unusual hieroglyphics (Khan, 1976, p. 71). The inscriptions were not secret writing, but incorporated one of the essential elements of cryptography: an intentional transformation of writing so that only certain people could read it.

The Spartans were probably the first to use cryptography for military purposes. Their crypto device, called the *scytale* (stick), consisted of a wooden stick around which a narrow piece of papyrus, leather, or parchment was wrapped in a spiral. The secret message was inscribed on the parchment over the whole length of the shaft, and the ribbon was then sent to its destination. The ribbon alone was useless to all but the recipient, who had a cylinder of the same diameter as the sender. The diameter of the cylinder determined the key.

The Arab civilization, with its advanced mathematics, was the first to establish specific rules to cryptoanalyze written messages (Khan, 1976, p. 97). The rules were the following:

- The cryptanalyst must know the language in which the crypto message is written and its linguistic characteristics.
- In every language, there are letters that are never found together in one word, letters that rarely come together in a word, and combinations of letters that are not possible.
- All letters are not used equally in any language, and the proportions in which the letters occur remain constant.

Unfortunately, with the decline of the Arab civilization, this knowledge of cryptology also vanished.

Figure 1-1. The Spartan Scytale

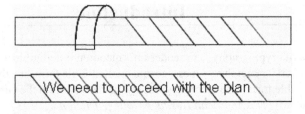

Classic Cipher Techniques

Many of the techniques employed over the centuries to attempt to **code** information were not very sophisticated. By today's standards, most of these techniques are considered too weak for serious applications; however, many of their basic principles are still used in modern cryptography and, therefore, it is worthwhile to review them.

These techniques include the following (Davies & Price, 1984, pp. 17-35):

- The Caesar substitution cipher
- Monoalphabetic substitution
- Polyalphabetic substitution (the Vigenere cipher)
- Transposition ciphers

Caesar Substitution Cipher

In his book, *The Gallic Wars*, Julius Caesar described the use of a military code in which a plaintext alphabet is shifted by three positions (Khan, 1976, p. 84).

Plain   a b c d e f g h i j k l m n o p q r s t u v w x y z

Cipher d e f g h i j k l m n o p q r s t u v w x y z a b c

This type of code, called a *Caesar substitution cipher*, is very weak because if the amount of displacement is known, there is no secret. Even if the displacement is not known, it can be discovered very easily because the number of possible cipher solutions is only 25.

Monoalphabetic Substitution

If the substitution of each letter is done at random, the cipher technique is called a *monoalphabetic substitution*.

Plain   a b c d e f g h i j k l m n o p q r s t u v w x y z

Cipher h o s b r g v k w c y f p j t a z m x i q d l u e n

The number of possible substitutions is 26! or 4.0329 x 10^{26}. With so many substitutions, monoalphabetic substitution might appear as a very strong cipher technique but, in reality, it is a very weak cipher. Cryptanalysis of a message enciphered using a monoalphabetic substitution takes into consideration that each plain letter is always transformed into the same encipher equivalent, and that in any language there are some letters that occur more often than others.

Polyalphabetic Substitution

In the 16th century, the Frenchman Blaise de Vigenere wrote the book, *Traite des Chiffres*, which described cryptology up to his day, and introduced a polyalphabetic substitution using one alphabet for each of the plain letters. Using Caesar's basic idea, he formed a square, the Vigenere Table, consisting of 25 horizontal alphabets, one below the other, with each shifted to the right by one letter. A vertical alphabet was used to define the key and, at the top, an additional alphabet was used for the plaintext letters (Khan, 1976, p. 149).

The Vigenere encryption could also be expressed as a modulo-26 addition of the letters of the key word, repeated as many times as necessary into the plaintext.

The Vigenere Tableau

(Plain Text)

	A B C D E F G H I J K L M N O P Q R S T U V W X Y Z
A	a b c d e f g h i j k l m n o p q r s t u v w x y z
B	b c d e f g h i j k l m n o p q r s t u v w x y z a
C	c d e f g h i j k l m n o p q r s t u v w x y z a b
D	d e f g h i j k l m n o p q r s t u v w x y z a b c
E	e f g h i j k l m n o p q r s t u v w x y z a b c d
F	f g h i j k l m n o p q r s t u v w x y z a b c d e
G	g h i j k l m n o p q r s t u v w x y z a b c d e f
H	h i j k l m n o p q r s t u v w x y z a b c d e f g
I	i j k l m n o p q r s t u v w x y z a b c d e f g h
J	j k l m n o p q r s t u v w x y z a b c d e f g h i
K	k l m n o p q r s t u v w x y z a b c d e f g h i j
L	l m n o p q r s t u v w x y z a b c d e f g h i j k
M	m n o p q r s t u v w x y z a b c d e f g h i j k l
N	n o p q r s t u v w x y z a b c d e f g h i j k l m
O	o p q r s t u v w x y z a b c d e f g h i j k l m n
P	p q r s t u v w x y z a b c d e f g h i j k l m n o
Q	q r s t u v w x y z a b c d e f g h i j k l m n o p
R	r s t u v w x y z a b c d e f g h i j k l m n o p q
S	s t u v w x y z a b c d e f g h i j k l m n o p q r
T	t u v w x y z a b c d e f g h i j k l m n o p q r s
U	u v w x y z a b c d e f g h i j k l m n o p q r s t
V	v w x y z a b c d e f g h i j k l m n o p q r s t u
W	w x y z a b c d e f g h i j k l m n o p q r s t u v

X   x y z a b c d e f g h i j k l m n o p q r s t u v w

Y   y z a b c d e f g h i j k l m n o p q r s t u v w x

Z   z a b c d e f g h i j k l m n o p q r s t u v w x y

In his book, Vigenere listed several key methods, such as words, phrases, and the progressive use of all the alphabets, as well as a running key in which the message itself is its own key —the so-called *autokey*.

All the possible keys can be grouped into three systems:

1.   A key word or key phrase is used, thus defining not only the key length (key period), but also the number of alphabets being used.

      Example:

      Key   D A L L A S D A L L A S

      Plain   N O W I S T H E T I M E

      Cipher   Q O H T S L K E E T M W

2.   A primary key consisting of a single letter is provided to encipher the first plaintext letter, and the plaintext is then used as a running key.

      Example:

      Key   D N O W I S T H E T I M

      Plain   N O W I S T H E T I M E

      Cipher   Q B K E A L A L X B U Q

3.   As in (2), the prime letter is used to encipher the first plaintext letter, but the ciphertext is used as a running key.

      Example:

      Key   D Q E A I A T A E X F R

      Plain   N O W I S T H E T I M E

      Cipher   Q E A I A T A E X F R V

It becomes apparent that example 1 uses only four alphabets (A and L are repeated), while B and C use all 26 alphabets, assuming that all 26 letters of the alphabet occur in the plaintext or in the cryptogram respectively.

Transposition Ciphers

With transposition ciphers, the successive letters of the plaintext are arranged according to the key. The key is a group of sequential numbers arranged at random. The plaintext is separated into groups of letters in which each group has the same number of letters as the number chosen as a key.

Plaintext	n o w i s / t h e t i / m e f o r / a l l x x /
Key	5 1 3 4 2
	s n w i o
	i t e t h
	r m f o e
	x a l x l
Ciphertext	s n w i o i t e t h r m f o e x a l x l

Early Cipher Machines

In the end, encryption without a cipher machine was too complex, the enciphering and deciphering processes were too slow, and the risk of making a mistake too high.

At the beginning of the 18th century, cryptographers started using mechanical aids to encipher information. The following were some of the most famous cipher devices used (Davies & Price, 1984, pp. 17-25):

- The Saint-Cyr Slide
- The Jefferson Cylinder
- The Wheatstone Disk
- The Vernam Cipher
- The Enigma (the rotor machine used by the German forces in World War II)
- The M-209 (used by the U.S. Army until the early 1950s)

The Saint-Cyr Slide

The construction, compilation, and use of complete enciphered tables in the polyalphabetic cipher system were inconvenient. This problem disappeared with a device called the *Saint-Cyr Slide*, invented by Kerckhoffs and named after the French military academy (Khan, 1976, p. 238). With this device, the process of modulo-26 addition could be conducted conveniently.

The Jefferson Cylinder

In the 1790's, Thomas Jefferson developed a device for polyalphabetic substitution that consisted of 36 discs or cylinders with their peripheries divided into 26 equal parts (Khan, 1976, pp. 192-195). Each of the discs was numbered and carried in its peripheral an alphabet with the letters placed, not alphabetically, but randomly. The discs were mounted on a shaft,

Figure 1-2. The Saint Cyr Slide

and the order was specified and agreed to between the correspondents. The discs' order constituted the key, and the number of possibilities was 36! or 3.72×10^{41}.

The message was enciphered by rotating the discs until the message letters stood in the same row. The ciphertext was any of the other 26 positions around the cylinder in which the letters appeared jumbled and meaningless. To decipher the message, the correspondent set the discs in the same specified order and rotated them to present a row with the same ciphertext; the correspondent then moved the wheel cipher device around until a meaningful row of letters was found.

The Wheatstone Disc

In the 19th century, the British scientist Sir Charles Wheatstone (Khan, 1976, p. 197) invented another famous cipher machine. The Wheatstone cryptograph machine consisted of two concentric discs that carried the letters of the alphabet in their peripheries. The outer disc contained the letters of the alphabet in alphabetic order, plus a symbol for a blank space after the letter **z**, while the inner disc had 26 letters at random. Over the discs, two clock-like hands were geared together in some way, so that when the larger hand completed one revolution, the smaller hand would move ahead only one letter. For enciphering, the two hands were first aligned at the blank space on the outer circle; then the outer hand was used to spell out the plaintext (always moving clockwise and including the space as a character), while the shorter hand automatically selected the cipher text equivalent from the inner disc. Whenever a double letter occurred, some unused letter (for example, q or x) was substituted for the repeated letter.

This cipher is a type of polyalphabetic substitution with a change of alphabet after each word because of the blank space. The variation in length of the alphabets means that as the larger hand is completing a revolution, the smaller is already one letter into its second revolution. This cipher has the property that the ciphertext representing a word depends on the preceding plaintext. This is called *chaining* and has great importance in today's applications.

The Vernam Cipher

In 1917, Gilbert Vernam (Kahn, 1976, pp. 94-97), an employee of AT&T, designed a security device for telegraphic communications that revolutionized modern cryptography: the bit-by-bit combination of random characters (keystream) with characters of plaintext using modulo-2 addition (the XOR function) —the *stream cipher*. Vernam's system, based upon the Baudot code, required punching a tape of random characters (chosen by picking numbers out of a hat) and electronically adding them to the plaintext characters.

A new tape, the ciphertext, was thus produced in a simple and reversible operation; all that was necessary to obtain the message was to subtract the ciphertext pulses from the keystream pulses.

Vernam decided to use the Baudot code pulses for his electronic addition so that if both pulses were mark or space, the result was space; if one was mark and the other was pulse, the result was mark. The four possibilities were the following:

Plaintext		Keystream		Ciphertext
Mark	+	Mark	=	Space
Space	+	Space	=	Space
Mark	+	Space	=	Mark
Space	+	Mark	=	Mark

The addition can be better visualized if, instead of using the Baudot code of mark and space, the mark is represented by a 1 and a space by a 0.

Plaintext		Keystream		Ciphertext
1	+	1	=	0
0	+	0	=	0
1	+	0	=	1
0	+	1	=	1

In accordance with this rule, and since in the Baudot code each character had five pulses, either a mark (pulse) or a space (no pulse), Vernam combined five pulses from the keystream with five pulses from the plaintext to obtain the ciphertext. For example:

Encipher

Plaintext	1 1 0 0 0 (letter A)	1 1 0 0 0 (letter A)
Keystream	1 0 1 0 1	1 1 0 0 1
Ciphertext	0 1 1 0 1 (letter P)	0 0 0 0 1 (letter T)

Decipher

Ciphertext	0 1 1 0 1 (letter P)	0 0 0 0 1 (letter T)
Keystream	1 0 1 0 1	1 1 0 0 1
Plaintext	1 1 0 0 0 (letter A)	1 1 0 0 0 (letter A)

Figure 1-3. Vernam's cipher

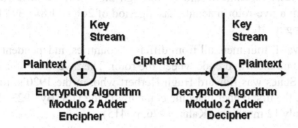

Vernam's addition, the modulo-2 (XOR), together with the use of the same keystream to encipher and decipher, are the basis of modern cryptography. Thanks to his contribution, enciphering and deciphering a message was made easy, simple, and fast.

Vernam's cipher required the sender to provide the receiver with identical tapes of keystream characters. Vernam's keystream consisted of a loop of tape with the alphabet on it, which was used over and over until the complete message was enciphered. The system was a polyalphabetic substitution, a 32 x 32 table, which permitted a Kasiski solution. To increase the difficulty of a Kasiski solution, which is the conjunction of a repeated portion of the key with a repetition in the plaintext producing a repetition of the ciphertext, the group of AT&T engineers working with Vernam at first made the keystream tapes extremely long. These tapes were difficult to handle, and they later decided to combine two short keystream tapes of different lengths to generate a longer number of keystream characters. For example, if one loop tape of 1000 keystream characters were combined with a keystream loop tape of 999 characters, the result would provide 999,000 combinations before the sequence would repeat.

If the keystream tapes are different for each message, and if each keystream tape is used only one time to encipher one message, then the cipher is perfect and unbreakable. Because of the randomness and the nonrepetition of the keystream, this system is called the *one-time system*.

The Rotor Crypto Machines

Rotor machines implemented polyalphabetic substitution ciphers with long periods (Davies & Price, 1984, p. 31; Kahn, 1976, p. 411; Way, 1977, p. 89). The body of the machine consisted of several *t* rotary discs made of insulated material, normally two to four inches in diameter, and half an inch thick. On each side of each disc were 26 electrical contacts in the form of metal studs. Each stud on one side of the disc was connected by wire to another stud on the other side of the disc. The wire did not go directly from one stud to the immediate opposite stud, but to a stud at random. For example, the stud from the letter *G* was connected internally not to *G*, but to another letter.

If the discs were immovable, an alphabet could be changed only to another alphabet. However, if after each letter were enciphered, one or more of the rotors were rotated one step, a new alphabet would be created to encipher each letter with a different ciphertext alphabet.

A machine with t rotors would not return to its starting position until after 26^t successive steps; a three-rotor machine would go through $26^3 = 17,576$ different alphabets before repeating itself; a five-rotor machine has a period of $26^5 = 11,881,376$ different alphabets before repeating itself.

After World War I, four men, all from different countries, independently created a crypto machine based on the wired code wheel, the rotor. The inventor of the first rotor machine in the United States was Edward Hugh Herbert who, in the 1920's, founded the Herbert Electric Code, the first cipher machine company in the U.S. By 1923, the firm had closed after selling only 12 machines (Kahn, 1976, p. 415).

In the Netherlands, Hugo Alexander Koch filed a patent for a secret writing machine and established a company called *Securitas*, but no machines were ever produced. In 1927, Kock transferred the patent rights to the German inventor of a rotor device (Kahn, 1976, p. 420).

In Germany, Arthur Scherbious designed a device with multiple switchboards. These boards connected each arriving lead with one of the outgoing leads and were adapted to make this connection with great facility and variation (Kahn, 1976, p. 421). This operation was the basis of a rotor machine. The first apparatus, which had only 10 contacts, was used to encipher code numbers into code words. In subsequent machines, Scherbious expanded the contacts from 10 to 26, so the machine could be used to encipher letters. He called his machine *Enigma*. Scherbious formed a company called *Cipher Machine Corporation*, which started operating in 1923. His advertisement, "One secret, well protected, may pay the whole cost of the machine ...," did not convince either commercial or military customers. The company survived 11 years before its dissolution and never paid a dividend. Scherbious went bankrupt and died prior to World War II before Germany decided to adopt the machine. When Hitler started rearming Germany, his cryptology experts chose the Enigma as the crypto machine for top army, navy, and air force communications.

These early inventors tried to commercialize their crypto machines too soon. Nations during the 1920's, after World War I, were not interested in crypto devices. In the 1930's, when European countries were rearming for World War II, the interest in crypto machines was renewed. At that time, Boris Caesar Wilhelm Hagelin, the only person who became a multimillionaire from the cipher machine business, was able to capitalize on the need for secure communications.

In 1916, Arvid Gerhard Damm founded in Stockholm a company called *Cryptograph, Inc.*, with money invested by Emanuel Nobel, nephew of Alfred Nobel, and K. W. Hagelin, man-

Figure 1-4. Rotor machine

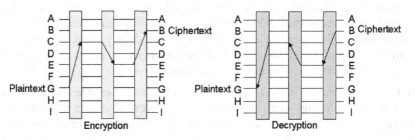

ager of the Nobel brothers' oil production in Russia. In October 1919, Damm applied for a patent for a rotor crypto machine (Kahn, 1976, p. 422). During the following years, Damm designed several crypto machines based on the rotor concept and even won some orders for a prototype, but the machines were not reliable, and he was not able to establish a market. In 1922, Boris Caesar Wilhelm Hagelin started to work in the factory to represent his father's and Emanuel Nobel's investments. With his degree in mechanical engineering, Hagelin had the technical background to enable him to modify and simplify the Damm mechanism; he was also able to get a large contract from the Swedish Army in 1926.

After Damm's death in 1927, Hagelin bought the company at a very good price and fulfilled the contract with the Swedish Army. By 1934, Hagelin had designed a more compact crypto machine, which was probably the first of its kind to print ciphertext in five-letter groups and the plaintext in normal word-lengths. In 1935, after witnessing a successful demonstration, the French government placed an order for 5,000 units. When World War II began, Hagelin packed blueprints and two dismantled ciphering machines and headed for the United States. The U.S Army, after exhaustive tests, adopted the crypto machine for medium-level cryptographic communications from divisions to battalions, and more than 140,000 units were manufactured by L.C. Smith & Corona Typewriters Inc. The Army's designation of Hagelin's crypto machine was the M-209 (Kahn, 1976, pp. 425-427).

The M-209

The M-209 was used by the U.S. Army until the early 1950's. A full description of the M-109 is given by Beker and Piper (1982).

The M-209 had six rotors, but not all the rotors had the complete alphabet. The following sequences of letters were engraved around the rotors' circumference:

Rotor	I	or	"26 wheel":	ABCDEFGHIJKLMNOPQRSTUVWXYZ
Rotor	II	or	"25 wheel":	ABCDEFGHIJKLMNOPQRSTUVXYZ
Rotor	III	or	"23 wheel":	ABCDEFGHIJKLMNOPQRSTUVX
Rotor	IV	or	"21 wheel":	ABCDEFGHIJKLMNOPQRSTU
Rotor	V	or	"19 wheel":	ABCDEFGHIJKLMNOPQRS
Rotor	VI	or	"17 wheel":	ABCDEFGHIJKLMNOPQ

The numbers 26, 25, 23, 21, 19, and 17 do not have common factors, so the rotors produced the following individual periods: 26 25, 23, 21, 19, and 17. Therefore, the ciphertext that the M-209 produced was polyalphabetic with a period of 26 x 25 x 23 x 21 x 19 x 17 = 101,405,850, nearly ten times greater than a five-rotor machine.

Cryptanalysis in World War II

The rotor machines used by Germany and Japan generated long keystreams, but they were not as random as they may have seemed. In August 1939, one month before World War II started, the British, with the help of some Polish ex-employees of the German factory that manufactured the Enigma, had somehow obtained a working replica of the machine. Getting the machine was only the first step, however; solving the mathematical computations involved was more difficult.

The head of the British Government's Codes and Cipher School, Alastair Denniston, hired the best mathematicians in Britain to work with him on a project called *ULTRA*, whose objective was to break the German Enigma machine. By early April 1940, Denniston and his personnel, using probably the first electronic computational machine, were able to decipher a short message from the Luftwaffe. During the rest of the war, the British were able to decipher all German messages. Churchill referred to ULTRA as "my most secret source."

In 1934, the Imperial Japanese Navy purchased several German Enigma machines. After making some modifications to the machine, they introduced it in 1937 with the name, *Alphabetic Typewriter 2597* (2597 was the Japanese year which corresponded to 1937). The *J machine*, as it was called by the Japanese Navy, was lent to the Foreign Office for its use. There it was adopted for the highest level, State Secret, diplomatic communications.

In the United States, this machine was called *PURPLE*, according to the color progression established by two previous Japanese codes, ORANGE and RED, which the Americans had solved (Way, 1977, p. 68). The task to break the PURPLE code was assigned directly to William Frederick Friedman, Chief Cryptanalyst of Signal Intelligence Service (S.I.S.). He and his team of codebreakers were able to put together a complicated maze of multicolored wires, contacts, switches, and relays, a perfect clone of the Japanese cipher machine. On September 25, 1940 (Bamford, 1982, p. 35), this replica issued its first totally clear, ungarbled text of a message from a PURPLE machine.

The British had an Enigma working model when they broke the German codes, but the Americans duplicated the PURPLE machine sight-unseen. Later on, the Americans were able to find out that the keys the Japanese were using were not random but did indeed have a special order, a terrible mistake in any crypto organization. The S.I.S found out that the keys used in a period of ten days were related, so after breaking the key used the first day, they were able to predict the keys for the next nine days. **They found the key to the keys!** Inexplicably, the Americans were able to break the highest level of messages from Japan, but sometimes they were not able to break low-level crypto messages.

Summary

The Saint-Cry Slide, the Jefferson Cylinder, the Wheatstone Disk, and the rotor machines, Enigma and M-209, used substitution and transposition techniques, which are still used in modern cryptography. However, the way these techniques were originally implemented made the encryption algorithms very vulnerable when today's computer power was utilized.

The number of possible substitutions in a monoalphabetic substitution is 26! or 4.0329 x 10^{26}, but, in reality, it is a very weak cipher technique because each plain letter is always transformed into the same encipher equivalent.

Rotor machines are based on substitution. A letter in one of the rotors is substituted for another letter in the following rotor. The technique is excellent; the only problem is that it is necessary to select many rotors and to make the rotors step in an unpredictable way. Today, some crypto companies are implementing rotors in electronic form by using an S-Box for each of the rotors. See Chapter 4 for more on the S-Box.

The one-time pad Vernam cipher is still used in ultra-secret communications for short messages. Furthermore, the XOR cipher algorithm used by Vernam, also called *modulo-2 addition*, is the most used cipher algorithm today.

In several places in this book, comparisons are made between encryption algorithms in order to make a determination about which one is more secure or more robust. If two encryption algorithms use the same techniques, it doesn't mean that both have the same ability to resist an attack or have the same cipher strength.

When talking about the strength of an encryption algorithm and to determine the minimum effort needed to break a crypto system, it is necessary to take into consideration the following:

- The cryptanalyst's processing capabilities
- The cryptanalyst's ability to find a weakness, that is, a fault in the design that allows circumventing the algorithm security
- Number of possible key combinations

A secure encryption algorithm is one in which it is not possible to use a short-cut attack because there is no fault in the design, and the only possible way of breaking the crypto algorithm is by brute force, trying all possible keys. If key exhaustion is the best attack, then the strength of an encryption algorithm is determined by its key size.

Learning Objectives Review

1. Cryptography is the art or science of rendering plaintext unintelligible and converting encrypted messages into intelligible form. (T/F)

2. The Calsar substitution cipher is very weak because there are only 25 different substitutions. (T/F)

3. The monoalphabetic cipher system has 4 x 1026 possible substitutions; therefore, it is a very strong cipher technique. (T/F)

4. The security of the Vernam cipher is based on its keystream randomness. (T/F)

5. A perfect cipher (unbreakable) is a cipher system in which:

   a. The cipher stream is random

    b.   The keystream is used to encipher only one message

    c.   A and B

6.   Make a histogram that shows the relative frequencies of alphabetic characters in the English language for one, two, and three letters

References

Bamford, J. (1982). *The puzzle palace: A report on NSA America's most secret agency*. Boston: Houghton, Mifflin Co.

Beker, H., & Piper, F. (1982) *Cipher system, the protection of communications*. New York: John Wiley and Sons.

Davies, D. W., & Price, W. L. (1984). *Security for computer networks*. New York: John Wiley & Sons.

Khan, D. (1976). *The codebreakers*. New York: Macmillan Publishing Co., Inc.

The American heritage college dictionary (3rd ed.). (n.d.). Boston: Houghton Mifflin Company.

Way, P. (1977). *The encyclopedia of espionage codes and ciphers*. London: The Danbury Press.

Chapter II

Information Assurance

Information Assurance

The TCP/IP protocol is becoming the world standard for network and computer communications. The number of TCP/IP applications on the Internet and in corporate networks is
continually growing, with a resulting increase in network vulnerability. When data communications security is discussed in this text, it refers to communications security for the
TCP/IP protocol and to the security mechanisms implemented at the different layers of the
TCP/IP stack protocol.

This chapter also describes, in a general way, which security mechanisms are used for
specific security services.

Objectives

* Provide some basic information about the TCP/IP protocol
* Introduce the security mechanisms used to provide security services

Introduction

The following definitions of terms used in security were taken from NSA Director of Information Assurance Daniel G. Wolf's (2003) statement before the House Select Committee
of Homeland Security on July 22, 2003 (pages 4 and 5).

COMSEC (1960's): Communications security provided protection against disclosure to unauthorized parties when information was transmitted or broadcasted from point-to-point. Security was accomplished by building secure "black boxes" using high-level encryption to protect the information.

COMPUSEC (Late 1970's): Computer security provided not only protection against unauthorized disclosure of information, but also against new threats, such as the injection of malicious code, or the theft of data on magnetic media.

INFOSEC (Early 1980's): Information security was the result of the convergence of COMSEC and COMPUSEC.

IA (Late 1990's): Information assurance dealt with providing protection against unauthorized disclosure of information (confidentiality), modification of information (integrity), denial of service (availability), authenticity, and non-repudiation.

When computer systems started to be interconnected within local and wide area networks, and, eventually, to Internet protocol networks, it was necessary, besides confidentiality, to provide the following:

- Protection against unauthorized modification of information to ensure data integrity
- Protection against denial-of-service attacks to ensure data availability
- Positive identification, or authentication, of parties in an electronic transaction
- Protection against parties denying their participation in a transaction—non-repudiation

Because the term *security* has been so closely associated with providing confidentiality for information, NSA and the Department of Defense adopted the term *information assurance* to encompass the five security services of confidentiality, integrity, availability, authenticity, and non-repudiation.

Computer Network Architecture

To be able to implement security in a communications network, it is necessary to understand how the network operates. Before discussing network security architecture, it is necessary to understand the reference model for computer network architecture from the standpoint of protocol design, physical construction, and topologies. The most common architectural computer models are the open system, interconnect (OSI), and the IP model. This section provides just enough information about networking architectures to understand the security model.

The term *computer network* is mostly used to describe several autonomous computers and servers interconnected in a complex structure (Tanenbaum, 1981). This structure consists of host computers and terminals in which communications paths are provided by routers and switches connected by several communications links. Computer networks are organized in a series of layers or levels. The purpose of each layer is to offer certain services to higher layers and to shield them from the details of service implementation. Between each pair of layers, an interface defines each layer's exchange of information with a lower layer. However, when layer *n* of one computer talks with layer *n* of another computer, no data is directly transferred from layer *n* of one machine to layer *n* of the other. Instead, the information is sent to the lowest layer where the physical communication is established with the other host computer through coaxial cables, fiber optics, telephone lines, microwaves, satellites, or any other type of communications channel.

The OSI Model

As an international organization dedicated to the writing and dissemination of technical standards for industry and trade, the International Standards Organization (ISO) has formulated a network structure for open system interconnection (OSI): the ISO IEC 7498-3: 1997—basic reference model. The OSI was developed in the mid 1980's, but the basics for the ARPANET Model (used by the Department of Defense and in today's IP networks) were already developed and implemented by that time. That is why the transmission control protocol/Internet protocol has it is own model.

The OSI divides communications into seven layers, each providing a specific set of services from a lower level, or physical layer, up to the top, or application layer. This division of the communication services allows for interoperability and flexibility. By defining standards for each layer, OSI attempts to ensure that a vendor providing a protocol at a certain layer can interoperate with a different vendor providing the same protocol at that layer.

The following are the seven layers in which the OSI model is divided:

1. Physical layer
2. Data Link layer
3. Network layer
4. Transport layer
5. Session layer
6. Presentation layer
7. Application layer

Flexibility is also obtained by the division of the stack into seven layers. Each layer can be developed independently and is constrained only by the services it provides to the *n + 1* layer and by the services provided by the *n - 1* layer.

Application Layer (Layer 7)

The application layer is where users process the information and determine which programs they will run and which protocols they will use. A single exchange at the application layer

Figure 2-1. The OSI and TCP/IP networking models

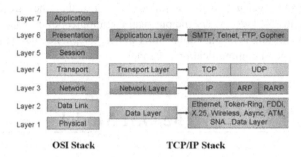

might include a person operating an automated banking terminal, an electronic-mail message transfer, or a database transaction with a database management system. The location in the network is either the user's terminal or the user's personal computer.

Simple mail transfer protocol (smtp), hypertext transfer protocol (http), file transfer protocol (ftp), telnet, and trivial transfer protocol (TFTP) are some examples of the protocols working at the application layer.

Presentation Layer (Layer 6)

The function of the presentation layer is to provide the users with certain useful, but not always essential, transformation services of the users' data. These services include conversion between character codes (8-bit ASCII, virtual terminal protocols), cryptographic transformations, text compression, terminal handling, file transfer, and manipulation of files. The presentation layer can take an electronic document and convert it to ASCII for transmission. On the other hand, it can also take a graphic and convert it to tagged image file format (TIFF), graphic interchange format (GIF), or joint photographic experts group (JPEG) format for transmission.

Session Layer (Layer 5)

The session layer is the user's interface with the network. The user must negotiate with this layer to establish a connection with another machine. Once the connection is established, the session layer manages the dialogue in an orderly manner. A connection between users (or between two presentation layers) is called a *session*. When the session is established, the two ends must agree on authentication and a variety of options; for example, if the communication should be simplex, half-duplex, or full-duplex.

The session layer often provides a facility by which a group of messages can be bracketed, so that none of them is delivered to the remote user until all of them arrive. In some networks, the session and transport layers are merged into a single layer, or the session layer is absent altogether.

The network file system (NFS), structured query language (SQL), and remote procedure call (RPC) are some examples of the protocols working at the session layer.

Transport Layer (Layer 4)

If computer network users do not believe that the carrier is technically capable of living up to its promise of 100% reliable service without error, loss, or duplication, they may decide to superimpose their own error and flow control on top of the carrier's. This error and flow control is done at the transport layer. The transport layer's task is to provide reliable and efficient end-to-end transport service between users' processes. The transport layer software splits the data up into messages and attaches a transport header to the front of each message.

Collectively, layers 1 through 4 provide a transport service, shielding the higher layers from the technical details of how communication is achieved. The difference is that for the transport layer, the communication channel is the entire communication subnetwork, or subnet. The task of the transport layer is to provide a network-independent transport service to the session layer. The transport and network layers establish the addresses to determine who wants to talk to whom. Each of the layers from 4 to 1 treats the message passed to them as data, wraps the data with its own header and trailer, and passes it to the layer below. By the time the original message exits the system at the physical layer, the message is enveloped in multiple nested wrappers, one for each protocol layer.

Network Layer (Layer 3)

The lowest three layers (3, 2, and 1) are concerned with the end-to-end transmission, framing, and routing of packets between machines. A network layer, sometimes called the *communication subnet layer*, controls the exchange of data between the user and the network, as well as the operation of the subnet. The network layer groups the binary digits, including data and control elements, into packets of information composed of header, data, and trailer, which are transmitted as a whole. Internet protocol (IP), Internet control message protocol ICMP), routing information protocol (RIP), open shortest path first (OSPF), and border gateway protocol (BGP) are some examples of the protocols working at the network layer.

The network layer provides network routing, flow and error control, request for network services, and logical multiplexing. Another function of the network layer is to ensure that the packets are not lost or duplicated during the transmission, and, in some models such as the virtual circuit networks, that the packets arrive in the same order that they were sent.

Data Link Layer (Layer 2)

When the packets from layer 3 arrive at layer 2, a frame header and trailer are attached for transmission. The data link layer breaks up the data from the network layer into data frames and transmits the frames sequentially; it also processes the received acknowledgment frames. If a frame is not received, the layer 2 software on the transmit side should retransmit the frame. Since layer 1 accepts and transmits a stream of bits, regardless of meaning or structure, it is at the data link layer that frames are created and frame boundaries are recognized. The main task of the data network is to provide node-to-node link initialization, block framing, data free of errors to the network layer (flow and error control across individual links), and data and control interchange. Advanced data communication control (ADCCP), layer 2 forwarding (L2F), layer 2 tunneling protocol (L2TP), and high-level data control (HDLC), asynchronous transfer mode (ATM) are some examples of the protocols working at the data link layer. All these protocols allow data frames to contain an arbitrary number of bits and are referred to as bit-oriented protocols.

Physical Layer (Layer 1)

The physical layer (layer 1) converts bits into electrical signals, and it is involved with the transmission and reception of the raw bits over a communication system. The main concern is how –from the mechanical, electrical, and procedural point of view– the computer interfaces to the transmission system. Integrated services digital network (ISDN), Ethernet physical layer, and SONET/SDH are some examples of the protocols working at the physical layer.

The main task of the physical layer is to make sure that when a 0 bit is sent, the other physical layer will receive a 0 bit and not a 1. Most of the time, the physical layer is connected to bridges, routers, switches, gateways, or modems.

The TCP/IP Model

TCP/IP, like most networking software, is modeled in layers, but these layers are not functionally the same as the layers in systems network architecture (SNA) or in the open system interconnection (OSI) model.

The TCP/IP protocol stack consists of four layers: applications layer, transport layer, network layer, and data layer.

Application Layer

The highest layer in the stack is the application layer. Applications communicate with each other over the network by using the data communication services of the transport layer. HTTP, file transfer protocol (FTP), SMTP, and SNMP telnet are some examples of the protocols working at the application layer.

Applications access the transport layer via uniquely assigned port numbers and sockets and communicate with each other via different transport protocols, depending on their needs.

The data formatted at the application layer are called *messages*.

Figure 2-2. TCP/IP model

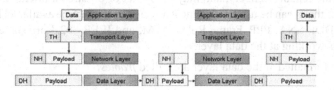

Transport Layer

The transport layer provides end-to-end data transfer by delivering data from an application to its remote peer. Two main protocols work at the transport layer: the transmission control protocol (TCP) and the user datagram protocol (UDP).

TCP is referred to as a connection-oriented protocol because handshaking takes place before any data is sent. TCP provides connection-oriented reliable data delivery via error correction, duplicate data suppression, congestion control, flow control, in-sequence delivery of data, and retransmission of lost data. TCP is called the *reliable protocol*.

UDP implements connectionless sessions via "best effort" delivery mechanisms. UDP is called the *unreliable protocol* because it sends out packets without first establishing a handshake and does not know if packets were received or dropped. As a result, applications using UDP as the transport protocol have to provide their own end-to-end integrity, flow control, and congestion control.

Network Layer

The network layer is also called the *Internet layer or the Internetwork layer*. The transport layer needs to determine the routes between endpoints to transfer the end-to-end data, and the network layer provides the network routing services or IP addresses. The protocol used to provide these services over the Internet is the Internet protocol (IP)

IP is a connectionless protocol that provides the address and routing information for each packet in an attempt to deliver transmitted messages to their destination. It does not provide reliability, flow control, or error recovery; these functions must be provided at a higher level. ICMP, IGMP, ARP, and RARP are some examples of the protocols working at the network layer.

Data Layer

The data layer is also called the *network interface layer* or the *link layer*.

Once the network route has been specified and the network headers added, the network layer relies on the data link interface to provide the device drivers to interface the data to the hardware components, such as Ethernet, Frame Relay, ATM, and so forth.

The data layer is the interface to the actual network hardware. This interface may or may not provide reliable delivery, and may be packet or bit-stream oriented. The flexibility of TCP/IP is that it can be used with almost any network interface available. IEEE 802.2, X.25 ATM, FDDI, SNA, PPP, Frame Relay, ATM, and IEEE 802.3 are some examples of the protocols working at the data layer.

The data formatted at the data layer are called *frames*.

Security Policies, Services, and Mechanisms

Security Policies is a document or set of documents that states an organization's intentions and decisions on what and how electronic information should be secured. A security policy is implemented using security mechanisms to provide security services.

The RFC 2828, "Internet Security Glossary" (Shirey, 2000), provides the following definitions for security policy, security services, and security mechanisms:

- **Security policy:** (1) A set of rules and practices that specify or regulate how a system or organization provides security services to protect sensitive and critical system resources. (2) The set of rules laid down by the security authority governing the use and provision of security services and facilities.

- **Security devices:** A processing or communication service that is provided by a system to give a specific kind of protection to system resources.

- **Security mechanisms:** A process (or a device incorporating such a process) that can be used in a system to implement a security service that is provided by or within the system.

The standards ISO 7498-2 (1989), "Reference Model for Security Architecture," "ITU-T X800," and "Security Architecture for Open System Interconnection," define the general security-related architectural elements that can be applied appropriately when communications between open systems needs to be protected. Both standards divide security services into five categories: authentication, access control, confidentiality, integrity, and non-repudiation.

Table 2.1 shows the relationship between security services and security mechanisms, based on information from both standards.

Figure 2-3 shows a one-to-one link between security services and a specific security mechanism. As shown in Table 2-1, in some cases more than one security mechanism can be used to achieve a security service. Some organizations do not require all five security services in IA, and the security policy of such an organization should specify which security services are required.

Table 2.1. Security services and mechanisms for the ISO model.

Mechanism Service	Encryption	Digital Signature	Access Control	Data Integrity	Authentication
Peer Entity Auth.	Y	Y			Y
Data Origin Auth.	Y	Y			
Access Control			Y		
Confidentiality	Y				
Traffic Flow Confidentiality	Y				
Data Integrity	Y	Y		Y	
Non-repudiation		Y		Y	
Availability				Y	Y

Figure 2-3. Security services and mechanisms

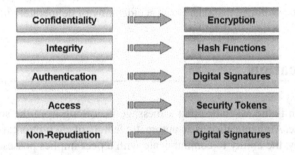

Confidentiality

Confidentiality is the assurance that information is not made available or disclosed to unauthorized individuals, entities, or processes. The confidentiality services are the following:

1. Connection confidentiality, which provides protection to all users in all connections
2. Connectionless confidentiality, which provides protection to all users in a single connectionless sessions
3. Selective field confidentiality, which provides protection to selected fields for n users on m connections or a single connectionless session
4. Traffic-flow confidentiality, which provides protection for information against wiretappers monitoring the traffic flow through passive wiretapping or eavesdropping

Figure 2-4. Confidentiality service and its security mechanisms

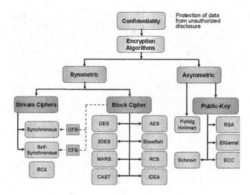

In this book, the term *confidentiality* is used to refer to *traffic-flow confidentiality*.

Integrity

Integrity is the assurance that data is not accidentally or deliberately modified in transit by replacement, insertion, or deletion.

Authentication

Authentication is the assurance that a message is coming from the source from which it claims to come. Authentication is an automatic feature of encryption; if nobody else has the encrypting key, the ability to communicate with a peer implies possession of the key and, therefore, proper authentication.

Figure 2-5. Integrity and its security mechanisms

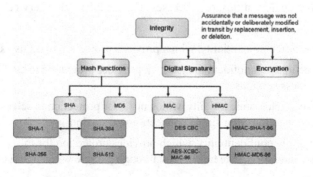

Figure 2-6. Authentication and its security mechanisms

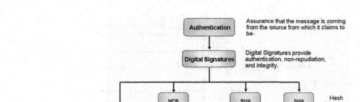

Authentication services include the following:

- Peer entity authentication is the corroboration (proof) of the sender's identity and authenticity—that the sender is who he claims to be. The service is provided for use when the connection is established, or during the data transfer phase, to confirm the identities of the entities connected.

- Data origin authentication is the corroboration of the original content of the data (data integrity) and that the source of data received is as claimed (authenticity). The data origin authentication service also provides the sender with proof of delivery of data to the receiver. This is also called a *non-repudiation service*. Digital signatures can be used for non-repudiation purposes.

Access Control Authentication

Access control provides protection against the unauthorized use of resources. It includes the prevention of the use of a resource in an unauthorized manner by identifying or verifying the eligibility of a station, originator, or individual to access specific categories of information.

Nonrepudiation

Repudiation means denial by one of the entities involved in a communication of having participated in all or part of the communication. Non-repudiation refers to protection against an individual denying sending or receiving a message. The non-repudiation service may take one or two forms:

1. **Non-repudiation with proof of origin:** The recipient of the data is provided with a proof of the origin of data. This proof will protect the recipient against any attempt by the sender to falsely deny sending the data or its original content. The sender cannot deny that he sent the message, nor can the sender deny its original content.

Figure 2-7. Access control authentication and its security mechanisms

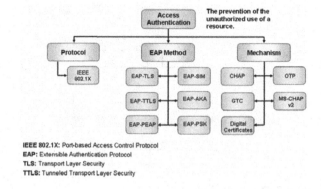

IEEE 802.1X: Port-based Access Control Protocol
EAP: Extensible Authentication Protocol
TLS: Transport Layer Security
TTLS: Tunneled Transport Layer Security

Figure 2-8. Non-repudiation and its security mechanisms

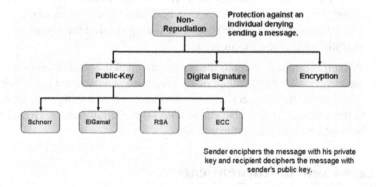

2.   **Non-repudiation with proof of delivery:** The sender of data is provided with proof of delivery of data. This proof will protect the sender against any subsequent attempt by the recipient to falsely deny receiving the data or its original content.

Placeholder Names Used in Cryptography

In the past, when describing an encryption protocol, writers would often say something like this: A sends an encrypted message to B, which has been signed with A's private key and encrypted with B's public key. Because the use of letters alone can be confusing, Ron Rivest used the names of "Alice" and "Bob" when he presented his RSA cryptosystem article at the 1978 Communications of the ACM conference. He reasoned that using names instead of the letters A and B would make a complex subject easier to explain.

Bruce Schneider (1996) added some other names to indicate the role of other parts in a protocol. The roles of the different names used as placeholders are described in a table that he called *dramatis personae*—the characters in a play. The following is the list of *dramatis personae*:

Alice	Participant in all protocols
Bob	Participant in two-, three-, and four-party protocols.
Carol	Participant in three- and four-party protocols
Dave	Participant in four-party protocols
Eve	Passive eavesdropper. While she can listen in on messages between Alice and Bob, she cannot modify them.
Mallet	Malicious active attacker. Mallet, also called Mallory, can modify messages, substitute his own messages, replay old messages, and so on. The problem of securing a system against Mallory is much greater than that against Eve.
Peggy	Prover
Victor	Verifier. Victor, a verifier, and Peggy, a prover, must interact in some way to show that the intended transaction between Alice and Bob has actually taken place.
Trent	Trusted arbitrator
Trudy	Intruder. Trudy can modify messages in transit; therefore, she is more dangerous than Eve. Bob and Alice ideally should use some integrity protocols to be able to detect any such modification and either ignore the changed message, or retrieve the correct message despite the intrusion.
Walter	Warden. He guards Alice and Bob in some protocols.

In cryptography and computer security, these placeholders are names widely used by writers in discussions about various security protocols. It is understood that in the protocol implementations where these placeholders are used, they do not refer to human parties, but rather to automated agents such as computer programs.

The Transformation of the Crypto Industry

When crypto equipment was used mainly by government agencies, developers and manufacturers of crypto equipment did not always need to design their equipment to be compatible with crypto equipment from other companies. Companies like Crypto AG, Cylink, TCC, Gretag, gmbh, and Datotek (subsequently AT&T Datotek), developed their own crypto algorithms, and it was up to their respective cryptographers to explain and demonstrate the level of security of their products. In addition, crypto equipment was designed to operate only with specific types of communications, for example, teletype, telex, facsimile, voice, radio, and data. Other equipment was developed for certain types of communication transmission protocols, such as X.25, T1, Frame Relay, Ethernet, or ATM.

In the early 1970's, large-scale integration (LSI), and, subsequently, very large scale integration (VLSI) technology permitted the implementation of highly complex key-generating algorithms in a single chip. Soon afterwards, several private companies started to carry out research in the development of key generators implemented in chips. In May 1973, the U.S. National Bureau of Standards (NBS), recognizing the need to adopt a standard algorithm to encipher digital communications used by the government, industry, and private organizations, asked several companies to propose techniques and algorithms that could be used to encipher computer data information. These techniques and algorithms might then be considered as the basis for the Federal Standard (subsequently, FIPS PUB 74, 1980). Thus, the Digital Encryption Standard (DES) was born. Some crypto manufacturers implemented DES in their crypto machines and sold them to U.S. government agencies and to domestic and foreign banking institutions, many of which were required to use DES technology. The use of the DES algorithm led to the possibility of network security equipment compatibility never before seen.

In 1976, Whitfield Diffie and Martin Hellman developed a key exchange cryptographic algorithm that allowed two parties to agree on a shared secret key over an insecure communications channel. Not many crypto manufacturers realized the importance of this new development, and it was not until the mid 1980's that companies like Cylink started developing applications using the Diffie-Hellman public-key key exchange to exchange the keys required in their proprietary encryption algorithms.

In the 1990's, the Internet, the standardization on IP networks, and Netscape's development of the secure socket layer (SSL) protocol caught many companies by surprise. After Netscape's SSL development, no longer was security associated with an exclusive group of crypto manufacturers. Now, anyone could implement a secure data link software program by using two standards: Diffie-Hellman to exchange a secret key and AES to encipher the data. Netscape is best known for developing a Web browser, but from the point of view of security, Netscape's SSL development was a major milestone for cryptography as it provided the pathway and tools for efficient secure communications. After Netscape's development of SSL, some providers of network equipment started using and implementing standard crypto algorithms in their routers and virtual private networks (VPNs) in order to try to capture the network security market from those crypto companies, which kept using their proprietary encryption algorithms.

The standardization on IP networks also led to a single crypto requirement, security for the IP protocol. Previously, companies needed to purchase crypto equipment that worked for a specific data layer and data rate (Frame Relay, ATM, Ethernet, etc.). With security being provided at the application, transport, and network layers, Internet protocol security (IPsec), secure e-mail, or transport layer security (TLS) could be used on any Frame Relay, ATM, or Ethernet network operating at any data rate.

U.S. Export Regulations for Encryption Equipment

Export and re-export controls on commercial encryption products are administered by the Bureau of Industry and Security (BIS) of the U.S. Department of Commerce (2007). Rules governing exports and re-exports of encryption items are found in the "Export Administration Regulations" (EAR), 15 C.F.R. Parts 730-774. Sections 740.13, 740.17 and 742.15 of the EAR are the principal references for the export and re-export of encryption items. In general, these are the regulations.

The following encryption items are eligible for export or re-export without a license, to most destinations, with notification only:

1. Up to (and including) 64-bit mass-market encryption commodities and software;

2. Encryption items (including key management products and company proprietary implementations) with key lengths not exceeding 56 bits for symmetric algorithms, 512 bits for asymmetric key exchange algorithms, and 112 bits for elliptic curve algorithms;

The following mass market encryption commodities and software exceeding 64 bits are eligible for export or re-export without a license, to most destinations, with notification only:

1. Up to (and including) 64-bit mass market encryption commodities and software

2. Encryption items (including key management products and company proprietary implementations) with key lengths not exceeding 56 bits for symmetric algorithms, 512 bits for asymmetric key exchange algorithms, and 112 bits for elliptic curve algorithms

3. Mass market encryption products include, but are not limited to, general purpose operating systems and desktop applications (e.g., e-mail, browsers, games, word processing, database, financial applications or utilities) designed for, bundled with, or preloaded on single CPU computers, laptops, or hand-held devices; commodities and software for client Internet appliances and client wireless LAN devices; home use networking commodities and software (e.g., personal firewalls, cable modems for personal computers, and consumer set top boxes); portable or mobile civil telecommunications commodities and software (e.g., personal data assistants (PDAs), radios, or cellular products); and commodities and software exported via free or anonymous downloads.

Other encryption commodities and software not considered mass-market encryption require a review request and a waiting period of 30 days after that request is registered. The following are some of the non-mass market encryption commodities, software and components listed in §740.17(b)(2)(iii):

1. Network infrastructure commodities and software parts and components thereof (including commodities and software necessary to activate or enable cryptographic functionality in network infrastructure products) providing secure wide area network (WAN), metropolitan area network (MAN), virtual private network (VPN), satellite, cellular or trunked communications for use with any of the following and having key lengths exceeding 64-bits for symmetric algorithms:

    a. Aggregate encrypted WAN, MAN, VPN or backhaul throughput (includes communications through wireless network elements such as gateways, mobile switches, controllers, etc.) greater than 44 Mbps.

    b. Wire (line), cable or fiber-optic WAN, MAN or VPN single-channel input data rate exceeding 44 Mbps

    c. Maximum number of concurrent encrypted data tunnels or channels exceeding 250

    d. Air-interface coverage (e.g., through base stations, access points to mesh networks, bridges, etc.) exceeding 1,000 meters, where any of the following applies:

        i.   Maximum data rates exceeding 5 Mbps (at operating ranges beyond 1,000 meters)

        ii. Maximum number of concurrent full-duplex voice channels exceeding 30

2. Cryptanalytic items

3. Encryption commodities and software that provide functions necessary for quantum cryptography

4. Encryption commodities and software that have been modified or customized

Summary

When assessing the security requirements of their organizations, managers need to define in which layer of the OSI and TCP/IP networking models the security service is required, and in which networking layer the security mechanism is going to be implemented. Brief descriptions of the various networking layers are provided in this chapter.

The standards ISO 7498-2, "Reference Model for Security Architecture," and ITU-T X.800, "Security Architecture for Open System Interconnection," define general security services and their related security mechanisms. Both standards divide security services into five categories: authentication, access control, confidentiality, integrity, and non-repudiation.

NSA defines *information assurance* (IA) as, "the set of measures intended to protect and defend information and information systems by ensuring their availability, integrity, authentication, confidentiality, and non-repudiation." The five pillars of IA, availability, integrity, authentication, confidentiality, and non-repudiation, are the same security services defined in ISO 7498-2 and ITU-T X800.

In this chapter, security services and mechanisms are described to provide readers with a complete view of what is going to be discussed in the rest of this book. In some cases, more than one security mechanism can be used to achieve a security service, but in this chapter, a one-to-one link between security services and a specific security mechanism is described in a fast and easy way to introduce readers to the whole concept of security.

At this point of the book, some of the figures showing security services and their security mechanisms may not have a lot of meaning to readers, but as they continue their reading, this chapter could be used to review security concepts.

Learning Objectives Review

1. Which of the following is Layer 3 in the International Standards Organization / Open Systems Interconnection (ISO/OSI)?

    a.   Application layer

    b.   Network layer

    c.   Data link layer

    d.   Presentation layer

2. Which of the following is a wide area network that was originally funded by the Department of Defense, and which uses TCP/IP for data interchange?

    a.   Intranet

    b.   Internet

    c.   Extranet

    d.   Ethernet

3. Which of the following protocols is considered connection-oriented?

    a.   IP

    b.   ICMP

    c.   UDP

    d.   TCP

4. Which best describes the IP protocol?

    a.   Connectionless protocol that deals with dialog establishment and routing of packets

    b.   Connectionless protocol that deals with addressing and routing of packets

    c.   Connection-oriented protocol that deals with addressing and routing of packets

    d.   Connection-oriented protocol that deals with sequencing, error detection, and flow control

5. Which best describes the TCP protocol?

    a.   Connectionless protocol that deals with dialog establishment and routing of packets

      b.   Connectionless protocol that deals with addressing and routing of packets

      c.   Connection-oriented protocol that deals with addressing and routing of packets

      d.   Connection-oriented protocol that deals with sequencing, error detection, and flow control

6.   What is the difference between confidentiality and integrity?

7.   Is confidentiality the same as security? Explain your answer.

8.   Repudiation means denial by one of the entities involved in a communication of having participated in all or part of the communication. (T/F)

9.   What are the Federal Information Processing Standard Publications?

10.   Which RFC provides a glossary of security terms?

11.   Why in cryptography and computer security are the names of Alice and Bob widely used by writers in discussions about various security protocols?

12.   What security provides access control?

13.   What is authentication?

14.   What is cleartext?

References

Department of Commerce, Bureau of Industry and Security. (2007). *Encryption export and re-export controls revisions* (15 CFR parts 740 and 742). Retrieved June 25, 2007, from http://www.gpo.gov/bis/ear/ear_data.html, http://www.gpo.gov/bis/ear/pdf/740.pdf, and http://www.gpo.gov/bis/ear/pdf/742.pdf

International Standards Organization (ISO). (1989). *(E) Security architecture*. ISO 7498-2-1989.

Schneier, B. (1994). *Applied cryptography*. New York: John Wiley & Sons.

Shirey, R. (2000). *Internet security glossary* (RFC 2828). Internet Engineering Task Force (IETF). Retrieved June 25, 2007, from http://www.ietf.org/rfc/rfc2828.txt?number=2828

Tanenbaum, A. (1981). *Computer networks*. Englewood Cliffs, NJ: Prentice-Hall.

Wolf, D. (2003). *Cybersecurity getting it right*. Homeland Security Subcommittee on Cybersecurity, Science, and Research & Development. Retrieved June 25, 2007, from http://frwebgate.access.gpo.gov/cgi-bin/getdoc.cgi?dbname=108_house_hearings&docid=f:98150.pdf

Chapter III

Number Theory and Finite Fields

Number Theory and Finite Fields

Mathematics plays an important role in encryption, public-key, authentication, and digital signatures. Knowing certain basic math concepts such as counting techniques, permutations, plotting a curve, raising a number to a power, modular arithmetic, and congruence would help to understand the material in this book.

Objectives

- Understand the Boolean Binary Expression and mathematical notations used in this book
- Understand the mathematical concepts upon which public-key algorithms are based

Introduction

When we talk about passwords and keys and how to break a password or a key, we are talking about counting techniques and probabilities. Number theory, the branch of mathematics concerned with the properties of natural numbers (1, 2, 3, …), plays an important role in public-key crypto systems. It is necessary to understand certain basic concepts of counting techniques and probabilities and number theory, for example, modular arithmetic and congruence.

In mathematics, it is possible to use any numeration system to count by using any number as the base in building that numeration system. The number of digits used in the numeration system is equal to the base. The decimal or base 10 system uses 10 digits; the binary or base 2 uses 2 digits, 0 and 1; the hexadecimal or base 16 uses the letters A – F to represent the tenth through fifteenth digits respectively. In encryption, numbers in base 2, 8, and 16 are very commonly used.

The mathematical operations of numbers, that is, multiplication and its multiplicative inverse (division), and addition and its additive inverse (subtraction), can be applied to any numeration system.

Principle of Counting

A procedure can be performed in n_1 different ways, a second procedure in n_2, a third procedure in n_3 different ways, and so forth. The number of ways the three procedures can be performed together is the product of $n_1 . n_2 . n_3$. This counting principle is used in passwords to determine the number of possible ways a password can be selected.

Suppose that a company's security policy states that a password should have four lower-case letters followed by four numbers, in that order. There are 26 lower-case letters and 10 possible numbers, 0 to 9. The password space is 26 . 26 . 26 . 26 . 10 . 10 . 10 . 10 = 4,569,760,000. At another company, the guidelines might be to use eight upper-case letters, lower case letters, or numbers, in any order. Now for each entry there are 26 + 26 + 10 possibilities and the total password space is 62 . 62 . 62 . 62 . 62 . 62 . 62 . 62 = 62^8, for a total of 8.39 x 10^{17}.

When talking about keys in cryptography, they are normally defined in numbers of bits. For example, a block encryption algorithm has a key of 128 bits; in this case, there are only two choices, either a 1 or a 0. Using the counting principle, the total number of possibilities is 2 . 2 . 2 . 2 . 2 . ... = 2^{128} = 3.40282 x 10^{38}.

How big is this number? Suppose that a computer software program can try ten million keys per second, and that it needs to try at least 50% of all possible combinations, 1.7014 x 10^{38}, to get the correct key. There are 3.1536 x 10^7 seconds in a year, so the computer will try 3.1536 x 10^{14} possible keys in a year. It will take 1.7014 x 10^{38} divided by 3.1536 x 10^{14} = 5.39514 x 10^{23} years for the computer to derive the correct key. According to the Big Bang theory, the age of the universe is about 13.7 billion years, which is 1.37 x 10^{10} years $\approx 2^{34}$.

This exhaustive procedure of trying all possibilities, one-by-one, is called a *brute force attack*.

Exponentiation and Prime Numbers

Exponentiation is used in encryption to describe the key size, and in public key to raise a number to a power. It is necessary to understand the following basic concepts about exponentiation:

- $2 \times 2 \times 2 \times 2 = 2^4$
- $(2 \times 2 \times 2 \times 2) \times (2 \times 2 \times 2) = 2^4 \times 2^3 = 2^{(4+3)} = 2^7$
- $(2 \times 2 \times 2 \times 2 \times 2) / (2 \times 2 \times 2) = 2^5 / 2^3 = 2^{(5-3)} = 2^2$

A prime number is a natural number that is only divisible by ± 1 and $\pm$ the integer itself. Prime numbers are the basis of a public-key crypto system such as RSA and key exchange algorithms such as Diffie-Hellman. Primes of the form $2^n - 1$ are known as Mersenne primes. If $2^n - 1$ is prime, then n is prime, but the converse, if n is a prime, then $2^n - 1$ is not always a prime. The largest Mersenne numbers are $2^{32,582,657} - 1$ and $2^{30,402,457} - 1$.

The Euclidean Algorithm

The Fundamental Theorem of Arithmetic, the most famous property of natural numbers, states that any number n can be written as a product of prime numbers.

$$n = p_1^{\alpha_1} + p_2^{\alpha_2} + \dots \ p_r^{\alpha_r}$$

where $p_1, p_2, \dots, p_r$ are primes and each $\alpha^i > 0$.

For example, $262,143 = 3^3 \cdot 7 \cdot 19 \cdot 73$.

It is often of interest in cryptography to find out whether two given numbers have any factors in common, and, if so, which ones. The greatest common divisor of two numbers is the largest number that evenly divides the two numbers. The notation $gcd(a, b)$ is generally used to indicate the greatest common divisor of a and b. The Euclidean algorithm gives us the common factors rolled into one in the form of the greatest common divisor. The Euclidean algorithm is based on the fact that if two numbers have a common factor k, then k is also a divisor of their difference. The Euclidean algorithm works as follows: (1) Find the $gcd(a, b)$ where $a > b$, divide b into a and write down the quotient q_1 and the remainder r_1 $a = q_1 + r_1$; (2) Perform a second division with b playing the role of a, and r_1 playing the role of b: $b = q_2 r_1 + r_2$; (3) Continue in this way until there is a remainder of zero. The final divisor is the $gcd(a, b)$.

Example: Find the greatest common divisor of 840 and 660 by means of the Euclidean algorithm:

840 = 660 . 1 + 180	840 = 180 mod 660
660 = 180 . 3 + 120	660 = 120 mod 180
180 = 120 . 1 + 60	180 = 60 mod 120
120 = 60 . 2	120 = 0 mod 60

Because 60 is the first divisor that yields a remainder of zero, then 60 is the greatest common divisor of 840 and 660.

If the greatest common divisor of two numbers is 1, the two numbers are relatively prime, sharing no common factor; the two numbers do not have to be prime in order to be relatively prime. The Euclidean algorithm discloses whether two numbers are relatively prime.

Example: Find out if 300 and 53 are relatively prime:

300	=	53 . 5 + 35	300	=	35 mod 53
53	=	35 . 1 + 18	53	=	18 mod 35
35	=	18 . 1 + 17	35	=	17 mod 18
18	=	17 . 1 + 1	18	=	1 mod 17
17	=	1 . 17 + 0	17	=	0 mod 17

Since 1 is the first divisor that yields a remainder of zero, then 1 is the greatest common divisor of 300 and 17, which means that both numbers are relatively prime.

Congruence Arithmetic

The notion of congruence arithmetic (modular arithmetic) was introduced by Gauss; it is a form of arithmetic in which only the remainders after division by a specific integer are used. If a is divided by p and has a remainder b, it can be said that a is congruent to b, modulo p. For example, if:

$$a = (k* p) + b$$ Equation 3-1

and, if $a = 32$ is divided by $p = 5$, the result will be $k = 6$ with a remainder of $b = 2$, and it can be written as a is congruent to b modulo $p = 5$.

This congruence is expressed as follows:

$a \equiv b \bmod p$ Equation 3-2

and it is read, *a is congruent to b modulo p*. Congruences with the same modulo can be added, subtracted, or multiplied (Ogilvy & Anderson, 1988).

Addition

If $a \equiv b \bmod p$ and $c \equiv d \bmod p$, then $(a + c) \equiv (b + d) \bmod p$.

For example, if $32 \equiv 2 \pmod 5$ and $49 \equiv 4 \pmod 5$, then $(32 + 49) \equiv (2 + 4) \pmod 5$ or $81 \equiv 6 \pmod 5 \equiv 1 \pmod 5$.

Subtraction

If $a \equiv b \bmod p$ and $c \equiv d \bmod p$, then $(a - c) \equiv (b - d) \bmod p$.

For example, if $49 \equiv 4 \pmod 5$ and $32 \equiv 2 \pmod 5$, then $(49 - 32) \equiv (4 - 2) \pmod 5$ or $17 \equiv 2 \pmod 5$.

Multiplication

Both sides of a congruence can be multiplied by the same number, just as both sides of an algebraic equation can be multiplied by the same number. If:

$a \equiv b \bmod p$ then, for any value of c, $(a* c) \equiv (b* c) \bmod p$ Equation 3-3

Example:

For   32 $\equiv$ 2 (mod 5) and c = 11:

           $(32 . 11) \equiv$ $(2 . 11)$ (mod 5)

           352        $\equiv$ 22 (mod 5)

           352        $\equiv$ 2 (mod 5)

Also, if $a \equiv b \bmod p$ and $c \equiv d \bmod p$, then $(a . c) \equiv (b . d) \bmod p$.

Example:

For   32 $\equiv$ 2 (mod 5)

and   49 $\equiv$ 4 (mod 5), then

           $(32 . 49) \equiv$ $(2 . 4)$ (mod 5)

$$1568 \equiv 8 \ (\text{mod } 5)$$
$$1568 \equiv 3 \ (\text{mod } 5).$$

Canceling

The rule for canceling a congruence by an integer is a little more complicated than multiplication. If:

$$(a* c) \equiv (b* c) \bmod p \hspace{4cm} \text{Equation 3-4}$$

then $a \equiv b \bmod \left[\dfrac{p}{(c, p)} \right]$

where (c, p) is the greatest common divisor of c and p. If c and p are relatively prime, then the $gcd\,(c, p) = 1$.

Example: $5800 \equiv 100 \ (\text{mod } 380)$. If the factor 100 is cancelled, then the module must be divided by the $gcd\,(100, 380)$, which is 20. Then, $58 \equiv 1 \bmod (19)$.

Exponentiation

Both sides of a congruence can be raised to the same exponent just as both sides of an equation can be raised to the same exponent. For any value of r:

$$a^r \equiv b^r \bmod p \hspace{4cm} \text{Equation 3-5}$$

Example:

For $32 \equiv 2 \ (\text{mod } 5)$ and r = 3:

$$32^3 \equiv 2^3 \ (\text{mod } 5)$$
$$32,768 \equiv 8 \ (\text{mod } 5)$$
$$32,768 \equiv 3 \ (\text{mod } 5)$$

If b is equal to 1, then Equations 3-1, 3-2, and 3-5 can be written as follows:

$$a = (k* p) + 1 \hspace{4cm} \text{Equation 3-6}$$
$$a \equiv 1 \bmod p \hspace{4cm} \text{Equation 3-7}$$
$$a^r \equiv 1 \bmod p \hspace{4cm} \text{Equation 3-8}$$

Fermat's Theorem indicates that if p is prime, and a is not divisible by p (a and p are relatively prime), they have no common factor other than 1 and -1). Then:

$$a^{p-1} = (k* p) + 1 \qquad\qquad\qquad\qquad \text{Equation 3-9}$$

$$a^{p-1} \equiv 1 \bmod p \qquad\qquad\qquad\qquad \text{Equation 3-10}$$

$$a^{p-1} \bmod p \equiv 1 \qquad\qquad\qquad\qquad \text{Equation 3-11}$$

In the same way:

$$(a^{p-1})^k \equiv 1 \bmod p \qquad\qquad\qquad\qquad \text{Equation 3-12}$$

For example, if $a = 6$ and $p = 17$ then:

$$6^{17-1} \equiv 1 \bmod 17$$

$$6^{16} \equiv 1 \bmod 17$$

This property can be used to exponentiate a to a large number. Having the restriction on a and p, it is possible to write:

$$6^{69} \ (\bmod\ 17) \equiv (6^{17 - 1})^4 \bmod 17. \ 6^5 \ (\bmod\ 17)$$

$$6^{69} \ (\bmod\ 17) \equiv 1 \ . \ 6^5 \ (\bmod\ 17) \equiv 7 \ (\bmod\ 17)$$

A faster way to do the exponentiation is to apply *modulo (p - 1)* to the exponent, and say that if $n \equiv m \bmod (p - 1)$, then $a^n \equiv a^m \bmod p$. In the example before, $a = 6$, $m = 69$, $p = 17$, and $n = 69 \bmod (17\text{-}1) = 5$; then, $6^{69} \ (\bmod\ 17) = 6^5 = 6^{69 \bmod (17 - 1)} = 6^5$ $(\bmod\ 17) = 7 \ (\bmod\ 17)$.

To exponentiate a to a large number when p is not a prime but a and p are relatively prime, $gcd\ (a, p) = 1$, it is necessary to use an extension of Fermat's Theorem, Euler's Theorem. Euler's Theorem states that:

$$a^{\varphi(p)} = (k*p) +1 \qquad\qquad\qquad\qquad \text{Equation 3-13}$$

$$a^{\varphi(p)} = 1 \bmod p \qquad\qquad\qquad\qquad \text{Equation 3-14}$$

where

1. a and p are relatively prime, they have no common factor other than 1 and -1.

2. $\varphi\ (p)$ is the Euler totien function, which is equal to the number of integers relatively prime to p in the range $1 \ . \ . \ . \ . \ (p - 1)$. For example, for $p = 15$, the relative prime

numbers are 1, 2, 4, 7, 8, 11, 13, 14; so, $\varphi\,(15) = 8$. In general:

a. If p is a prime, then $\varphi\,(p) = (p - 1)$

b. If p is a prime, then $\varphi\,(p^k) = (p^k - p^{k-1})$

d. If p is a prime and $k = 2$, then $\varphi\,(p^2) = p\,(p - 1)$

c. If p and q are primes, then $\varphi\,(p \cdot q) = (p - 1)\,(q - 1)$

3. If $gcd\,(p, q) = 1$, the Euler totien function is multiplicative denoting $\varphi\,(pq) = \varphi\,(p) * \varphi\,(q)$

Using Equation 3-14, it is possible to exponentiate a to a large number by reducing the exponent to:

$$a^{\varphi(p)} = 1 \bmod p$$

Example: For $a = 2$, $p = 15$ and $\varphi\,(15) = 8$:

$$2^{22} \text{ (mod 15)} \qquad \equiv \qquad [2^8 \text{ (mod 15)}] \,.\, [2^8 \text{ (mod 15)}] \,.\, [2^6 \text{ (mod 15)}]$$

$$2^{22} \text{ (mod 15)} \qquad \equiv \qquad 1 \,.\, 1 \,.\quad [2^6 \text{ (mod 15)}] \equiv 4 \text{ (mod 15)}$$

or,

$$2^{22} \text{ (mod 15)} \qquad \equiv \qquad [2^{22 \text{ (mod 8)}} \text{ (mod 15)}] \equiv [2^6 \text{ (mod 15)}] \equiv 4 \text{ (mod 15)}$$

Even if a is not relatively prime with p, it is possible to reduce the exponent to modulo φ (p), except in the case of exponents reduced to 0. For example, for $a = 3$, $p = 15$ and $\varphi\,(15) = 8$:

$$3^{22} \text{ (mod 15)} \qquad \equiv \qquad [3^8 \text{ (mod 15)}] \,.\, [3^8 \text{ (mod 15)}] \,.\, [3^6 \text{ (mod 15)}]$$

$$3^{22} \text{ (mod 15)} \qquad \equiv \qquad 1 \,.\, 1 \,.\quad [3^6 \text{ (mod 15)}] \equiv 9 \text{ (mod 15)}$$

or, $$3^{22} \text{ (mod 15)} \qquad \equiv \qquad [3^{22 \text{ (mod 8)}} \text{ (mod 15)}] \equiv [3^6 \text{ (mod 15)}] \equiv 9 \text{ (mod 15)}$$

According to Equation 3-5, Equation 3-14 can be written as follows:

$$a^{k\varphi(p)} = 1^k \bmod p = 1 \bmod p \qquad\qquad \text{Equation 3-15}$$

In addition, from Equation 3-3 it follows that:

$$a \cdot a^{k\varphi(p)} = a \cdot 1 \bmod p \qquad\qquad \text{Equation 3-16}$$

$$\text{or, } a^{k\varphi(p)+1} = a \bmod p \qquad\qquad \text{Equation 3-17}$$

Another exponentiation property is:

$a^{x \bmod p-1} \bmod p = a^x \bmod p$ Equation 3-18

Proof: Make $x = k(p-1) + y$, y being the remainder; by symmetry, if:

$x = y \bmod (p-1)$ then $y = x \bmod (p-1)$;
so $x = k(p-1) + x \bmod (p-1)$

Replacing x on the right side of Equation 3-18, we can say that:

$a^{x \bmod p-1} \bmod p = a^{k(p-1)+x \bmod p-1} \bmod p$
$a^{x \bmod p-1} \bmod p = [a^{k(p-1)}] * [a^{x \bmod p-1}] \bmod p$
$a^{x \bmod p-1} \bmod p = [(a^{p-1})^k \bmod p] * [a^{x \bmod p-1} \bmod p]$

Since according to Equation 3-12, $(a^{p-1})^k \bmod p = 1$, then:

$a^{x \bmod p-1} \bmod p = [1] * [a^{x \bmod p-1}] \bmod p = a^{x \bmod p-1} \bmod p$

Summary of Properties

The following is a summary of the properties of modulo (congruence) arithmetic mentioned in earlier paragraphs:

1. $(a+b) \bmod p \equiv a \bmod p + b \bmod p$
2. $(a * b) \bmod p \equiv a \bmod p * b \bmod p$
3. $(a^b)^c \bmod p \equiv a^{b*c} \bmod p$
4. $(a^{b+c}) \bmod p \equiv a^b * a^c \bmod p$-
5. If $a \equiv b \bmod p$, then

    $(a+x) \bmod p \equiv (b+x) \bmod p$

    $\quad (a * x) \equiv (b * x) \bmod p$

    $\quad\quad -a \equiv -b \bmod p$
6. By symmetry, if $a \equiv b \bmod p$ then $b \equiv a \bmod p$
7. If the $gcd(a, p) = 1$, then $a = (k * p) + a \bmod p$
8. By reflexivity, $a \equiv a \bmod p$
9. By transitivity, if $a \equiv b \bmod p$, and $b \equiv c \bmod p$, *then* $a \equiv c \bmod p$
10. If $a \equiv b \bmod p$, and $c \equiv d \bmod p$, then $a \pm c \equiv b \pm d \bmod p$ and $a * c \equiv b * d \bmod p$

11.   If $a \equiv b \bmod p$, then $a \equiv b \bmod d$ for any divisor $d \mid p$

12.   If $a \equiv b \bmod p$, and $a \equiv b \bmod q$, and p and q are relatively prime, then $a \equiv b \bmod (p * q)$

13.   Multiplication and exponentiation

$$(a \cdot c) \equiv (b \cdot c) \bmod p$$
$$a^k \equiv b^k \bmod p$$
$$a^{k \bmod (n-1)} \equiv a^k \bmod n$$

14.   **Cancellation:** If $a * c \equiv b * c \bmod p$, then $a \equiv b \bmod \lfloor \frac{p}{(c, p)} \rfloor$; but, if c and p are relatively prime, then $gcd(c, p) = 1$ and $a \equiv b \bmod p$.

15.   **Fermat's Theorem:** If p is prime and a and p are relatively prime, then:

$$a^{p-1} \equiv 1 \bmod p$$
$$(a^{p-1})^k \equiv 1 \bmod p$$

16.   **Fermat's Little Theorem:** If p is prime, any integer a satisfies $a^p \equiv a \pmod p$, and any integer a not divisible by p satisfies:

$$a^{p-1} \equiv 1 \bmod p$$

17.   If $gcd(a, p) = 1$ and if $b \equiv c \bmod (p-1)$, then $a^b \equiv a^c \bmod p$.

   Example: Find $38^6 \bmod 5$.

   Since $6 = 2 \bmod (5-1)$, then

   $38^6 \bmod 5 = 38^2 \bmod 5$

18.   **Euler's function:** If p is a composite number (not prime), and if: $gcd(a, p) = 1$, then, $a^{\varphi(n)} = 1 \bmod p$ and $a^{k\varphi(n)+1} = a \bmod n$

19.   If $a \equiv b \bmod p$, and $c \equiv d \bmod p$, and if $gcd(c, p) = gcd(d, p) = 1$, then, $a * c^{-1} = b * d^{-1} \bmod p$

where c^{-1} and d^{-1} are the multiplicative inverses of c and d *modulo p*.

Calculation of the Reciprocal (Multiplicative Inverse)

In modulo p arithmetic, the reciprocal of a number a is the solution of the equation $a \cdot x = 1 \pmod p$, when a and p are relatively prime. Relatively prime means that the only number that divides a and p is 1, that is, that the greatest common divisor of a and p is 1. The Euclidian algorithm can be modified to find x; x is called the reciprocal a or the multiplicative inverse of a. The following is one of the easiest procedures for finding the multiplicative inverse (Davies & Price, 1984).

Table 3-1. Multiplicative inverse

Col. 1	Euclid's Algorithm (Column 2)	K (Col. 3)	(Col. 4)	(Col. 5)
(a)			a = 0	a = 0
(b)			b = 1	b =1
(c)	341 = 6 * 53 + 23	6	c = (a – kb)	c = 0 - 6(+1) = -6
(d)	53 = 2 * 23 + 7	2	d = (b – kc)	d = 1 - 2(-6) = 13
(e)	23 = 3 * 7 + 2	3	e = (c – kd)	e = -6 - 3(+13) = -45
(f)	7 = 3 * 2 + 1	3	f = (d – ke)	f = 13 - 3(-45) = 148

For example, to find 53^{-1} mod 341, that is, the inverse of 53 mod 341, the steps necessary to find the *gcd* (341, 53) are put in column 2; in column 5, the results of the equations written in column 4 are listed. The equations in column 4 are continued until there is a remainder of 1 in Euclid's algorithm. The number in the fifth column, 148, is the multiplicative inverse of 53 mod 341; then 53 * 148 = 1 mod (341) and is written as 148 = inv (53, 341) or 148 = 53^{-1} mod 341.

In this example, 53 * (1/53) = 1 mod 341; replacing 1/53 = 148 mod 341, yields 53 * 148 = 1 mod 341.

There are situations in which the result of the multiplicative inverse is a negative number, so to convert it to positive number, the result is subtracted from the module. For example, 17^{-1} mod 23 = -4 mod 23 = (23 -4) mod 23 = 19 mod 23.

Multiplication and Exponentiation in Modulo *p*

The idea of preventing a number from getting too big is very useful in public-key exponentiation where the exponents are very large. As an example, raising the number 56 to the power of 118 and then finding its modulo would take a lot of time, even with the use of a very powerful computer application. By using modulo *p*, the number of operations could be reduced considerably. There are several algorithms that perform exponentiation in modulo *p*. The following algorithm, based on the binary expansion of the exponent, is one of the easiest to understand, and is used in the RSA algorithm.

The following are some of the properties of exponentiation modulo *p*:

56^1 (modulo 8191) = 56 (modulo 8191)

56^2 (modulo 8191) = 56 . 56 (modulo 8191) = 3,136 (modulo 8181)

56^4 (modulo 8191) = 3,136 . 3,136 (modulo 8191) = 5,296 (modulo 8191)

56^8 (modulo 8191) = 5,296 . 5,296 (modulo 8191) = 1,632 (modulo 8191)

56^{16} (modulo 8191) = 1,632 . 1,632 (modulo 8191) = 1,349 (modulo 8191)

56^{32} (modulo 8191) = 1,349 . 1,349 (modulo 8191) = 1,399 (modulo 8191)

56^{64} (modulo 8191) = 1,399 . 1,399 (modulo 8191) = 7,743 (modulo 8191)

To find the exponent (modulo p) of a large number, for example, 56^{118} (modulo 8191), first, the exponent, 118, is converted to binary:

118 (decimal)	=	3/2	7/2	14/2	29/2	59/2	118/2	118
(disregard decimals)		1	3	7	14	29	59	118
(0 if even, 1 if odd)		1	1	1	0	1	1	0

Next, to find the exponent (modulo p) up to the maximum binary exponent, as above, the rest of the operation is carried out as follows:

118 (decimal) =	1	1	1	0	1	1	0
(binary)							
56^{118} =	56^{64}	56^{32}	56^{16}		56^4	56^2	

which is equal to

56^{118} (mod 8191) = [56^{64} (mod 8191)] . [56^{32} (mod 8191)] . [56^{16} (mod 8191)] . [56^4 (mod 8191)] . [56^2 (mod 8191)]

By solving 56^2 (mod 8191) first and squaring and solving the results, the following is obtained:

56^{118} (mod 8191) = [7,743 (mod 8191)] . [1,399 (mod 8191)]. [1,349 (mod 8191)] . [5,296 (mod 8191)] . [3,136 (mod 8191)]

56^{118} (mod 8191) = [3,955 (mod 8191)] . [1,752 (mod 8191)] . [3,136 (mod 8191)]

56^{118} (mod 8191) = [7,765 (mod 8191)] . [3,136 (mod 8191)]

56^{118} (mod 8191) = [7388 (mod 8191)]

RSA Algorithm

The following is the RSA algorithm suggested for encryption (Rivest, Shamir, & Adleman 1978) and described by Muftic (1989):

RSA Algorithm (Encryption)

Step 0: Given *input*, a sequence of bits for encryption,

Step 1: Let $e_k e_{k-1} ... e_1 e_o$ be the binary representation of the encrypting key, *e*.

Step 2: Set the variable C to 1.

Step 3: Repeat steps 3a and 3b for $i = k, k - 1, k - 2, ..., 1, 0$.

Step 3a: Set C to the remainder of C^2 when divided by *n* (C^2 mod *n*).

Step 3b: If $e_1 = 1$, then set C to the remainder of C *input* when divided by *n* (C mod *n*).

Step 4: Stop. C is the encrypted form of *input*.

Finite Fields

A *set* is any collection of objects specified in such a way that it is possible to determine whether any given object is or is not in the collection (Hankerson, Menezes, & Vanstone, 2004). Capital letters are often used to designate particular sets. Symbolically:

$a \in E$ means   *a* is an element of *E*.

$a \notin E$ means   *a* is not an element of *E*.

$a \subset E$ means   *a* is a subset of *E*.

Table 3-2. Set of real numbers

Symbol	Number System	Description	Examples
N	Natural Numbers	Counting numbers (also called positive integers).	1, 2, 3, 4, 5, ...
Z	Integers	Set of natural numbers, their negatives, and zero.	.., -2, -1, 0, 1, 2, ...
Q	Rational	Any number that can be represented as *a/b*, where *a* and *b* are integers and $b \neq 0$.	-7, -2/5, 0, ¾, 5.42
R	Real	Set of all rational and irrational numbers.	-7, -2/5, 0, 1, ¾, 5.42, $\sqrt{2}, \sqrt{5}, \pi$

$a \not\subset E$ means a is not a subset of E.

$a = E$ means a and E are exactly the same elements.

A *field F* is a set of numbers with multiplication and addition operations that satisfies the following axioms (Koblitz, 1994):

- The operations $+$ and $*$ are associative, that is, $a + (b + c) = (a + b) + c$ and $a * (b * c) = (a * b) * c$ for any a; b; $c \in F$.

- There exists a multiplicative identity 1, such that $a * 1 = 1 * a = a$, for each element $a \in F$.

- There exists an additive identity 0, such that $a + 0 = 0 + a = a$, for each element $a \in F$.

- Each element $a \in F$ has an inverse $b \in F$ satisfying $a * b = b * a = 1$.

- The operation is commutative, that is, $a * b = b * a$ for any two elements $a, b \in F$. The group is called *abelian*.

The set of real numbers shown in Table 4-3 is not generally applicable to cryptography because in arithmetic, information is lost through round-off errors, or truncation in integer division, and, also, because real numbers are infinite fields.

In cryptography, it is necessary to have cyclic groups and this can be achieved using congruences. An integer field modulo q, denoted Z_q, has a finite number q of elements in it. The set Z_n is a cyclic group under addition, but if $q = ab$ is a composite number with $a > 1$ and $b > 1$, then the set $\{1 \ldots n-1)$ is not a group under multiplication modulo n because the product of a and b is equal to 0 modulo n. The set is not closed under multiplication.

When the modulo is a prime p, every integer $a \in \{1...p-1\}$ is relative prime to p and, therefore has a unique multiplicative inverse mod p. This field is denoted $F_p = Z / pZ$ and is called a *finite field*.

Another type of *finite field* with applications in cryptography is the field F_{q^m}, in which the modulo is an irreducible polynomial of degree m whose coefficients are integers modulo q, where q is a prime. When talking about polynomials, the term *prime* is replaced by the term *irreducible*. A polynomial is irreducible if it cannot be expressed as the product of two other polynomials.

Of particular interest in computer applications is the field F_{2^m} because the coefficients of the polynomial are 0s or 1s. Computation in F_{2^m} can be quickly implemented in hardware using linear feedback shift registers. The cost of hardware or software to compute F_{2^m} depends on the module that is selected. Using the primitive irreducible trinomial of the form $x^m + x + 1$ implements multiplication efficiently in F_{2^m}. The trinomial must be primitive, and the following are the values for m for which $x^m + x + 1$ is irreducible: 1, 3, 4, 6, 9, 15, 22, 28, 30, 46, 60, 63, 127, 153, 172, 303, 471, 532, 865, 900 (Schneier, 1994, p. 354).

Characteristic Prime Finite Fields

The finite field F_p is the prime finite field containing p elements. If p is an odd prime number, then there is a unique field F_p that consists of the set of integers $\{0, 1, 2, ..., p-1\}$ with the following arithmetic operations:

- **Addition:** If $a, b \in F_p$, then $a + b \equiv r \bmod p$.
- **Multiplication:** If $a, b \in F_p$, then $a * b \equiv r \bmod p$.
- **Inversion:** If a is a nonzero element in F_p, the inverse of a modulo p, denoted as a^{-1}, is the unique integer $c \in F_p$ for which $a * c \equiv 1 \bmod p$.

Characteristic Two Finite Fields

A characteristic two finite field (also known as a binary finite field) is a finite field whose number of elements is 2^m. If m is a positive integer greater than 1, the *binary finite field* $F_2{}^m$ consists of the 2^m possible bit strings of length m.

Thus, for example, $F_2{}^3 = \{000, 001, 010, 011, 100, 101, 110, 111\}$. The integer m is called the *degree* of the field.

A way to represent the elements of F_{2^m} is by the set of binary polynomials of degree m:

$$\{a_{m-1}x^{m-1} + a_{m-2}x^{m-2} + \ldots\ldots + a_1x + a_0 : a_i \in \{0,1\}\}$$

The following operations are defined in the elements of F_{2^m}:

- **Addition:** $a + b \equiv r \bmod 2$. This is equivalent to bitwise exclusive-OR (XOR) where $a, b,$ and r are bit strings.

Table 3-3. Bitwise logical operations

p	q	$p \wedge q$ (AND)	$p \vee q$ (OR)	$p \oplus q$ (XOR)	$p \rightarrow q$	$p \leftrightarrow q$
0	0	0	0	0	1	1
0	1	0	1	1	1	0
1	0	0	1	1	0	0
1	1	1	1	0	1	1

- **Multiplication:** If $a, b \in F_{2^m}$, then $a * b \equiv r$. Multiplication is done using polynomials.

  Then:

  $r = \{a_{m-1} x^{m-1} + a_{m-2} x^{m-2} + \ldots + a_1 x + a_0\} * \{b_{m-1} x^{m-1} + b_{m-2} x^{m-2} + \ldots + b_1 x + b_0\}$

  $r = \{r_{m-1} x^{m-1} + r_{m-2} x^{m-2} + \ldots + r_1 x + r_0 \bmod f(x)$

  For example, if $f(x) = x^4 + x + 1$, $a = x^3 + x^2 + 1$, and $b = x^3 + 1$,

  then, $r = a * b = (x^3 + x^2 + 1) * (x^3 + 1)$

  $r = x^6 + x^5 + x^2 + 1 \bmod (x^4 + x + 1) = x^3 + x^2 + x + 1$

- **Inversion:** If a is a nonzero bit stream element in F_{2^m}, the inverse of a, denoted as a^{-1}, is the unique integer $c \in F_{2^m}$ for which $a * c \equiv 1$.

Boolean Binary Expressions

Some of the Boolean Binary Expressions that are used in cryptography are $\wedge$ (AND), $\vee$ (inclusive OR), $\oplus$ (exclusive OR, all called XOR), $\rightarrow$ (conditional), and $\leftrightarrow$ (biconditional). They are shown in Table 3-3. Other expressions include:

AND: The operation yields the result TRUE when both of its operands are TRUE, otherwise the result is FALSE.

Inclusive OR: The operation yields the result FALSE when both of its operands are FALSE, otherwise the result is TRUE.

Exclusive OR: The operation yields the result TRUE when one, and only one, of its operands is TRUE, otherwise, the result is FALSE.

Conditional (if-then): The operation yields the result TRUE only if either p is FALSE or if q is TRUE, otherwise the result is FALSE.

Biconditional (If-and-only-if): The operation yields the result TRUE only if both operands are TRUE or False, otherwise, the result is FALSE.

With binary numbers, addition is done using XOR: $0 + 0 = 0$, $0 + 1 = 1$, $1 + 0 = 1$, and $1 + 1 = 0$ and carry a 1.

For example, adding binary 111001 (decimal 57) to 10011 (decimal 19) is as follows:

1		1	1	0	0	1
		1	0	0	1	1
1	0	0	1	1	0	0 (decimal 76)

In binary, multiplication is done using AND: $0 \times 0 = 0$, $0 \times 1 = 0$, $1 \times 0 = 0$, and $1 \times 1 = 1$ and carrying a 1.

For example, multiplying binary 10011 (decimal 19) by binary 111001 (decimal 57) works in this way:

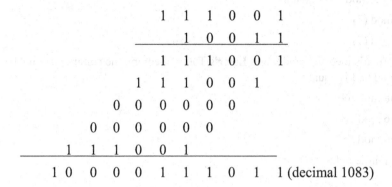

$$
\begin{array}{ccccccccccc}
 & & & & 1 & 1 & 1 & 0 & 0 & 1 \\
 & & & & & 1 & 0 & 0 & 1 & 1 \\
\hline
 & & & & 1 & 1 & 1 & 0 & 0 & 1 \\
 & & & 1 & 1 & 1 & 0 & 0 & 1 \\
 & & 0 & 0 & 0 & 0 & 0 & 0 \\
 & 0 & 0 & 0 & 0 & 0 & 0 \\
 1 & 1 & 1 & 0 & 0 & 1 \\
\hline
1 & 0 & 0 & 0 & 0 & 1 & 1 & 1 & 0 & 1 & 1 \text{ (decimal 1083)}
\end{array}
$$

Other binary definitions used in this book are *byte*, which is a group of eight bits, and *word*, which is a group of 32 bits that is treated either as a single entity or as an array of four bytes.

Summary

The following operation, 2^{53} mod 77201053 = 6352370, could be performed in a spreadsheet. However, in trying to do 2^{54} mod 77201053, there is an overflow error. In public-key, large numbers in the order of 50 or 100 digits are raised to the power of numbers with 300 or 400 digits. So how are computers able to perform these calculations? Euler's and Fermat's properties are used, as well as binary expansion of the exponent, to raise large numbers to a large exponent. In the same above-mentioned spreadsheet, it is possible to do $143634389^{4036961}$ mod 77201053 before overflow occurs by implementing the RSA algorithm explained in this chapter. Quite a difference!

Note that in encryption, it is necessary to use natural numbers (1, 2, 3, 4, 5, ...) because arithmetic operations using real numbers lead to round-off errors and truncation. Besides, encryption requires cyclic groups and finite fields. Cyclic groups and finite fields can be achieved using congruences.

Learning Objectives Review

1. If 4657 is divided by 9, the congruence is expressed as follows:

  a. $4657 \equiv 4 \bmod 9$

  b. $517 \equiv 4 \bmod 9$

2.   6 mod 7 + 3 mod 7 is equal to

  a.   4 mod (7)

  b.   2 mod (7)

3.   Using Fermat's theorem mod p and Euler's Totien theorem, the congruence of $1103^{317214570} \bmod 683$ is equal to

  a.   258 mod 683

  b.   186 mod 683

  c.   420 mod 683

4.   What is a finite field?

References

Davies, D. W., & Price W. L. (1984). *Security for computer networks*. New York: John Wiley & Sons.

Hankerson, D., Menezes A., & Vanstone, S. (2004). *Guide to elliptic curve cryptography*. New York: Springer-Verlag.

Koblitz, N. (1994). *A course in number theory and cryptography* (3rd ed.). New York: Springer-Verlag.

Muftic, S. (1989). *Security mechanisms for computer networks*. Chichester West Sussex, UK: Ellis Horwood Limited.

Ogilvy, C. S., & Anderson, J. T. (1988). *Excursion in number theory*. Mineola, NY: Dover Publications, Inc.

Schneier, B. (1994). *Applied cryptography*. New York: John Wiley & Sons.

Chapter IV

Confidentiality:
Symmetric Encryption

Confidentiality: Symmetric Encryption

In the world of communications, assurance is sought that (1) a message is not accidentally or deliberately modified in transit by replacement, insertion, or deletion; (2) the message is coming from the source from which it claims to come; (3) the message is protected against unauthorized individuals reading information that is supposed to be kept private; and (4) there is protection against an individual denying that the individual sent or received a message. These assurances are provided through the use of security mechanisms.

Chapters IV, V, VI, and VII discuss security mechanisms such as confidentiality, integrity, and access authentication that are used to implement the security services listed above.

This chapter covers two types of symmetric encryption: stream ciphers and block ciphers. The theory behind using shift registers as stream ciphers, as well as the DES and the Advanced Encryption Standard (AES), are also covered in this chapter.

Objectives

- Understand the differences between symmetric and asymmetric encryption
- Learn the design theory of the shift register as a random keystream generator
- Understand DES and AES design principles

Introduction

With the advent of computers and integrated circuits, mechanical cipher machines were replaced by encryption software, link encryption (Frame Relay or IP encryption), or encryption embedded in a data communications box such as a router or a switch. The use of microprocessor technology has made crypto machines more secure, reduced the encryption and decryption time processes, and made possible the manufacture of more compact units. Smart cards with an EPROM of 32K support public key infrastructure applications such as hashing, AES encryption, and RSA 1024-bit key generation.

Modern cryptographic equipment allows only carefully controlled access to the information it handles. The equipment is tamper resistant: the electronic design of the equipment does not reveal how to break the code, and the cryptographic variables are automatically dumped out of the electronic memory (erased) if the equipment is tampered with or altered. Furthermore, tests are used to check the operation of the key generator and the encryption algorithm.

Today there are crypto units to encipher any form of information: video, voice, messages, data, facsimile, satellite and microwave links, television signals, computer files, computer transmissions, signal authentication, and many more. A simplified block diagram of a crypto system is shown in Figure 4.1. The information to be enciphered, which can be voice, message, data, or any of the examples mentioned above, is called *plaintext*.

The microprocessor controls all the functions of the crypto unit. At a certain time, it may load the crypto variables into the key generator or get keystream bits to send them to the encryption algorithm block section whenever it is required.

The key generator is a device that produces an extremely long pseudorandom keystream, which consists of 1's and 0's.

The input interface block transforms the information to be enciphered into a format required by the machine for enciphering. For example, it may convert analog voice signals into digital for digital encryption; in a bulk encrypter, it may separate the framing bits from the data to encipher the data only and leave the framing bits in clear.

An encryption algorithm consists of a set of rules. These rules transform (1) the plaintext into ciphertext and (2) the ciphertext into plaintext (restored to its original unencrypted form) in the case of deciphering.

Figure 4-1. Crypto system

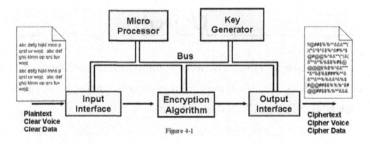

The output interface block transforms the ciphertext into a format suitable for transmission in a communications network.

The following are some of the terms used in modern cryptography. (Appendix B, "Glossary of Terms," provides an extended list of terms.)

- **Cipher system**: A cryptographic system in which cryptography is applied to information to transform it in such a way that unauthorized persons cannot understand it.

- **Encryption:** The transformation of plaintext into an unintelligible form (ciphertext) so that the original plaintext cannot be obtained without using the inverse decryption process.

- **Plaintext:** Information to be enciphered, or ciphertext that has been deciphered to intelligible information.

- **Cleartext:** Information that is transmitted in clear—it is not enciphered.

- **Ciphertext:** The plaintext that has been enciphered.

- **Cryptographic variables:** Any of the randomly generated variables (keys) that the user can change frequently to control the operation of the cipher algorithm that enciphers or deciphers information. The crypto variables are loaded into the keystream generator to change its output.

- **Keystream generator:** Device that produces the keystream. Also called *key generator*.

- **Keystream:** Pseudorandom stream of bits used by the ciphering algorithm to combine with the plaintext to form the ciphertext.

- **Encryption algorithm:** Set of rules implemented in software or hardware and used in conjunction with the cryptographic variables to encipher plaintext and decipher ciphertext.

- **Encipher**: To convert plaintext into unintelligible form by means of a cipher system.

- **Decipher:** To convert the ciphertext back to intelligible information by means of a cipher system.

Figure 4-2. Enciphering and deciphering a message

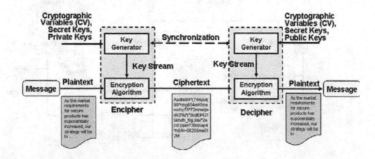

Crypto Systems

Essentially, there are two main types of modern crypto systems: symmetric and asymmetric encryption.

The type of crypto system in which enciphering and deciphering keys are the same is called *symmetric* (i.e., secret key) encryption. The system is analogous to having a box with a lock on it that can be locked and unlocked with the same key.

If a number of individuals wish to send secure information, symmetric cryptosystems require that initial arrangements be made for the individuals to share a unique secret key. The key must be distributed to the individuals via some secure, protected means to ensure key confidentiality and integrity. Transporting the key by courier, for example, is risky, slow, and expensive. Knowledge of the ciphering key implies knowledge of the deciphering key and vice versa.

An asymmetric crypto system, Figure 4-5, uses a pair of keys, mathematically related but different, to encipher and decipher messages. Messages encoded with either one of the keys can be decoded by the other. It is possible to make one of the keys public; however, the other one must be kept secret.

There are two main types of symmetric encryption: stream ciphers and block ciphers.

Stream Cipher Symmetric Encryption

Stream ciphers can be synchronous or self-synchronous (Denning, 1983). In a stream cipher, plaintext is broken into successive bits, and each one is enciphered with a bit from a keystream produced by a key generator. If the keystream repeats itself after p characters, the stream cipher is periodic; otherwise, it is nonperiodic. The Vernam cipher (one-time pad) and running-key ciphers are nonperiodic.

Figure 4-3. Symmetric and asymmetric encryption algorithms

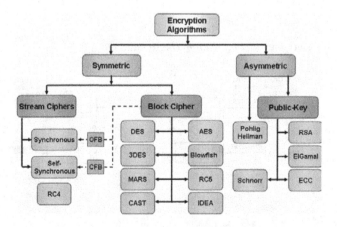

Figure 4-4. Symmetric cryptosystem

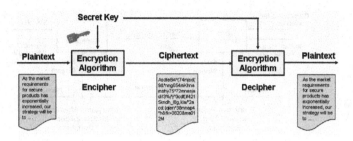

Figure 4-5. Public key crypto system

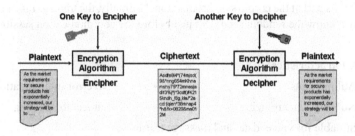

In a synchronous stream cipher, the keystream is generated independently of the clear or cipher text. In the self-synchronous stream cipher, each bit of the keystream depends on a fixed number *n* of the preceding ciphertext bits. To explain the synchronous and self-synchronous stream ciphers, the XOR function will be used as the encryption algorithm in the following diagrams.

Synchronous Stream Cipher

A stream cipher is synchronous when the plaintext bits that have been enciphered previously do not influence the keystream. This type of encryption, also called *Key-Auto-Key* (KAK), XORs the plaintext to the keystream output of the key generator. The deciphering process also involves the addition of the keystream to the ciphertext.

Since the key generator algorithm is fixed, a variable keystream is obtained by varying the cryptographic variables, which are loaded by the user. The Initialization Vector (IV), also called *random seed*, is the randomly generated variable which causes each cryptographic session to start at a different point in the keystream.

The initialization vector/random seed (IV) is normally generated by the transmitting cipher machine, and then transmitted to the receiving unit in clear. This cleartext transmission does not compromise the system's security because both sender and receiver use a shared secret method (H*) to transform the publicly known random seed into a secret H*(IV) called the

Figure 4-6. Synchronous stream cipher

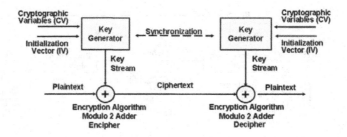

message key. The transmitting and receiving machines load the message key into the key generator as part of the crypto synchronization. Normally, the transmitting and the receiving machines know the random seed (IV) just before the communication session begins.

KAK Characteristics

- Autonomous
- Not self-synchronizing
- Suitable for voice, data, and message traffic

- No error multiplication
- Subject to spoofing

If the units lose synchronization, they must reinitialize, that is, begin a new communication session with a new initialization vector. Thus, KAK stream ciphers are not self-synchronizing. For security reasons, the keystream should be different for each session; this is achieved by having a different message key each time the unit synchronizes.

The Key-Auto-Key (KAK) stream ciphers have the advantage that there is no error propagation. If there is an error in the ciphertext bits (receiving a 1 for a 0 or a 0 for a 1), that bit error will produce an error only in the corresponding bit position of the plaintext. This factor is highly desirable in digital voice encryption over the telephone, microwave-link encryption with several hops, or any system that cannot operate with error propagation.

The disadvantages of KAK stream ciphers are that a special initialization effort is necessary to establish synchronism, and, as long as imitative deception is employed (the spoofer replaces the genuine ciphertext segment with a bogus segment, which is equally long), there will be no discernible hint that the ciphertext has been modified. However, imitative deception of real-time messages, data, or voice is almost impossible. Deception is more of a concern with formatted message communication than with real-time information.

Self-Synchronous Stream Ciphers

In a self-synchronous stream cipher, also called *Ciphertext-Auto-Key* (CTAK), part of the ciphertext is continuously fed back into the key generator. Consequently, each bit of the keystream depends on a fixed number n of ciphertext bits, n being the length of the feedback shift register used. The key generator's keystream is a function of the ciphertext.

There is no real need for an initialization vector (IV). The sender unit starts transmitting ciphertext, and, after just n incorrectly deciphered bits, the receiving unit begins deciphering the traffic correctly; the system is self-synchronizing. In broadcast communications, it is not necessary to be listening from the beginning of a communication session to decipher correctly the last parts of the message —late entry is possible.

The CTAK stream cipher prevents an active wiretapper (spoofer) from altering a segment of the ciphertext bit-stream. When the spoofer changes k bits in the ciphertext, due to the n-bit error propagation, it will produce $n + k$ bad ciphertext bits; on the average, half of the corresponding deciphered bits will be incorrect. If this is not normal in the communications environment in which the cipher system is operating, the receiver will suspect that spoofing has occurred.

The self-synchronization and authentication characteristics of CTAK self-synchronous stream ciphers are very attractive because they make the key generator design much less complicated than the synchronous stream cipher, and their features are widely used for message verification.

CTAK Characteristics

- Authentication
- Self-synchronization
- Unsuitability for high-error rate channels
- Error multiplication
- Ciphertext dependency

The poor signal performance of this technique detracts from the concept. If the feedback is n bits, and a single error appears in the ciphertext, the decryption process expands (multiplies) the error to a burst error n bits long, and then resynchronizes by itself after n correct bits have been received. In order to avoid exhaustive cryptanalysis, n is a number between 50 and 200 in most cipher systems. In some communications environments, like optical cable (fiber optics) with error rates of 10^{-9}, this is not a problem. However, the CTAK technique is not recommended for use in communications circuits with bit error rates of 10^{-4} or higher, or in systems subject to electronic warfare techniques. The cipher dependency and the resulting error multiplication make the system subject to failure due to noise and interference.

Figure 4-7. Self-synchronous stream ciphers

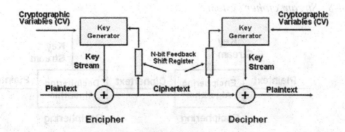

There is a noise-related range effect. As the distance between the transmitting and receiving units increases, the signal-to-noise ratio decreases (the signal strength at the receiver is inversely proportional to the square distance from the transmitter). KAK stream cipher systems work where CTAK systems become disabled by noise. In general, KAK systems have three times the range of CTAK systems for any given signal strength.

Self-synchronous stream ciphers are nonperiodic because the keystream depends on the plaintext; however, they are weak because they expose the key in the ciphertext stream. Passing the keystream through a nonlinear function increases the strength of the cipher stream. This technique is called *Cipher Feedback Mode* (CFB), and it has been approved by the National Bureau of Standards for use with block ciphers (NIST Special Publication 800-38A (Dworkin, 2001).

Basic Theory of Enciphering

Stream ciphers use a keystream to transform the plaintext into ciphertext. The set of rules used by the cipher system to mix the plaintext information with the keystream in order to obtain the ciphertext is called the *encryption algorithm.*

The keystream can be produced by a random noise (one-time tape) generator or by a pseudorandom bit generator. The one-time tape cannot be reproduced, and it needs to be delivered to the receiving side. The pseudorandom bit generator has the properties of random noise and can be duplicated at the receiving unit if both the sending and receiving units use the same cryptographic variables. If the keystream is obtained from shift registers, the inputs or initial states of the shift registers on the transmitting and receiving sides need to be the same.

In the following examples, the XOR function is used as the encryption algorithm, whose values are represented in the following table:

$$1 + 0 = 1 \qquad\qquad 1 + 1 = 0$$
$$0 + 1 = 1 \qquad\qquad 0 + 0 = 0$$

In a stream cipher system, to encipher a plaintext sequence of 1's and 0's each bit of the plaintext is XORed to one bit from the keystream to get the ciphertext. At the receiving

Figure 4-8. Stream cipher system

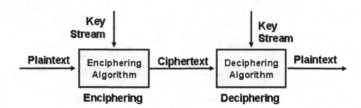

side, the ciphertext is again XORed to the same keystream to obtain the plaintext. If both keystream sequences are not the same, the message cannot be correctly deciphered.

Enciphering

Plaintext	1 0 0 1 1 0 0 0 1 0 1 0 0 0 1 1 0
Keystream	1 0 1 1 0 0 1 1 1 0 0 1 0 0 0 1 1

Ciphertext	0 0 1 0 1 0 1 1 0 0 1 1 0 0 1 0 1

Deciphering

Ciphertext	0 0 1 0 1 0 1 1 0 0 1 1 0 0 1 0 1
Keystream	1 0 1 1 0 0 1 1 1 0 0 1 0 0 0 1 1

Plaintext	1 0 0 1 1 0 0 0 1 0 1 0 0 0 1 1 0

When transmitting a long sequence of 1's and 0's, the received ciphertext may not be the same as it was transmitted, either because there was an error in receiving one of the bits (a 1 for a 0, or a 0 for a 1) or because one of the bits was missing. These two types of problems, errors or missing bits, produce different effects in the deciphering text.

Effects of Errors on Deciphering

In the following example, the first bit of the ciphertext was not received correctly (bit flip); for example, a 1 was received instead of a 0.

Enciphering

Plaintext	1 0 0 1 1 0 0 0 1 0 1 0 0 0 1 1 0
Keystream	1 0 1 1 0 0 1 1 1 0 0 1 0 0 0 1 1

Ciphertext	0 0 1 0 1 0 1 1 0 0 1 1 0 0 1 0 1

Deciphering

Ciphertext	**1** 0 1 0 1 0 1 1 0 0 1 1 0 0 1 0 1
Keystream	1 0 1 1 0 0 1 1 1 0 0 1 0 0 0 1 1

Plaintext	**0** 0 0 1 1 0 0 0 1 0 1 0 0 0 1 1 0

It can be seen that the only difference between the plaintext and the deciphered text is the first bit; the rest of the bits are the same. When the receiver's crypto unit gets a bad ciphertext bit, it will not interfere with the deciphering of the next ciphertext bit. In a message communication, one character will be incorrectly deciphered, and in a voice communication, only a hiss or a click will be heard.

Effect on Missing Bits during Transmission

When one bit is missed, the keystream is offset and the deciphered plaintext after the missing bit is garbled. If, for example, the sixth bit was missed during transmission:

Enciphering

Plaintext	1 0 0 1 1 <u>0 0 0 1 0 1 0 0 0 1 1 0</u>
Keystream	1 0 1 1 0 0 1 1 1 0 0 1 0 0 0 1 1

| Ciphertext | 0 0 1 0 1 0 1 1 0 1 1 1 0 0 1 0 1 |

Deciphering

Ciphertext	0 0 1 0 1 **1 1 0 1 1 1 0 0 1 0 1**
Keystream	1 0 1 1 0 0 1 1 1 1 0 1 0 0 0 1 1

| Plaintext | 1 0 0 1 1 **1 0 1 0 0 1 1 0 1 0 0** |

It can be noted that the first five bits of the deciphered text are the same as the plaintext but, later on, the deciphered text goes awry.

Synchronous Data with Unrestricted Cipher

Figure 4-9 shows an unrestricted cipher algorithm in which the XOR function is used to encipher synchronous data. In this type of encryption, if the keystream is random, the ciphertext will be random. The correct decryption requires that the keystream be the same in the enciphering and deciphering processes.

Unrestricted ciphers encipher bit by bit and are mainly used in data encryption to encipher microwave links, computer data, digital facsimiles, and digital voice. In some situations, the crypto unit enciphers whatever sequence of bits enters the encryptor. In others, the crypto unit separates the data from the framing bits and communications protocols to encipher only the data.

Figure 4-9. Unrestricted encryption algorithm

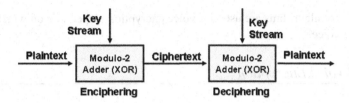

Character-Formatted Ciphertext

In the character-formatted encryption machine shown in Figure 4-10, the ASCII plaintext is enciphered using a symmetric encryption algorithm and the ciphertext is formatted into ASCII. The cipher characters can have any value; for example, if the ciphertext is in Baudot, the characters can be figures, letters, line feed, carriage return, and so forth.

Since the ciphertext is unrestricted and can have any value, it may produce some ciphertext characters which are not compatible with certain e-mail systems or carriers and networks, such as Frame Relay. Consequently, the network must allow the transmission of the ciphertext characters without any change or disruption to the communications channel.

There are situations in which the transmission system may require that only the characters A-Z, a-z, and numbers 0-9 be used, as in the case of e-mail. In those situations, a Base-64 substitution table is used to convert raw encrypted data to only printable ASCII characters. Six bits at a time of raw cipher data are converted to one of the characters in the string "ABCDEFGHIJKLMNOPQRSTUVWXYZabcdefghijklmnopqrstuvwxyz0123456789+/". For example, 000000 (Dec 0) is converted to A, 011010 (Dec 26) is converted to a, and 111111 (Dec 63) is converted to /. Base-64, also know as Radix-64, is used mainly for transfer encoding for e-mail in Pretty Good Privacy (PGP) and Secure Email (S/MIME). See Chapter 10 for more information on Base-64 and Radix-64.

If only the characters A-Z are allowed in the ciphertext, then modulo-26 could be applied to five or seven bits of the raw encrypted data.

Figure 4-10. Character-formatted encryption algorithm

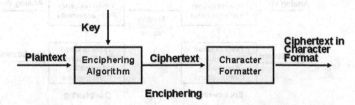

Voice Encryption

Two types of algorithms are used for voice encryption, depending on whether it is digital or analog voice.

Digital Voice Encryption

Digital voice encryption, Figure 4-11, is similar to synchronous data encryption. The enciphering algorithm is typically bit-by-bit encryption or block encryption.

Analog Voice Scrambling

Analog voice scrambling, Figure 4-12, rearranges the time and frequency of the voice signal. In this method, the keystream does not act directly on the encryption algorithm. The way in which the frequencies and time portions of the voice signal are arranged is based on the encryption algorithm.

Perfect Secrecy

In the section, "Basic Theory of Enciphering," the way in which keystream bits produced by the key generator are used by the encryption algorithm to convert the plaintext into ciphertext

Figure 4-11. Digital voice encryption

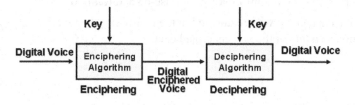

Figure 4-12. Analog voice scrambling

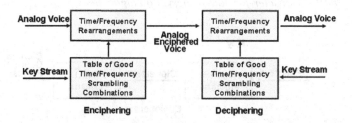

was described. In encryption, the keystream and the encryption algorithm should provide perfect secrecy and make the system unbreakable. A system provides perfect secrecy if the enciphering of a character or a bit is not based on any previous or subsequent character or bit; this means that the intercepted ciphertext does not provide enough information for the cryptanalyst to break the cipher.

From the theoretical point of view, the only system that offers perfect secrecy is the one in which the keystream is totally random, infinitely long, and used only one time. A perfect crypto system is achieved only with Vernam's cipher, the one-time key, in which the keystream is random, as long as the message, and used only one time. However, Vernam's cipher system is not widely used because of the following problems:

- The length of the key should be at least as long as the plaintext.
- There is an immense volume of key material that needs to be sent to the receiver.
- It is imperative that the cryptographer finds a safe way of letting the recipient know the key that was used to encipher the message.

In today's communications, there is a great volume of traffic, and the number of messages sent and received in any corporation, army, or branch of government is immense. If a one-time key system is used, a great deal of equipment and resources are necessary to ensure that each keystream sequence is used only once. This is the reason why a one-time key system is only used for top-secret messages in high-level strategic communications.

Several mathematicians and cryptologists have proven that Vernam's cipher, the one-time pad, is unbreakable. As a result, many cryptographers believed that if they could emulate the one-time key system in some way, without the key management problems mentioned before, they would have a system with a guaranteed high level of security. Vernam's conditions led to the introduction of the keystream generator, most commonly known as key generator, which emulates the conditions for perfect secrecy.

Characteristics of a Perfect Key Generator

The following are some of the characteristics of a perfect key generator, if one could be built:

1. **Infinite Number of Crypto Variables (Keys).** In order to maintain the highest level of security, a different key would be used to encipher each message. Therefore, the perfect key generator would have an infinite number of keys from which to choose.

2. **Completely Random Keystream.** Ideally, the keystream from a perfect key generator would be completely random, such as the output of a white noise generator. The value of this concept lies in the inability to re-create exactly the same keystream.

3. **Infinite Cycle Length.** Each keystream of the perfect key generator would be infinitely long to ensure that the keystream in use would never repeat itself.

4. **Random Starting Places**. The perfect key generator would never start enciphering a message with a portion of the keystream already used to encipher a previous message. To prevent this occurrence, the key generator would start at a different place on its infinitely long cycle length each time a new message was enciphered.

5. **Fail Safe-Alarms.** An alarm system would be used to prevent any transmissions if the key generator fails.

In the real world, a key generator is very close to being perfect by having the following characteristics and advantages:

1. **Code-Setting Control.** A code-setting control actually changes the generated keystream; thus, two identical devices can "talk to each other" only if they have the same code setting or crypto variables. A good key generator should have more than 10^{80} crypto variables.

2. **Pseudorandom Keystream**. A completely random keystream would be impractical because it could not be re-created and, thus, could not be deciphered. A more practical unit would be a key generator that produces a pseudorandom keystream that is random for all statistical tests, but which can be recreated, by the same type of key generator, when the same crypto variables are loaded into both key generators.

3. **A Very Long Cycle Length**. A very long cycle period more than 10^{90} is satisfactory.

4. **Random Starting Places**. By randomizing the starting position for the enciphering sequence, the keystream is changed for every single message. This concept is called *message key* or *initialization vector (IV)*. With many different message keys (starting positions in the key generator), the probability that the key used to encipher a message is used only one time is very high. This is one of the most important of Vernam's conditions for a perfect keystream. In some crypto systems, the IV size is the same size as the block, that is, in AES the IV is 128 bits.

5. **Fail-Safe Alarms**. Most key generators employ an alarm system to monitor their own operation to prevent transmission if a failure is detected.

Shift Registers

As mentioned before, information written in binary digits can be enciphered by XORing the plaintext and keystream. An electrical-noise, random bit generator could be used to generate a stream sequence of 1's and 0's, with the great advantage that it is totally random; however, since the sequence cannot be reproduced, the keystream must be sent to the receiver to decipher the message. This situation would lead back to the key management problem of Vernam's cipher, the one-time key system.

A shift register, implemented as a random sequence generator, generates the same keystream sequence used to encipher and decipher information. Key generators based on shift registers

Figure 4-13. A four-stage shift register

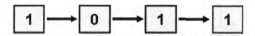

generate the sequence using only 1's and 0's, the sequence **looks** random, and slight modifications to the shift register generate different sequences or keystreams.

Shift registers are devices consisting of n consecutive, 2-state memory-storage units (usually flip-flops). These registers are connected so that the state of each stage memory can be transferred to its neighbor to the immediate left or right under the control of a single clock signal (Jay, 1984).

An n-stage shift register consists of n consecutive storage or memory units regulated by a clock signal. Each storage unit stores a 1 or a 0. At each clock signal, the state (1 or 0) of each memory stage is shifted to the next stage in line.

Figure 4-13 shows a four-stage shift register with an initial input of 1, 0, 1, and 1. At each clock signal, the state of each stage will be as follows:

Clock	Stages	Clock	Stages	Clock	Stages
0	1 0 1 1	3	0 0 0 1	6	0 0 0 0
1	0 1 0 1	4	0 0 0 0		
2	0 0 1 0	5	0 0 0 0		

Since no new signal is introduced into the first stage during this process, at the end of the four clock signals, the state of all the stages is 0 and will remain like that from then on. Therefore, depending on the input, the period is $p \le 4$.

Linear Shift Registers

The shift register can be kept active during a longer period by including a feedback loop, which computes a new term for the first stage based on the states of certain other stages. To compute the new state (1 or 0) for the first stage, AND, OR, and XOR gates (or a combination of them) are used. Linear shift registers use only XOR gates.

The term *Linear Feedback Shift Register (LFSR)* is used to refer to a shift register with an XOR function and a feedback line; shift register sequence is used to refer to the output, which is normally from the last stage, but it can be from any stage.

A shift register can be represented as follows:

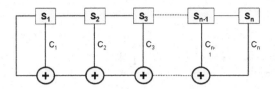

in which the new value for location S1 is given by

$$f(S_1, S_2\ S_3\ \cdots\ S_n) = C_1 S_1 \oplus C_2 S_2 \oplus C_3 S_3 \oplus \cdots \oplus C_n S_n \qquad \text{Equation 1}$$

Each of the feedback coefficients, C_i, is either 1 or 0, and the symbol $\oplus$ denotes addition using an XOR function.

Polynomial notation is a very convenient way to represent LFSRs. For example, the vector 110110001 may be represented as $f(x) = x_0 + x_1 + x_3 + x_4 + x_8$, where the first bit starting from left to right indicates the coefficient of x_0. The polynomial $f(x)$ of any shift register, called the *characteristic polynomial*, can be determined as the sum of the values of $C_i x_i$ for which the S_i stage is fed back into the XOR function.

In the above shift register, $f(x)$, the characteristic polynomial, is equal to:

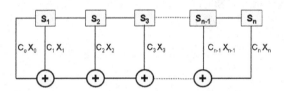

$$f(x) = \sum_{n=0}^{n} C_n\ x^n \qquad \text{Equation 2}$$

$$f(x) = C_0 x^0 + C_1 x^1 + C_2 x^2 + C_3 x^3 + \cdots C_{n-1} x^{n-1} + C_n x^n \qquad \text{Equation 3}$$

or, for $C_0 = 1$ and $C_n = 1$

$$f(x) = 1 + C_1 x^1 + C_2 x^2 + C_3 x^3 + \cdots C_{n-1} x^{n-1} + x^n \qquad \text{Equation 4}$$

C_i is either 1 when the feedback is connected or 0 when it is disconnected. $C_n = 1$ means that the last feedback switch is always connected; otherwise, the last stage is not used. $C_0 = 1$ refers to the fact that the new computed term is always loaded into the first stage. The characteristic polynomial is expressed as an addition in which the content of each of the feedback coefficients, C_i, is either 1 or 0.

Advantages of Linear Shift Registers

Linear shift registers have the following advantages:

1. They produce sequences of 1's and 0's.
2. Identical shift registers with the same initial input behave alike and produce exactly the same outputs.
3. They easily produce long cycles.
4. Their outputs are statistically balanced.
5. They have well-known properties.

Disadvantages of Linear Shift Registers

Linear shift registers have the following disadvantages:

1. They are described by a single recursion equation.
2. Previous stages are easily calculated.
3. In the initial starting condition, all zeros must be avoided to prevent collapse. Setting at least one of the stages to 1 prevents this problem.
4. Improper selection of the feedback taps may not produce maximum length periods.

In the following examples, certain characteristics and properties of shift registers will be explained, as well as aspects to be considered when choosing the taps for feedback.

Example 1

The example below illustrates a four-stage linear shift register in which stages 1 and 4 are tapped and XORed, with the result being fed back to stage 1. The state diagram shows the initial state and the sequence of successive states of the shift register.

	Clock	States	Clock	States	Clock	States
(Initial)		0 0 0 1				
	1	1 0 0 0	7	0 1 0 1	13	0 1 0 0
	2	1 1 0 0	8	1 0 1 0	14	0 0 1 0
	3	1 1 1 0	9	1 1 0 1	15	0 0 0 1
	4	1 1 1 1	10	0 1 1 0	16	1 0 0 0
	5	0 1 1 1	11	0 0 1 1	17	1 1 0 0
	6	1 0 1 1	12	1 0 0 1	18	1 1 1 0

$$f(x) = C_0 x^0 + C_1 x^1 + C_4 x^4 = 1 + x + x^4$$

At the 15th clock signal, the state of the shift register returns to the initial state and starts repeating itself. It can be said that the sequence is periodic with a period of $p = 15 = 2^4 - 1$. Because all possible binary vectors of length 4, except 0000, occur in the shift register, it is possible to say that $p = 15 = 2^4 - 1$ is the maximum length of a four-stage shift register.

The shift register sequence is the output of the shift register, which can be taken from any of the stages. If the output is taken from the fourth stage, the sequence will be the following:
0 0 0 1 1 1 1 0 1 0 1 1 0 0 1 **0 0 0 1 1 1 1 0 1 0 1 1 0 0 1**.

Note that the sequence starts repeating itself after the 15th bit, even if the output sequence is taken from any of the stages. Also, in the output sequence of any of the stages, there is one more one than zeros. In this case, there are eight 1's and seven 0's. This is the balance property of maximum sequences in which there are 2^{n-1} ones and $2^{n-1} - 1$ zeros.

In polynomial algebra, the degree of a polynomial is the largest power of a term of the polynomial having a nonzero coefficient. Thus, the degree of $f(x) = x^0 + x^1 + x^3 + x^4 + x^8$ is 8. A polynomial $f(x)$ which is not divisible by any polynomial of a degree less than n but greater than 0 is called *irreducible*. Irreducible polynomials play the same role among polynomials that the prime numbers play among integers. An irreducible polynomial of degree n is a primitive polynomial if, and only if, it divides $x^m - 1$ (where $m = 2^n - 1$) and does not divide $x^k - 1$ for $k < m$. A sequence generated by a shift register will be said to have maximum length if the characteristic polynomial is primitive.

In example 1, the characteristic polynomial of the shift register is given by $f(x) = x^0 + x^1 + x^4 = 1 + x^1 + x^4$. Since the shift register has a maximum-length sequence, then its characteristic polynomial is primitive.

Note the following property: If each of the exponents of the above characteristic polynomial is deducted from the highest exponent in the polynomial (x^{n-k}), the result is the characteristic polynomial of a shift register that has the same period and, in some cases, identical sequences. For the example given above, the reciprocal polynomial will be the following:

$$f(x) = (x^{4-0}) + (x^{4-1}) + (x^{4-4})$$
$$f(x) = x^4 + x^3 + x^0 = 1 + x^3 + x^4$$

which is the shift register of Example 2.

For any characteristic polynomial, $f(x) = \sum_{n=0}^{n} C_n x^n$ the reciprocal polynomial is given by:

$$f^*(x) = \sum_{i=0}^{n} C_i x^{n-i} = x^n f\left(\frac{1}{x}\right)$$

Equation 5

and the degree of $f(x)$ is equal to the degree of $f^*(x)$.

Example 2

The same four-stage shift register with stages 3 and 4 tapped and with the initial states is shown below.

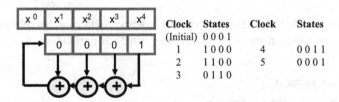

x^0	x^1	x^2	x^3	x^4
	1	0	0	0

Clock	States	Clock	States	Clock	States
1	1 0 0 0	6	0 1 1 0	11	1 1 1 0
2	0 1 0 0	7	1 0 1 1	12	1 1 1 1
3	0 0 1 0	8	0 1 0 1	13	0 1 1 1
4	1 0 0 1	9	1 0 1 0	14	0 0 1 1
5	1 1 0 0	10	1 1 0 1	15	0 0 0 1

$$f(x) = C_0 x^0 + C_3 x^3 + C_4 x^4 = 1 + x^3 + x^4$$

This shift register also has a maximum-length sequence of $p = 2^n - 1$, which indicates that there is more than one way to obtain a maximum-length sequence in a shift register. Also, the characteristic polynomial of the shift register is primitive and is given by $f(x) = x^0 + x^3 + x^4 = 1 + x^3 + x^4$.

Example 3

The same four-stage shift register, but now with stages 1, 2, 3 and 4 tapped, and with the same initial states, is shown below.

The sequence starts repeating itself after five clock signals, and the period is not maximum; therefore, the length of a shift register sequence is not always $p = 2^n - 1$, depending on how the feedback taps are selected. Also, even if the characteristic polynomial of the shift register below is irreducible, the sequence is not maximum.

Golomb (1982) established that if a shift-register sequence has a maximum length, its characteristic polynomial is irreducible. That is the case in Examples 1 and 2. Golomb also stated that the converse of the theorem does not hold, and that there actually exist irreducible polynomials that correspond to no maximum-length sequences. For example, $f(x) = 1 + x^1 + x^2 + x^3 + x^4$ (Example 3) is irreducible (it is not divisible by any polynomial of a degree less than 4), but since it divides $1 - x^5$, it is not primitive, and it has a period of five rather than the maximum period of $2^4 - 1 = 15$.

x^0	x^1	x^2	x^3	x^4
0	0	0	1	

Clock	States	Clock	States
(Initial)	0 0 0 1		
1	1 0 0 0	4	0 0 1 1
2	1 1 0 0	5	0 0 0 1
3	0 1 1 0		

$$f(x) = C_0 x^0 + C_1 x^1 + C_2 x^2 + C_3 x^3 + x^4 = 1 + x^1 + x^2 + x^3 + x^4$$

Zierler has demonstrated (Zierler, 1955) that the number of irreducible polynomials modulo-2 of degree n is given by:

$$N_1 = \frac{1}{n} \sum_{d|n} 2^d \, \mu(\frac{n}{d})$$

Equation 6

where the sum is extended over all positive divisors d of n, including 1.

The Möbius function $\mu(n)$ is defined as follows (Hardy & Wright, 1989):

1. $\mu(1) = 1$
2. $\mu(n) = 0$ if n has a squared factor
3. $\mu(p_1 \, p_2 \dots p_k) = (-1)^k$ if all the primes $p_1, p_2, \dots, p_k$ are different
4. $\mu(p^k) = 0$ if $k \geq 2$
5. $\mu(p^i q^j) = 0$ if p and q are primes and if $i + j > 2$

Thus $\mu(4) = -1$, $\mu(5) = -1$, $\mu(5 \times 3) = 0$, $\mu(5) = 0$, $\mu(5^2) = 0$, $\mu(5^2 \times 3^4) = 0$.

For example, to compute the number of irreducible polynomials modulo-2 of a shift register of $n = 4$, the divisors of 4 are d = 1, 2, and 4. Then:

$$N_1(4) = 1/4 \, [2^1 \, \mu(4/1) + 2^2 \, \mu(4/2) + 2^4 \, \mu(4/4)]$$
$$N_1(4) = 1/4 \, [2^1 \, (0) + 2^2 \, (-1) + 2^4 \, (1)] = 3$$

In this case, examples 1, 2, and 3 are the only irreducible polynomials of degree 4.

Zierler also has shown that the N_m number modulo-2 logic yielding the maximum length of $p = 2^n - 1$ is given by:

$$N_m(n) = \frac{\varphi(2^n - 1)}{n}$$

Equation 7

where φ is the Euler function. The Euler phi-function $\varphi(n)$ is defined as the number of non-negative integers b less than n, which are prime to n (Riesel, 1985). In particular:

1. $\varphi(p) = (p - 1)$ for any prime p
2. $(p^k) = (p^k - p^{k-1}) = p^{k-1}(p - 1)$ for any prime p
3. $(pq) = \varphi(p) \, \varphi(q) = (p - 1)(q - 1)$ if p and q are primes

For $n = 4$, then

$$N_m(n) = \frac{\varphi(2^n - 1)}{n} = \frac{\varphi(15)}{4} = \frac{\varphi(3.5)}{4} = \frac{(2).(4)}{4} = 2$$

Zierler's formula indicates that for a four-stage shift register, there are only two ways to achieve maximum length. In this case, Examples 1 and 2 are the only feedback configurations that yield a maximum length, $p = 2^4 - 1 = 15$.

An approximation to this formula, when n is greater than 5, is the following:

$$N_m(n) = \frac{\varphi(2^n - 1)}{n} \approx \frac{2^n}{n} \qquad \text{Equation 8}$$

Example 4

Examples with the same four-stage shift register with stages 2 and 4 tapped, but this time, with two initial states, 0 0 0 1 and 1 0 1 1, are shown below.

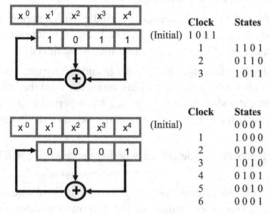

	Clock	States
(Initial)	1 0 1 1	
	1	1 1 0 1
	2	0 1 1 0
	3	1 0 1 1

	Clock	States
(Initial)		0 0 0 1
	1	1 0 0 0
	2	0 1 0 0
	3	1 0 1 0
	4	0 1 0 1
	5	0 0 1 0
	6	0 0 0 1

$$f(x) = C_0 x^0 + C_2 x^2 + C_4 x^4 = 1 + x^2 + x^4$$

In the examples above, (1) When the initial state is 0 0 0 1, the sequence starts repeating itself after six clock signals; (2) When the initial state is 1 0 1 1, the period is 3; (3) The characteristic polynomial, $f(x) = x^0 + x^2 + x^4$, is reducible (that is, it can be factored). Therefore, if the characteristic polynomial $f(x)$ is reducible, the period depends on the initial conditions.

In Example 3, the polynomial is irreducible, but this time with an initial state of 0 1 0 1.

	Clock	Stages	Clock	Stages
(Initial)		0 1 0 1		
	1	0 0 1 0	4	1 0 1 0
	2	1 0 0 1	5	0 1 0 1
	3	0 1 0 0		

$$f(x) = C_0 x^0 + C_1 x^1 + C_2 x^2 + C_3 x^3 + x^4 = 1 + x^1 + x^2 + x^3 + x^4$$

Even if the initial condition (input) is different, the period is still $p = 5$, as in Example 3, and the period 5 is a factor of the maximum length of 15. This suggests that the length of shift registers with irreducible polynomials is always the same, regardless of their initial state.

Properties of Shift Registers

Shift registers have some important properties when used as key generators; most of these properties have been mathematically proven (Golomb, 1982).

- **Property 1:** A shift register produces sequences that depend upon the number of stages, feedback tap connections, and initial conditions.

- **Property 2:** The succession of states in a shift register is periodic, with a period $p \leq 2^n - 1$, where n is the number of stages (Golomb, 1982). The value of p depends on the feedback coefficients, but a period of $(2^n - 1)$ can sometimes be achieved.

- **Property 3:** A sequence generated by an n-stage shift register is said to have maximum length if its period is $p = 2^n - 1$. This maximum length holds, no matter what the initial state of the shift register is. Also, if a shift register sequence has a period of $p = 2^n$, then every possible binary vector (except all zeros) of length n occurs exactly once in each period.

- **Property 4:** In any LFSR, the feedback tabs determine whether the sequence will be maximum or not.

- **Property 5:** In LFSRs with reducible characteristic polynomials (nonmaximal sequences), the initial conditions (the initial sequence loaded into the shift register) determine which sequence is generated and the period of said sequence.

- **Property 6:** If all the exponents of a polynomial are even (Golomb, 1982), then the characteristic polynomial is reducible, and it cannot have a maximum length sequence', for example, the characteristic polynomial $f(x) = 1 + x^2 + x^4$ of Example 4 is reducible.

- **Property 7:** If a shift register sequence has maximum length, its characteristic polynomial is irreducible; however, the converse of this property does not hold true. There actually are irreducible polynomials that correspond to no maximum-length sequences (Golomb, 1982).

- **Property 8:** If the characteristic polynomial of a LFSR is primitive, the shift register sequence has maximum length.

- **Property 9:** A maximum length sequence cannot be generated from a shift register that has an odd number of taps because this means that $f(x)$ is divisible by $(x - 1)$.

- **Property 10:** The number of ways to achieve maximum length ($p = 2^n - 1$) in a shift register is given by:

$$N_m(n) = \frac{\phi(2^n - 1)}{n} \approx \frac{2^n}{n}$$

- **Property 11:** If a sequence has an irreducible characteristic polynomial of degree n, the period of the sequence is a factor of $2^n - 1$, and it may or may not be maximum.

The period is always the same, regardless of the initial state. However, if the maximal length, $p = 2^n - 1$, is prime, every irreducible polynomial of degree n corresponds to a shift register sequence of maximum length (Golomb, 1982). When $p = 2^n - 1$ is prime, it is known as Mersenne prime.

- **Property 12:** If a sequence has an irreducible characteristic polynomial of degree n, its maximum length does not depend on the initial conditions, except for the initial condition, "all 0's."

- **Property 13:** If a sequence has a primitive characteristic polynomial of degree n, its period is the smallest positive integer p for which the characteristic polynomial $f(x)$ divides $x^p - 1$, modulo 2.

Nonlinear Combinations of LFSR Devices

A key generator based on LFSR is similar to a large turning wheel made up of $2^n - 1$ memory spaces. At a certain point, all these memory spaces are filled with 1's and 0's; whether a 1 or a 0 is stored in each memory space depends on the crypto variables loaded by the user of the crypto machine. These are the initial conditions of the key generator. After the memory spaces are loaded, a starting position around the virtual cipher wheel is chosen by selecting an initial variable (IV); and the 1's and 0's of each memory location constitute the keystream.

Golomb (1982) demonstrated that shift register sequences satisfy all three of his randomness properties. Shift registers are thus very good candidates to generate the sequences needed for stream ciphers. In the examples above, however, linear shift registers with periods $p \leq 2^n - 1$ have certain disadvantages: (1) The entire sequence is known once it has been determined how the feedback taps are connected; and (2) If the input is not changed before 2^n clocks signals, the keystream reverts to its initial state—it starts repeating the original sequence.

Key generator algorithms based on only one LFSR are not used because by solving $2n$ independent equations involving the feedback coefficients and the initial states, a cryptanalyst would be able to obtain the entire sequence. Instead, cryptosystem designers use the algebra of Galois fields to design cryptosystems that incorporate several LFSRs. These LFSRs are connected in nonlinear ways to increase the amount of effort and time (work factor) a cryptanalyst must use in order to read the traffic. A key generator should have a well-balanced sequence, so the designer should be careful when selecting nonlinear combinations of LFSRs because some nonlinear combinations produce keystreams that exhibit bad statistical properties.

Implementation of Nonlinear Key Generators

Most key generators consist of several mostly maximum-length LFSRs whose output sequences are combined in a nonlinear function F to produce the keystream. See Figure 4-14. Some of the functions used to introduce some nonlinearity into the keystream are multiple registers, dynamic interconnection between registers, stepping between registers, and random starting points.

Figure 4-14. Nonlinear LFSR key generator

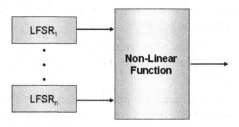

Beker and Piper (1982) established the following requirements for a sequence to be considered for use in a cipher system:

1. The keystream produced by the key generator must have a large period, and that period should be at least as long as any message to be enciphered. Only messages that are shorter than the keystream sequence will be enciphered.

2. The sequence must appear to be random.

3. The sequence must exhibit maximum linear complexity (nonlinearity). The linear complexity of a sequence is defined as the length of the shortest LFSR that can generate the sequence.

As Beker and Piper indicate, having a sequence with a large linear equivalent is necessary, but not sufficient. The sequence also needs to be random, so that the cryptanalyst cannot use statistical methods to attack the system.

There are many ways to implement the nonlinear function F. Some of the techniques used are explained below.

Generating Long Sequences Using Multiple LFSRs

The first requirement in the design of a key generator is that it should produce a very long sequence; this means that it will only repeat itself after a very long period. This requirement could be achieved, as in Vernam's cipher, by having a long, random, never-repeating, one-time-pad or by combining two short one-time-pads of different lengths to produce a very long sequence (Morgan, 1989). Today, the equivalent of Vernam's cipher is a very long shift register with many stages (200 or more), or a combination of several small shift registers of different lengths, each one with its own feedback. The key generator used by today's crypto machine normally has sequences longer than 10^{60} (equivalent to using one shift register with 200 stages).

Establishing the similarity between shift registers and gears helps explain how to produce long sequences using small shift registers. In a gear with t teeth, one of the teeth of the gear is marked, and the gear is rotated one step at a time; after t clock signals, the marked tooth will return to its original position.

Figure 4-15. Key generators with the shift registers output XORed

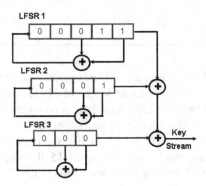

The period of the gear is the same as the number of teeth in the gear. However, if two gears in which the numbers of teeth do not have any common factors are used (for example, 5 and 7), then the period is equal to 5 x 7 = 35.

Likewise, if there are three gears with lengths of 31, 15, and 7, then the period is 31 x 15 x 7. This is equivalent to having three shift registers, each one with a number of stages n_1 = 5; n_2 = 4; and n_3 = 3. If the feedbacks are chosen correctly, the maximum length of each shift register sequence will be 2^n -1, or 31, 15, and 7.

In the example presented in Figure 4-15, three shift registers with their outputs XORed are used: one with five stages, another with four, and another with three. Since the feedback taps in each of the shift registers have been selected so as to produce a maximum length, the combination of the three shift registers will produce a sequence that will start repeating itself, for S.R.1 $\oplus$ S.R.2 at 31 x 15 = 465, and for SR1 $\oplus$ SR2 $\oplus$ SR3 at 31 x 15 x 7 = 3255, or $(2^5 - 1)$ x $(2^4 - 1)$ x $(2^3 - 1)$.

Will there be a longer sequence if a shift register with a greater number of stages is used instead of the shift register with five stages? Perhaps not; for example, the maximum sequence obtained with a shift register that has periods of 63, 15, and 7 is 315 instead of $(2^6 - 1)$ x $(2^4 - 1)$ x $(2^3 - 1)$ or 63 x 15 x 7 = 6615. Quite a difference! The reason is that when several shift registers are combined to produce a long sequence, the maximum length M_1 of the sequence is equal to:

$$M_1 = \frac{(P_1 \times P_2 \times P_3 \times .... P_n)}{Any\ common\ factors\ of\ P_1, P_2, P_3, ... P_n} \qquad \text{Equation 9}$$

In this case, P_1, P_2, P_3, ..., P_n are the periods of each of the shift registers.

For example, if the shift registers have periods of 63, 15, and 7, the maximum length of the sequence they will produce is:

$$M_1 = \frac{(63 \times 15 \times 7)}{(3 \times 7)} = 315$$

because 3 and 7 are common factors. The factors of 63 are (3) . (3) . (7); the factors of 15 are (3) . (5), with 7 being a prime number.

Exclusive-OR (XOR)

In XOR, the outputs of shift registers are XORed together. In the previous example, the three shift registers, each one with a maximum length of 31, 15, and 7 were XORed; the result was a sequence with a length of 3255, since there is no common factor among 31, 15, and 7. The XOR function provides a balanced sequence, since for the four pairs of sequence entries, i.e., $(1 + 1 = 0)$, $(1 + 0 = 1)$, $(0 + 1 = 1)$, $(0 + 0 = 0)$, there is the same number of 1's and 0's, in this case, 2 zeros and 2 ones. In Figure 4-15, the output is well balanced because the number of ones is 1,628, and the number of zeros is 1,627.

Multiplication

In this type of key generator, the outputs of the shift registers are multiplied, as indicated in Figure 4-16. The period of the sequence generated by $SR1 \equiv SR2 \equiv SR3$ can be determined as indicated in Equation 4-9. Staffelbach and Rueppel (1987) have considered multiplication as a mode of nonlinear combinations. They proved the following theorem:

The product of the output sequences of any n maximum-length LFSRs of different lengths (greater than two) will always exhibit maximum linear complexity.

They continued, saying:

From the cryptographic viewpoint, a single product of many sequences is of little interest since the resulting statistics tend to be poor, and thus the influence of the product sequence is only limited.

Figure 4-16. Shift registers with their outputs multiplied

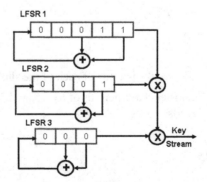

What they meant is that the keystream of such devices is mostly zeros. When two bits are multiplied, the product is unbalanced. This can be seen in the following: The four possibilities for the pairs of entries of the sequences, that is, (1 x 1 = 1), (1 x 0 = 0), (0 x 1 = 0), (0 x 0 = 0) results in more zeros than ones. In Figure 4-16, the output of the three shift registers is multiplied and the result is an output sequence that has 512 ones and 2743 zeros. This sequence is highly unbalanced because the proportion of ones is equal to 512/3255 = 0.15729646.

The number of ones in a maximum-length LFSR is equal to 2^{n-1}. The proportion of ones is:

$$\theta = \frac{2^{n-1}}{(2^n - 1)}$$

Equation 10

The keystream output of the combined three LFSRs of Figure 4-16 has a proportion of ones equal to:

$$\theta = \prod_{J=3}^{5} \left(\frac{2^{j-1}}{(2^j - 1)} \right) = \frac{4}{7} x \frac{8}{15} x \frac{16}{31} = 0.15729646$$

Equation 11

Random-Stepping

Random-stepping is a parallel combination mode in which one or several LFSRs drive several others simultaneously. Their various outputs can be later XORed, multiplexed, or combined using any other nonlinear technique. Random-stepping adds some confusion/diffusion to the keystream generated by the LFSRs.

In Figure 4-15, with three LFSRs, it can be seen that each LFSR moves **one** step at a time. Random-stepping involves using the output of the small shift register; in this case, the one with three stages randomly steps the other two shift registers. The example in Figure 4-17 shows three LFSRs in which the output of LFSR 3 determines the number of clock signals that will step LFSRs 2 and 3.

Figure 4-17. Key generator with random stepping

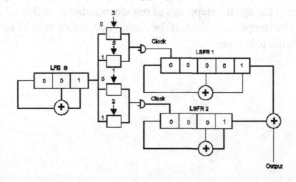

For example, if the output of LFSR3 is 1, then LFSR1 is stepped five times and LFSR2 twice; if the output is 0, LFSR1 is stepped three times and LFSR2 once. The maximum sequence of a shift register with three stages and a characteristic polynomial $f(x) = 1 + x^2 + x^3$ (feedback tap on stages two and three) is the following:

LFSR 3 Sequence			LFSR1 Stepping	LFSR2 Stepping
Output			(31)	(15)
0	0	1	5	2
1	0	0	3	1
0	1	0	3	1
1	0	1	5	2
1	1	0	3	1
1	1	1	5	2
0	1	1	5	2

When random-stepping is used, the maximum length of the combined shift registers is established by determining the driver's equation for each of the shift registers. This equation will be the number of times the shift register is stepped times the number of steps. In the key generator just designed (Figure 4-17), LFSR1 three times is stepped 3, and four times is stepped 5; LFSR2 three times is stepped 1, and four times is stepped 2. Thus, the driver's equations for LFSR1 and LFSR2 are as follows:

LFSR1 $3(3) + 4(5) = 29$ LFSR2 $3(1) + 4(2) = 11$

Since there is no common factor between 31 and 29 and between 15 and 11, the period of LFSR1 is $31 \times 7 = 217$, and the period of LFSR2 is $15 \times 7 = 105$. The combined period of SR1 $\oplus$ SR2 is then $(217 \times 105) \div 7 = 3255$, where 7 is a common factor of 217 and 105.

By using the appropriate random-stepping, some confusion and diffusion have been added to the sequence while still achieving the same period. However, there are certain disadvantages to using random stepping: (1) It takes (in this case) seven clock signals to generate one bit of the keystream, thus reducing the maximum speed at which the key generator can generate random bits; and (2) If the steppings are not chosen correctly, the period may be reduced.

For example, to change the steppings of register number 2, so that when the output of LFSR 3 is 1, it will be stepped one time; if the output is 0, then it will be stepped twice. The steppings will be the following:

LF	SR3 Output	Sequence (31)	LFSR1 Stepping (15)	LFSR2 Stepping
0	0	1	5	1
1	0	0	3	2
0	1	0	3	2
1	0	1	5	1
1	1	0	3	2
1	1	1	5	1
0	1	1	5	1

For this new example, the driver's equations for LFSR1 and LFSR2 are the following:

LFSR1: 3(3) + 4(5) = 29, and LFSR2: 3(2) + 4(1) = 10 = (5) (2)

Since there is no common factor between 31 and 29, the period of LFSR1 is (31 x 7) = 217; however, since 5 is a common factor in the driver's equation (15 x 7), then the period of SR2 will be [(15 x 7) ÷ 5 = 21)]. The period of SR1 $\oplus$ SR2 will be (217 x 21) ÷ 7 = 651 divided by 7 because 7 is a common factor of 217 and 21. It should be noted that the period of SR1 $\oplus$ SR2 has been reduced from 3,255 to 651.

Multiplexing (Geffe Generator)

Figure 4-18 shows a technique that uses a multiplexer for generating random number sequences. This method combines several shift registers with linear feedback and multiplexes them to obtain a nonlinear sequence. The outputs of several LFSRs (in this example, B_i) provide an address for the multiplexer. Several inputs to the multiplexer are provided by another set of LFSRs, in this case A_i. The output of the multiplexer, called *multiplexed se-*

Figure 4-18. Multiplexer

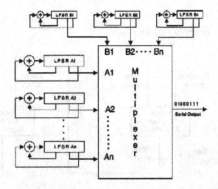

quence, is a member of set *A*, the inputs. Basically, all that the multiplexer does is pick as an output one of the LFSR connected to its input.

If the shift registers do not have common factors, the period of a multiplexed sequence is determined as follows:

$$p = (M_A 1) x (M_A 2) x ....x (M_{A2^n}) x (M_B 1) x (M_B 2) x ....x (M_{Bn})$$ Equation 0-12

where M_{Ai} is the maximum length of LFSRs used as a set of inputs to the multiplexer, and M_{Bi} is the maximum length of LFSRs used as a set of addresses to the multiplexer. Note that the elements of **B** determine a binary number that gives the address for **A**. Thus if | **A** | = *n*, there will be 2^n addresses.

The multiplexing method meets all the requirements by Beker and Piper for nonlinear sequence generators.

Block Encryption Algorithms

A block cipher uses an encryption algorithm, in conjunction with cryptographic variables, to transform a plaintext block of *x* bits into a ciphertext block of *x* bits (Denning, 1983). The positive integer *x* is the *block size*. In the block cipher system, the block of *x* bits is encrypted by the encryption algorithm. The enciphering and deciphering functions are such that every bit in the ciphertext block depends jointly on every bit in the plaintext and on the cryptographic variable. Block cipher systems are similar to codebooks in which, for every possible plaintext block, there is a corresponding ciphertext block. A block cipher cryptosystem can be configured as a block cipher or as a block stream cipher.

Each block is treated independently, and there is no influence between blocks; i.e., two identical plaintext blocks will produce identical ciphertext blocks. As in codebooks, decryption can be performed on isolated blocks in an arbitrary order without any loss of crypto synchronization. This was the initial mode of the DES algorithm known as the Electronic Code Book (ECB).

Figure 4-19. Block encryption algorithm

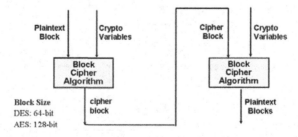

The best-known block ciphers are the Data Encryption Standard (DES) and the Advanced Encryption Standard (AES).

Data Encryption Standard (DES)

In the early 1970's, Large-Scale Integration (LSI) technology permitted the implementation of a highly complex key-generating algorithm in a single chip. Soon afterwards, several private companies started to carry out research in the development of key generators implemented in chips. In May 1973, the National Bureau of Standards (NBS), recognizing the need to adopt a standard algorithm to encipher digital communications used by the government, industry, and private organizations, asked several companies to propose techniques and algorithms that could be used to encipher computer data information and which then might be considered for use in a federal standard (FIPS PUB 74, 1981).

Several companies presented their proposals. Among them was IBM, which on August 6, 1974, submitted a block cipher product based on the LUCIFER design, an algorithm that IBM had been trying to implement for years. IBM made the specifications of the algorithm available to NBS for publication as a Federal Information Processing Standard (FIPS) and provided nondiscriminatory and royalty-free licensing procedures for building electronic devices that implement the algorithm. The National Security Agency, NSA, tested all the algorithms presented, and, according to the NBS, only the algorithm submitted by IBM was found acceptable. On March 17, 1975, the National Bureau of Standards published the algorithm in the Federal Register for public comment and published the proposed standard in the Federal Register in August 1975. In January 1977, the proposed algorithm became the Data Encryption Standard (DES) and was later then published as a federal standard (1977), FIPS PUB 46-3.

Figure 4-20. DES block diagram

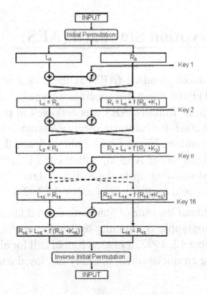

As a Federal Information Standard for encryption, the DES was only used by the private sector and nonmilitary federal department agencies to encipher sensitive, nonclassified computer data. The DES was also adopted by the American National Standards Institute (ANSI) and was recommended for use by the American Bankers Association (ABA).

The DES algorithm enciphers a 64-bit block of plaintext into a 64-bit block of ciphertext, under the control of a 56-bit crypto variable. DES keys are 64-bit binary vectors consisting of 56 independent information bits and 8 parity bits. The parity bits are reserved for error detection purposes and are not used by the encryption algorithm. The encryption process consists of 16 separate rounds of encryption. First, the 64-bit block of data undergoes a permutation that rearranges the bits according to a matrix; then the 64-bit permuted block of data is split into two 32-bit halves. The right half is enciphered with a key K_1, obtained from the original 56-bit crypto variable, and then is XORed to the left half.

For the second round of encryption, the result just obtained becomes the right half, and the unaltered right half from the first round becomes the left. The procedure is repeated 16 times with a different key, K, used each time. Figure 4-20 shows the enciphering compilation. After the 16 rounds of encryption, the 64-bit block of data undergoes a final permutation, the inverse initial permutation, thus producing the ciphered 64-bit block.

By the time the DES was adopted, several reports had been written by Diffie and Hellman (1976) and Diffie (1982) stating that the DES had three major weaknesses:

1.   The 56-bit key size may not provide adequate security

2.   The number of rounds should be at least 32

3.   The S-boxes may have hidden trap doors

In addition, Hellman and Diffie predicted in 1976 that by 1990 the cost of building a machine to break DES would be considerably low. Their prediction was correct because since the mid 1990's, NSA has not endorsed the DES.

Advanced Encryption Standard (AES)

The Advanced Encryption Standard (AES) is the new Federal Information Processing Standard (FIPS) (2001) Publication that specifies a cryptographic algorithm for use by U.S. government organizations. Initially, AES was endorsed to protect sensitive (unclassified) electronic data. In June 2003, the National Security Agency conducted a review (Committee on National Security Systems, 2003), CNSS Policy 15, and determined that the design and strength of all key lengths of the AES algorithm (i.e., 128, 192, and 256) were sufficient to protect classified information up to the SECRET level. NSA's policy stated that TOP SECRET information would require use of either the 192 or 256 key lengths.

For some time, the National Institute of Standards and Technology (NIST) had worked with industry and the cryptographic community to develop an Advanced Encryption Standard (AES) and, on September 12, 1997, it made a formal call for algorithms. The call stipulated that the AES would be an unclassified, publicly disclosed encryption algorithm(s), available royalty-free, worldwide. In addition, the algorithm(s) must implement symmetric key cryptography as a block cipher and (at a minimum) support block sizes of 128-bits and key sizes of 128, 192, and 256 bits.

By August 20, 1998, members of the cryptographic community from around the world submitted fifteen AES candidate algorithms. After an initial review of the algorithms, the NIST selected five algorithms for the second round:

- MARS, submitted by IBM (United States)

- RC6, submitted by RSA Laboratories (United States)

- Rijndael, submitted by Joan Daemen and Vincent Rijmen (Belgium)

- Serpent, submitted by Ross Anderson (United Kingdom), Eli Bihar (Israel), and Lars Knudsen (Norway)

- Twofish, submitted by Bruce Schneier, John Kelsey, Doug Whiting, David Wagner, Chris Hall, and Niels Ferguson (United States)

On October 2, 2000, the NIST announced that it had selected Rijndael for the AES. The standard became effective on May 26, 2002.

Implementation

The AES is a symmetric block cipher that can process data blocks of 128 bits, using cipher keys with lengths of 128, 192, and 256 bits. The Rijndael algorithm is designed to handle additional block sizes and cipher key lengths, but they were not adopted in the AES algorithm (Daemen & Rijmen, 1999, p. 41)

The input and the output for the AES algorithm each consists of block sequences of 128 bits (digits with values of 0 or 1). The cipher key for the AES algorithm is a sequence of 128, 192, or 256 bits. Other input, output, and cipher key lengths are not permitted by the AES standard.

Figure 4-21. Input sequence and array conversion

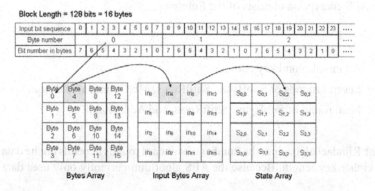

Figure 4-22. Pseudo code to encipher

```
Cipher(byte in[4*Nb], byte out[4*Nb], word w[Nb*(Nr+1)])
begin
        byte state[4,Nb]
        state = in
        AddRoundKey(state, w[0, Nb-1])
        for round = 1 step 1 to Nr-1
                SubBytes(state)
                ShiftRows(state)
                MixColumns(state)
                AddRoundKey(state, w[round*Nb, (round+1)*Nb-1])
        end for
        SubBytes(state)
        ShiftRows(state)
        AddRoundKey(state, w[Nr*Nb, (Nr+1)*Nb-1])
        out = state
End
```

The basic unit for processing in the AES algorithm is a byte, a sequence of eight bits treated as a single entity. During the ciphering and deciphering processes, the input, output, and cipher key bit sequences are processed as bytes (eight continuous bits) in array form. The bytes in the resulting array are referenced as in_n or as $S_{r,c}$ where r is the row number in the array and c is the column number in the array. Internally, the AES algorithm's operations are performed in a two dimensional array of bytes called the *state*.

The array's number of rows is always 4, so there are 32 bits per column. The number of columns depends on the cipher key length. The cipher keys may have lengths of 128, 192, or 256, so the number of columns is calculated as follows:

- Cipher Key length = 128 bits, columns = 128 / 32 = 4
- Cipher Key length = 192 bits, columns = 192 / 32 = 6
- Cipher Key length = 256 bits, columns = 256 / 32 = 8

The AES encryption consists of the following:

- Key expansion
- An initial round key addition
- Several rounds of SubBytes, ShiftRows, MixColumns, and AddRoundKey
- Final round of SubBytes, ShiftRows, and AddRoundKey

In the Rijndael algorithm, the number of standard rounds depends on the data block size and the cipher key length. Because the AES algorithm currently only uses data blocks of 128 bits, the number of standard rounds is 10 rounds for a 128-bit cipher key length, 12 rounds for a 192-bit cipher key length, or 14 rounds for a 256-bit cipher key length.

Blocks \ Keys→	128	192	256
128	10	12	14
192	12	12	14
256	14	14	14

The Standard Round Function is composed of four steps:

- **SubBytes:** Nonlinear byte substitution using a substitution table S-box, 8 x 8.

- **ShiftRows:** m bits of the State Array row are moved from the left to the right for intercolumn diffusion (linear mixing).

- **MixColumns:** Every column in the State Array is transformed using a matrix multiplication for inter-byte diffusion within columns (Linear Mixing). In the last round, the column mixing is omitted.

- **AddRoundKey:** Subkey bytes are XORed into each byte of the array.

Cipher Key Expansion

The AES algorithm takes the cipher key, K (128, 192, or 256 bits), and performs a key expansion routine to generate a key schedule with a total number of sub-keys equal to the required

Figure 4-23. AES implementation (N_r = Number of rounds)

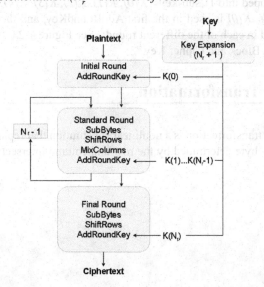

Figure 4-24. Cipher key expansion

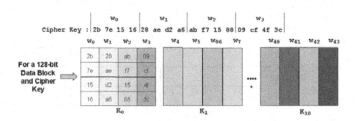

number of rounds. First, the cipher key is grouped into words. A word is a group of 32 bits that is treated either as a single entity or as an array of four bytes. See Figure 4-24.

Then, the key expansion routine generates a total of $N_b\ (N_r + 1)$ words where:

- N_b is equal to number of columns in the data block. For a data block of 128 bits, N_b is equal to 4.

- N_r is the number of rounds.

For a 128-bit data block and cipher key, the key expansion generates $4 \times (10 + 1) = 44$ words. The cipher key becomes the first word. All other words are calculated using the following transformation:

temp = SubWord (RotWord (temp)) xor Rcon [i / nk]

In the case of a key length of 128, the cipher key, K, will be expanded to generate 44 words which are grouped into 11 sub-keys; $K(0)$, $K(1)$, $K(2)$, $K(3)$, $K(4)$, ..., $K(10)$. Each sub-key has four words. $K(0)$ is used in the first AddRoundKey, and the cipher sub-keys $K(1)$ to $K(10)$ are used in each of the different rounds. See Figure 4-23, "AES Implementation for a 128-bit Data Block and Cipher Key."

SubBytes Transformation

The SubBytes transformation is a nonlinear substitution that replaces the bytes in the State Array with the byte determined by the row and column intersection in a substitution box, S-box.

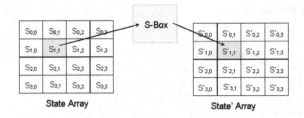

State Array   State' Array

For example, if $S_{1,1} = 0\ 1\ 0\ 1\ 0\ 0\ 1\ 1 = S\{53\}$, then the substitution value is determined by the intersection of row 5 and column 3. This would be the value of $S'_{1,1} = S'\{ed\} = 1\ 1\ 1\ 0\ 1\ 1\ 0\ 1$.

Figure 4-25. S-box substitution values for the Byte xy (in Hexadecimal Format)

	0	1	2	3	4	5	6	7	8	9	a	b	c	d	e	F
0	63	7c	77	7b	f2	6b	6f	c5	30	01	67	2b	fe	d7	ab	76
1	Ca	82	c9	7d	Fa	59	47	f0	ad	d4	a2	af	9c	a4	72	C0
2	b7	Fd	93	26	36	3f	F7	cc	34	a5	e5	f1	71	d8	31	15
3	04	c7	23	c3	18	96	05	9a	07	12	80	e2	eb	27	b2	75
4	09	83	2c	1a	1b	6e	5a	a0	52	3b	d6	b3	29	e3	2f	84
5	53	d1	00	ed	20	Fc	B1	5b	6a	cb	be	39	4a	4c	58	cf
6	d0	Ef	Aa	fb	43	4d	33	85	45	f9	02	7f	50	3c	9f	A8
7	51	a3	40	8f	92	9d	38	f5	bc	b6	da	21	10	ff	f3	D2
8	Cd	0c	13	ec	5f	97	44	17	c4	a7	7e	3d	64	5d	19	73
9	60	81	4f	dc	22	2a	90	88	46	ee	b8	14	de	5e	0b	db
A	e0	32	3a	0a	49	06	24	5c	C2	d3	ac	62	91	95	e4	79
B	e7	c8	37	6d	8d	D5	4e	a9	6c	56	f4	ea	65	7a	ae	08
C	Ba	78	25	2e	1c	A6	B4	c6	E8	dd	74	1f	4b	bd	8b	8a
D	70	3e	b5	66	48	03	f6	0e	61	35	57	b9	86	c1	1d	9e
E	e1	f8	98	11	69	D9	8e	94	9b	1e	87	e9	ce	55	28	df
F	8c	a1	89	0d	Bf	E6	42	68	41	99	2d	0f	b0	54	bb	16

Figure 4-26. ShiftRows transformation

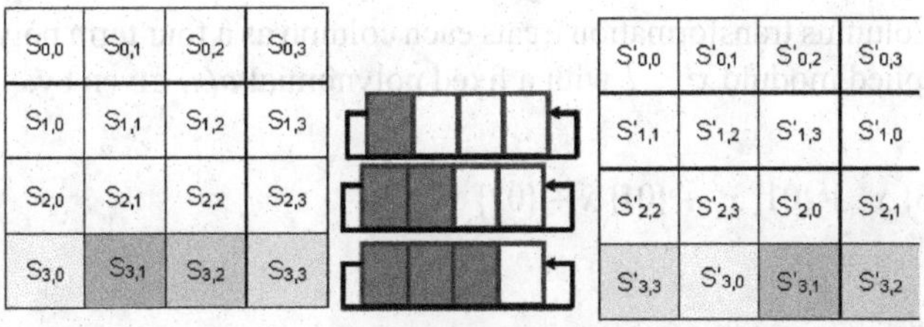

Figure 4-27. MixColumns transformation

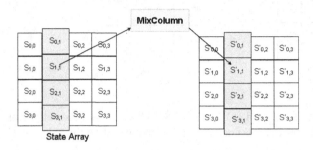

Figure 4-28. AddRoundKey transformation

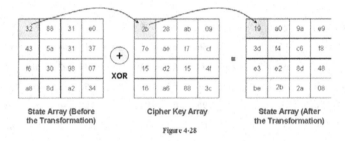

The S-box has a mathematical structure based on the combination of inversion over a Galois field and an affine transformation. Although this mathematical structure might conceivably aid an attack, the structure is not hidden, as would be the case for a trapdoor. The Rijndael specification asserts that if the S-box were suspected of containing a trapdoor, then the S-box could be replaced.

ShiftRows Transformation

In the ShiftRows transformation, the bytes in the last three rows of the State Array are shifted 1, 2, or 3 times to the left.

MixColumns Transformation

The MixColumns transformation treats each column as a four term polynomial over $GF(2^8)$ and multiplied modulo $x^4 + 1$ with a fixed polynomial $a(x)$ given by:

$$a(x) = \{03\} \, x^3 + \{01\} \, x^2 + \{01\} \, x + \{02\}$$

AddRoundKey Transformation

In the AddRoundKey transformation, every entry in the state array is XORed with its corresponding entry in the cipher sub-key.

AES Advanced Validation Suite

FIPS Pub 197, "Advanced Encryption Standard" provides information on how to implement the AES algorithm. When the AES is implemented in software or hardware, the Implementation Under Test (IUT), as it is called for testing purposes, needs to be used to determine if the design is correct. The AES Advanced Validation Suite (Bassham, 2002) provides the basic design and configuration of a battery of tests designed to perform automated testing on the IUT.

The battery of tests includes the following: Known Answer Test (KAT), the Multi-Block Message Test (MMT), and the Monte Carlo Test (MCT). The successful completion of the tests, as they are described in the AES Advanced Validation Suite, is required to claim conformity to the Advanced Encryption Standard FIPS 197.

Known Answer Test (KAT)

For a specific key, input vector (IV), and plaintext, the IUT should produce (Response) the same ciphertext after encryption or plaintext after decryption. The following is a sample data set:

Key = 00000000000000000000000000000000
IV = 00000000000000000000000000000000
PT = 6a84867cd77e12ad07ea1be895c53fa3
CT = 732281c0a0aab8f7a54a0c67a0c45ecf

Multi-Block Message Test

Block ciphers have several modes of operation in which the encryption process "chains" successive ciphertext and plaintext blocks together until the last plaintext block of data is enciphered. The Multi-Block Message Test checks that the IUT is able to chain information from one block to another.

Monte Carlo Test

The Monte Carlo Test uses a specific algorithm to generate 100 pseudorandom texts. The 100 texts are enciphered by the AES Algorithm Validation Suite and by the IUT. The results, the cipher text after encryption or plaintext after decryption, from the AES Algorithm Validation Suite and from the IUT should be the same.

AES Analysis

Nechvatal, Barker, Dodson, Dworkin, Foti, & Roback (2000) concluded the following about the Rijndael algorithm:

- Appears to be a very good performer in both hardware and software across a wide range of computing environments, regardless of its use in feedback or nonfeedback modes

- Has an excellent key setup time and good key agility

- Has very low memory requirements, which makes it very well suited for restricted-space environments

- Is designed with some flexibility in terms of block and key sizes and can accommodate alterations in the number of rounds

- Has an internal round structure, which appears to have good potential to benefit from instruction-level parallelism

Block Cipher Modes of Operation

NIST Special Publication 800-38A (Dworkin, 2001) provides recommendations regarding modes of operation to be used with symmetric key block cipher algorithms. The five modes of operation are the Electronic Codebook (ECB) mode, the Cipher Block Chaining (CBC) mode, the Cipher Feedback (CFB) mode, the Output Feedback (OFB) mode, and the Counter (CTR) mode.

Figure 4-29. Electronic Codebook mode (ECB)

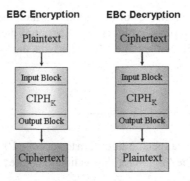

In any of the mode operations, there are two functions that are inverses of each other. These two functions are encryption and decryption. In the recommendation, one of these functions is designated as *forward cipher function*, denoted $CIPH_k$, meaning that a data block x was enciphered by a block cipher algorithm using the key K. The other function is called *inverse cipher function* and is denoted $CIPH^{-1}_k$.

The plaintext consists of n bit strings called *blocks* with a bit length b and represented as P_1, P_2, P_3, ..., P_n. The ciphertext is represented as C_1, C_2, C_3, ..., C_n. In ECB and CBC modes, padding bits may be added to the plaintext, so the total number of bits in the plaintext would be nb.

Electronic Codebook (ECB)

The ECB mode is a basic, block cryptographic mode that transforms x bits of input to x bits of output, as specified in FIPS 800-38A. See Figure 4-29.

In this mode of operation, x bits of data are loaded into the block input register, and the output register yields the encrypted x bits of ciphertext. This method establishes a reference for cryptanalysis because the same plaintext always produces the same ciphertext for a given set of crypto variables, thus its comparison to a codebook. In addition, a one-bit error is propagated throughout the entire x-bit block, which causes the deciphered plaintext to have an average error rate of fifty percent. All block ciphers support the ECB mode of operation.

When each block is enciphered independently with the same key variable, block ciphers are especially susceptible to spoofing because one enciphered block can be replaced by another, or blocks can be inserted or deleted. These changes do not affect surrounding blocks.

From the viewpoint of cryptanalysis, if certain blocks of the plaintext are the same in several messages, the corresponding ciphertext blocks will be the same, thus enabling the attacker to compile a codebook of plaintext/ciphertext pairs.

Figure 4-30. Cipher Block Chaining mode

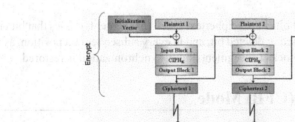

Cipher Block Chaining (CBC) Mode

In the CBC mode, the data to be encrypted is divided into blocks, and the first input block is formed by XORing the first block of data to an x-bit initialization vector (IV). The IV does not need to be secret, but it must be unpredictable. See Figure 4-30.

The CBC mode is defined as follows:

CBC Encryption:
$$C_1 = CIPH_K \ (P_1 \oplus IV);$$
$$C_j = CIPH_K \ (P_j \oplus C_{j-1}) \quad \text{for } j = 2 \ldots n$$

CBC Decryption:
$$P_1 = CIPH^{-1}{}_K \ (C_1 \oplus IV);$$
$$P_j = CIPH^{-1}{}_K \ (C_j \oplus C_{j-1}) \quad \text{for } j = 2 \ldots n$$

An initialization vector or random seed is used as the first block. Two identical, plaintext blocks in different parts of the message will produce two different ciphertext blocks if the previous plaintext blocks are not identical.

The input block is processed through the block cipher algorithm in the encrypting state, and the resulting output block is used as the ciphertext. The first ciphertext block is then XORed to the second plaintext block of data to produce the second input block. The latter is processed through the cipher block algorithm in the encrypting state to produce the second block of ciphertext block. This encryption process continues to "chain" successive ciphertext and plaintext blocks together until the last plaintext block of data is enciphered. A one-bit error during transmission will affect the deciphering of two blocks, the block with the error and the next block. Block synchronization between the enciphering and deciphering units is required and is accomplished by loading the same initialization vector into both units.

A bit error is the substitution of a 0 bit for a 1 bit, or vice versa. In the CBC mode, any bit positions that contain **C** will also contain bit errors in the decryption of the succeeding ciphertext block; the other bit positions are not affected. If bit errors occur in the IV, then the first ciphertext block will be decrypted incorrectly, and bit errors will occur in exactly the same bit positions as in the IV. The decryptions of the other ciphertext blocks are not affected.

The deletion or insertion of bits into a ciphertext block (or segment) causes that bit errors in the bit position of the inserted or deleted bit, and in every subsequent bit position, as well as all subsequent ciphertext blocks (or segments) until synchronization is restored.

Cipher Feedback (CFB) Mode

The CFB mode is a stream method of encryption. In this method, the block cipher is used to generate pseudorandom bits that are XORed to binary plaintext to form ciphertext. See Figure 4-31.

The CFB mode is defined as follows:

CFB Encryption:
$$I_1 = IV;$$
$$I_j = LSB_{b-s}(I_{j-1}) \mid C_{j-1} \quad \text{for } j = 2 \dots n$$

$$O_j = CIPH_k(I_j)$$
$$C_j = P_j \oplus MSB_s(O_j) \text{ for } j = 1, 2 \dots n$$

CFB Decryption:
$$I_1 = IV;$$
$$I_j = LSB_{b-s}(I_{j-1}) \mid C_{j-1} \quad \text{for } j = 2 \dots n$$

$$O_j = CIPH_k(I_j)$$
$$P_j = C_j \oplus MSB_s(O_j) \text{ for } j = 1, 2 \dots n$$

The plaintext and ciphertext consist of data units each containing s bits, such that ($1 \leq s \geq b$). The value of s is sometimes incorporated into the name of the mode, e.g., the 1-bit CFB mode, the 8-bit CFB mode, the 64-bit CFB mode, or the 128-bit CFB mode.

In CFB encryption, the first input block is the IV and the most significant s bits of the forward cipher function are XORed to the s-bit plaintext to produce an s-bit of ciphertext. The unused bits of the forward cipher function, $b - s$, are discarded.

The second input block is created by concatenating the $b - s$ least significant bits of the IV with the s bits of the ciphertext. This is done by shifting the first input block s positions to the left, and then filling the empty bits with the s bits from the ciphertext. The process is repeated, and each successive ciphertext block is input into the next input block to form the new input block.

The cipher feedback method does not pass data directly through the block encryption algorithm; instead, it uses the algorithm as a random-number generator.

Figure 4-31. Cipher Feedback (CFB) mode

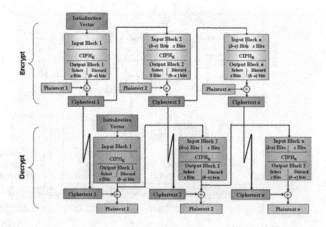

In the CFB mode, bit error(s) in the ciphertext will cause bit error(s) in the decrypted ciphertext block (or segment) in the same bit position(s) as in the ciphertext block (or segment), as well as the next b/s (rounded up to the nearest integer) ciphertext segments. A one-bit error in any s-bit unit of ciphertext will affect the deciphering of succeeding ciphertexts until the bits in error have been shifted out of the CFB input block. This normally occurs *b* bits after the s-bit boundaries have been reestablished. In the CFB mode, bit errors in the IV affect, at a minimum, the decryption of the first ciphertext segment, and possibly successive ciphertext segments, depending on the bit position of the rightmost bit error in the IV. In general, a bit error in the ith most significant bit position affects the decryptions of the first i/s (rounding up) ciphertext segments.

The deletion or insertion of bits into a ciphertext block (or segment) causes that bit errors in the bit position of the inserted or deleted bit, and in every subsequent bit position, as well as all subsequent ciphertext blocks (or segments) until synchronization is restored. When the 1-bit CFB mode is used, then the synchronization is automatically restored b+1 positions after the inserted or deleted bit. For other values of *s* the synchronization must be restored externally.

Output Feedback (OFB) Mode

The OFB mode operates in a way similar to the CF mode, except that the feedback is taken directly from the output block and not from the ciphertext. See Figure 4-32.

In the OFB mode, the IV is transformed by the forward cipher function to produce the first output block, which is fed back as the second input block and so on. Each output block is XORed with the plaintext block producing the ciphertext block.

The OFB mode is defined as follows:

Figure 4-32. Output Feedback (OFB) mode

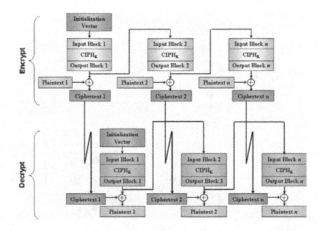

OFB Encryption: $\begin{aligned} I_1 &= IV; \\ I_j &= O_{j-1} \end{aligned}$ for $j = 2 \ldots n$

$$O_j = CIPH_k(I_j) \text{ for } j = 1, 2 \ldots n$$

$$C_j = P_j \oplus O_j$$
$$C_n = P_n \oplus MSB_u(O_n) \text{ for } j = 1, 2 \ldots n - 1$$

OFB Decryption: $\begin{aligned} I_1 &= IV; \\ I_j &= J_{j-1} \end{aligned}$ for $j = 2 \ldots n$

$$O_j = CIPH_k(I_j) \text{ for } j = 1, 2 \ldots n$$

$$P_j = C_j \oplus O_j$$
$$P_n = C_n \oplus MSB_u(O_{nj}) \text{ for } j = 1, 2, \ldots, n - 1$$

For the last block, which may be a partial block of u bits, only the most significant bits of the last output block of the forward cipher function are used for the XOR operation. The remaining $b - u$ bits are discarded.

This feedback is completely independent of all plaintext and all ciphertext. As a result, there is no error extension in the OFB mode.

A one-bit error in the ciphertext causes only a one-bit error in the decrypted ciphertext block. Bit errors within a ciphertext block do not affect the decryption of any other blocks. In the OFB mode, bit errors in the IV affect the decryption of every ciphertext block until cryptographic initialization is performed again. The OFB mode is not a self-synchronizing cryptographic mode.

Figure 4-33. Counter (CTR) mode

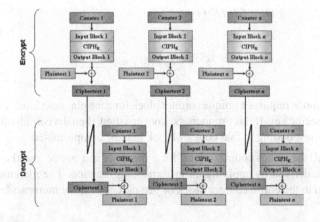

The deletion or insertion of bits into a ciphertext block (or segment) causes bit errors in the bit position of the inserted or deleted bit, and in every subsequent bit position, as well as all subsequent ciphertext blocks (or segments) until synchronization is restored.

Counter (CTR) Mode

The CTR mode, as well as the CFB and OFB modes, is a stream method of encryption. In this method, the block cipher is used to generate pseudorandom bits that are XORed to binary plaintext to form ciphertext. See Figure 4-33.

In CFB and OFB modes, the bits in the input blocks (initialization vectors) $I_2 \ldots I_n$ depend on the previous ciphertext blocks or output blocks. In the CRT mode, input blocks don't depend on the ciphertext nor the output blocks. The input blocks are blocks of bits called *counters* that must have the property that each counter block in the sequence is different from every other counter block. The counters for a given message are denoted T_1, T_2, T_3, ..., T_n and there are several methods to generate them.

The forward cipher function is invoked on each counter block, and the resulting output blocks are XORed with the corresponding plaintext blocks to produce the ciphertext blocks. As in the OFM mode, for the last block, which may be a partial block of u bits, only the most significant bits of the last output block of the forward cipher function are used for the XOR operation. The remaining $b - u$ bits are discarded.

The CRT mode is defined as follows:

CRT Encryption: $O_j = CIPH_k (T_j)$ for $j = 1, 2 \ldots n$

$$C_j = P_j \oplus O_j$$
$$C_n = P_n \oplus MSB_u (O_n) \text{ for } j = 1, 2 \ldots n$$

CRT Decryption:
$$I_1 = IV;$$
$$I_j = J_{j-1} \quad \text{for } j = 2 \ldots n$$

$$O_j = CIPH_k (I_j)$$
$$P_j = C_j \oplus O_j$$
$$P_n = C_n \oplus MSB_u (O_{nj}) \text{ for } j = 1, 2, \ldots n$$

The CRT mode requires a unique counter block for each plaintext block that is ever encrypted under a specific key. If this uniqueness is not satisfied, then the confidentiality of all plaintext blocks corresponding to that counter block may be compromised.

In general, the initial counter block for a message is a nonce and the successive counter blocks are derived by applying an incrementing function. The incrementing function can be applied to the entire counter block or just part of it. If the incremental function is m bits, then the number of message blocks, n, to encipher should be less than 2^m, so no counter block is repeated.

Bit error(s) in the decrypted ciphertext block (or segment) occur in the same bit position(s) as in the ciphertext block (or segment); the other bit positions are not affected. Bit errors within a ciphertext block do not affect the decryption of any other blocks.

Summary

There are various security mechanisms for symmetric encryption including stream and block ciphers. One of the most used methods for stream ciphers is linear shift registers. They have well known rules, produce very long cycles, and are easy to implement in hardware or in software. Shift registers are implemented in Global System Mobile (GSM) and in Bluetooth. See Chapter XIV, "Wireless Security," for more information.

When selecting the length of shift registers, their prime factorization numbers should not be repeated to ensure maximum length. Feedback taps should be such that the polynomials are irreducible.

The Advanced Encryption Standard (AES) block encryption has become the default standard for all data encryption. It is implemented in all new security protocols and is required by government agencies for their security devices. Initially, AES was endorsed by NSA to protect sensitive (unclassified) electronic data, but in June 2003, NSA conducted a review and determined that the design and strength of all key lengths of the AES algorithm (i.e., 128, 192, and 256) were sufficient to protect classified information up to the SECRET level. NSA's policy stated that TOP SECRET information would require use of either the 192 or 256 key lengths.

Enciphering the same plaintext with the same key always produces the same ciphertext. To avoid this predictability, encryption systems have an additional key that changes with every message, block, or IP packet. In stream ciphers, the additional key is called the *message key* or *initialization vector*; in block ciphers, it is called the *initialization vector*. The initialization vector doesn't need to be secret, but it should not be used twice with the same key.

In block ciphers, the initialization vector could be XORed with the first plaintext block, as is done in the Cipher Block Chaining (CBC) mode, or used as a dummy plaintext in the Cipher Feedback (CFB) mode, Output Feedback (OFB) mode, or Counter (CTR) mode. Note that in the Counter mode, the nonce is the same thing as an initialization vector (IV).

CFB and OFB modes turn a block cipher into a stream cipher. The OFB mode turns into a synchronous stream cipher and the CFB turns into a self-synchronous stream cipher.

Learning Objectives Review

1.   The type of crypto system in which enciphering and deciphering keys are the same is called *symmetric encipherment*. (T/F)

2.   In a symmetric crypto system:

   a.   Security is based on the secret key, not on the encryption algorithm

   b.   The sharing of secret keys is necessary

   c.   A and B

3.   In an asymmetric crypto system:

   a.   Two mathematically related keys are used

   b.   Either key can be used to encipher

   c.   One of the keys can be made public and the other kept private

   d.   All of the above

4.   In a stream cipher, the plaintext is broken up into successive bits, and each one is enciphered with a bit from a keystream. (T/F)

5.   From the theoretical point of view, the only system that offers perfect secrecy is the one in which the keystream is totally random, infinitely long, and used only one time. (T/F)

6.   Key generators based on shift registers generate a sequence of 0's and 1's and the sequence looks pseudorandom. (T/F)

7.   A block cipher uses an encryption algorithm, in conjunction with the cryptographic variables, to transform a plaintext block of x bits into a ciphertext block of x bits. (T/F)

8.   The DES is considered to be a weak encryption algorithm because:

   a.   The key length is too small, 56 bits

   b.   It has some intrinsic weaknesses in its design

9.   What is the effective key size of DES?

   a.   56 bits

   b.   64 bits

   c.   128 bits

   d.   256 bits

10.   Block cipher systems can be used as stream ciphers. (T/F)

11.   As an approved encryption algorithm, the AES can be used by U.S. government organizations to protect secret (classified) information. (T/F)

12.   Which of the following is a weakness in a symmetric crypto system?

   a.   Limited security

   b.   Key distribution

   c.   Speed

   d.   Scalability

13.   Which of the following is best provided by symmetric cryptography?

   a.   Confidentiality

   b.   Integrity

      c.   Availability

      d.   Non-repudiation

14.   Which encryption algorithm was selected by NIST for the new Advanced Encryption Standard?

      a.   Twofish

      b.   Serpent

      c.   RC6

      d.   Rijndael

15.   AES uses the following data block and secret key sizes:

      a.   256bit block size; 128/192/256bit key size

      b.   128bit block size; 64/128/256bit key size

      c.   128bit block size; 128/192/256bit key size

      d.   None of the above

16.   Which of the following statements pertaining to stream ciphers is correct?

      a.   Stream ciphers encipher bit by bit.

      b.   Stream ciphers are asymmetric encryption algorithms.

      c.   Stream ciphers are slower than a block ciphers.

      d.   Stream ciphers are not appropriate for hardware-based encryption.

17.   AES symmetric block encryption algorithm uses substitution and transposition. (T/F)

18.   In asymmetric encryption, why is one of the keys called the *private key*?

19.   Asymmetric cryptosystems are normally used to encipher large amounts of data. (T/F)

20.   Is there anything incorrect in the following statement: "DES supports an 8-bit block cipher with a 56-bit encryption key length, while AES supports 128-bit, 192-bit, and 256-bit block cipher lengths and encryption (key) sizes." Explain.

References

Bassham L. (2002). *The advanced encryption standard algorithm validation suite (AESAVS)*. National Institute of Standards and Technology (NIST), Information Technology Laboratory, Computer Security Division. Retrieved June 25, 2007, from http://csrc.nist.gov/cryptval/aes/AESAVS.pdf

Beker, H., & Piper, F. (1982) *Cipher system, the protection of communications*. New York: John Wiley & Sons.

Committee on National Security Systems (CNSS). (2003). *National policy on the use of the advanced encryption standard (AES) to protect national security systems and national security information* (CNSS Policy No. 15, Fact Sheet No. 1). Retrieved June 25, 2007, from http://csrc.nist.gov/cryptval/CNSS15FS.pdf

Daemen, J., & Rijmen, V. (1999). *AES proposal: Rijndael.* Retrieved June 25, 2007, from http://csrc.nist.gov/CryptoToolkit/aes/rijndael/Rijndael-ammended.pdf

Denning, D. (1983). *Cryptography and data security.* Reading, MA: Addison-Wesley.

Diffie, W. (1982). Cryptographic technology: Fifteen-year forecast. *ACM SIGACT News, 14*(4), 38-57

Diffie, W., & Hellman, M. E. (1976). A critique of the proposed data encryption standard (DES). *Communication ACM, 19*(3), 164-165.

Dworkin, M. (2001). *Recommendation for block cipher modes of operation methods and techniques* (NIST Special Publication 800-38A). National Institute of Standard and Technology (NIST). Retrieved June 25, 2007, from http://csrc.nist.gov/publications/nistpubs/800-38a/sp800-38a.pdf

Federal Information Processing Standards (FIPS). (2001). *Advanced encryption standard (AES)* (FIPS PUB 197). Retrieved June 25, 2007, from http://csrc.nist.gov/publications/fips/fips197/fips-197.pdf

Federal Information Processing Standards (FIPS). (1981). *Guidelines for implementing and using the NBS data encryption standard* (FIPS PUB74).

Federal Information Processing Standards (FIPS). (1977). *Data encryption standard.* (FIPS PUB 46-3). http://csrc.nist.gov/publications/fips/fips46-3/fips46-3.pdf

Golomb, S. (1982). *Shift register sequences.* Laguna Hills, CA: California Aegean Park Press.

Hardy, G. H., & Wright, E. M. (1980). *An introduction to the theory of numbers.* New York: Oxford University Press.

Jay, F. (Ed.). (1984). *IEEE Standard Dictionary of Electrical and Electronics Terms* (IEEE Std 100-1984). New York: The Institute of Electrical and Electronic Engineers, Inc.

Morgan, B. (1989). *The building of customizable and configurable key generators.* Dallas, TX: Datotek, Inc.

Nechvatal J., Barker, E., Dodson, D., Dworkin, M., Foti, J., & Roback, E. (2000). *Status report on the first round of the development of the advanced encryption standard.* National Institute of Standards and Technology (NIST), Computer Security Resource Center. Retrieved June 25, 2007, from http://csrc.nist.gov/encryption/aes/round1/r1report.htm

Riesel, H. (1985). *Prime numbers and computer methods for factorization.* Boston: Birkhäuser.

Staffelbach, O., & Rueppel, R. (1987). Products of linear recurring sequences with maximum complexity. *IEEE Transactions on Information Theory, 33*(1), 128

Zierler, N. (1955). *Several binary sequence generators.* Lexington, MA: MIT Lincoln Lab.

Chapter V

Confidentiality:
Asymmetric Encryption

Confidentiality: Asymmetric Encryption

Asymmetric encryption is a form of cryptography in which one key is used to encipher and the other to decipher. The two keys are mathematically related, and if it is possible to make one of the keys public and still maintain the algorithm security, then the system is called *public-key*.

The most used public-key ciphers, the Pohlig-Hellman algorithm, the RSA algorithm, the ElGamal algorithm, and Diffie-Hellman, are discussed in this chapter.

Objectives

- Learn the design theory of Pohlig-Hellman, RSA, ElGamal, and Diffie-Hellman public-key algorithms
- Understand how public-key algorithms can be used to exchange crypto keys

Introduction

Originally, the security of crypto systems depended on the secrecy of the encryption algorithm. Eventually, however, crypto manufacturers started developing crypto equipment in which the encryption algorithm could be revealed, yet, the security would remain intact because of the secret key. When the security of a crypto system depends exclusively on the secrecy of the key, the key must be transmitted by means of a protected channel. In general, most crypto equipment implements a secret key that is known only to the sender and to the receiver.

If a number of individuals wish to send secure information, symmetric cryptosystems require that initial arrangements be made for the individuals to share a unique secret key. First the secret key must be agreed upon by the users; then the key must be distributed to the individuals via some secure means to ensure key confidentiality and integrity. Knowledge of the ciphering key implies knowledge of the deciphering key and vice versa. In order to establish the secure channel, it is necessary to deliver the secret key to the individuals using a protected medium such as a courier. Of course, transporting the key in this way is risky, troublesome, slow, and expensive.

In their paper "New Directions in Cryptography," Diffie and Hellman (1976) proposed a new kind of cipher system in which the enciphering and deciphering keys are related but different: one is made public, while the other is kept private. This type of crypto system is called *asymmetric*, since it provides encryption in only one direction —a second pair of keys is needed to communicate in the other direction. Once the two mathematically related keys are calculated, there is no way to find out the private key from the public key. Asymmetric public cryptosystems allow two users to communicate securely over an insecure channel without any key prearrangement.

By definition, a public-key cryptosystem has the property that knowledge of the encryption algorithm and the encryption key does not imply knowledge of the decipherment key or vice versa because it is not computationally feasible to derive one key from the other. In mathematical terms, this implies that the enciphering algorithm must be a one-way function. However, the legitimate recipient with his private deciphering key should be able to decipher the message, implying that the enciphering algorithm should not only be a one-way function but a trapdoor one-way function as well. Being computationally infeasible depends on state-of-the-art computer technology; a trapdoor one-way enciphering transformation today may lose its one-way status in several years.

Figure 5-1. Public key cryptosystem

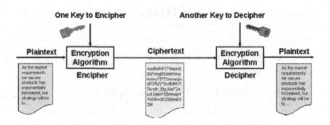

In a public-key crypto system, privacy is achieved without keeping the enciphering key secret because it is not used for deciphering. Instead of agreeing on a specific key before the transmission through a secure channel, the sender and the receiver generate two distinct keys: a *Pub* (public) key and a *Priv* (private) key. Anything enciphered with one of the keys can be deciphered by the other.

Since, practically speaking, no one could derive the deciphering key, *Priv*, from the enciphering key, *Pub*, the enciphering key could be in the public domain; for example, it could be published in a public file like the telephone book. That is the reason for the name *public-key crypto system*. Anyone who wants to send information to a particular person would simply encipher the message with that person's listed encrypting key *Pub*, and then send the secure message over non-secure channels. Only the intended receiver who knows the corresponding deciphering key *Priv*, which is kept secret, would be able to decipher the message.

Public-key cryptography provides solutions to two problems (Diffie, 1988):

1. If two persons want to communicate through a crypto system, the key must be distributed by secure means, such as a trusted courier. This is a key management problem.

2. The other problem is message authentication and digital signature. In a message exchange between two persons, it is not possible to prove that the receiver actually received the message, that it came from a particular person, or that a person has not sent messages to himself and made it appear as though they had come from a bona fide sender.

Contributors to the development of public-key cryptography include Whitfield Diffie and Martin Hellman who, in 1976, developed the exponential key agreement; in the same year, Martin E. Hellman and Ralph Merkle developed the trap-door knapsack system. Ronald Rivest, Adi Shamir, and Leonard Adleman (1977) developed the RSA public-key system based on factoring large prime numbers in May 1977, and Taher ElGamal presented his digital signature concept at the Crypto '84 Conference.

The RSA public-key algoritm bases its strength on the difficulty of factoring large numbers and when the RSA paper was written, it was recommended that the prime number should be a 40-digit number. However, because of the progress in factoring during the last several years, the numbers used in an RSA system have been increased to 100 digits (332 bits) and to 200 digits (664 bits). Some manufacturers have public-key chips that use numbers with 308 digits (1024 bits). The RSA system runs very slowly compared to other crypto systems such as AES or stream ciphers, and it requires keys that are very large, 664 bits, compared to 128 bits in the AES and around 180 bits in stream ciphers. To use public-key systems in cryptography requires chips that can perform high-speed calculations; this is why public-key systems are restricted to key management and signature applications.

Virtually all of the surviving public-key crypto systems and signature/ message authentications employ exponentiation over products of primes and, therefore, have the ability to carry out large arithmetic computations.

Exponentiation and Public-Key Ciphers

An exponentiation cipher is a technique in which the encryption and decryption processes involve raising plaintext and ciphertext messages to specific powers. Diffie-Hellman, Pohlig-Hellman, RSA, ElGamal, and many others are all exponentiation ciphers, each one implemented in a slightly different way. By definition, a public-key cipher is a one-way crypto system, so, from this point of view, all exponentiation ciphers are public-key cryptosystems. However, from the standpoint that the enciphering key can be made public, not all exponentiation ciphers are public. For the sake of discussion, this distinction will be kept, the term exponentiation cipher used for all, and public key reserved for use with those cryptosystems in which the enciphering key can be made public.

Most of the exponentiation cipher techniques are based in the following procedures:

Equation 3-17 $a^{k\varphi(p)+1} = a \bmod p$ can be written as:

$$a^{E*D} = a \bmod p \qquad\qquad \text{Equation 5-1}$$

where

$$E * D = k\varphi(p) + 1 \qquad\qquad \text{Equation 5-2}$$

or, once again according to Equations 3-1 and 3-2,

$$E * D = 1[\bmod \varphi(p)] \qquad\qquad \text{Equation 5-3}$$
$$E * D = [\bmod \varphi(p)] = 1 \qquad\qquad \text{Equation 5-4}$$

The reciprocal of the number E is the inverse or multiplicative inverse of D. Normally, E is selected first and then the corresponding D must be derived.

Another modular arithmetic property that should be mentioned is the one that applies to exponentiation. By symmetry, the exponents E and D are commutative and mutual inverses, so it is possible to say that:

$$a^{E*D} \bmod p = [a^e \bmod p]^D \bmod p \ 1 \qquad\qquad \text{Equation 5-5}$$

Note: In exponentiation ciphers and public-key ciphers, large prime numbers should be used, but in the examples given in this book, small integers are used for clarity.

Example:

$5^{3.2} \bmod(7) = 15{,}625 \ (\bmod 7) = 1$

$[\{5^3 \ (\bmod 7)\}^2 \ (\bmod 7)] = 1$

Exponentiation ciphers encipher a message block by computing the exponentiation according to Equation 5-1.

$$M^{E*D} \bmod p = M$$

then, according to Equation 5-5,

$$[M^E \bmod p]^D = \bmod p = M \qquad \text{Equation 5-6}$$

The equations illustrate that if M the plaintext is enciphered with the following algorithm **{(plaintext)^E (mod p)}** to produce a ciphertext, and that if at the receiver's end, the ciphertext is deciphered using the algorithm **[(Ciphertext)^D] (mod p)**, the same plaintext M will be obtained. In other words, by raising the ciphertext to the D th power and reducing it modulo p, the plaintext will be recovered. This can be written as follows:

$$C = M^E \bmod p \qquad \text{Equation 5-7}$$
$$M = C^D \bmod p \qquad \text{Equation 5-8}$$

where M is the plaintext, C is the ciphertext, and E and D are the enciphering and deciphering key.

Pohlig-Hellman Algorithm

The Pohlig-Hellman (1978) algorithm is not a public-key system, but it is based on exponentiation. In the Pohlig-Hellman algorithm, the modulo is chosen to be a large prime number p and the arithmetic is performed in the Galois field GF (n). The enciphering and deciphering are carried out according to Equations 5-7 and 5-8:

$$C = M^E \bmod p$$
$$M = C^D \bmod p$$

According to Equation 5-3, the enciphering key E and the deciphering key D should satisfy the requirement that
$$E * D = 1 \ [\bmod \varphi \ (p)] = 1 \bmod (p\text{-}1), \text{ where } \varphi \ (p) = (p\text{-}1)$$

Example

Let $p = 73$; then $\varphi\ (p) = (p - 1) = 72$. Select $E = 29$, and compute D the reciprocal of E; D = inv (29, 72) = 5. Suppose that the plaintext $M = 2$; then:

$C = M^E \pmod{p} = 2^{29} \pmod{73} = 4 \pmod{73}$

$M = C^D \pmod{p} = 4^5 \pmod{73} = 2$

The message $M = 2$ has been enciphered with $E = 29$ and the cipher message $C = 4$ has then been deciphered with $D = 5$ to obtain again the message $M = 2$.

Pohlig and Hellman recommended choosing $p = (2\ q + 1)$, where p and q are large prime numbers.

The difference between the Pohlig-Hellman cipher and the RSA is that with the former, p is not defined in terms of two large numbers, so the information necessary to encipher a message (E and p) can also be used to determine the deciphering key D. It is necessary, then, to keep secret both the enciphering and the deciphering keys.

The RSA Algorithm

In the RSA public-key algorithm (named after the algorithm's inventors Ronald Rivest, Adi Shamir, and Leonard Adleman), the encryption and decryption are also based on exponentiation, but with the difference that the *modulo n* is based on two large prime numbers, p and q (Rivest, Shamir, Adleman, 1978). Every user in the system must have a distinct composite number made up of two large primes. This differs from Diffie-Hellman and ElGamal techniques where only a single prime number is required. The RSA is the most versatile public-key cryptosystem since it supports both secrecy and authentication, and therefore can be used for encryption, key transport, authentication (digital signature), and certification. The RSA algorithm uses Equation 5-1 as follows:

$M^{Pub\ *\ Priv} = M \bmod n$ $\hspace{4cm}$ Equation 5-9

where,

M = Plaintext

Pub = Enciphering Key = $n = p\ .\ q$

$Priv$ = Deciphering Key

For confidentiality, the enciphering key, *Pub, n,* is made public and the deciphering key *Priv* is kept secret.

According to Equation 5-3, the private key and the public key should satisfy the requirement that:

$Pub * Priv = 1 \ [\text{mod}\varphi\ (n)]$ Equation 5-10

where $\varphi\ (n) = (p\text{-}1)(q\text{-}1)$

According to Equation 5-5, the RSA algorithm, Equation 5-9, can be written as follows:

$M^{Pub * Priv} \bmod n = [M^{Pub} \bmod n]^{Priv} \bmod n$ Equation 5-11

and the enciphering and deciphering processes are carried out according to the equations:

$C = M^{Pub} \bmod n$
$M = C^{Priv} \bmod n$

In the RSA system, for Alice to be able to send a message to Bob, Bob must publish or send Alice his public numbers n and Pub.

The following procedure describes how to select the public key (Pub) and the private key ($Priv$) in the RSA algorithm:

1.   Select at random two large prime numbers, p , q.
2.   Make n, the modulo, equal to $n = p \cdot q$.
3.   Calculate Euler's function, $\varphi\ (n) = \varphi\ (p \cdot q) = (p - 1)(q - 1)$.
4.   Select a number Pub, and test to verify that is relatively prime to $\varphi\ (n)$ by using Euclid's algorithm.
5.   Find $Priv$ so that it satisfies Equation 5-10, $Pub \cdot Priv = 1 \ mod \ \varphi\ (n)$, by calculating the multiplicative inverse of Pub using Euclid's algorithm. The properties of $\varphi\ (n)$ guarantee that if Pub is relatively prime to $\varphi\ (n)$, then there is always a multiplicative inverse, which in our case is $Priv$.
6.   Make n and Pub public; keep $\varphi\ (n)$ and $Priv$ secret.

Example
1.   For $p = 11, q = 31$.
2.   The modulo $n = 11 * 31 = 341$.
3.   Euler's function $\varphi\ (341) = 10 * 30 = 300$.
4.   Select $Pub = 53$ which is relatively prime to $\varphi\ (300)$.
5.   Find $Priv$ so it satisfies $53 * Priv = 1 \ mod \ (300)$. The result of the multiplicative inverse procedure is $Priv = 17$.
6.   Make $n = 341$ and $Pub = 53$ public; keep $\varphi\ (341) = 300$ and $Priv = 17$ secret.

7. If Alice wants to encipher, for example, the number 2 and send it to Bob, she enciphers it using Bob's public number, in this case, $n = 341$, and $Pub = 53$.

    Enciphering

    Plaintext   2

    Ciphertext $2^{53} \pmod{341} = 8$

8. When Bob receives the ciphertext (here the number 8), he proceeds to decipher it using his private key (which for this example is 17) to obtain the plaintext of 2.

    Deciphering

    Ciphertext   8

    Plaintext $8^{17} \pmod{341} = 2$

The strength of the RSA algorithm is based on the fact that multiplying two large primes to get n is far easier than, given n, to find the two primes; this is called a *one-way* property. One approach a cryptanalyst might use to break an RSA algorithm is to find p and q, the factors of n, calculate $\varphi\ (n)$, and then calculate *Priv* from $\varphi\ (n)$ and *Pub*, using Euclid's algorithm. The difficulty of computing *Priv* from the public information, $\varphi\ (n)$ and *Pub*, depends on the difficulty of factoring n or of deriving p and q from n, because $\varphi\ (n) = (p - 1) * (q - 1)$, $\varphi\ (n)$ can only be found if p and q are known. Since factoring large numbers is a very difficult problem, the difficulty of breaking the RSA algorithm increases when n is a very large number. When p and q are chosen so that n is a 300-digit number, it seems to be computationally infeasible for anyone, even using the fastest computer available today, to break the RSA algorithm.

Today, RSA Data Security recommends using a 768-bit RSA modulo for personal use, 1024-bits for corporate use, and 2048-bits for protecting extremely valuable data (RSA 1999).

RSA has been implemented in hardware, but the fastest chip is about 100 times slower than AES. Even in software, AES is also around 100 times faster than RSA. This is why RSA is mainly used to transport AES keys, and then AES encryption used to encrypt the information.

Table 5-1. Factorization of RSA numbers

Number	Month	Number	Month
RSA-100	April 1991	RSA-110	April 1992
RSA-120	June 1993	RSA-129	April 1994
RSA-130	April 1996	RSA-140	February 1999
RSA-155	August 1999	RSA-160	April 2003
RSA-576	December 2003	RSA-640	November 2005
RSA-704	Open	RSA 768	Open

ElGamal Algorithm

A modification of the ElGamal (1985) digital signature can be used to encipher messages. The public and private keys, or key pair, are generated as follows:

1. Choose a prime p to be the modulo and choose two random numbers g and $Priv_A$ that are less than p.

2. Calculate $y_A = g^{PrivA} \pmod{p}$.

The public key is y_A, g, and p.

Suppose Bob wishes to send a message m to Alice. Bob first generates a random number k less than p. He then computes:

$$y_1 = g^k \ (\bmod \ p)$$

$$y_2 = m \ y_A^{\ k} \ (\bmod \ p)$$

Bob sends $(y_1; y_2)$ to Alice. Upon receiving the ciphertext, Alice computes:

$$y_3 = y_1^{\ (p-1-yA)} \pmod{p}$$

and then deciphers the message, m, by calculating $m = y_3 \ y_2 \pmod{p}$

Example (Menezes, Oorschot, & Vanstone, 1996).

1. Alice selects the prime $p = 2357$ to be the modulo, and two random numbers $g = 2$ and $Priv_A = 1751$.

2. Alice calculates $y_A = g^{PrivA} \ (\bmod \ p) = 2^{1751} \ (\bmod \ 2357) = 1185$.

3. Bob's message $m = 2035$ and random number $k = 1520$.

4. Bob computes:
$$y_1 = 2^{1520} \ (\bmod \ 2357) = 1430$$

$$y_2 = 2035 \ . \ 1185^{\ 1520} \ (\bmod \ 2357) = 697$$

5. Bob sends $(y_1$ and $y_2)$ to Alice.

6. Upon receiving the ciphertext, Alice computes:
$$y_3 = y_1^{\ (p-1-yA)} \ (\bmod \ p \ ) = 1430^{\ (2357-1-1751)} \ (\bmod \ 2357 \ ) = 872$$

7. And then deciphers the message, m, by calculating:
$$m = y_3 \ y_2 \ (\bmod \ p \ ) = 872 \ . \ 697 \ (\bmod \ 2357 \ ) = 2035.$$

Key Management

Conventional crypto networks using symmetric cryptosystems typically have a Key Distribution Center (KDC) to distribute or load the keys into each of the crypto units. Secret keys are then sent using a secure channel such as a courier, but there is no way to know if the courier has compromised the keys to an unauthorized person who wants to read the messages in the network. Security may increase if the keys are loaded into the equipment before it is deployed; however, it is very difficult and inconvenient to bring the equipment to the KDC in order to change the keys. The problem is compounded if a new key for each day—or for each session—is desired.

There are three ways to send information about the secret key needed to decipher a message:

1.   **Pre-shared secret keys:** The secret keys are preloaded into both parties' crypto systems, and it is only necessary to define which of the secret keys was used to encipher the message. In general, every loaded secret key is associated with a name; therefore, only the name associated with the key needs to be sent to the recipient.

2.   **Transport and wrapping keys:** A secret key can be sent by transporting the key using public-key algorithms or by wrapping the key using symmetric key algorithms. Key transport algorithms are public-key encryption algorithms specifically for encrypting and decrypting keys. Symmetric key-wrap algorithms are algorithms specifically for wrapping, enciphering and deciphering symmetric keys. Both parties need to share a key-encrypting-key that is used to wrap (encipher) the key that is going to be used to encipher the information.

3.   **Key agreement:** A key agreement algorithm allows a sender and a receiver to share a secret key computed from public-key algorithms. Normally, the shared secret key is not used as a key, but instead, as a way of arriving at key material. Diffie-Hellman is used for key agreement.

Security Services and Public-Key Encryption

When using public key, a message can be enciphered either with the public key or with the private key. Figure 5-2 shows the different ways in which a message that Alice is sending to Bob can be enciphered.

Combining Asymmetric and Symmetric Ciphers

In many instances, symmetric public cryptosystems, either public or exponential, are relatively slow compared to classic symmetric cryptosystems. However, asymmetric cryptosystems can be used for the secure and authenticated process of transporting or agreeing

Figure 5-2. Public key encryption and security services

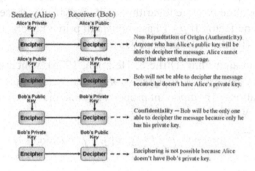

on a session key that will be used to encipher the message. Therefore, it is not necessary to send the session key beforehand, but it can be exchanged in a secure way over non-secure public networks like the Internet.

In most applications, asymmetric encryption algorithms (public key) are used to exchange, agree upon, or transport a key and the symmetric algorithms used to encipher the data. Normally, the shared or transported key is not used as a secret key or crypto variable key; instead, it is used as an entropy source to generate random values for MACS, secret keys, and initialization values (IV) required to encipher the data using symmetric algorithms like AES. The steps required to generate a key used to encrypt the message depend on the protocol. See Figure 5-3.

The Diffie-Hellman Key Agreement System

Another process in number theory that has a one-way property is raising a number to a power in a large finite field. When working with real numbers, finding $y = g^x$ is as easy as finding $x = log_g y$. But when we have a finite group such as $GF(p)$, exponentiation becomes a one-way process for a large prime p. Given g and x, it is easy to compute $y = g^x \bmod p$,

Figure 5-3. Combining public-key exchange and symmetric encryption

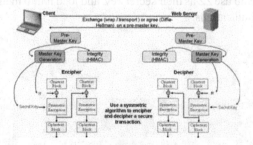

but how can we compute $x = \log_g y \bmod p$ when $\log$ has a different but analogous meaning than before? This type of logarithm is called a *discrete logarithm*, and it is computationally difficult to compute discrete logarithms in *GF(p)* if p is chosen such that $p - 1$ has at least one large prime factor. If $p - 1$ has only small prime factors, then computing discrete logarithms is easy (Pohlig & Hellman, 1978).

The Diffie-Hellman algorithm (Diffie & Hellman, 1976), which is based on the discrete logarithm problem, can be used to agree on keys between two units that want to establish secure communications. An important property exponentiation using modulo p is the commutative property, where:

$$[X^{E_1}(\bmod p)]^{E_2}(\bmod p) = [X^{E_2}(\bmod p)]^{E_1}(\bmod p)] \qquad \text{Equation 5-12}$$

This property allows two users in a network to share a secret crypto key by exchanging only non-secret numbers using a non-secure channel like the Internet. The secret key is used as a conventional crypto variable where the key is loaded into the key generator of a symmetric crypto system.

The procedure is as follows:

1. Before the units are deployed, two fixed constants, p and g, which do not need to be kept secret, are loaded into both units; p is a large prime number, and g is any integer between 0 and $p - 1$.

2. When communication between Alice and Bob is established, Alice and Bob randomly generate a secret number: $Priv_A$ and $Priv_B$.

3. Alice and Bob generate their corresponding public numbers:

    $Pub_A = g^{PrivA} (\bmod p)$

    $Pub_B = g^{PrivB} (\bmod p)$

4. Alice and Bob exchange Pub_A and Pub_B over the nonsecure channel. For a large prime number p, it is practically impossible to find $Priv_A$ and $Priv_B$ from Pub_A and Pub_B.

5. Alice and Bob compute *ZZ*, the session key, by:

    $$ZZ = Pub_B^{PrivA} (\bmod p) \qquad \text{Equation 5-13}$$

    $$ZZ = Pub_A^{PrivB} (\bmod p)$$

6. Alice and Bob use *ZZ* as their secret key, and load it into their key generators to secure their communications.

Example

Alice	Bob
p = prime number = 47	p = prime number = 47
g = any integer < $(p - 1)$	
$g = 12$	$g = 12$
$Priv_A = 3$	$Priv_B = 5$
$Pub_A = 12^3 \pmod{47} = 36$	$Pub_B = 12^5 \pmod{47} = 14$
36	→
←	14
$ZZ = 14^3 \pmod{47} = 18$	$ZZ = 36^5 \pmod{47} = 18$

Alice and Bob end up with the same crypto key, 18, but they do not have control of the key that was generated. This procedure is good for a link encryption, server to client, in which one unit establishes communications with another, but it cannot be used when a secure message is broadcasted to several units. If the user wants to compartmentalize the user's crypto network, several p's and g's (DH group) should be used with one group designated for each of his crypto organizations; these groups should then be stored in the crypto units and kept secret. Whenever an operator establishes a connection to send a secure message, the operator designates the organization to which the secure message is going to be sent, and the crypto unit automatically selects from its memory the corresponding p and g numbers.

Another problem with the Diffie-Hellman technique is that it can be spoofed very easily. A spoofer can intercept communications between Alice and Bob and make Alice believe that she is talking to Bob, and at the same time, make Bob believe that he is taking to Alice when, in reality, both are talking to the spoofer. The spoofer generates a secret number $Priv_S$ and computes:

$$Pub_S = g^{Privs} \pmod{p}.$$

The spoofer intercepts Pub_A and transmits Pub_S to Bob. The spoofer also intercepts Pub_B and transmits Pub_S to Alice. Bob computes a key based on Pub_S and $Priv_B$, and Alice computes a key based upon Pub_S and $Priv_A$; the spoofer computes both keys. When Alice transmits enciphered data to Bob, this data is decrypted by the spoofer and reencrypted for transmission to Bob. Alice and Bob establish crypto communications with a key —or keys— supplied by the spoofer who is able to intercept the messages and to read or to modify them at will.

A way to avoid this problem is to combine the Diffie-Hellman algorithms with an unforgeable digital electronic signature or a certificate that provides user authentication. Another way is to apply a hash function to the negotiated key and to present the result in the unit display. If the hash function that appears in both units is the same, then there is no man-in-the-middle. With the digital signature, or with the hash function, Alice is sure that she is talking to Bob and not to the spoofer.

Figure 5-4. Diffie-Hellman key agreement

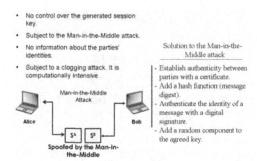

The Diffie-Hellman Key Agreement Method

The Diffie-Hellman (DH) key agreement protocol involves the derivation of shared secret information (*ZZ*) based on compatible DH keys from the sender and recipient. *ZZ* may then be converted into cryptographic keying material for other (symmetric) algorithms.

The Diffie-Hellman specified in RFC 2631 (Rescorla, 1999) standardizes one particular Diffie-Hellman variant, based on the ANSI X9.42 (National Institute of Standards and Technology), developed by the ANSI X9F1 working group. This variation of the Diffie-Hellman is used for converting the shared secret, *ZZ*, into an arbitrary amount of keying material. The resulting keying material is used as a symmetric encryption key. The Diffie-Hellman variant described requires the recipient to have a certificate, but the originator may have a static key pair (with the public key placed in a certificate) or an ephemeral key pair.

The RFC 2631describes one such variant, based on the ANSI X9.42 specification. X9.42 specifies that both parties generate the shared secret *ZZ* as follows:

$$Pub_A = g^{Priv_A} \pmod p$$
$$Pub_B = g^{Priv_B} \pmod p$$
$$ZZ = Pub_B^{Priv_A} \; (\bmod \; p \;) = y_B^{\,x_A} \; (\bmod \; p \;)$$

$$ZZ = Pub_A^{Priv_B} \; (\bmod \; p \;) = y_A^{\,x_B} \; (\bmod \; p \;)$$

where,

$$Pub_A = y_A = g^{x_A} \pmod p$$
$$Pub_B = y_B = g^{x_B} \pmod p$$

x_A is party A's private key and x_B is party B's private key; p and q are large prime numbers. $g = h^j \pmod p$, with g being >1,

where,

h is any integer with $1 < h < p$ - 1 such that $h\{(p - 1)/q\} \bmod p > 1$

j a large integer such that $j = (p - 1) / q$

RFC 2631 specifies the following algorithm for generating an essentially arbitrary amount of key material, KM:

$KM = H (ZZ \mid OtherInfo)$ Equation 5-14

H is the message digest function SHA-1, ZZ is the shared secret value computed before, and the OtherInfo includes a random string provided by the sender. Note that the only source of secret entropy in this computation is ZZ.

Ephemeral-Static Mode

In the ephemeral-static mode, the recipient has a static (and certified) key pair, but the sender generates a new key pair for each message and sends it using the originator key production. If the sender's key is freshly generated for each message, the shared secret ZZ will be similarly different for each message.

Static-Static Mode

In the static-static mode, both the sender and the recipient have a static (and certified) key pair. Since the sender's and recipient's keys are the same for each message, ZZ will be the same for each message.

The RSA Key Transport System

The RSA public key cryptosystem can be used to transport an encrypting key. First, the sender's unit (Alice) randomly selects a session key and enciphers it using the receivers's unit (Bob) public key. Alice then sends the enciphered session key to Bob over a nonsecure channel. Bob deciphers the session key with his own secret key. Because the deciphering private key is known only to Bob, only Bob can decipher the session key. After exchanging the session key, both Alice and Bob use the session key in a symmetric cryptosystem to securely communicate with each other.

Figure 5-5. Key management using RSA public-key cryptosystem

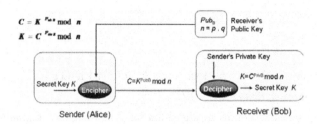

Sender (Alice)   Receiver (Bob)

The secrecy of the public key is not required, but it is essential that the integrity of the key in the public directory be guaranteed. If an attacker could replace an organization's public key with an enciphering key produced by the attacker—who would also hold the corresponding deciphering key—then the secret information destined to an organization would be available to the attacker. The attacker would receive the information, decipher it, and send it again to the organization. This type of attack is called *playback attack*.

To avoid this type of attack, it is possible to have both units contribute to the session key. A session key would consist of a random component from the transmitting unit and a random component from the receiving unit. The random components prevent a playback attack, since both units have to contribute to the construction of the session key. The implementation could be as follows:

1.   Alice sends a random component enciphered with Bob's public key.

2.   Bob uses his private key to decipher the random component sent by Alice.

3.   Bob generates a random component, encrypts it using Alice's public key, and sends it to Alice.

4.   Alice adds hers and Bob's random components to the previously transported key to obtain the session key.

5.   Bob adds his and Alice's random components to the previously transported key to obtain the same session key.

6.   Both key generators are initialized with the session key and encryption begins.

Variation of ElGamal System

This public key crypto system is based on a variation of ElGamal public key exchange. The differences between the two are the way the modulo p is selected and the way ZZ is calculated. A public-key cryptosystem, as with the ElGamal cryptosystem, relies on the difficulty of computing logarithms over finite fields.

g and p are generated with the following restrictions and loaded into all the units:

- p must be a large prime with the same length in bits as g.

- $q = p - 1$ must have a large prime factor. For example, $q = 2 . t$, with t being a prime number.

- g can be any number, but it is recommended that it be an element of $GF(p)$. This can be verified by checking that $g^x ! \bmod p = 1$, for all values of the divisor x of $p - 1$. For example, if $q = 2^t$, it is only necessary to verify that $g^2 ! \bmod p = 1$ and that $g^t ! \bmod p = 1$.

The following is the procedure used when two units would like to agree on a crypto variable ZZ that later on will be used as the crypto variable to load into their key generators:

1. Each unit generates a secret random number R:

    $$R_A \qquad\qquad R_B.$$

2. Each unit generates V according to ElGamal:

    $$V_A = g^{R_A} \bmod p \qquad V_B = g^{R_B} \bmod p \qquad\qquad \text{Equation 5-15}$$

3. Each unit generates Pub according to Diffie-Hellman:

    $$Pub_A = g^{Priv_A} \bmod p \quad Pub_B = g^{Priv_B} \bmod p \qquad\qquad \text{Equation 5-16}$$

4. Both units exchange Vs and public keys:

    $$Pub_A, V_A \qquad\qquad \rightarrow$$
    $$\qquad\qquad\qquad \leftarrow \quad V_B, Pub_B$$

5. Each unit generates the crypto variable ZZ:

    $$ZZ_A = (V_B * Pub_B)^{\ (Priv_A + R_A)\, \bmod q}\ \bmod p \qquad\qquad \text{Equation 5-17}$$

    $$ZZ_B = (V_A * Pub_A)^{\ (Priv_B + R_B)\, \bmod q}\ \bmod p$$

    where $Z_A = Z_B$

Demonstration that $ZZ_A = ZZ_B$

If $q = p - 1$, then Equation 5-17 ZZ_A can be written as:

$$ZZ_A = (V_B * Pub_B)^{\ (Priv_A + R_A)\, \bmod (p-1)}\ \bmod p$$

and according to Equation 3-18, it can be written as

$$ZZ_A = (V_B * Pub_B)^{\ (Priv_A + R_A)}\ \bmod p$$

$$ZZ_A = [(V_B * Pub_B)^{\ Priv_A}] * [(V_B * Pub_B)^{\ R_A}]\ \bmod p$$

From Equations 5-15 and 5-16, it can be said that:

$$ZZ_A = [\ (\ a^{R_B}\ \bmod p\ )\ ^{Priv_A} * (\ a^{Priv_B} \bmod p\ )^{Priv_A}\ ] *$$

$$[\ (a^{R_B} \bmod p)^{R_A} * (a^{Priv_B} \bmod p)^{R_A}\ \bmod p \qquad\qquad \text{Equation 5-18}$$

In the same way:

$$ZZ_B = (\ V_A * Pub_A)^{\ (Priv_B + R_B)\ \bmod q}\ \bmod p$$

since $q = p -1$, then Z_B can be written as:

$$ZZ_B = (\ V_A * Pub_A)^{\ (Priv_B + R_B)}\ \bmod p$$

$$ZZ_B = [\ (\ V_A * Pub_A)^{\ Priv_B}\ ] * [\ (\ V_A * Pub_A)^{\ R_B}\ ]\ \bmod p$$

From Equations 5-15 and 5-16, it can be concluded that:

$$ZZ_B = [\ (\ a^{R_A} \bmod p\ )^{Priv_B} * (\ a^{Priv_A} \bmod p\ )^{Priv_B}\ ] * \qquad \text{Equation 5-19}$$

$$[\ (\ a^{R_A} \bmod p\ )^{R_B} * (\ a^{Priv_A} \bmod p\ )^{R_B}\ ]\ \bmod p$$

Since all the terms in ZZ_A and ZZ_B are the same, it can be stated can say that $Z_A = Z_B$.

Summary

One very important issue about asymmetric cryptosystems, public key crypto, is that they are very slow compared to symmetric crypto systems. That is why they are rarely used to encipher large amounts of data. Keys and hashes are very small, 128, 192, and 256 bits for AES keys, and 160, 256, and 512 bits for SHA; for this reason in general, asymmetric cryptosystems are used to encipher keys for key transport or key wrapping, for key agreement, and for authentication and integrity.

Keys that are transported, wrapped, or exchanged go through several transformations before they are used in a symmetric crypto system such as AES.

Diffie-Hellman is the de-facto key exchange system used today in most IP protocols. Since Diffie-Hellman has a problem with man-in-the-middle attacks, several protocols have been created as countermeasures to this problem. To avoid the man-in-the-middle attack, the parties are first authenticated, and a pseudo random function (prf) is applied to the exchanged key using nonces from the initiator (Ni) and the responder (Nr).

The Diffie-Hellman exchange has three components: a generator g, the modulo p, and a secret key called the *private key*. During the key exchange, the initiator and responder use the same generator g and the same modulo p to calculate ZZ, the shared public value. Since both parties need to agree on the same generator g and the same modulo p, several RFCs have specified certain Diffie-Hellman groups that include specific g and p values. For example, Diffie-Hellman Group 2 has a generator $g = 2$ and modulo $p = 2^{1536} - 2^{1472} - 1 + 2^{64}$ * { $[2^{1406}$ pi] + 741804 }. The initiator only has to indicate to the responder that DH Group 2 will be used, and both know what g and p to use.

The RSA public key crypto system is a very versatile algorithm; it can be used for encryption, digital signatures, and for authentication. The problem is that it could be broken by factoring the module n to find p and q; as computer power increases, it would then be necessary to use longer keys. Today, an RSA system using 640 bits (193 digits) has been broken, and RSA's recommendation is to use key sizes of 1024 bits or more.

Also, the National Institute of Standards and Technology recommends that when using AES 128, 192, and 256, the RSA and Diffie-Hellman key sizes should be of 3072, 7680, or 15360 bits in order to be able to provide equivalent security. However, using larger keys increases the computational effort and requires a much larger number of bits transmitted to perform key exchanges.

Learning Objectives Review

1. In a Diffie-Hellman key exchange system, the sender and the receiver do not need to agree on any initial value to arrive at a common key. (T/F)

2. The Diffie-Hellman key exchange system has the problem that:

    a. There is no control over the generated session key

    b. It is subject to the man-in-the-middle attack

    c. There is no information about the parties' identities

    d. It is subject to a clogging attack

    e. All of the above

3. Public-key cipher systems are mainly used to encipher long messages and files because they are relatively fast compared to classic symmetric cryptosystems. (T/F)

4. In public-key encryption, the secrecy of the public key is not required, but the authenticity of the public key is necessary to guarantee its integrity and to avoid spoofing and playback attacks. (T/F)

5. The Diffie-Hellman algorithm is used for:

    a. Encryption

    b. Digital signature

    c. Key exchange

    d. Non-repudiation

6. A public-key crypto system requires the sender and receiver to agree on a specific key, which must be distributed through a secure means. (T/F)

7. How is non-repudiation achieved with public-key algorithms?

8. Public Key algorithms are:

    a. 100 to 1,000 times slower than secret key algorithms

    b. 100 to 1,000 times faster than secret key algorithms

9. In a _____ attack, the attacker replaces an organization's public key with his and then is able to receive information, decipher it, and send it again to the organization.

    a. Man-in-the-middle attack

    b. Playback attack

    c. Hide-and-seek attack

    d. Loop attack

10. Which of the following is a major problem of the Diffie-Hellman key exchange system?

    a. It reveals numbers that are used to generate the key

    b. Each party has control over the session key

    c. It is subject to a man-in-the-middle attack without digital certificates that verify identities

    d. The generated session key is used in a symmetric key algorithm

11. Which of the following is NOT a characteristic of the Diffie-Hellman key exchange system?

    a. No control over the generated session key

    b. Subject to the Man-in-the-middle attack

    c. Subject to a clogging attack

    d. Provides information about the parties' identities

12. Public-key algorithms use symmetric encryption based on mathematical functions. (T/F)

13. In symmetric key algorithms, the sender and the receiver use the same key for encryption and decryption. (T/F)

14. Symmetric key algorithms can provide confidentiality, but not authentication or non-repudiation. (T/F)

15. The size of modulus n refers to the size of a key in the RSA algorithm. (T/F)

16. What is the recommended key size when using an RSA algorithm?

    a. 64-bits

    b. 1024-bits

    c. 128-bits

    d. 512-bits

17.   If two parties exchange crypto messages using asymmetric encryption, the public key needs to be published or exchanged. (T/F)

References

Diffie, W. (1988). The first ten years of public-key cryptography. In *Proceedings of the IEEE, 76*(5), 560.

Diffie, W., & Hellman, M. E. (1976). New directions in cryptography. *IEEE Transactions on Information Theory, 22*(6) 29-40.

ElGamal, T. A. (1985). Public key cryptosystem and a signature scheme based on discrete logarithms. *IEEE Transactions on Information Theory, 31*, 469-472.

Menezes, A., Oorschot, P., & Vanstone, S. (1996). *Handbook of applied cryptography*. Boca Raton, FL: CRC Press

Pohlig, S. C., & Hellman, M. E. (1978). An improved algorithm for computing logarithms in GF(p) and its cryptographic significance. *IEEE Transactions on Information Theory, 24*, 106-110.

Rescorla, E. (1999). *Diffie-Hellman key agreement method* (RFC 2631). Internet Engineering Task Force (IETF). Retrieved June 26, 2007, from http://www.ietf.org/rfc/rfc2631. txt?number=2631

Rivest, R., Shamir, A., & Adleman, L. (1978). A method for obtaining digital signatures and public-key cryptosystem. *Communications ACM, 21*, 120-126.

RSA. (1999). *The factorization of RSA-140* (RSA Laboratories' Bulletin #10). Retrieved June 26, 2007, ftp://ftp.rsasecurity.com/pub/pdfs/bulletn10.pdf

Chapter VI

Integrity and Authentication

Integrity and Authentication

In this chapter, methods that can check if a message was modified are explained; this includes the Message Authentication Code (MAC), hash functions, and the Keyed-Hash Message Authentication Code (HMAC). Also discussed are ways to verify a sender's identity by using digital signatures.

Objectives

- Understand the SHA-1 and MD5 hash algorithms
- Learn how digital signatures are used to verify the message sender's identity
- Understand how digital certificates are used to validate public keys

Introduction

In the world of communications, it is very important to ensure that messages are not modified by unauthorized persons.

The mechanism for ensuring that data is not altered when transmitted from source to destination, or when it is stored, is called *integrity*. Message Digest 5 (MD5), Secure Hash Standards (SHA-1, SHA-256, SHA-384, and SHA-512), Message Authentication Codes (MACs), and Keyed-Hash Message Authentication Codes (HMAC) are mechanisms that check the integrity of a message.

Encryption provides intrinsic integrity because if a ciphertext block has been modified, the block will not be deciphered properly. Digital signature also provides integrity because it uses hash functions.

Message Authentication Code (MAC)

The mechanisms that provide integrity checks based on a secret key are usually called *Message Authentication Codes* (MACs). Typically, Message Authentication Codes are used between two parties who share a secret key in order to authenticate information transmitted between these parties.

MAC is a key-dependent one-way hash function. One popular way to construct a MAC algorithm is to use a block cipher in conjunction with the Cipher Block Chaining (CBC) mode of operation with the IV = 0. The Message Authentication Code is the ANSI standard DES-based checksum, also known as the U.S. Government Standard Computer Data Authentication Code, FIPS PUB 113 (Federal Information Processing Standards (FIPS), 1985).

The integrity provided by the MAC is based on the fact that it is not possible to generate a MAC without knowing the cryptographic key. An adversary without knowledge of the key will not be able to modify data and then generate an authentic MAC on the modified data.

Figure 6-1. Secure mechanisms for integrity

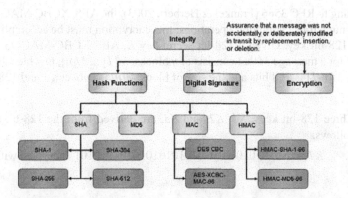

Figure 6-2. Message authentication code

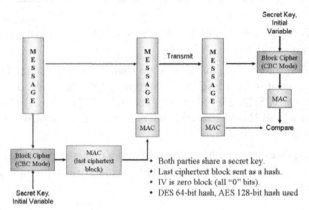

- Both parties share a secret key.
- Last ciphertext block sent as a hash.
- IV is zero block (all "0" bits).
- DES 64-bit hash, AES 128-bit hash used

It is, therefore, crucial that keys be protected so that their secrecy is preserved. If the key is known only by the source and the destination, this algorithm will provide both data origin authentication and data integrity for datagrams sent between the two parties. In addition, only a party with the identical key can verify the hash.

AES-XCBC-MAC-96

According to RFC 3566 (Frankel & Herbert, 2003), the classic CBC-MAC algorithm, while secure for messages of a pre-selected fixed length, has been shown to be not secure across messages of varying lengths such as the type found in typical IP datagrams. The new algorithm, AES-XCBC-MAC-96 RFC 3566 (Frankel & Herbert, 2003), specifies the use of AES in CBC mode with a set of extensions to overcome this limitation.

AES-XCBC-MAC-96 is used as an authentication mechanism within the context of IPsec in the Encapsulating Security Payload (ESP) and the Authentication Header (AH) protocols.

As with MAC, data integrity and data origin authentication, as provided by AES-XCBC-MAC-96 depend on the secrecy of the secret key, K, distribution.

According to RFC 3566 (Frankel & Herbert, 2003), the AES-XCBC-MAC-96 calculations require numerous encryption operations; this encryption must be accomplished using AES with a 128-bit key. Given a 128-bit secret key K, AES-XCBC-MAC-96 is calculated as follows for a message M that consists of n blocks, $M[1]$ ... $M[n]$, in which the size of blocks $M[1]$ ... $M[n-1]$ is 128 bits and the size of block $M[n]$ is between 1 and 128 bits:

1. Three 128-bit keys, $K1$, $K2,$ and $K3$, are derived from the 128-bit secret key K as follows:

    a. $K1 = 0x010101010101010101010101010101010101$ encrypted with Key K

Figure 6-3. AES-XCBC-MAC-96

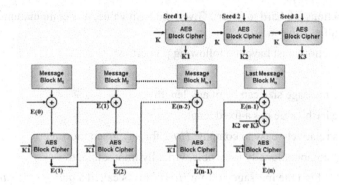

b. $K2 = 0x02020202020202020202020202020202$ encrypted with Key K

c. $K3 = 0x03030303030303030303030303030303$ encrypted with Key K

2. $E[0]$ is defined as $0x00000000000000000000000000000000$

3. For each block M[i], where $i = 1 ... n-1$: XOR M[i] with E [i-1], the result is encrypted with Key K1, yielding E[i].

4. For block $M[n]$:

    a. If the block size of $M[n]$ is 128 bits: XOR $M[n]$ with $E[n-1]$ and Key $K2$, the result is encrypted with Key $K1$, yielding $E[n]$.

    b. If the block size of $M[n]$ is less than 128 bits:

        i. $M[n]$ is padded with a single 1 bit, followed by the number of 0 bits (possibly none) required to increase $M[n]$'s block size to 128 bits.

        ii. XOR $M[n]$ with $E[n-1]$ and Key $K3$, then the result is encrypted with Key $K1$, yielding $E[n]$.

5. The authenticator value is the leftmost 96 bits of the 128-bit $E[n]$.

AES-XCBC-MAC produces a 128-bit authenticator value. AES-XCBC-MAC-96 is derived by truncating this 128-bit value in the same way as is done in HMAC. No other authenticator value lengths are supported by AES-XCBC-MAC-96. The length of 96 bits was selected because it is the default authenticator length for use with either ESP or AH.

Hash Functions

Hash functions are used to prove that transmitted data was not altered. A hash function H takes an input message m and transforms it to produce a hash value h that is a function of the message $h = H(m)$; the input is a variable string and the output is a fixed-size string.

The hash value is also called a *message digest* or a *fingerprint* of the message because there is a very low probability that two messages will produce the same hash value.

Hash functions are hard to invert. Given the hash value, it is computationally infeasible to find the initial value *m*.

A hash function must have the following properties:

- The message size can be of any length.
- The hash value has a fixed length.
- It is relatively easy to compute *H(m)* for any given message.
- It is computationally infeasible, virtually impossible, to:
  a. Find the message *m* from *H(m)* (this is called a *one-way function*)
  b. Have two messages, *m1* and *m2*, in which *H(m1) = H(m2)*
  c. Find two messages, *m1* and *m2*, such that *H(m1) = H(m2)*

A hash function is a "strong hash function" if it satisfies all of the above properties.

Figure 6-4. Hash function (one-way function)

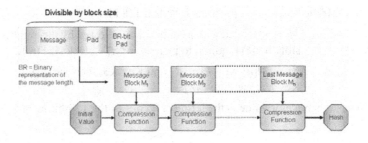

Figure 6-5. Checking integrity

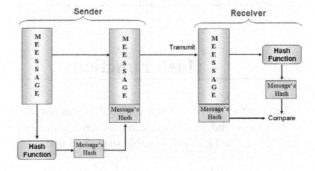

Checking Integrity with a Hash Function

The message and the message's hash are sent to the receiver. The receiver compares the received hash with a newly generated hash. If the hashes are the same, it is highly probable that the message has not been changed.

Secure Hash Standard

On April 17, 1995, the National Institute of Standards and Technology, NIST, approved the Secure Hash Standard, FIPS PUB 180-1, which included one secure hash algorithm, the SHA-1 (Federal Information Processing Standards (FIPS), 1995a). On February 1, 2003, a new Secure Hash Signature Standard (SHS) (FIPS PUB 180-2) was approved; it added three hash algorithms that are capable of producing larger message digests, superseding FIPS 180-1. The Secure Hash Standard is required for use with the Digital Signature Algorithm (DSA), as specified in the Digital Signature Standard (DSS), and, also, whenever a secure hash algorithm is required for federal applications.

FIPS PUB 180-2 (Federal Information Processing Standards (FIPS), 1995b) specifies four secure hash algorithms, SHA-1, SHA-256, SHA-384, and SHA-512. The message digests range in length from 160 to 512 bits, depending on the algorithm. The SHA-1 algorithm specified in the FIPS PUB 180-2 is the same algorithm that was specified previously in FIPS 180-1, although some of the notation was modified to be consistent with the notation used in the SHA-256, SHA-384, and SHA-512 algorithms.

All four of the algorithms are iterative, i.e., one-way hash functions that can process a message in a condensed representation called a *message digest*. They are called secure because according to the standard, it is computationally infeasible (1) To find a message that corresponds to a given message digest, or (2) To find two different messages that produce the same message digest. Therefore, these hash algorithms enable the determination of a message's integrity: any change to the message will, with a very high probability, result in a different message digest. This will result in a verification failure when the secure hash algorithm is used with a digital signature algorithm or a keyed-hash message authentication algorithm. Secure hash algorithms are typically used with other cryptographic algorithms,

Table 6-1. Basic properties of all four secure hash algorithms

Algorithm	Message Size (bits)	Block Size (bits)	Word Size (bits)	Message Digest Size (bits)	Security (bits)
SHA-1	$< 2^{64}$	512	32	160	80
SHA-256	$< 2^{64}$	512	32	256	128
SHA-384	$< 2^{128}$	1024	64	384	192
SHA-512	$< 2^{128}$	1024	64	512	256

such as digital signature algorithms and keyed-hash message authentication codes, or in the generation of random numbers (bits).

The number of bits of security that are provided for the data being hashed is directly related to the message digest length. When a secure hash algorithm is used in conjunction with another algorithm, the FIPS PUB 180-2 recommends the use of the hash algorithm that corresponds according to the number of bits of security. For example, if a message is being signed with a digital signature algorithm that provides 128 bits of security, then that signature algorithm may require the use of a secure hash algorithm that also provides 128 bits of security (e.g., SHA-256). Table 6-1 presents the basic properties of all four secure hash algorithms.

Each secure hash algorithm has two stages, those being preprocessing and hash computation. Preprocessing involves padding a message, parsing the padded message into *m-bit* blocks, and setting initialization values to be used in the hash computation. The hash computation generates a message schedule from the padded message and uses that schedule, along with functions, constants, and word operations to iteratively generate a series of hash values. The final hash value generated by the hash computation is used to determine the message digest.

The purpose of padding a message is to ensure that the padded message is a multiple of 512 or 1024 bits, depending on the algorithm.

Bit Strings and Integers

The following terminology related to bit strings and integers is used in FIPS PUB 180-2 (Federal Information Processing Standards (FIPS), 1995b):

1.   A *hex digit* is an element of the set {0, 1, ..., 9, a, ..., f}. A hex digit is also the representation of a 4-bit string. For example, the hex digit "7" represents the 4-bit string "0111", and the hex digit "a" represents the 4-bit string "1010."

2.   A *word* is a *w-bit* string that is represented as a sequence of hex digits. To convert a word to hex digits, each 4-bit string is converted to its hex digit equivalent, as described in (1) above. For example, the 32-bit string 1010 0001 0000 0011 1111 1110 0010 0011 can be expressed as "a103fe23", and the 64-bit string 1010 0001 0000 0011 1111 1110 0010 0011 0011 0010 1110 1111 0011 0000 0001 1010 can be expressed as "a103fe2332ef301a."

Symbols

According to FIPS PUB 180-2, the following bitwise logical operator symbols are used to calculate the hash function:

∧   Bitwise logical "and" of X and Y

∨   Bitwise logical "inclusive-or" of X and Y

$\oplus$ Bitwise logical "exclusive-or" of X and Y

$\neg$ Bitwise logical "complement" of X

$+$ Addition modulo 2

$<<$ Left-shift operation, where $x << n$ is obtained by discarding the left-most n bits of the word x and then padding the result with n zeros on the right

$>>$ Right-shift operation, where $x >> n$ is obtained by discarding the rightmost n bits of the word x and then padding the result with n zeros on the left

The "and" function sets the resulting bit to 1, if the corresponding bit in both operands is 1, otherwise the result is 0.

Inclusive OR means that if either or both of the operands are 1, the result is 1, otherwise the result is 0.

Exclusive OR means that if just one of the operands is 1, the result is 1, otherwise the result is 0.

The "complement" operator inverts the value of each bit of the operand: if the operand bit is 1, the result is 0, and if the operand bit is 0, the result is 1.

See Table 3-1, Bitwise Logical Operations.

Parameters

The following parameters are used in the secure hash algorithm specifications:

- $a, b, c, ..., h$: Working variables that are the w-bit words used in the computation of the hash values, $H^{(i)}$.

- $H^{(i)}$: The ith hash value. $H^{(0)}$ is the *initial* hash value; $H^{(N)}$ is the *final* hash value and is used to determine the message digest.

- $H_j^{(i)}$: The jth word of the ith hash value, where $H_0^{(i)}$ is the left- most word of hash value i.

- K_t: Constant value to be used for iteration t of the hash computation.

- k: Number of zeroes appended to a message during the padding step.

- l: Length of the message, M, in bits.

- m: Number of bits in a message block, $M^{(i)}$.

- M: Message to be hashed.

- $M^{(i)}$: Message block i, with a size of m bits.

- $M_j^{(i)}$: The jth word of the ith message block, where $M^{(i)}$ is the left-most word of message block i.

- n: Number of bits to be rotated or shifted when a word is operated upon.

- N: Number of blocks in the padded message.
- T: Temporary w-bit word used in the hash computation.
- w: Number of bits in a word.
- W_t: The tth w-bit word of the message schedule.

Operation in Word

The following operations are applied to w-bit words in all four secure hash algorithms. SHA-1 and SHA-256 operate on 32-bit words (w = 32), and SHA-384 and SHA-512 operate on 64-bit words (w = 64).

1. Bitwise *logical* word operations: $\wedge$, $\vee$, $\oplus$, $\neg$.

2. Addition modulo 2^w

    The operation $x + x$ is defined as follows: words x and x represent integers X and Y, where $0 \leq X \leq 2^w$ and $0 \leq Y \leq 2^w$. For positive integers U and V, let U mod V be the remainder upon dividing U by V. Compute:

    $Z = (X + Y)$ mod 2^w.

    Then $0 \leq Z \leq 2^w$. Convert Z to a word, z, and define $z = x + y$.

3. The *right shift* operation $SHR^n(x)$, where x is a w-bit word and n is an integer with $0 \leq n < w$, is defined by $SHR^n(x) = x >> n$.

    This operation is used in the SHA-256, SHA-384, and SHA-512 algorithms.

4. The *rotate right* (circular right shift) operation $ROTL^n(x)$, where x is a w-bit word and n is an integer with $0 < n < w$, is defined by

    $ROTL^n(x) = (x >> n) \vee (x << w - n)$.

    Thus, $ROTL^n(x)$ is equivalent to a circular shift (rotation) of x by n positions to the right. This operation is used by the SHA-256, SHA-384, and SHA-512 algorithms.

5. The *rotate left* (circular left shift) operation $ROTL^n(x)$, where x is a w-bit word and n is an integer with $0 < n < w$, is defined by $ROTL^n(x) = (x << n) \vee (x >> w - n)$.

Thus, $ROTL^n(x)$ is equivalent to a circular shift (rotation) of x by n positions to the left. This operation is used only in the SHA-1 algorithm. Note that in FIPS PUB 180-1, this operation was referred to as "$S^n(X)$"; however, the notation was modified in FIPS PUB 180-2 for clarity and consistency with the notation used for operations in the other secure hash algorithms.

In the above, $X << n$ is obtained as follows: the left-most n bits of X are discarded and then the result is padded with n zeros on the right (the result will still be 32 bits). $X >> 32 - n$ is obtained by discarding the right-most n bits of X and then padding the result with n zeros on the left.

Secure Hash Algorithm: SHA-1

The SHA-1 is designed so it is computationally infeasible to find a message that corresponds to a given message digest, or to find two different messages which produce the same message digest.

The SHA-1 (Federal Information Processing Standards (FIPS), 1995a):

- Works on messages up to 2^{64} in length
- Produces a 160-bit message digest
- Pads a message to a multiple of 512 bits (length = 448 mod 512)
- Carries eighty operations in its main algorithm
- Performs a nonlinear operation on three of the five variables A, B, C, D, and E, in each operation

SHA-1 uses a sequence of logical functions, $f_0, f_1, ..., f_{79}$. Each function f_t, where $0 \leq t < 79$, operates on three 32-bit words, x, y, and z, and produces a 32-bit word as output. The function $f_t(x, y, z)$ is defined as follows:

$$f_t(x,y,z) = \begin{cases} Ch\,(x,y,z) = (x \wedge y) \oplus (\neg x \wedge z) & 0 \leq t \leq 19 \\ Parity\,(x,y,z) = x \oplus y \oplus z & 20 \leq t \leq 39 \\ Maj\,(x,y,z) = (x \wedge y) \oplus (x \wedge z) \oplus (y \wedge z) & 40 \leq t \leq 59 \\ Parity\,(x,y,z) = x \oplus y \oplus z & 60 \leq t \leq 79 \end{cases}$$

Message Padding

The message, M, shall be padded before hash computation begins. The purpose of this padding is to ensure that the padded message is a multiple of 512 for SHA-1 and SHA-256 or 1024 bits for SHA-384 and SHA-512.

The SHA-1 sequentially processes blocks of 512 bits when computing the message digest and padding is required, even if the message is a multiple of 512. Suppose that the length of the message, M, is l bits and k is the number of zero bit. Padding is done as follows:

$$\underbrace{01100001}_{\text{"a"}} \quad \underbrace{01100010}_{\text{"b"}} \quad \underbrace{01100011}_{\text{"c"}} \quad 1 \quad \overbrace{00...00}^{423} \quad \overbrace{\underset{L=24}{00...011000}}^{64}$$

- A 1 bit followed by 0 bits is appended until the length is 64 bits less than a multiple of 512, $(l + 1 + k = 448 \bmod 512)$.

- A 64-bit block that is equal to the number l expressed using a binary representation is appended. The padded message length is $512 \times n$.

For example, the (8-bit ASCII) message abc has the length $8 \times 3 = 24$, so the message is padded with a one bit, then $448 - (24 + 1) = 423$ zero bits.

The length of the padded message is now a multiple of 512 bits.

Parsing the Padded Message

After a message has been padded, it must be parsed into N m-bit blocks before the hash computation can begin. For SHA-1, the padded message is parsed into N *512-bit* blocks, $M^{(1)}, M^{(2)}, ..., M^{(N)}$. Since the 512 bits of the input block may be expressed as sixteen 32-bit words, the first 32 bits of message block i are denoted $M_0{}^i$, the next 32 bits are $M_1{}^i$, and so on up to $M_{15}{}^i$.

Computing the Message Digest

The SHA-1 computation uses two buffers, each consisting of five 32-bit words, and a sequence of eighty 32-bit words. The words of the first 5-word buffer are labeled H_0, H_1, H_2, H_3, H_4. The words of the second 5-word buffer are labeled a, b, c, d, and e. The words of the 80-word sequence are labeled $W_0, W_1, ..., W_{79}$.

The following steps show the calculations to generate the message digest for a 512-bit message block for $i = 1$ to $i = N$. N is the number of 512-bit message blocks.

Figure 6-6. SHA-1 compression function

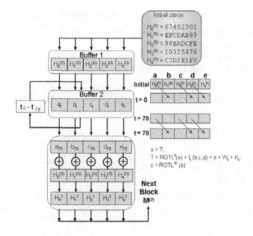

1. In Buffer 1, $H_j^{(0)}$ is initialized as follows:

    $H_0^{(0)} = 67452301$

    $H_1^{(0)} = \text{EFCDAB89}$

    $H_2^{(0)} = \text{98BADCFE}$

    $H_3^{(0)} = 10325476$

    $H_4^{(0)} = \text{C3D2E1F0}.$

2. The 512-bit message block is divided into 16 words $W_0,\ W_1,\ ...,\ W_{15}$, where W_0 is the left-most word.

    For $t = 0$ to 16, let W_t be equal to the message $W_0,\ W_1,\ ...,\ W_{15}$

    For $t = 16$ to 79, let $W_t = \text{ROTL}^1\ (W_{t-3} \oplus W_{t-8} \oplus W_{t-14} \oplus W_{t-16}).$

3. Buffer 2 is initialized as follows:

    $a = H_0^{(i-1)}$

    $b = H_1^{(i-1)}$

    $c = H_2^{(i-1)}$

    $d = H_3^{(i-1)}$

    $e = H_4^{(i-1)}$

4. Let $a = H_0,\ b = H_1,\ c = H_2,\ d = H_3,\ e = H_4.$

    For $t = 0$ to 79, do $e = d;\ d = c;\ c = ROTL^{30}\ (b);\ b = a;\ a = T.$ T is the temporary $w\text{-}bit$ word used in the hash computation and is calculated as follows:

    $T = ROTL^5(a) + f_t\ (b,\ c,\ d) + e + W_t + K_t;$

    $ROTL^5(a) = (a << 5) \vee (a >> 32\text{-}5)$

    $K_t = 5A827999 \qquad (0 \le t \le 19)$

    $K_t = 6ED9EBA1 \qquad (20 \le t \le 39)$

    $K_t = 8F1BBCDC \qquad (40 \le t \le 59)$

    $K_t = CA62C1D6 \qquad (60 \le t \le 79)$

    $f_t\ (b,\ c,\ d) = (b \wedge c) \oplus (\neg\ b \wedge d) \qquad (0 \le t \le 19)$

    $f_t\ (b,\ c,\ d) = b \oplus c \oplus d \qquad (20 \le t \le 39)$

    $f_t\ (b,\ c,\ d) = (b \wedge c) \oplus (\ b \wedge d) \oplus (\ c \wedge d) \qquad (40 \le t \le 59)$

    $f_t\ (b,\ c,\ d) = b \oplus c \oplus d \qquad (60 \le t \le 79).$

5. The ith intermediate hash value $H^{(i)}$ is computed as follows:

    $H_0^i = a + H_0^{(i-1)}$

    $H_1^i = b + H_1^{(i-1)}$

    $H_2^i = c + H_2^{(i-1)}$

    $H_3^i = d + H_3^{(i-1)}$

    $H_4^i = e + H_4^{(i-1)}$

After repeating steps one through four a total of N times (i.e., after processing $M^{(N)}$), the resulting 160-bit message digest of the message is M, is $H_0^N \parallel H_1^N \parallel H_2^N \parallel H_3^N \parallel H_4^N$.

Secure Hash Algorithm: SHA-256

SHA-256 may be used to hash a message, M, having a length of l bits, where $0 \le l < 2^{64}$. The algorithm uses (1) a message schedule of sixty-four 32-bit words, (2) eight working variables of 32 bits each, and (3) a hash value of eight 32-bit words. The final result of SHA-256 is a 256-bit message digest.

SHA-256 uses six logical functions, where *each function operates on 32-bit words*, which are represented as x, y, and z. The result of each function is a new 32-bit word.

$Ch(x, y, z) = (x \wedge y) \oplus (\neg x \wedge z)$

$Maj(x, y, z) = (x \wedge y) \oplus (x \wedge z) \oplus (y \wedge z)$

$$\sum_0^{\{256\}} (x) = ROTR^2(x) \oplus ROTR^{13}(x) \oplus ROTR^{22}(x)$$

$$\sum_0^{\{256\}} (x) = ROTR^6(x) \oplus ROTR^{11}(x) \oplus ROTR^{25}(x)$$

$$\sigma_0^{\{256\}}(x) = ROTR^7(x) \oplus ROTR^{18}(x) \oplus SHR^3(X)$$

$$\sigma_0^{\{256\}}(x) = ROTR^{17}(x) \oplus ROTR^{19}(x) \oplus SHR^{10}(X)$$

SHA-256 Constants

SHA-256 uses a sequence of sixty-four constant 32-bit words:

$K_0^{\{256\}}, K_1^{\{256\}}, \ldots, K_{63}^{\{256\}})$.

These words represent the first 32 bits of the fractional parts of the cube roots of the first 64 prime numbers. In hex, these constant words are (from left to right)

```
428a2f98  71374491  b5c0fbcf  e9b5dba5  3956c25b  59f111f1  923f82a4  ab1c5ed5
d807aa98  12835b01  243185be  550c7dc3  72be5d74  80deb1fe  9bdc06a7  c19bf174
e49b69c1  efbe4786  0fc19dc6  240ca1cc  2de92c6f  4a7484aa  5cb0a9dc  76f988da
983e5152  a831c66d  b00327c8  bf597fc7  c6e00bf3  d5a79147  06ca6351  14292967
```

27b70a85 2e1b2138 4d2c6dfc   53380d13 650a7354 766a0abb 81c2c92e 92722c85

a2bfe8a1 a81a664b c24b8b70 c76c51a3 d192e819 d6990624 f40e3585 106aa070

19a4c116 1e376c08 2748774c 34b0bcb5 391c0cb3 4ed8aa4a 5b9cca4f 682e6ff3

748f82ee 78a5636f 84c87814 8cc70208 90befffa   a4506ceb bef9a3f7 c67178f2.

Message Padding

SHA-256 message padding is the same as in SHA-1.

Parsing the Padded Message

SHA-256 parsing is the same as in SHA-1.

Computing the Message Digest

The words of the message schedule are labeled W_0, W_1, ..., W_{63}. The eight working variables are labeled a, b, c, d, e, f, g, and h. The words of the hash value are labeled $H_0^{(i)}$, $H_1^{(i)}$, ..., $H_7^{(i)}$, which will hold the initial hash value, $H^{(0)}$ replaced by each successive intermediate hash value (after each message block is processed), $H^{(i)}$ and ending with the final hash value, H^N. SHA- 256 also uses two temporary words, T_1 and T_2.

The following steps show the calculations to generate the message digest for a 512-bit message block for $i = 1$ to $i = N$. N is the number of 512-bit message blocks.

1. $H_j^{(i)}$ is initialized as follows:

    $H_0^{(0)} = 6a09e667$

    $H_1^{(0)} = bb67ae85$

    $H_2^{(0)} = 3c6ef372$

    $H_3^{(0)} = a54ff53a$

    $H_4^{(0)} = 510e527f$

    $H_5^{(0)} = 9b05688c$

    $H_6^{(0)} = 1f83d9ab$

    $H_7^{(0)} = 5be0cd19$

    These words were obtained by taking the first 32 bits of the fractional parts of the square roots of the first eight prime numbers.

2. $\{W_t\}$ message schedule is prepared as follows:

    For $0 \leq t \geq 15$, let $W_t = M_t^{(i)}$

    For $16 \leq t \geq 63$, let $W_t = \sigma_1^{\{256\}}(W_{t-2}) + W_{t-7} + \sigma_0^{\{256\}}(W_{t-15}) + W_{t-16}$

3.   The eight working variables, a, b, c, d, e, f, g, and h are initialized the with the $(i-1)^{th}$ hash value:

$$a = H_0^{(i-1)}$$
$$b = H_1^{(i-1)}$$
$$c = H_2^{(i-1)}$$
$$d = H_3^{(i-1)}$$
$$e = H_4^{(i-1)}$$
$$f = H_5^{(i-1)}$$
$$g = H_6^{(i-1)}$$
$$h = H_6^{(i-1)}$$

4.   For $t = 0$ to 63, the following values are calculated:

$$T_1 = h + \sum_1^{\{256\}} (e) + Ch(e, f, g) + K_t^{256} + W_t$$

$$T_2 = \sum_0^{\{256\}} (a) + Maj(a, b, c)$$

$$a = T_1 + T_2$$
$$b = a$$
$$c = b$$
$$d = c$$
$$e = d + T_1$$
$$f = e$$
$$g = f$$
$$h = g$$

5.   The ith intermediate hash value $H^{(i)}$ is computed as follows:

$$H_0^{(i)} = a + H_0^{(i-1)}$$
$$H_1^{(i)} = b + H_1^{(i-1)}$$
$$H_2^{(i)} = c + H_2^{(i-1)}$$
$$H_3^{(i)} = d + H_3^{(i-1)}$$
$$H_4^{(i)} = e + H_4^{(i-1)}$$
$$H_5^{(i)} = f + H_4^{(i-1)}$$
$$H_6^{(i)} = g + H_4^{(i-1)}$$
$$H_7^{(i)} = h + H_4^{(i-1)}$$

After repeating steps one through four a total of N times (i.e., after processing $M^{(N)}$), the resulting 160-bit message digest of the message is M, is $H_0^{(N)} \| H_1^{(N)} \| H_2^{(N)} \| H_3^{(N)} \| H_4^{(N)} \| H_5^{(N)} \| H_6^{(N)} \| H_7^{(N)}$.

MD5 Message Digest Algorithm

MD2, MD4, and MD5 are message-digest algorithms developed by Ronald Rivest in 1989, 1990, and 1991. All three algorithms produce a 128-bit message digest of the message input that may have any length, but, in reality, it is expected that the message will have less than 2^{64} bits. The MD5 message-digest algorithm is described in the RFC 1321 (Rivest, 1992).

Message Padding

Padding is similar to SHA-1. Padding is done as follows:

- A single 1 bit followed by 0 bits is appended until the length is 64 bits less than a multiple of 512 (length = 448 mod 512), then,

- A 64-bit representation of the prepadded message length is appended.

The padded message length is $512 \times n$.

Computing the Message Digest

MD5 uses a four-word buffer (A, B, C, D) to compute the message digest. A, B, C, and D are 32-bit registers and are initialized with the following values in hexadecimal:

A = 01 23 45 67

B = 89 ab cd ef

C = fe dc ba 98

D = 76 54 32 10

The algorithm to generate the message digest for a 512-bit message block has four rounds, and each round consists of 16 operations. Each operation performs a non-linear operation on three of the four variables A, B, C, D.

The function a_n is different for each of the four rounds:

$$a_1 = b + ((a + F(b, c, d) + X[k] + T[i]) \lll s)$$
$$a_2 = b + ((a + G(b, c, d) + X[k] + T[i]) \lll s)$$
$$a_3 = b + ((a + H(b, c, d) + X[k] + T[i]) \lll s)$$
$$a_4 = b + ((a + I(b, c, d) + X[k] + T[i]) \lll s)$$

Figure 6-7. MD5 compression function

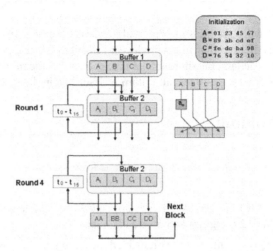

where the nonlinear functions, very similar to the SHA-1 nonlinear functions (different notation), are the following

$F(b, c, d) = bc \vee$ not $(b) d$

$G(b, c, d) = bd \vee c$ not (d)

$H(b, c, d) = b$ XOR c XOR d

$I(b, c, d) = c$ XOR $(b \vee$ not $(d))$

$X[k]$ represents the kth sub-block of the message (from 0 to 15).

$T[i]$ is the integer part of 4294967296 times abs(sin(i)), where I is in radians. Note 4294967296 is 2^{32}.

$<<< s$ represents a left shift of s bits.

After the 512-bit block has been processed, the results are called AA, BB, CC, and DD. Then, A = A + AA, B = B + BB, C = C + CC, and D = D + DD. After processing M_n, the message digest is the 128-bit string represented by the word ABCD.

Table 6-2 shows a comparison between SHA-1 and MD5.

Keyed-Hash Message Authentication Code (HMAC)

The Federal Information Processing Standards FIPS PUB 198 (2002) describes HMAC as a mechanism for message authentication using cryptographic hash functions. HMAC can be used with any approved cryptographic hash function in combination with a shared secret key. The cryptographic strength of a HMAC depends on the properties of the underlying hash

Table 6-2. SHA-1 and MD5 comparison

Secure Hash Algorithm (SHA-1)	Message Digest 5 (MD5)
• Developed by NSA and is required for use with the digital signature algorithm (DSA).	• Developed by Ronald Rivest in 1991 (MD2 in 89, MD4 in 90).
• Works on messages up to 2^{64} bits in length.	• Works on messages up to 2^{64} bits in length.
• Produces a 160-bit message digest.	• Produces a 128-bit message digest.
• Processes block messages of 512 bits.	• Processes block messages of 512 bits.
• Has four rounds of twenty operations in main loop of algorithm.	• Has four rounds of 16 operations in main loop of algorithm.
• Performs a nonlinear operation on three of the five variables a, b, c, d, e in each operation.	• Performs a nonlinear operation on three of the four variables a, b, c, d in each operation.

function. The HMAC specified in FIPS PUB 198 is a generalization of Internet RFC 2104 (Krawczyk, Bellare, & Canetti, 1997), HMAC, "Keyed-Hashing for Message Authentication," and ANSI X9.71, "Keyed Hash Message Authentication Code."

HMAC Parameters and Symbols

The following are the HMAC parameters and steps to calculate HMAC as they are described in FIPS PUB 198:

- **B:** Block size (in bytes) of the input to the approved hash function.
- **H:** An approved hash function.
- **Ipad:** Inner pad; the byte x'36' repeated B times.
- **K:** Secret key shared between the originator and the intended receiver(s).
- K_0: The key K after any necessary pre-processing to form a B byte key.
- **L:** Block size (in bytes) of the output of the approved hash function.
- **Opad:** Outer pad; the byte x'5c' repeated B times.
- **t:** The number of bytes of an MAC.
- **text:** The data on which the HMAC is calculated; text does not include the padded key. The length of text is n bits, where $0 \leq n < 2^B - 8B$.
- **x'N':** Hexadecimal notation, where each symbol in the string N represents 4 binary bits.
- **||:** Concatenation
- **XOR:** Exclusive-OR operation.

Figure 6-8. Keyed-Hash Message Authentication (HMAC)

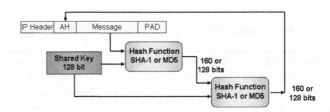

Calculating the HMAC

The HMAC is calculated using the following operation:

$\text{MAC(text)}_t = \text{HMAC(K, text)}_t = H((K_0 \text{ XOR opad})\| H((K_0 \text{ XOR ipad}) \| \text{text}))_t$

1. If the length of $K = B$: set $K0 = K$. Go to step 4.

2. If the length of $K > B$: K is hashed to obtain an *L-byte* string, then append $(B - L)$ zeros to create a *B-byte* string $K0$ (i.e., *K0 = H (K)* || *00...00)*. Go to step 4.

3. If the length of $K < B$: zeros are appended to the end of K to create a *B-byte* string K_0 (e.g., if K is 20 bytes in length and $B = 64$, then K will be appended with 44 zero bytes 0x00).

4. XOR $K0$ with *ipad* is done to produce a *B-byte* string: $K0 \oplus ipad$.

5. The stream of data *text* is appended to the string resulting from step 4: $(K0 \oplus ipad) \| text$.

6. H is applied to the stream generated in step 5: $H ((K0 \oplus ipad) \| text)$.

7. XOR K_0 with *opad*: $K0 \oplus opad$ is done.

Figure 6-9. HMAC implementation

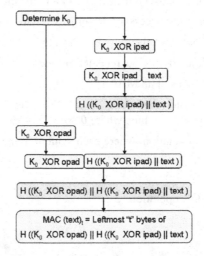

8.   The result from step 6 is appended to step 7: $(K0 \oplus opad) \parallel H\ ((K0 \oplus ipad) \parallel text)$.

9. H is applied to the result from step 8: $H\ ((K0 \oplus opad) \parallel H\ ((K0 \oplus ipad) \parallel text))$.

10.   The leftmost t bytes of the result of step 9 are selected as the MAC.

Some HMAC implementation truncates the output H to a given length t, so only part of the hash is outputted. RFC-2104 (Krawczyk, Bellare, & Canetti, 1997) recommends that t should not be less than half of the original hash output. The HMAC notation is as follows: HMAC – Hash algorithm – t. For example, HMAC-SHA-1-96 is a HMAC that uses SHA-1 for its hash function, and the resulting hash is truncated to 96 bits. The SHA-1 output is 160 bits.

Authentication (Digital Signatures)

Authentication is the act of identifying or verifying the entity that originated the message. It can also mean the corroboration (proof) of the sender's identity and authenticity, that the sender is the one the sender claims to be. When a written message is sent, the message is authenticated with a handwritten signature so the receiver of the message is able to validate the message.

Note that the ElGamal digital signature signs the message and not the message's hash, as do RSA and the DSA.

While passwords can be used for establishing identity, it is better to use public-key digital signatures, such as the DSS and the RSA because of their strong authentication mechanisms.

When using public-key digital signatures, each entity requires a public key and a private key. Certificates are an essential part of a digital signature authentication mechanism. Certificates bind a specific entity's identity (be it host, network, user, or application) to its public keys, and possibly, to other security-related information such as privileges, clearances, and compartments. Authentication based on digital signatures requires a trusted third party or certificate authority to create, sign, and properly distribute certificates. See Chapter IX, "Certificates and PKI."

Digital signatures provide a way to verify that a message has not been altered in transit, and for a recipient to be certain of the originator's identity. Digital signatures provide the following:

•   **Authentication:** It should be possible for the recipient of a message to ascertain its origin

•   **Non-repudiation:** A sender should not be able to later deny having sent and signed a message

•   **Integrity:** It should be possible for the recipient of a message to verify that the message has not been modified in transit

Figure 6-10. Secure mechanisms for authentication

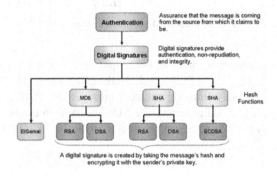

Figure 6-11. Authentication using digital signature

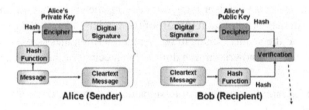

A digital signature must provide the following assurances:

- The signature is not forgeable
- The signature can be validated
- Once a message is signed, the sender must not be able to repudiate it

Figure 6-11 shows how authentication is achieved using digital signatures. Alice hashes the message and the hash is encrypted using Alice's private key. Alice transmits the message in clear concatenated with the digital signature. When Bob receives the message, he deciphers the digital signature using Alice's public key and obtains the message hash. Bob then hashes the cleartext message and compares both hashes. If both hashes are the same, then the message has not been modified and it came from Alice.

Digital Signature Standard (FIPS 186-2)

The FIPS Pub 186-2 (Federal Information Processing Standards (FIPS), 2000), issued on January 27, 2000, is the specification for the Digital Signature Standard (DSS), which prescribes three algorithms suitable for digital signatures: the Digital Signature Algorithm (DSA), the RSA algorithm, and the ECDSA algorithm.

For a digital signature to work, the signatory and the verifier need to have their public and private keys. The private key is used in the signature generation process, and the public key is used in the signature verification process. Also, the Secure Hash Algorithms (SHAs), specified in FIPS 180-2 are used for both signature generation and verification.

If a message is signed with Alice's private key, then it is possible to assume that only Alice signed the message because she is the only one who has that private key. A spoofer, who does not know Alice's private key, cannot generate Alice's correct signature. In other words, digital signatures cannot be forged. In the same way, if a message is enciphered with Bob's public key, only Bob will be able to decipher the message because it is assumed that only Bob has Bob's private key.

Because there is the possibility that a spoofer may post his own public key as Alice's or Bob's, it is necessary to have a means of associating a user's identity and the user's public key. A mutually trusted party, a certifying authority, could sign credentials containing the user's public key and identity by creating a digital certificate that binds the certificate to the user.

Digital Signature Algorithm (ANSI X9.30)

According to the FIPS Pub 186-2 (Federal Information Processing Standards (FIPS), 2000), the DSA makes use of the following parameters:

1. p is a prime modulus, where $2^{L-1} < p < 2^L$ for L = 1024
2. q is a prime divisor of $p - 1$, where $2^{159} < q < 2^{160}$
3. $g = h^{(p-1)/q} \bmod p$, where h is any integer with $1 < h < p - 1$ such that $h^{(p-1)/q} \bmod p > 1$ (g has order $q \bmod p$)
4. x = a randomly or pseudo randomly generated integer with $0 < x < q$
5. $y = g^x \bmod p$
6. k = a randomly or pseudo randomly generated integer with $0 < k < q$

The integers p, q, and g can be public and can be common to a group of users. A user's private and public keys are x and y, respectively. Parameters x and k are used for signature generation only, and must be kept secret. Parameter k must be changed for each signature.

The signature of a message m is the pair of numbers r and s computed according to the following equations:

Figure 6-12. DSA algorithm

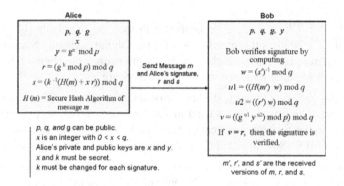

$r = (g^k \bmod p) \bmod q$, and $s = (k^{-1}(\text{SHA-1}(m) + x\,r)) \bmod q$.

In the above, k^{-1} is the multiplicative inverse of k, mod q, i.e., $(k^{-1}\,k) \bmod q = 1$ and $0 < k^{-1} < q$. The value of SHA-1(m) is a 160-bit string output by the Secure Hash Algorithm specified in FIPS 180-1 and must be converted to an integer. The signature is transmitted along with the message to the verifier.

Prior to verifying Alice's signature, Bob needs to have access to p, q and g. Once Alice has signed the message, she sends the message, m, and her digital signature r and s.

Let m', r', and s' be the received versions of m, r, and s, respectively, and let y be Alice's public key. To verify Alice's signature, Bob first checks to see that $0 < r' < q$ and $0 < s' < q$.

If either condition is violated, the signature will be rejected. If these two conditions are satisfied, then the verifier computes:

$w = (s')^{-1} \bmod q$

$u1 = ((\text{SHA-1}\,(m')\,w)) \bmod q$

$u2 = ((r')\,w) \bmod q$

$v = ((g^{u1}\,y^{u2}) \bmod p) \bmod q$.

If $v = r'$, then the signature is verified and the verifier can have high confidence that the received message was sent by the party holding the private key, x, corresponding to the public key, y.

If v does not equal r', then the message may have been modified, the message may have been incorrectly signed by Alice, or the message may have been signed by an impostor, and, therefore, the message should be considered invalid.

RSA Digital Signature (ANSI X9.31)

When Alice wants to send a secure message to Bob, she enciphers the message with Bob's public key. Bob will then be the only one able to decipher the message using his private key. In addition, it is possible to sign a message in such a way that the signature positively identifies the sender. For example, if Alice wants to send an authenticated message to Bob, she enciphers the message using her own private key and sends the message to Bob; when Bob receives the enciphered message, he uses Alice's public key to decipher it.

$$C = M^{Priv_A} \bmod p$$
$$M = C^{Priv_A} \bmod p$$

Example

Let Alice's p, *Pub*, and *Priv* be 341, 53, and 17. To authenticate the message, Alice enciphers her message with her private key using her own modulo. When Bob receives the enciphered message, he deciphers it with Alice's public key using Alice's modulo. Suppose that the plaintext $M = 2$, then:

$$C = M^{Priv_A} \bmod p = 2^{17} (\bmod\ 341) = 128 (\bmod\ 341)$$
$$M = C^{Priv_A} \bmod p = 128^{53} (\bmod\ 341) = 2$$

The receiver, Bob, or anyone else, knows that the message could have only been enciphered by Alice and not by any other person. Thus, the message has been signed (authenticated) by Alice. However, there is no secrecy in the message because anyone could decipher it using Alice's public key.

If Alice wants to send a signed (authenticated) and enciphered message to Bob, first she needs to authenticate it by enciphering the message with her own private key, and then, she enciphers the message using Bob's public key. At the receiver end, Bob first deciphers the message using his own private key, and then authenticates it by deciphering again with Alice's public key. This only applies if Alice's modulo p is smaller than Bob's modulo p. If Alice's modulus is greater than Bob's, then Alice should encipher the message first and then authenticate it (Kohnfelder, 1978). When Bob receives the message, he proceeds first to authenticate and then to decipher it.

$$p_A \leq p_B \quad p_A \leq p_B$$

$$C = Pub_B{}^{M^{Priv_A}} \bmod p \qquad C = Priv_A{}^{M^{Pub_B}} \bmod p$$

$$M = Pub_A{}^{C^{Priv_A}} \bmod p \qquad M = Priv_B{}^{C^{Pub_A}} \bmod p$$

Figure 6-13 shows how RSA encryption and MD5 hash algorithms can be used for encryption and digital signature. When Alice, the sender, enciphers the hash created using MD5 with her private key, she is signing the message.

Figure 6-13. RSA digital signature

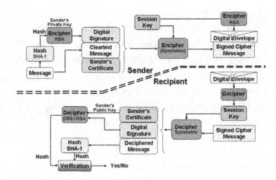

Elliptic Curve Digital Signature Algorithm (ANSI X9.62)

According to the FIPS Pub 186-2 (Federal Information Processing Standards (FIPS), 2000), the Elliptic Curve Digital Signature Algorithm (ECDSA) is the approved cryptographic algorithm for digital signature generation and verification. Appendix 6 of the FIPS Pub 186-2 describes the recommended elliptic curves for federal government use. See Chapter 8, "Elliptic Curve Cryptography," for a description of ECDSA.

ElGamal Digital Signature

In August 1984, at the '84 IEEE Crypto conference, Taher ElGamal presented a new signature scheme derived from a modification of exponentiation ciphers (ElGamal, 1985). In this scheme, the security of the system relies on the difficulty of computing discrete logarithms over finite fields. This technique uses only exponentiation in *GF (p)*. The procedure is as follows:

1. *M* is a document to be signed, where $0 \leq m \geq p - 1$.
2. A large prime number *p*, the modulus, is selected.
3. A random number R^A, uniformly between 0 and *p - 1*, such that $gcd(R^A, p - 1) = 1$ is selected.
4. V_A is computed:

   $V_A = a^{R_A} \bmod p$ Equation 6-1

   where, *a*, the base, is a primitive root modulus *p*.
5. The private and public keys are generated according to Diffie-Hellman:

   $Pub_A = a^{PrivA} \bmod p$ Equation 6-2

6. I_{RA}, the multiplicative inverse of R^A is computed, such that:

$$R^A * I_{RA} \equiv 1[\bmod (p\text{-}1)]$$

7. S_A, the signature, is computed:

$$S_A = [I_{RA} * (M\text{-}V_A * Priv\,A)]\bmod (p\text{-}1)$$ Equation 6-3

8. M, V_A, and S_A are sent to B

9. For authentication, B computes:

$$C_B = a^M \bmod p$$ Equation 6-4

$$C_{B'} = [\,Pub_A^{V_A} * V_A^{S_A}\,]\bmod p$$ Equation 6-5

10. If $C_B = C'_B$ the M is authentic.

Proof that $C_B = C'_B$

From Equation 6-3, it can be said that M is equal to:

$$S_A = [\,I_{RA} * (M\text{-}V_A * Priv_A)\,]\bmod (p\text{-}1)$$

$$S_A * I_{RA}^{-1} = (M\text{-}V_A * Priv_A)\bmod (p\text{-}1)$$

$$S_A * R_A = (M\text{-}V_A * Priv_A)\bmod (p\text{-}1)$$ Equation 6-6

According to equation $a^{\,x\bmod(p\text{-}1)} = a^x \bmod p$, then, a^M is equal to:

$$a^M = a^{[\,Priv_A * V_A + R_A * S_A\,]\bmod (p\text{-}1)}$$

$$a^M = a^{(Priv_A * V_A + R_A * S_A)}\bmod p$$

$$a^M = (a^{Priv_A}\bmod p)^{V_A} * (a^{R_A}\bmod p)^{S_A}\bmod p$$

and C_B is equal to:

$$C_B = (a^{Priv_A}\bmod p)^{V_A} * (a^{R_A}\bmod p)^{S_A}\bmod p$$ Equation 6-7

Replacing Equations 6-1 and 6-2 in 6-5, it is determined that $C_{B'}$ is equal to:

$$C_{B'} = (a^{Priv_A}\bmod p)^{V_A} * (a^{R_A}\bmod p)^{S_A}\bmod p$$

then $C_B = C_{B'}$

The ElGamal digital signature is a variation of the Diffie-Hellman public key algorithm in which the use of V_A introduces another public-key encryption. Several public key variations have been developed from ElGamal.

Summary

Has data been changed while at rest (data storage) or in transit (going from point A to point B)? After confidentiality, this question relates to one of the most important security services, i.e., checking message integrity. Hash algorithms, SHA and MD5, and message authentication codes, HMAC and AES-XCBC-MAC-96, allow us to verify message integrity.

Another security requirement is to check if a message really is coming from the entity that claimed to send it. If a message is enciphered with the sender's private key and the receiver is able to decipher with the sender's public key, then the sender cannot deny that the sender sent the message, because supposedly, the sender is the only one with the private key. Authentication and non-repudiation security services are provided by digital signatures.

As stated previously, public key crypto systems are very slow and are mainly used to encipher short messages. If a message is hashed first, then the message length is reduced to the hash size, which is 128 bits for MD5, and 160, 256, 384, or 512 for SHA. A digital signature is created by taking the message's hash and encrypting it with the sender's private key. Digital signatures are used to provide authentication, non-repudiation, and integrity. Note that the ElGamal digital signature signs the message and not the message's hash as is done for other types of digital signatures.

The Digital Signature Standard (FIPS 186-2) prescribes three algorithms suitable for digital signatures: the Digital Signature Algorithm (DSA), the RSA algorithm, and the ECDSA algorithm.

Learning Objectives Review

1. SHAs are required for use with the Digital Signature Algorithm (DSA), as specified in the Digital Signature Standard (DSS), and whenever a secure hash algorithm is required for federal applications. (T/F)

2. Which one of the following is appended to the message and is used by the receiver to verify the data's origin and integrity?

    a.   A digital envelope

    b.   A digital signature

    c.   A cryptographic hash

    d.   A message authentication code

3. Which security services provide digital signatures?

    a.   Integrity, confidentiality, and authorization

    b.   Integrity, authentication, and non-repudiation

    c.   Authentication, authorization, and non-repudiation

    d.   Authentication, authorization, confidentiality

4.   Authentication is the act of identifying or verifying:

    a.   The entity that originated the message

    b.   That the CA is who he claims to be

5.   Which of the following is NOT a property of a hash function?

    a.   It converts a message of a fixed length into a message digest of arbitrary length

    b.   It is computationally infeasible to construct two different messages with the same digest

    c.   It converts a message of arbitrary length into a message digest of a fixed length

    d.   Given a digest value, it is computationally infeasible to find the corresponding message

6.   SHA-1 output is 160 bits. The HMAC notation HMAC - SHA-1 - 96 is an HMAC that uses SHA-1 for its hash function, and the resulting hash is truncated to:

    a.   96 bits

    b.   64 bits

7.   Which of the following services is not provided by the Digital Signature Standard (DSS)?

    a.   Authentication

    b.   Digital signature

    c.   Integrity

    d.   Encryption

8.   A digital signature is created by taking the hash function of a message and encrypting it with the sender's private key. (T/F)

9.   Digital signatures can prevent messages from being:

    a.   Erased

    b.   Disclosed

    c.   Repudiated

10.   Hash functions create hashes that can easily be inverted. (T/F)

11.   The Secure Hash Algorithm (SHA-1) is used for both signature generation and verification. (T/F)

12.   A hash function is considered a one-way function if it is computationally infeasible to:

    a.   Determine the original message from the hash value

    b.   Have two messages resulting in the same hash value

    c.   Both A and B

    d.   Neither A nor B

13.   Integrity is an intrinsic feature of encryption. (T/F)

14.   A one-way hash function provides:

    a.   Authentication

    b.   Confidentiality

    c.   Integrity

    d.   Availability

15.   Which of the following algorithms is NOT a hash function?

    a.   SHA-1

    b.   MD5

    c.   MD2

    d.   RC4

16.   The hash of a message is called:

    a.   A ciphertext

    b.   A digital signature

    c.   A plaintext

    d.   A message digest

17.   How is integrity achieved using hash functions?

18.   What is a one-way function?

19.   Any approved cryptographic hash function may be used to create an HMAC. (T/F)

20.   Authentication is an intrinsic feature of encryption. (T/F)

References

ElGamal, T. A. (1985). Public key cryptosystem and a signature scheme based on discrete logarithms. *IEEE Transactions on Information Theory, 31*, 469-472.

Federal Information Processing Standards (FIPS). (1985). *Computer data authentication* (FIPS PUB 113). Retrieved June 26, 2007, from http://www.itl.nist.gov/fipspubs/fip113.htm

Federal Information Processing Standards (FIPS). (1995a). *Secure hash standard* (FIPS PUB 180-1). Retrieved June 26, 2007, from http://www.itl.nist.gov/fipspubs/fip180-1.htm

Federal Information Processing Standards (FIPS). (1995b). *Secure hash standard* (FIPS PUB 180-2). Retrieved June 26, 2007, from http://csrc.nist.gov/publications/fips/fips180-2/fips180-2withchangenotice.pdf

Federal Information Processing Standards (FIPS). (2000). *Digital signature standard (DSS)* (FIPS PUB 186-2 (+Change Notice)). Retrieved June 26, 2007, from http://csrc.nist.gov/publications/fips/fips186-2/fips186-2-change1.pdf

Federal Information Processing Standards (FIPS). (2002). *The keyed-hash message authentication code* (FIPS PUB 198). Retrieved June 26, 2007, from http://csrc.nist.gov/publications/fips/fips198/fips-198a.pdf

Frankel, S., & Herbert, H. (2003). *The AES-XCBC-MAC-96 algorithm and its use with IPsec* (RFC 3566). Internet Engineering Task Force (IETF). Retrieved June 26, 2007, from http://www.ietf.org/rfc/rfc3566.txt?number=3566

Kohnfelder, L. M. (1978). On the signature reblocking problem in public-key cryptosystems. *Communications of the ACM, 21*(2), 179.

Krawczyk, H., Bellare, M., & Canetti, R. (1997) *HMAC: Keyed-hashing for message authentication* (RFC 2104). Internet Engineering Task Force (IETF). Retrieved June 26, 2007, from http://www.ietf.org/rfc/rfc2104.txt?number=2104

Rivest, R. (1992). *The MD5 Message-Digest Algorithm* (RFC 1321). Internet Engineering Task Force (IETF). Retrieved June 26, 2007, from http://www.ietf.org/rfc/rfc1321.txt?number=1321

Chapter VII

Access Authentication

Access Authentication

Unless a corporation can reliably authenticate its network users, it is not possible to keep unauthorized users out of its networks. Authentication is essential for two parties to be able to trust in each other's identities. Authentication is based on something you know (a password), on something you have (a token card, a digital certificate), or something that is part of you (fingerprints, voiceprint). A strong authentication requires at least two of these factors. The following mechanisms of authentication are described in this chapter: (1) IEEE 802.1X Access Control Protocol; (2) Extensible Authentication Protocol (EAP) and EAP methods; (3) traditional passwords; (4) Remote Authentication Dial-in Service (RADIUS); (5) Kerberos authentication service; and (6) X.509 authentication.

Objectives

- Understand the IEEE 8021X and EAP methods of authentication
- Learn how RADIUS is used to authenticate dial-in users
- Understand how the Kerberos service is used to provide authentication and authorization to a user
- Learn how X.509 provides user authentication

Introduction

Authentication has been used to verify that an individual is authorized to access property, resources, and information. In today's communications, users access information from everywhere; for example, individuals can travel with their laptops and IP phones and are able to access their networks and receive phone calls as if they were at their offices. There is an increasing demand to provide strong authentication for users, devices, and applications across all type of networks.

Ideally, a subject's identity should be initially established and verified at a specified point in the network, and some type of credentials that assert the subject's identity should be given to the subject by the authenticator. When access to several networks or Web domains are involved in a transaction, the subject should be able to show credentials and assertions to other networks or Web domains to prove the subject's identity to complete the transaction. This requires making the assertion portable. For example, in Web services, the security assertion markup language (SAML) allows users to gain access to different resources in multiple domains without having to re-authenticate after initially logging into to the first domain.

Regardless of whether the authentication can be made portable, or if authentication is at the access point or end-to-end, or if individuals and or devices are authenticated, secure and trusted networks require strong authentication. This means that people and devices are reliably identified so transactions can be conducted without compromise.

VoIP technology requires the same level of reliability as public switch telephone networks (PSTN) to ensure that services will not be interrupted or compromised. The VoIP service can only be secure by strongly authenticating every element in the VoIP system.

For the purpose of providing authentication and authorization mechanisms for devices connected to a network, it is necessary to establish the following:

1. An authentication protocol between the devices that require authentication, i.e., client/supplicant and the authenticator

Figure 7-1. Access authentication

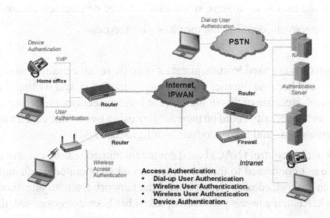

Figure 7-2. Authentication mechanisms, methods, and protocols

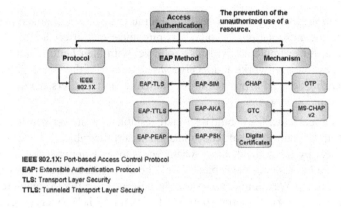

IEEE 802.1X: Port-based Access Control Protocol
EAP: Extensible Authentication Protocol
TLS: Transport Layer Security
TTLS: Tunneled Transport Layer Security

2.   An authentication method used between the authenticator and an authentication server

3.   An authentication mechanism to carry the access control that authenticates a client or supplicant

Authentication Concepts

Authentication is the process of reliably verifying the identity of a user or device and should not to be confused with identification, which is only an assertion of identity. Authentication is usually a prerequisite to authorization since entitlements depend upon verifying the identity of the user.

User authentication is usually based on one or a combination of the following:

- What the user knows—passwords
- What the user has—tokens, smart cards, digital certificates, and so forth
- What personal identifier the user has—biometrics

When passwords are used to authenticate a user, there are certain limitations on the length of the password because the user will have to memorize it, and writing the password is not recommended. Because of this limitation, the level of security offered by passwords is very low. The level of security could be increased by using two or three factor authentication, for example, passwords and tokens, or passwords, tokens and biometrics.

A network access control (NAC) based device for authentication ensures that unauthorized devices are not connected to the network, even when operated by an authorized user. For example, an authorized user cannot access the network from an unauthorized PC at home or at a kiosk. Also, if a user's password or token has been compromised, the network is still protected because the attacker needs to use an authorized device to access the network. Device authentication is also used when two network devices, for example, two switches or routers, authenticate each other. Device-to-device authentication is not constrained by the need to remember passwords. Encryption keys can be used to provide strong authentication.

Device authentication provides the following benefits:

- Provides identity information for electronic devices connected to the network
- Adds another layer of protection by establishing control regarding the equipment connected to the network
- Increases the device's trustworthiness

IEEE 802.1X Authentication

The IEEE 802.1X-2004 is a data link layer transport protocol that defines port-access control standards for wireless and physical networks. The Extensible Authentication Protocol is used to provide authentication credentials. Within this framework, port access refers to user port access controlled by a wireless access point or wired switch. Users do not get IP-connectivity until they have successfully authenticated.

IEEE802.1X (Institute of Electrical and Electronic Engineers (IEEE), 2004) deployment requires the installation of three components, which are the same three main components for EAP: the supplicant, the authenticator, and the authentication server.

1. **Supplicant authentication software and hardware:** They run on a device that requires authentication. The network adapter needs to be 802.1X-compatible.

2. **Authenticator 802.1X EAP compatible:** The authenticator is nothing more than a gateway. Its function is to convert the supplicant's EAP packets from 802.1X to RADIUS format and pass the packets to the authentication server. It also converts the authentication server's EAP packets from RADIUS format to 802.1X and passes the packets to the supplicant. The authenticator should not only be 802.1X EAP compatible, but also should be compatible with the authentication method the system is using.

3. **Authentication server:** The authentication server needs to support EAP. Usually the authentication server is a RADIUS, although 802.1 X does not specify RADIUS. The authentication server also needs to support: (1) the inner authentication method for TTLS and PEAP, if these methods were selected; (2) the database, LDAP server, or Windows 2000; (3) the platform operating system, UNIX or Windows.

In IEEE 802.1X, the access point acts as an authenticator, while a wireless station (e.g., a laptop) is the supplicant. A Port Access Entity (PAE) is an entity that is able to control the authorized/unauthorized state of its controlled port.

Figure 7-3. 802.1X port-based access control protocol

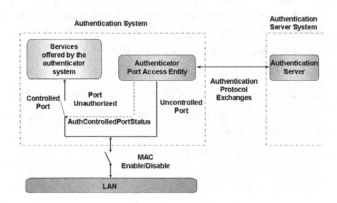

In IEEE 802.1X-2004, an authenticator establishes a dialog with a single supplicant in order to establish credentials. This process prevents unauthorized access by supplicants to the services offered by the system. Access control is achieved by the system requiring authentication from the supplicants who attach to the authenticator's controlled ports. In a port-based access control, the authentication occurs at the edge rather than in the core of the LAN.

Figure 7-3 illustrates the operation of a port-based access. The authenticator uses a dual-port model with two ports, the uncontrolled port and the controlled port. The uncontrolled and controlled ports have the same point of attachment to the LAN. Any access to the LAN is subject to the current administrative and operational state of the MAC (or logical MAC) associated with the port, in addition to Auth_Controlled_Port_ Status. If the MAC is physically or administratively inoperable, then no protocol exchanges of any kind can take place using that MAC on either the controlled or the uncontrolled port.

Connection through the uncontrolled port access allows uncontrolled exchange of data information between the authenticator and the client on the LAN, regardless of the authorization state (the uncontrolled port). The uncontrolled port filters all network traffic and allows only EAP packets to pass. Authentication occurs when a supplicant is connected to an authenticator's port. Until authentication has been successfully completed, the supplicant only has access to the authenticator to perform authentication exchanges. Depending on the result of the authentication process, the authenticator can determine whether or not the supplicant is authorized to access its services on that controlled port. A possible outcome is that when the supplicant is successfully authenticated, its traffic is directed to a particular virtual LAN (VLAN). If the supplicant is not authorized for access, the authenticator sets the controlled port state to "unauthorized." In the unauthorized state, the use of the controlled port is restricted, thus preventing unauthorized data transfer between the supplicant and the services offered by the authenticator. In order to perform the authentication, the authenticator makes use of an authentication server.

As an authentication protocol, 802.1X can be used in Ethernet, Token Ring, or wireless LAN.

Figure 7-4. IEEE 802.1X stack

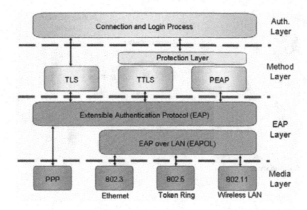

Extensible Authentication Protocol (EAP)

EAP, RFC 3748 (Aboba, Blunk, Vollbrecht, Carlson, & Levkowetz, 2004) was originally created for use with PPP; it has since been adopted for use with IEEE 802.1X (2004) "Port-Based Network Access Control."

EAP is extensible because any authentication mechanism can be encapsulated within EAP messages. It supports authentication mechanisms such as smart cards, Kerberos, digital certificates, one-time passwords, and others. Authentication mechanisms are implemented in a number of ways called *EAP methods*, for example, EAP-TLS, EAP-TTLS, EAP-PEAP, and so forth.

EAP as specified in RFC 3748 allows the deployment of new protocols between the supplicant and the authentication server. The encapsulation technique used to carry EAP packets between the supplicant and authenticator in a LAN environment is known as EAP over LANs, or EAPOL.

The EAP Authentication Process

Secure user authentication is obtained through the encrypted exchange of the user's security credentials or challenges. Security credentials are used in this context to mean something that the authentication server knows about a particular user or device, for example, the knowledge of a valid user name, password, token, PIN, challenge, or in the case of an authentication device, the device's ID.

The process of authenticating a user or device involves the following parties and protocols:

Figure 7-5. Authentication process

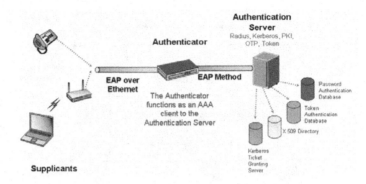

1. The supplicant is an entity at one end of a point-to-point LAN segment that is being authenticated by an authenticator attached to the other end of that link.

2. The authenticator is an entity at one end of a point-to-point LAN segment that enables authentication of the entity attached to the other end of that link, the supplicant.

3. The 802.1X port-based network access control protocol provides the means to authenticate and authorize devices attached to a LAN port that has point-to-point connection characteristics; it can also prevent access to that port in cases in which the authentication and authorization process fails.

4. An EAP authentication method such as EAP-TLS, EAP-TTLS, EAP-PEAP, and so forth, provides specific authentication mechanisms between the client and the authentication server. The choice of method often implies a choice of mechanisms.

5. An authentication mechanism such as one-time passwords, token cards, biometrics, Kerberos, pre-shared keys, or digital certificates, authenticates a client or supplicant.

6. An authentication server performs the authentication function necessary to check the credentials of the supplicant on behalf of the authenticator and indicates whether the supplicant is authorized to access the authenticator's services.

Authentication Exchange

Figure 7-6 shows the authentication exchange among a supplicant, the authenticator, and the authentication server.

1. The supplicant connects to the authenticator; the authenticator's port is always in the unauthorized state, so it only accepts 802.1X, EAPOL traffic and discards any other type of traffic such as HTTP, FTP, dynamic host configuration protocol, and simple mail transfer protocol.

Figure 7-6. IEEE 802.1X stack

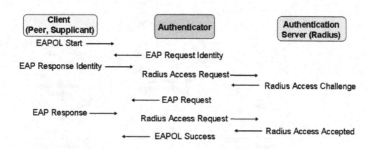

2. The supplicant sends an EAPOL start message.

3. The authenticator replies with an EAP request identity message to obtain the client's identity.

4. The supplicant sends the EAP response identity. The authenticator passes the client's identity on to the authentication server (RADIUS) encapsulated in RADIUS protocol.

5. The authentication server sends back a supplicant access challenge.

6. The authenticator unpacks the client access challenge using RADIUS protocol, repacks it using EAP protocol, and forwards the access challenge to the supplicant.

7. The supplicant responds to the challenge and sends it to the authenticator, which passes the response on to the authentication server.

8. The result is an accept or reject packet from the authentication server to the authenticator.

9. The authenticator enables the port to offer the services and allows the supplicant's traffic to be forwarded.

10. At logoff, the supplicant sends an EAP-logoff message that forces the authenticator to transition the port from the services offered to a disabled state.

EAP Methods

Several EAP methods are available but only four are currently standardized; those are EAP-MD5, EAP-OTP, EAP-GTC, and EAP-TLS. With the exception of EAP-TLS, none of these methods offer very good security if an attacker has access to the EAP traffic. EAP-MD5 is no longer recommended because it provides neither mutual authentication nor key derivation. No simple, shared-key EAP method seems to be widely available to replace EAP-MD5.

Several drafts describing EAP methods have been presented to the IETF. The following information describes some of the EAP standard methods, as well as proposed EAP drafts.

Figure 7-7. Protected EAP

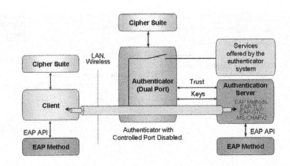

- First a TLS tunnel ((⊙▭▭▭)) is established, and then the tunnel is used
  to run legacy authentication protocols in the inner tunnel (⊂▭▭▭▭▭▭▷).

EAP Certificate Methods

EAP-TLS: The Extensible Authentication Protocol-Transport Layer Security leverages X.509 digital certificates for secure mutual authentication using digital signatures but requires client-side and server-side certificates to perform authentication. It ensures authenticity, message integrity, and non-repudiation. It is generally appropriate for enterprises that have already deployed a PKI infrastructure. EAP-TLS is an experimental RFC and it is defined in RFC 2716 (Aboba & Simon, 1999).

EAP Hybrid Methods

EAP-TTLS: The Extensible Authentication Protocol-Tunneled Transport Layer Security is a third-party alternative to PEAP-MS-CHAPv2 that provides similar benefits when using client software from Funk Software and Certicom. It is an EAP method based on asymmetric cryptography reusing TLS mechanisms. In EAP-TTLS, the TLS handshake can be mutual, or it can be one way, in which only the server is authenticated to the client. The secure connection established by the handshake could then be used to allow the server to authenticate the client using existing, widely deployed authentication infrastructures such as RADIUS. The authentication of the client may itself be EAP, or it may be another authentication protocol such as PAP, CHAP, MS-CHAP, or MS-CHAP-V2.

PEAP: The Protected Extensible Authentication Protocol is an EAP method based on asymmetric cryptography reusing TLS mechanisms that provide an encrypted and authenticated tunnel based on transport layer security (TLS) that encapsulates EAP authentication mechanisms.

Figure 7-7 shows the authenticator's port to the services offered in the disabled state. If access is authenticated, the authentication server informs the authenticator, which enables the port to the services offered.

The following are some of the advantages of tunneled and protected EAP:

- Offers message integrity by using encryption so no one can interfere with authentication and confidentiality
- Has simple deployment because it does not require certificates/PKI
- Can be used in inner tunnel to protect existing authentication methods
- Protects user identity because no client ID is exchanged until a TLS secure channel is established
- Uses mutual authentication, TLS for the client and legacy authentication for the server

PEAP uses TLS to protect against rogue authenticators and against attacks on the confidentiality and integrity of the inner EAP method exchange; it also provides EAP peer identity privacy.

In summary, PEAP and TTLS are very similar. Both are not as secure as TLS, but they have the advantage of being able to use username/password authentication instead of certificate authentication for backward compatibility with legacy authentication methods. PEAP only allows EAP methods for client authentication whereas TTLS allows any method, including PAP and CHAP. Another difference is the way payload encoding is done, whereas TTLS uses the TLS channel to exchange attribute-value-pairs (AVP) much like RADIUS, PEAP uses type-length-value. Thus, TLS is EAP friendly and TTLS is better aligned with RADIUS. PEAP-EAP-MS-CHAPv2 requires that the client trust certificates provided by the server.

EAP SIM-Based Methods

EAP-AKA: Authentication and key agreement is an EAP method based on the 3rd generation authentication and key agreement mechanism (AKA) specified for Universal Mobile Telecommunications System (UMTS) and for cdma2000. AKA typically runs in a UMTS Subscriber Identity Module (USIM) or a cdma2000 (removable) User Identity Module ((R)UIM). It could be used without a USIM (e.g., with a software-based virtual USIM), thus becoming a generic shared-key EAP method.

EAP-AKA is based on challenge-response mechanisms and symmetric cryptography. It uses shared secrets between the user and the authenticator together with a sequence number to perform the authentication. EAP-AKA uses AES with a 128-bit key in the cipher block-chaining (CBC) mode of operation. It uses SHA-1 to check the integrity of all EAP-Request/AKA-Identity and EAP-Response/ AKA-Identity packets used in the authentication exchange. It also uses SHA-1 to create the master key by hashing certain concatenated parameters. EAP-AKA is defined in RFC 4187 (Arkko & Haverinen, 2006).

EAP-SIM: The Subscriber Identity Module is an EAP method based on symmetric cryptography that reuses the GSM authentication infrastructure. The lack of mutual authentication is a weakness in GSM authentication. Also, the derived 64-bit cipher key (Kc) is not strong enough for use in data networks for which stronger and longer keys are required. To overcome the key size problem, several RAND challenges are used for generating various 64-bit Kc keys, which are combined to get longer keys. EAP-SIM is defined in RFC 4186 (Haverinen & Salowey, 2006).

EAP-SIM could be implemented for backward compatibility with the millions of GSM/GPRS SIM cards already deployed. However, since AKA architecture for the UMTS includes mutual authentication, replay protection, and derivation of longer session keys, EAP-AKA, which is a more secure protocol, may be used instead of EAP-SIM, if 3rd generation identity modules and 3G network infrastructures are available.

EAP Pre-Shared Key Methods

EAP-TLS-PSK: This EAP method based on TLS supports authentication based on pre-shared keys. The TLS-PSK, RFC 4764 (Bersani & Tschofenig, 2007), describes methods for using symmetric keys, also called *pre-shared keys* or PSKs, shared in advance among the communicating parties, to establish a TLS connection.

TLS-PSK uses one of the following:

1.   Symmetric key operations for authentication

2.   Diffie-Hellman exchange authenticated with a pre-shared key

3.   A combination of the public key authentication of the server with pre-shared key authentication of the client

EAP-IKEv2: This is an EAP method based on the symmetric and asymmetric cryptography of IKEv2. Its main advantages are that it uses the IKEv2 standard protocol, RFC 4306 (Kaufman, 2005), whose security features have received considerable favorable expert review. EAP-IKEv2 also provides support for cryptographic ciphersuite negotiation, has hash function agility, identity confidentiality (in certain modes of operation), fragmentation, and an optional fast reconnect mode. Currently, IKEv2 supports authentication techniques that are based on passwords, high-entropy shared keys, and public-key certificates.

EAP-IKEv2 might not be an appropriate EAP method under certain circumstances because DH computations and potential server side authentication make EAP-IKEv2 computationally expensive. Whereas in TLS-PSK, DH exchange is optional, in EAP-IKEv2, it is not the case.

EAP-PSK: EAP pre-shared key is an EAP method based on symmetric cryptography defined in RFC 4764 (Bersani & Tschofenig, 2007). Some of the advantages it has are the following:

- **Simplicity:** It is easy to implement and to deploy without any pre-existing infrastructure. EAP-PSK uses only AES-128.

- **Wide applicability:** It is possible to use this method to authenticate over any network. In particular, it complies with IEEE 802 EAP method requirements for wireless LANs.

- **Security:** It is based on AES.
- **Extensibility:** It is possible to add to this method any required extensions as needed.

Password-Based EAP Methods

EAP-PAX: The EAP Password Authenticated Exchange, RFC 4746 (Clancy & Arbaugh, 2006), is an EAP method designed for device authentication using a shared key and a personal identification number (PIN). Instead of using a symmetric key exchange, the client and server perform a Diffie-Hellman key exchange, which provides forward secrecy.

EAP-PAX uses two separate subprotocols, PAX_STD and PAX_SEC. PAX_STD is a simple, lightweight protocol for mutual authentication using a shared key supporting authenticated data exchange (ADE). PAX_SEC uses public key. In the weakest mode, PAX_SEC allows the use of raw public keys, eliminating the need for a PKI. In the strongest mode, PAX_SEC requires that EAP servers use certificates signed by a trusted certification authority (CA).

EAP-PAX supports the generation of strong key material; mutual authentication; resistance to desynchronization, dictionary, and man-in-the-middle attacks; ciphersuite extensibility with protected negotiation; identity protection; and the authenticated exchange of data, useful for implementing channel binding. EAP-PAX is ideal for wireless environments such as IEEE 802.11.

EAP-SPEKE (simple password encrypted key exchange): An EAP method based on symmetric cryptography and asymmetric key cryptography to provide password-only authenticated key exchange. EAP-SPEKE is only useful when authentication is based on user-provided password information. It is unnecessarily complex for device authentication (e.g., it makes heavy use of public key cryptography). The improved EAP-SPEKE protocol supports mutual authentication and key exchange and it works on the Elliptic Curve Cryptosystems (ECC) base, as well as the DH (Diffie-Hellman) base.

Figure 7-8. Authentication decision tree

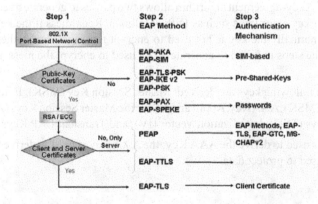

Evaluating and Selecting an EAP Method

Where EAP messages are not encrypted, it must be assumed that an attacker could be passively listening during the EAP exchange or act as a man-in-the-middle. Therefore, EAP methods must not leak secret or sensitive information (e.g., passwords or password hashes, as in the case of EAP-MD5). When selecting an EAP method, it is necessary to consider the fact that EAP transmits identity in clear; consequently, it is possible for an attacker to learn the identity of authenticating users. Password compromise should be avoided by using EAP methods that employ strong encryption.

Another consideration when selecting an EAP method is to determine if the authentication mechanism will use either pre-shared keys, or keys that are created and exchanged during the authentication process using public keys and digital certificates.

When selecting an EAP method, consideration must be given to whether mutual or one-way authentication is required. In a rogue attack, the attacker replaces the device with a suitably modified one. This attack can be prevented by using an EAP method that supports mutual authentication and that indicates whether mutual authentication has been completed. It is also necessary to have the supplicant refuse to process an EAP success received prior to that indication.

EAP Key Material

User authentication protocols perform two functions:

1. Verifying the identity of one or both parties
2. Producing ephemeral secret keys shared between the parties and that are used subsequently for data origin authentication

During authentication, key material is transported or agreed to, and this key material is used to authenticate and, possibly, to encrypt data transmitted between the device and the network. In key transport, also called *key exchange* or *key wrapping*, both parties share a key-encrypting key that is used to wrap (encipher) the key that is going to be transported, exchanged. A key-agreement algorithm allows two parties to generate a secret key computed from public-key algorithms such as Diffie-Hellman. Regardless if the key is exchanged or generated, normally the key is not used to encrypt messages, but, rather, to arrive at key material. The steps required to generate a key used to encrypt the message depends on the protocol.

In EAP, the following keys are derived: Master Session Key (MSK), Extended Master Session Key (EMSK), AAA Key, Application-Specific Master Session Keys (AMSK), Transient Session Keys (TSK), Initialization Vector (IV), and Transient EAP Keys (TEK).

The MSK is used to derive the AAA Key; the AAA Key is used to derive the TSKs, and the TSKs are used to protect data.

EAP Password Mechanisms

The use of EAP-TLS requires digital certificates for authentication. Digital certificates provide strong methods of authenticating, but they can require a public-key infrastructure (PKI). Rather than deploying a PKI, or using EAP methods based on pre-shared keys, the use of legacy authentication systems, based on passwords, or token-based authentication systems is still preferred.

A way to use EAP with legacy authentication systems is to first establish a secure tunnel (e.g., TLS), and then to use that tunnel to run the legacy authentication protocols, so the authentication is running in an inner tunnel. Two EAP methods, TTLS and PEAP, have been proposed to support legacy authentication methods.

The EAP-TTLS supports all EAP methods, as well as CHAP, PAP, MS-CHAP, and MS-CHAPv2. EAP-PEAP supports all EAP methods, EAP-TLS, EAP-GTC, and MS-CHAPv2. PAP and CHAP are not recommended for use as authentication methods with EAP-PEAP.

EAP MS-CHAP-v2

The EAP MS-CHAP-v2 protocol is based on Microsoft MS-CHAP-v2. The authentication mechanism is password-based and supports mutual authentication. Integrity is supported but confidentiality is not. The name field, in both the challenge and response packets, is sent in the clear. While key derivation is supported, the key strength is limited by the password policy.

EAP-Generic Token Card (EAP-GTC)

The generic token card is defined for use with various token card implementations that require user input. The use of EAP-GTC was standardized in EAP RFC 3748 (Aboba, Blunk, Vollbrecht, Carlson, & Levkowetz, 2004). EAP-GTC allows the exchange of cleartext passwords and token information across the network. However, because of the GTC two-factor

Figure 7-9. Generic token card

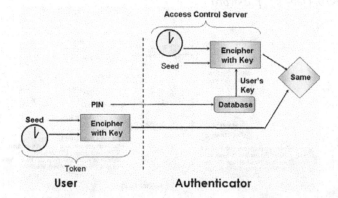

authentication, this method is not vulnerable to a replay attack. Even though EAP-GTC can be used alone and does not need to be tunneled, it is recommended that it be used inside of TTLS or PEAP to provide server authentication.

The generic token card is used in those implementations that require a two-factor authentication mechanism. Typically, this would be information from the user's token card device, entered as ASCII text, and a PIN.

Generic token cards are dynamic in the sense that the information that they display changes in time, that is, every 60 seconds. Each end user is assigned a token, which is bonded to the user's PIN. The user logs into the system by entering his PIN and the pass code from the token.

The server gets the user's key from the database, computes the token value, and compares it with the token value entered by the user. If the value is correct, access is granted; if incorrect, the user is allowed to try again for certain number of times. After x failed attempts, the user should be locked out until the administrator re-enables the user access.

One-Time Password

The one-time password system is defined in RFC 2289 (Haller, Metz, Nesser, & Straw, 1998), "A One-Time Password System." The request contains a displayable message containing an OTP challenge. A response must be sent in reply to the request. The response must be of type 5 (OTP) or type 3 (Nak). The Nak reply indicates the peer's desired authentication mechanism type.

The one-time password only allows a password to be used one time; this prevents the unauthorized used of an intercepted password. In the S/Key system, the user generates a secret password to which a one-way function is applied. The secret password does not leave the user terminal, but what is sent is the hashed password.

The RFC 2289 (Haller, Metz, Nesser, & Straw, 1998) describes the procedure as follows:

Figure 7-10. One-time password

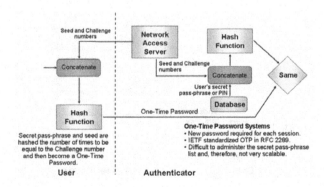

1. The authenticator, a network access server, sends a seed and a challenge number, N, to the user.

2. The user's pass phrase is concatenated with a seed that is transmitted from the server in clear text. This nonsecret seed allows clients to use the same secret pass-phrase on multiple machines (using different seeds) and to recycle safely their secret pass-phrases by changing the seed.

3. A sequence of one-time passwords is produced by applying the secure hash function multiple times to the output of step 2 (called S). That is, the first one-time password to be used is produced by passing S through the secure hash function the number of times (N) specified by the authenticator challenge number. The next one-time password to be used is generated by passing S though the secure hash function $N - 1$ times. An eavesdropper who has monitored the transmission of a one-time password would not be able to generate the next required password because doing so would mean inverting the hash function.

4. The authenticator server gets the user's pass-phrase from the database, concatenates the user pass-phrase with his seed, and applies the one-way hash function. If the hashed password matches, the user is allowed to log in. All pass-phrases must be of at least 63 characters.

EAP-MD5 (MD5 Challenge)

The EAP-MD5 challenge is analogous to the PPP CHAP protocol with MD5 as the specified algorithm, RFC 1994 (Simpson, 1996). The request contains a challenge message to the peer. A response must be sent in reply to the request. The response may be either Type 4 (MD5-challenge) or Type 3 (Nak). The Nak reply indicates the peer's desired authentication mechanism type. All EAP implementations must support the MD5-challenge mechanism.

Due to new security requirements, EAP-MD5 is no longer recommended because it has the following security problems: it provides neither mutual authentication nor key derivation, and it has high vulnerability to active brute-force/dictionary attacks. In addition, cryptographers tend to favor SHA instead of MD5 because MD5's output is only 16 bytes and because collisions have been found in the MD5 compression function.

Other Password Mechanisms

The following password mechanisms are not supported in EAP, but are described here as a reference for the reader.

Point-to-Point Protocol (PPP)

The Point-to-Point Protocol, RFC 1661 (Simpson, 1994), is designed for simple links that transport packets between two peers. These links provide full-duplex, simultaneous, bidirectional operation and are assumed to deliver packets in order. It is intended that PPP provide a common solution for easy connection of a wide variety of hosts, bridges, and routers. PPP establishes the connection between the client and network access server.

In order to establish communications over a point-to-point link, each end of the PPP link must first send link control protocol (LCP) packets to configure and test the data link. After the link has been established, PPP provides for an optional authentication phase before proceeding to the network-layer protocol phase. After authentication, PPP must send network control protocol (NCP) packets to choose and configure one or more network-layer protocols. Once each of the chosen network-layer protocols has been configured, datagrams from each network-layer protocol can be sent over the link. The link will remain configured for communications until explicit LCP or NCP packets close the link down, or until some external event occurs (an inactivity timer expires or intervention by the network administrator).

By default, authentication is not mandatory. If authentication of the link is desired, an implementation must specify the authentication-protocol configuration option during the link establishment phase.

These authentication protocols are intended for use primarily by hosts and routers that connect to a PPP network server via switched circuits or dial-up lines, but might be applied to dedicated links as well. The server can use the identification of the connecting host or router in the selection of options for network layer negotiations.

Challenge and Response Systems

Challenge and response systems are based on identification and authentication (Kosiur, 1998). When a user is signing on to a computer system, the computer will ask for the user's name or identification number. If the computer wants to verify (authenticate) the user's identity (challenge), it asks for some special information related to or only known to the user. If the response generated at the user's terminal matches the one generated by the host end computer, then the host authenticates the user's identity. Challenge and response network control requires using a matched set of hardware protection devices at the user's computer and the authentication server that are intelligent enough to perform the identification and authentication. The special information used for a challenge and response could be the following:

1. A piece of hardware belonging to the user (unique token) such as a mechanical key or a smart card placed into a device connected to the terminal. Magnetic strip cards and smart cards may contain algorithms that decipher the challenge from the host computer and encipher the user's answer.

2. A personal feature of the user, such as fingerprints, retinal patterns, body dimensions, voice patterns, biochemical body properties, and so forth, can be used as a biometric access.

3.   Real-time skill capabilities and habits of the user, such as signature dynamics, typing style and ability, reading speed, and so forth, can be used to detect intrusions.

4.   Skills, knowledge, and characteristics that the user possesses due to education, training, history, culture, hobbies, and so forth, can be used to query the person trying to log on.

Many terminals or workstations already support the assignment of unique terminal identifiers: hardware or, more commonly, codes located at special memory locations that can be loaded during the terminal setup. This feature is used by the host computer to identify the terminal (challenge) when the terminal logs in.

Password Security Considerations

Passwords are prearranged identifiers that the user possesses, such as words, special coded phrases, personal identification numbers (PINs), and so forth.

Password systems require a single coded response from the user to be allowed access to the host computer. In the case of an organization, to make password systems secure, it is important to consider the following:

- How the password will be selected
- How often the password will be changed
- How long the password will be used
- How the system will handle (transmit) the password

Practice has shown that leaving the choice of a password to the user often results in the use of unsatisfactory or poor passwords, such as words from a dictionary, words spelled backwards, first names, surnames, address numbers, telephone numbers, and social security numbers. For this reason, it is recommended that a series of random characters be generated and assigned to each user. The composition of the password should require a minimum of a possible 100 million passwords for the lowest level of security.

A password used for a long time has the probability of falling into an intruder's hands. The greater the length of time a password is used, the more opportunities there are for breaking security. The recommended maximum lifetime of a password should be not more than one year. The password should be changed immediately if a compromise is suspected, or if the owner is no longer authorized to access the computer. The maximum lifetime of a password depends on the size of the password space, how fast an intruder could execute a login attempt, and the level of security (probability that a password will be guessed during its lifetime). The following formula (Department of Defense, 1985) may be used to determine the lifetime of a password:

$$L = \frac{P \times S}{R}$$

where L =   Maximum lifetime for a password.

P =   Probability that a password can be guessed within its lifetime, assuming continuous guesses for that period.

R =   Number of guesses possible to make per unit of time.

S =   Password space; the total number of passwords that can be generated.

S = A^M (A = number of alphabet symbols, M = password length).

The following is an example of a typical scenario: In a high-speed connection where the host computer is connected to a 3 M bits/sec cable modem, 500,000 guesses can be made per second (or 43.2×10^8 per day), with a probability of 10^{-6} for guessing the password in its lifetime, and a combination of ten upper and lower case letters and numbers is used for the password. Then A = 26+26+10 (52 upper and lower alphabet characters and the numbers 0 – 9). Therefore, $S = A^M = 62^{10} = 8.39 \times 10^{17}$ and:

$$L = \frac{10^{-6} \times 8\,39 \times 10^{17}}{43.2 \times 10^8} = 19.43 \ days.$$

It can be seen from this example that it is unlikely that guessing, even with the use of advanced technology, would be considered an effective way to obtain a password. However, precaution should be taken that a password is handled in such way that its storage, entry, and transmission are protected from disclosure to unauthorized individuals. For this reason, any password that is transmitted from a terminal to a central location should be enciphered. Further, in an automatic teller machine, the response from the host computer should also be enciphered because an intruder may reproduce the response and defraud the teller machine.

Another method of identity verification consists of gathering some personal information, such as the color of a first car, names of friends from childhood, and so forth. This system has the advantage that it is easy for the user to remember the information, but it is unlikely that an intruder could find it out. The computer selects one of the challenge questions at random every time the user signs on, just in case somebody taps the line and tries to sign on using the password obtained from the last session.

The use of passwords may be considered appropriate for user authentication but for device authentication, the use of a very complex and much longer secret key or password is more appropriate.

A premise in authentication is that passwords provides weak authentication. This is true because of the way passwords are selected and how authentication is implemented. Simple passwords are not a good idea because they can be broken using dictionary attacks. A better option is a random combination of 20 alphanumeric characters including alphabetic (lower and upper case), numeric, and special (e.g., punctuation) characters. When the password is hashed using SHA-256 and sent to the authentication server, then a good password authentication system is enabled. That password implementation, in which the hash is truncated from

256 to 80 bits, reduces considerably the security of the password because of collisions. It is not necessary to have the same password to breach security, but a password that produces the same 80 bits of the stored hash could do so.

EAP Authentication Servers

In EAP and 802.1X protocols, the use of an authentication server to centrally manage authentication, authorization, and accounting is optional. However, RADIUS and Diameter are considered suitable AAA servers and both are supported in EAP.

The use of RADIUS for purposes of authentication, authorization, and accounting in IEEE 802.1X makes the EAP implementation vulnerable to all the threats that are present in other RADIUS applications. The RADIUS implementation in IEEE 802.1X should follow the recommendations in RFC 3579 (Aboba & Calhoun, 2003), RADIUS & EAP, which state in Section 4.2 that encryption should be used to provide per-packet confidentiality, authentication, integrity, and replay protection.

Remote Authentication Dial-in User Service (RADIUS)

Two different sets of protocols are used to provide access authentication. For LAN-to-LAN, X.509 is used, and for dial-in or client-to-LAN, a protocol called *Remote Authentication Dial-in User Service* (RADIUS) is used.

Remote access using dial-in systems requires access security, authorization, and accounting (AAA). RFC 2865 (Rigney, Willens, Rubens, & Simpson, 2000) describes a protocol for carrying authentication, authorization, and configuration information between a network access server that needs to authenticate its links and a RADIUS server. A RADIUS server is connected to a database that maintains access profiles for all trusted users. Access to this database allows for authentication (verifying user name and password), access privileges (authorization), as well as configuration information detailing the types of services to deliver to the user (for example, SLIP, PPP, telnet, rlogin).

Client/Server Model

RADIUS servers handle requests from a network access server (NAS) that is installed as a gateway or network entry point and that operates as a client of RADIUS. The NAS client is responsible for passing user information to designated RADIUS servers, and then acting on the response that is returned.

RADIUS servers are responsible for receiving user connection requests, authenticating the user, and then returning all configuration information necessary for the client to deliver service to the user.

Network Security

Transactions between the client and a RADIUS server are authenticated with a shared secret, which is never sent over the network. In addition, all user passwords are sent encrypted between the client and the RADIUS server to eliminate the possibility that someone snooping on an unsecured network could determine a user's password.

RADIUS Authentication Mechanisms

The RADIUS server can support several methods to authenticate a user. RADIUS is the preferred protocol for use with point-to-point tunneling protocol (PPTP) and Layer 2 tunneling protocol (L2TP), but it also can support password authentication protocol (PAP), challenge handshake authentication protocol (CHAP), UNIX login, and other authentication mechanisms.

The authentication process begins with the user submitting an "access-request" to the NAS. The NAS submits the "access-request" plus NAS-identifier, NAS-port, user-name, and user-password. Once the RADIUS server receives the request, it validates the sending client. A request from a client for which the RADIUS server does not have a shared secret is discarded. If the client is valid, the RADIUS server consults a database of users to find the user whose name matches the request. The user entry in the database contains a list of requirements that must be met to allow access for the user. This always includes verification of the password, but can also specify the port(s) to which the user is allowed access.

If any condition is not met, the RADIUS server sends an "access-reject" response indicating that this user request is invalid. If all conditions are met, the RADIUS server generates a

Figure 7-11. RADIUS

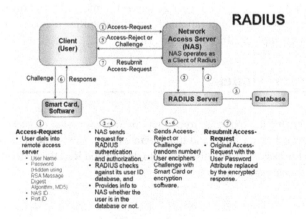

random number and sends back an "access-challenge" packet with state and a reply-message along the lines of "challenge {random number}, enter your response at the prompt," thus challenging the user to encrypt the random number and send back the result.

The user enciphers the challenge using a special device such as a smart card or encryption software. Unauthorized users, lacking the appropriate device or encryption software and lacking knowledge of the secret key, are not able to generate the response. The user then resubmits its original "access-request" with a new request ID, in which the user-password attribute is replaced by the response (encrypted). If the response matches the expected response, the RADIUS server replies with "access-accept," otherwise it sends an "access-reject."

Needham and Schroeder

The authentication protocol invented by Needham and Schroeder (1978) uses symmetric key encryption and a trusted entity, which, for this example, will be called Trent.

The procedure is as follows:

1.   Alice sends a message to Trent with her name, A, and the name of the server, B, to which she wants access and a random value, R_A.

2.   Trent generates a session key, K, concatenates the generated session key with Alice's name and enciphers it with Bob's secret key. This enciphered message is concatenated with Alice's random number, Bob's name, the key, and everything else is enciphered with Alice's key.

3.   Alice deciphers the message using her key, gets the session key, K, and confirms that R_A is the same value that she sent to Trent in step 1. Then, she sends Bob the message $E_B \{K \| A\}$ that Trent sent her.

4.   Bob deciphers the message and gets the session key, K. He then generates another random value, R_B, enciphers R_B with the session key, K, and sends the message to Alice.

Figure 7-12. Needham and Schroeder authentication

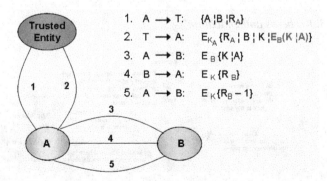

5.   Alice deciphers the message with the session key, K and generates $R_B - 1$ and enciphers it with the session key, K. Then, she sends the message back to Bob.

R_A, R_B, and R_B -1 are used to ensure that there will not be any replay attacks during the authentication process, and that intruders will not be able to use Alice's messages in future sessions.

Kerberos

Kerberos Version 5.2 is an Internet security standard protocol, RFC 4120 (Neuman, Yu, Hartman, & Raeburn, 2005), based on a trusted third-party authentication to offer authentication services to users and servers in an openly distributed environment. Kerberos relies on secret-key symmetric ciphers for encryption and authentication and does not use public-key encryption; therefore, it does not produce digital signatures or authentication of authorship of documents. The authentication requires trust in a third party (the Kerberos server), so if the server is compromised, the integrity of the whole system is lost. Kerberos version 4 uses DES and version 5.2 uses any encryption algorithm; in version 5.2, DES has to be used in the CBC mode. The Kerberos authentication server (KAS) keeps a database with the names of all the users and their secret keys.

Suppose that Alice would like to generate a session secret key for a communication with the server, Bob. The basic Kerberos authentication process for this procedure is as follows:

•   Alice sends a request to the KAS requesting credentials to talk with the application server, Bob.

•   The KAS responds with the credentials, encrypted in Alice's secret key. The credentials consist of (1) A ticket to communicate with the application server B and (2) a temporary encryption key (often called a *session key*). The ticket is encrypted with application server B secret key.

Figure 7-13. Kerberos authentication

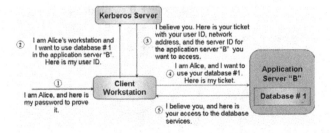

Figure 7-14. Kerberos abbreviations and protocols

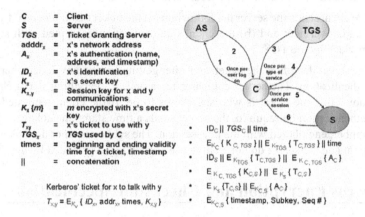

C	=	Client
S	=	Server
TGS	=	Ticket Granting Server
adddr$_x$	=	x's network address
A$_x$	=	x's authentication (name, address, and timestamp)
ID$_x$	=	x's identification
K$_x$	=	x's secret key
K$_{x,y}$	=	Session key for x and y communications
K$_x\{m\}$	=	m encrypted with x's secret key
T$_{xy}$	=	x's ticket to use with y
TGS$_x$	=	TGS used by C
times	=	beginning and ending validity time for a ticket, timestamp
||	=	concatenation

Kerberos' ticket for x to talk with y

$T_{x,y} = E_{K_y}\{ ID_x, addr_x, times, K_{x,y}\}$

- $ID_C \| TGS_C \|$ time
- $E_{K_C}\{ K_{C,TGS}\} \| E_{K_{TGS}}\{T_{C,TGS}\} \|$ time
- $ID_S \| E_{K_{TGS}}\{T_{C,TGS}\} \| E_{K_{C,TGS}}\{A_C\}$
- $E_{K_{C,TGS}}\{K_{C,S}\} \| E_{K_S}\{T_{C,S}\}$
- $E_{K_S}\{T_{C,S}\} \| E_{K_{C,S}}\{A_C\}$
- $E_{K_{C,S}}\{$ timestamp, Subkey, Seq #$\}$

- Alice transmits the ticket, which contains her identity and a copy of the session key, all encrypted with the application server B secret key, to the application server B.

- The session key, now shared by Alice and application server B, may be used to provide three different levels of protection: (1) authenticate Alice and application server B at the beginning of the network connection; (2) authenticate and encipher further communications between Alice and application server B; (3) to exchange a separate sub-session key to be used to encrypt further communications between Alice and application server B.

The Kerberos process has two components: the authentication and the ticket generation. The component that does the authentication is called an *authentication server* and the component that generates the ticket is called *ticket granting service*.

The following describes the Kerberos protocol:

1. The client sends the client's identification and the name of the clients's TGS to the Kerberos authentication server.

2. The Kerberos authentication server looks in its database to see if the client identification is correct. If the client ID is correct, the Kerberos authentication server sends a ticket to be presented to the TGS and a message that has a session key, enciphered with the client's secret key. The client deciphers the message and retrieves the session that it is going to use to communicate in secure with the Ticket Granting Service (TGS).

3. The client sends the TGS the following: (a) the server ID to which the client wants to communicate; (b) the ticket that it received from the Kerberos authentication server; and (c) the client's authentication (client's name & address, and time stamp) enciphered with the session key sent by the Kerberos authentication server.

4. The TGS deciphers the ticket and the client's authentication and compares them. If everything is correct, the TGS sends a ticket for the client to present to the server, and a message for the client that has a new session key, enciphered with the client's

secret key. The client deciphers the message and retrieves session key 2 that is going to be used to communicate in secure with the server.

5. The client sends the server the following: (a) the ticket that it received from the ticket granting service; and (b) the client's authentication encrypted with session key 2 provided by the TGS.

6. The server deciphers the ticket, and, after getting session key 2, deciphers the client's authentication. The server compares them and, if everything is correct, the server knows that the client is who she claims to be. If the client requested that mutual authentication be required, the server sends a time stamp, a subkey, and a sequence number, enciphered with the new session. The subkey is an optional key, in case the client and the server do not want to use session key 2 provided by the TGS.

Kerberos Encryption and Checksum Specifications

Kerberos is designed to encipher messages, using block encryption ciphers or stream encryption ciphers. Encryption is used as an authentication mechanism to prove the identities of the network entities participating in message exchanges. However, the Kerberos protocol does not require a specific encryption algorithm be used, as long as the algorithm includes certain operations.

RFC 3961 (Raeburn, 2005a), "Encryption and Checksum Specifications for Kerberos 5," specifies the encryption and checksum mechanisms for Kerberos, as well as a framework for defining future mechanisms. RFC 3962 (Raeburn, 2005b), "Advanced Encryption Standard (AES) Encryption for Kerberos 5," defines how to generate encryption keys and checksum types for Kerberos 5 using the AES 128-bit block encryption and key sizes of 128 or 256 bits. AES is used in the CBC mode with ciphertext stealing (CTS) to avoid message expansion. SHA-1 is the associated checksum function. CTS is defined in RFC 2040 (Baldwin & Rivest, 1996), "The RC5, RC5-CBC, RC5-CBC-Pad, and RC5-CTS Algorithms."

According to RFC 3961 (Raeburn, 2005a), the format for the data to be encrypted includes a one-block confounder, the plaintext, and any necessary padding. Then, the concatenated block is enciphered using an encryption algorithm and an HMAC function (possibly truncated), using the specified hash function H. The ciphertext output is the concatenation of the output of the basic encryption function E and the hash function as shown below.

The confounder, a random number, is included so that an observer cannot know if two messages contain the same plaintext, or even if the cipher state and specific keys are the same. Decryption is performed by removing the (partial) HMAC, decrypting the remainder, and verifying the HMAC. The cipher state is an initial vector, initialized to zero. In some of the algorithms proposed in RFC 3961, the confounder and the hash result are enciphered using a cipher encryption.

The following are some of the encryption and checksum algorithms proposed in RFC 3661 (Raeburn, 2005a) and 3962 (Raeburn, 2005b) for Kerberos:

Figure 7-15. Kerberos encryption and checksum

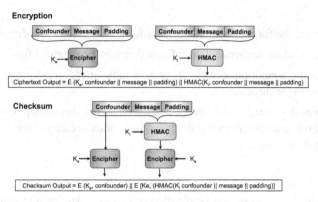

Encryption	Checksum
des3-cbc-md5	rsa-md5
des3-cbc-sha1	rsa-md5-des
aes128-cts-hmac-sha1-96	rsa-md5-des3
aes256-cts-hmac-sha1-96	hmac-sha1-des3
	hmac-sha1-96-aes128
	hmac-sha1-96-aes256

ITU-T X.509: Authentication Framework

The International Telecommunication Union (ITU) is the United Nations Specialized Agency in the field of telecommunications. The ITU Telecommunications Standardization Sector (ITU-T), a permanent group in the ITU, is the body that sets world telecommunications standards (Recommendations). Many countries, telecom operating entities, scientific and industrial organizations, and international organizations participate in the ITU-T.

According to Shuh (1997), the purpose of electronic directories is not much different from that of printed directories, that is, to provide names, locations and other information about people and organizations. This directory information may be used for e-mail addressing, user authentication (e.g., logins and passwords), and network security (e.g., user-access rights). Several ITU-T Recommendations have been made to facilitate the interconnection of information processing systems to provide directory services. A set of such systems, together with the directory information that they hold, can be viewed as an integrated whole called the *directory*.

The ITU-T X.509 Recommendation defines a framework for the provision of authentication services by the directory to its users. These users include the directory itself, as well as other applications and services. The directory is a natural place from which communicating parties can obtain authentication information from each other.

The ITU-T X.509 Recommendation includes the following information:

- Specifies the form of authentication information held by the directory
- Describes how authentication information may be obtained from the directory
- States the assumptions made about how authentication information is gathered and placed in the directory
- Defines three ways in which applications may use this authentication information to carry out authentication and describes how other security services may be supported by authentication

The ITU-T X.509 Recommendation describes two levels of authentication: simple authentication, using a password as a verification of claimed identity, and strong authentication, involving credentials created by using cryptographic techniques. The strong authentication method specified in ITU-T X.509 is based upon public-key cryptosystems.

ITU-T X.509 Recommendation focuses on defining a mechanism by which information can be made available in a secure way to a third party either by a password or by using certificates. The public keys and user certificates are created off-line by an off-line certificate authority and subsequently placed in the directory. The directory server merely provides an easily accessible location for users to obtain certificates. No special requirements are placed upon directory providers to store or communicate user certificates in a secure manner.

Simple Authentication

In a simple authentication, the password is sent in clear. The general procedure for achieving simple authentication is shown in Figure 7-16.

1. Alice sends her ID and password to Bob
2. Bob sends Alice's ID and password to the directory, where the password is checked against the information held for Alice

Figure 7-16. Simple authentication

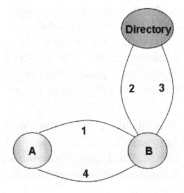

Figure 7-17. Protected authentication

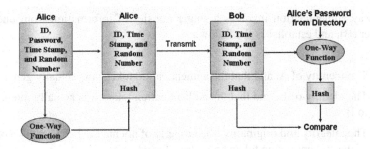

3.   The directory confirms (or denies) to Bob that the credentials are valid

4.   The success (or failure) of authentication may be conveyed to Alice

Protected Authentication

In a protected authentication, the password is not sent. The general procedure for achieving protected authentication is shown in Figure 7-17.

1.   Using a one-way function, Alice creates a hash of her ID, password, time stamp and a random number.

2.   Alice sends in clear her ID, time stamp and random number; the timestamp and/or random number (when used) are used to minimize replay and to conceal the password.

3.   Bob generates Alice's hash by using Alice's ID and optional timestamp and/or random number, together with the directory's local copy of Alice's password.

4.   Bob checks the authentication by comparing Alice's hash with the locally generated hash value.

Strong Authentication

The basic approach to authentication is the corroboration of identity by demonstrating possession of a private key. ITU-T X.509 includes three strong authentication procedures all based on public key.

The three procedures provide different types of authentication: (1) Only the identity of the initiating party, Alice, is verified; (2) The identity of both parties, Alice and Bob, is verified; (3) The identity of both parties is verified but without the need for time-stamp checking.

It is assumed that prior to any exchange of information, Alice has Bob's public key, as well as the return certification path from Bob to Alice, so Bob will know how to get Alice's public key.

One-Way Authentication

One-way authentication involves a single transfer of information from one user (A) to another (B), and establishes the following:

- The identity of A, and that the authentication token was actually generated by A
- The identity of B, and that the authentication token was actually intended to be sent to B
- The integrity and originality (the property of not having been sent two or more times) of the authentication token being transferred

The following steps are involved, as shown in Figure 7-17:

1. Alice generates r^A, a non-repeating number, which is used to detect replay attacks and to prevent forgery.
2. Alice sends the following message to Bob:

    $A\{t^A,\ r^A, ID^B, \text{sgn}\,Data, E_{Pub_B}\,[encData]\}$

    where B→A is Alice's certification authority path, and t^A is a timestamp. t^A consists of one or two dates: the generation time of the token (which is optional) and the expiration date. sgnData is used if the digital signature provides data origin authentication. [encData] is used in cases when information conveyed will subsequently be used as a secret key. [encData] is enciphered with Bob's public key, Pub_B.

    The use of [encData] as a secret key implies that it shall be chosen carefully, so as to be a strong key for whatever cryptosystem is used.

Figure 7-18. One-way authentication

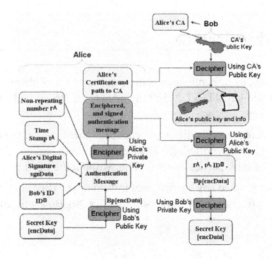

3.   Bob carries out the following actions:

    a.   Obtains Alice's public key, p, from the certificate authority (B→A), checking that Alice's certificate has not expired

    b.   Verifies the signature, and thus the integrity, of the signed information

    c.   Checks ID^B to verify that Bob himself is the intended recipient

    d.   Checks that the time stamp is current

    e.   Checks that r^A has not been replayed (optional). r^A is valid until the expiration date indicated by t^A, so Alice will not repeat the token during the time range t^A

Two-Way Authentication

In two-way authentication, the two parties authenticate themselves. First Alice authenticates herself and, then, Bob does the same for himself. To authenticate, they use the two-way authentication method. The only difference between one-way and two-way authentication is that since Alice already has Bob's public key, Bob does not need to send a path to his certificate authority. The following steps are involved, as shown in Figure 7-19:

1.   Same as Step 1 of one-way authentication

2.   Same as Step 2 of one-way authentication

3.   Same as Step 3 of one-way authentication

4.   Bob generates r^B, a non-repeating number, used for similar purpose(s) to r^A.

5.   Bob sends the following authentication token to Alice:

$$B\{t^B,\ r^B, ID^A, \text{sgn}\, Data, E_{Pub_A}\,[encData]\}$$

Figure 7-19. Two-way authentication

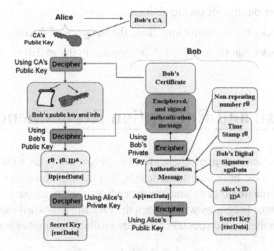

t^B is a timestamp defined in the same way as t^A. sgnData is used if the digital signature provides data origin authentication, [encData] is used in cases where information being conveyed will subsequently be used as a secret key. [encData] is enciphered with Alice's public key, Pub_A.

6.   Alice carries out the following actions:

    a.   Verifies the signature, and thus the integrity of the signed information

    b.   Checks ID^A to verify that Alice herself is the intended recipient

    c.   Checks that the timestamp t^B is current

    d.   Checks that r^B has not been replayed (optional)

Three-Way Authentication

Three-way authentication involves the same properties as two-way authentication, but does so without the need for timestamp checking. The following steps are involved:

1.   Same as Step 1 of two-way authentication

2.   Same as Step 2 of two-way authentication. Time stamp t^A may be zero

3.   Same as Step 3 of two-way authentication, except that the time stamp need not be checked

4.   Same as Step 4 of two-way authentication

5.   Same as Step 5 of two-way authentication. Time stamp t^B may be zero

6.   Same as Step 6 of two-way authentication, except that the time stamp need not be checked

7.   Alice checks that the received r^A is identical to the r^A that she sent

8.   Alice sends the following authentication token to Bob:

    $A \{r^B, ID^B\}$

9.   Bob carries out the following actions:

    a.   Checks the signature and, thus, the integrity of the signed information

    b.   Checks that the received r^B is identical to the r^B that was sent by him

Hash and Encryption Recommendations

Where hash functions are used, there are two approaches to try to break the hash, exploiting a weakness in the hash algorithm design, that is, collision attacks, or using brute force attacks. Brute force involves exhaustive procedures that try all password possibilities, one-by-one. Brute force programs will attempt to crack the password using every combination of numeric, alphabetic, and special characters available no matter how long it takes.

Table 7-1. Key length equivalent strengths

Security (Bits)	Symmetric Encryption Algorithm	Hash Algorithm	Diffie-Hellman and RSA Modulus Size		ECC
80	SKIPJACK	SHA-1	1024	1024	160
112	3DES	SHA-1	2048	2048	224
128	AES-128	SHA-256	3072	3072	256
192	AES-192	SHA-384	7680	7680	384
256	AES-256	SHA-512	15360	15360	512

There have been several reports questioning the resiliency of the MD5 (128-bit) and, more recently, the SHA-1 (160-bits) hashing algorithms. New algorithms have called into question the resiliency of the SHA-1 hashing algorithm because those new algorithms can find collisions in an estimated work factor of 2^{69} hash computations.

The current NIST recommendation is to consider migrating to the stronger hash functions (SHA-256, SHA-512). There is no immediate risk to products in deploying SHA-1, especially for message authentication requirements. In fact, companies might be forced to support SHA-1 for legacy support in customer networks.

In order to guard against brute force and collision attacks, EAP authentication methods should use encryption key size and hash functions that have appropriate cryptographic strength. The National Institute of Standards and Technology (NIST) has specified in FIPS 180-2 the correct combination of hash size, AES key size, and public-key modulo for specific authentication levels of security. In Table 7-1, the minimum RSA public-key size refers to the bit-length of the RSA modulo. The RSA public key algorithm uses a nonprime large number, RSA *modulo n*, that is equal to the product of the two large prime factors *p* and *q*.

AES should be used in any authentication protocol that requires encryption. Furthermore, the recommendation is to match the AES crypto strengths with their corresponding hash functions as shown in Table 7-1.

When considering a public-key system for access authentication, it sould be noted that elliptic curve cryptography (ECC) offers security equivalent to RSA, but it uses a smaller key size. An ECC key of 160-bits is roughly equivalent in security to a 1024-bit RSA key, and a 210-bit ECC key is roughly equivalent to a 2048-bit RSA. The smaller ECC key results in less computational overhead and a more efficient cryptosystem. Diffie-Hellman key exchange, ElGamal encryption, digital signatures, and the Digital Signature Algorithm (DSA) can all be implemented in elliptic curve cryptography. This makes ECC a very attractive algorithm for any type of device, especially for those with limited bandwidth and processing power. Certicom, the leading ECC vendor, documents that an IKE exchange on a Palm wireless device can be reduced from 39 seconds with Diffie-Hellman to less than a second with ECC.

Summary

The process of selecting authentication protocols can be simplified by narrowing the selection to a group of EAP methods. In general, when implementing any access authentication control, the starting point is the IEEE 802.1X – 2004 Port-Based Network Access Control Protocol, and then a type of EAP method that is appropriate for the type of application selected.

Recommended Authentication Protocols, Methods, and Mechanisms

- Use EAP-TLS for device authentication
- Use EAP-PEAP for those applications requiring one-way authentication; the certificate is only required for the infrastructure, not the end-user
- Use EAP-MS-CHAP v2 as the inner authentication method for those situations in which authentication is done by using passwords and/or tokens

Pre-Shared-Key

EAP-TLS-PSK is recommended for those situations in which a shared-key EAP method would be used instead of digital certificates to authenticate the device.

Recommended User Authentication

- Use EAP-TTLS and SSL certificates for generic token card-based methods
- Use EAP-AKA where appropriate compliance with 3GPP is required

Authentication Server

Use Diameter, RFC 3588 (Calhoun, Loughney, Guttman, Zorn, & Arkko, 2003), as the default, backend authentication, authorization, and accounting server and Radius for back compatibility. Currently, there are two RADIUS documents, one providing suggestions on usage with IEEE 802.1X Authenticators, RFC 3580 (Congdon, Aboba, Smith, Zorn, & Roese, 2003), and another defining support for EAP, RFC-3579 (Aboba, & Calhoun, 2003). Diameter is defined in RFC 4072 (Eronen, Hiller, & Zorn, 2005).

In RADIUS/EAP, HMAC-MD5 and HMAC-SHA1 are used or supported as key-dependent, one-way hash functions. However, it is recommended that AES-XCBC-MAC, RFC 3566 (Frankel & Herbert, 2003), a new key-dependent, one-way hash function proposed for use in IPsec, AH, and ESP, be used instead of HMAC-MD5 and HMAC-SHA1.

Encryption Algorithm, Hash, and Key Sizes

• Use AES encryption algorithm, SHA, and Elliptic Curve Cryptography

• Use the appropriate cryptographic strength and match the correct combination of hash size, AES key size, and public-key modulo for a specific authentication level of security

Storing Digital Certificates and Pre-Shared Keys

A number of certificates should be selected for loading at the time of manufacturing a device. The number of certificates loaded into a device depends on the device's code, space, and functionality. Space should be reserved for customers to add their own certificates after deleting all or some of the certificates loaded at the time of manufacture.

When pre-shared key authentication is used, the pre-shared keys must be loaded prior to connecting the equipment to the network. Companies that are deploying the equipment must be able to load their own pre-shared keys. Pre-shared keys must be loaded out-of-band and never over the network.

Learning Objectives Review

1. Using the 802.1 X standard, a user is not connected to the network until he is properly authenticated. (T/F)

2. When using a one-time password, the password is:

    a. Sent encrypted

    b. Sent in clear

    c. Not sent

3. What does a packet sniffer do?

4. With X.509 _____ Authentication, the password is sent in clear.

5. Spoofing can be described as:

    a. Eavesdropping on a communications link

    b. Working through a list of words

    c. Pretending to be someone or something else

6. IEEE 802.1X Authentication can only be used for wireless networks. (T/F)

7. The IEEE 802.1X Standard does not mandate that TTL, TTLS, and PEAP authentication methods MUST be used. (T/F)

8. Authentication is not essential for two parties to be able to trust in each other's identities. (T/F)

9. What type of attack attempts all possible solutions?

10. The dual-port system in IEEE 802.1X allows:

    a. The authenticator to connect two supplicants to the network at the same time

    b. The authenticator to control a port through which the supplicant has access to the network

    c. Both

11. Authentication means:

    a. Authorizing a user

    b. Identifying a user

    c. Registering a user

    d. Validating a user

12. EAP TTL requires digital certificates for its implementation. (T/F)

13. The maximum lifetime of a password depends on:

    a. The size of the password space

    b. How fast an intruder can execute a login attempt

    c. The probability that a password will be guessed during its lifetime

    d. All of the above

14. In PAP, the password is:

    a. Sent encrypted

    b. Sent in clear

    c. Not sent

15. What is a challenge-response technique?

16. EAP is an authentication protocol for:

    a. PPP

    b. Multiple protocols

    c. Both

17. EAP supports multiple authentication mechanisms. (T/F)

18. The Kerberos process has three components: the authentication server, the ticket-granting service, and the X.509 directory. (T/F)

19. Kerberos relies on public-key asymmetric ciphers for encryption and authentication; therefore, it produces digital signatures and authentication of authorship of documents. (T/F)

20. Which of the following is not part of Kerberos authentication implementation?

    a. Message authentication code

    b. Ticket-granting service

    c. Authentication service

    d. Users, programs, and services

References

Aboba, B., Blunk, L., Vollbrecht, J., Carlson, J., & Levkowetz, E. (2004). *Extensible authentication protocol (EAP)* (RFC 3748). Internet Engineering Task Force (IETF). Retrieved June 28, 2007, from http://www.ietf.org/rfc/rfc3748.txt?number=3748

Aboba, B., & Calhoun, P. (2003). *RADIUS (Remote authentication dial in user service) support for extensible authentication protocol (EAP)* (RFC 3579). Internet Engineering Task Force (IETF). Retrieved June 28, 2007, from http://www.ietf.org/rfc/rfc3579.txt?number=3579

Aboba, B., & Simon, D. (1999). *PPP EAP TLS authentication protocol* (RFC 2716). Internet Engineering Task Force (IETF). Retrieved June 28, 2007, from http://www.ietf.org/rfc/rfc2716.txt?number=2716

Arkko, J., & Haverinen, H. (2006). *Extensible authentication protocol method for 3rd generation authentication and key agreement (EAP-AKA)* (RFC 4187). Internet Engineering Task Force (IETF). Retrieved June 28, 2007, from http://www.ietf.org/rfc/rfc4187.txt?number=4187

Baldwin, R., & Rivest, R. (1996). *The RC5, RC5-CBC, RC5-CBC-Pad, and RC5-CTS Algorithms* (RFC 2040). Internet Engineering Task Force (IETF). Retrieved June 28, 2007, from http://www.ietf.org/rfc/rfc2040.txt?number=2040

Bersani, F., & Tschofenig, H. (2007). *The EAP-PSK protocol: A pre-shared key extensible authentication protocol (EAP)* (RFC 4764). Internet Engineering Task Force (IETF). Retrieved June 28, 2007, from http://www.ietf.org/rfc/rfc4764.txt?number=4764

Calhoun, P., Loughney, J., Guttman, E., Zorn, G., & Arkko, J. (2003). 3588 *Diameter base protocol* (RFC 3588). Internet Engineering Task Force (IETF). Retrieved June 28, 2007, from http://www.ietf.org/rfc/rfc3588.txt?number=3588

Clancy, T., & Arbaugh, W. (2006). Extensible authentication protocol (EAP) password authenticated exchange. (RFC 4746). Internet Engineering Task Force (IETF). Retrieved June 28, 2007, from http://www.ietf.org/rfc/rfc4746.txt?number=4746

Congdon, P., Aboba, B., Smith, A., Zorn, G., & Roese, J. (2003). *IEEE 802.1X remote authentication dial-in user service (RADIUS)* (RFC 3580). Internet Engineering Task Force (IETF). Retrieved June 28, 2007, from http://www.ietf.org/rfc/rfc3580.txt?number=3580

Department of Defense. (1985). *Password management guideline* (CSC-STD-002-85). Fort George G. Meade, MD: DoD Computer Security Center (DoDCSC). Retrieved June 28, 2007, from http://www.alw.nih.gov/Security/FIRST/papers/password/dodpwman.txt

Eronen, P. (Ed.), Hiller, T., & Zorn, G. (2005). *Diameter extensible authentication protocol (EAP) application* (RFC 4072). Internet Engineering Task Force (IETF). Retrieved June 28, 2007, from http://www.ietf.org/rfc/rfc4072.txt?number=4072

Frankel, S., & Herbert, H. (2003). *The AES-XCBC-MAC-96 algorithm and its use with IPsec* (RFC 3566). Internet Engineering Task Force (IETF). Retrieved June 28, 2007, from http://www.ietf.org/rfc/rfc3566.txt?number=3566

Haller, N., Metz, C., Nesser, P., & Straw, M. (1998). *A one-time password system* (RFC 2289). Internet Engineering Task Force (IETF). Retrieved June 28, 2007, from http://www. ietf.org/rfc/rfc2289.txt?number=2289

Haverinen, H., & Salowey, J. (Eds). (2006). *Extensible authentication protocol method for global system for mobile communications (GSM) subscriber identity modules (EAP-SIM)* (RFC4186). Internet Engineering Task Force (IETF). Retrieved June 28, 2007, from http://www.ietf.org/rfc/rfc4186.txt?number=4186

Institute of Electrical and Electronic Engineers (IEEE). (2004). *Port-based network access control* (IEEE Standard 802.1X).

Kaufman, C. (Ed.) (2005). *Internet key exchange (IKEv2)* (RFC 4306). Internet Engineering Task Force (IETF). Retrieved June 28, 2007, fromhttp://www.ietf.org/rfc/rfc4306. txt?number=4306

Kosiur, D. (1998). *Building and managing virtual private networks*. New York: John Willey & Sons.

Needham, R., & Schroeder, M. (1978). Using encryption for authentication in large networks of computers. *Communications of the ACM, 21*(12).

Neuman, C., Yu, T., Hartman, S., & Raeburn, K. (2005). *The Kerberos network authentication service (V5)* (RFC 4120). Internet Engineering Task Force (IETF). Retrieved June 28, 2007, from http://www.ietf.org/rfc/rfc4120.txt?number=4120

Raeburn, K. (2005a). *Encryption and Checksum Specifications for Kerberos 5* (RFC 3961). Internet Engineering Task Force (IETF). Retrieved June 28, 2007, from http://www. ietf.org/rfc/rfc3961.txt?number=3961

Raeburn, K. (2005b). Advanced Encryption Standard (AES) Encryption for Kerberos 5 (RFC 3962). Internet Engineering Task Force (IETF). Retrieved June 28, 2007, from http://www.ietf.org/rfc/rfc3962.txt?number=3962

Rigney, C., Willens, S., Rubens, A., & Simpson, W. (2000). *Remote authentication dial-in user service (RADIUS)* (RFC 2865). Internet Engineering Task Force (IETF). Retrieved June 28, 2007, from http://www.ietf.org/rfc/rfc2865.txt?number=2865

Shuh, B. (1997). *Directories and X.500: An introduction*. Information Technology Services, National Library of Canada. Retrieved June 28, 2007, from http://www.lac-bac. gc.ca/9/1/p1-244-e.html

Simpson, W. (1994). *The point-to-point protocol (PPP)* (RFC 1661). Internet Engineering Task Force (IETF). Retrieved June 28, 2007, from http://www.ietf.org/rfc/rfc1661. txt?number=1661

Simpson, W. (1996). *PPP challenge handshake authentication protocol (CHAP)* (RFC 1994). Internet Engineering Task Force (IETF). Retrieved June 28, 2007, from http://www.ietf.org/rfc/rfc1994.txt?number=1994

Chapter VIII

Elliptic Curve Cryptography

Elliptic Curve Cryptography

For the same level of security that public-key cryptosystems such as RSA have, elliptic curve cryptography (ECC) offers the benefit of smaller key sizes, hence smaller memory and processor requirements. The Diffie-Hellman key exchange, ElGamal encryption, digital signatures, and the Digital Signature Algorithm (DSA) can all be implemented in ECC. This makes ECC a very attractive algorithm for wireless devices such as handhelds and PDAs, which have limited bandwidth and processing power. Running on the same platform, ECC runs more TLS/SSL transactions per second than RSA.

This chapter describes the basic concepts and definitions of elliptic curve cryptography.

Objectives

*   Understand finite fields
*   Learn about elliptic curves and points
*   Select an elliptic curve
*   Learn how to use the elliptic curve in cryptography
*   Utilize EC for digital signatures

Introduction

An elliptic curve E, is the set of solutions $\{x; y\}$ of the equation $y^2 = f(x)$, where $f(x) = x^3 + \ldots$ is a polynomial of degree three. E is defined over the rational numbers q; that is, the coefficients of f are in q. Elliptic curves are not ellipses.

ECC is an encryption system that uses the properties of elliptic curves to provide the same functionality of other public-key cryptosystems such as encryption, key agreements, and digital signatures. Bit-by-bit key size, elliptic curve crypto-system provides the greatest security of any cryptosystem known today.

Elliptic curve cryptography was independently introduced in 1985 by Victor Miller and Neal Koblitz and has become an essential public-key system in electronic banking and financial institutions.

ECC's smaller key size and unmatched level of security ranks it above other public systems such as RSA and DSS. ECC's properties make it a good choice for smart card applications. ECC offers similar security to established public-key cryptosystems with reduced key sizes and is especially useful in applications for which memory, bandwidth, or computational power is limited (Brown, Cheung, Hankerson, Lopez, Kirkup, & Menezes, 2000).

Elliptic curve cryptography uses plane curves, which are sets of points satisfying the equation $F(x, y) = 0$. Examples of plane curves are lines ($2x + y = 0$), conic sections ($3x^2 + 5y^2 = 0$), and cubic curves ($y^2 + xy = x^3 + ax^2 + b$), which include elliptic curves.

There are several standards for elliptic curve cryptography.

- **IEEE P1363:** This standard specifies common public-key cryptographic techniques, including elliptic curve cryptography.

- **ANSI X9:** An ANSI-accredited standards committee for the financial services industry has developed two elliptic curve standards: ANSI X9.62 for digital signatures and ANSI X9.63 for key agreement and key transport.

- **IETF:** RFC 2412 (Orman, 1998), "The OAKLEY Key Determination Protocol," includes elliptic curve groups over the field F_2^m. RFC 2412 provides group identifier, GRP, only for elliptic curve groups over F_2^{155}, and F_2^{185}.

- **FIPS 186.2:** The Digital Signature Standard (DSS)

Notation

The following notation used in ANSI X9.62 will be used in this chapter:

- $a \in E$: a is an element of E
- $a \notin E$: a is not an element of E
- $a \subset E$: a is a subset of e
- $a \not\subset E$: a is not a subset of E

- $a = E$: a and E are exactly the same elements

- $\lfloor x \rfloor$: The floor function rounds the number down to the nearest integer. Examples: $\lfloor 2.4 \rfloor$ = 2; $\lfloor 2.6 \rfloor$ = 2; $\lfloor -2.4 \rfloor$ = -3; $\lfloor -2.6 \rfloor$ = -3. The floor function is also called the *integer part function* and is denoted int(x).

- $\lceil x \rceil$: The ceiling function rounds the number up to the nearest integer. Examples: $\lceil 2.4 \rceil$ = 3; $\lceil 2.6 \rceil$ =3; $\lceil -2.4 \rceil$ = -2; $\lceil -2.6 \rceil$ = -2.

- a, b: The coefficients defining the elliptic curve E, elements of F_q (part of the EC domain parameters)

- E : Elliptic curve equation

- $E(F_q)$: The set of all points on an elliptic curve E defined over F_q and including the point at infinity O

- $\#E(F_q)$: If E is defined over F_q, then $\#E(F_q)$ denotes the number of points on the curve (including the point at infinity). $\#E(F_q)$ is called the *order of the curve* E.

- $F_2{}^m$: The finite field containing $q = 2^m$ elements, where m is a positive integer

- F_p: The finite field containing $q = p$ elements, where p is a prime

- F_q: The finite field containing q elements. For ANSI X9.62, q shall be either an odd prime number ($q = p$, $p > 3$) or a power of 2 ($q = 2m$).

- h: $h = \#E(F_q)/n$, where n is the order of the base point G. h is called the *cofactor*.

- G: A distinguished point on an elliptic curve called the *base* point or *generating point*. It generates a subgroup of order n (part of the EC domain parameters).

- n: The order of the base point G; for ANSI X9.62, n shall be greater than 2^{160} and $4\sqrt{q}$ and shall be a prime number; n is the primary security parameter.

- O: A special point on an elliptic curve, called the *point at infinity*; this is the additive identity of the elliptic curve group

- p: An odd prime number

- P: An EC point

- q: The number of elements in the field F_q

- Q: Elliptic curve public key

- t: According to Hasse's theorem $\#E(F_q) = q + 1 - t$, where $|t| \leq 2\sqrt{q}$ is called the *trace of Frobenius*.

- x_P: The x-coordinates of point P

- y_P: The y-coordinates of point P

- z: Shared secret values, elements of GF (q), derived by a key exchange algorithm such as Diffie-Hellman

- ZZ: The octet string of the shared secret value

- *Singular*: A curve is said to be singular if all the partial derivatives $\partial F / \partial x$, $\partial F / \partial y$ are zero at the point P.

- *Supersingular*: An elliptic curve over F_q is supersingular if the characteristic p divides the trace of E, $tr(E) = t = q + 1 - \#E(F_q)$.

- *Anomalous*: An elliptic curve over F_p is said to be prime-field anomalous if the trace of E, $tr(E) = t$. Therefore, $\#E(F_p) = p$.

Finite Fields

A field is a set F in which the usual mathematical operations (addition, subtraction, multiplication, and division by nonzero quantities) are possible; these operations follow the usual commutative, associative, and distributive laws. Rational numbers (fractions), real numbers, complex numbers, and the integer modulo n are elements of infinite fields. The mathematical operations in a field are multiplication and addition, meaning that for them, the additive inverse is subtraction and the multiplicative inverse is division.

Finite fields are fields that are finite. F_q denotes a field that has a finite number q of elements.

Discrete logarithm cryptography (DLC), which includes finite field cryptography (FFC) and elliptic curve cryptography (ECC), requires that the public- and private-key pairs be generated within a finite field. For cryptography applications, the finite fields that are usually used in ECC and in FFC are the fields of characteristic F_p and the fields of characteristic two $F_2{}^m$. The finite field is also denoted as *GF(q)*.

Characteristic Prime Finite Fields

The finite field F_p is the prime finite field containing p elements. If p is an odd prime number, then there is a unique field F_p that consists of the set of integers $\{0, 1, 2, ..., p-1\}$ with the following arithmetic operations:

- **Addition:** If $a, b \in F_p$, then $a + b \equiv r \bmod p$
- **Multiplication:** If $a, b \in F_p$, then $a * b \equiv r \bmod p$
- **Inversion:** If a is a nonzero element in F_p, the inverse of a modulo p, denoted as a^{-1}, is the unique integer $c \in F_p$ for which $a * c \equiv 1 \bmod p$.

Characteristic Two Finite Fields

A characteristic two finite field (also known as a binary finite field) is a finite field whose number of elements is 2^m. If m is a positive integer greater than 1, the binary finite field $F_2{}^m$ consists of the 2^m possible bit strings of length m.

Thus, for example, $F_2{}^3 = \{000, 001, 010, 011, 100, 101, 110, 111\}$. The integer m is the *degree of the field*.

A way to represent the elements of F_{2m} is by the set of binary polynomials of degree m:

$$\{a_{m-1}x^{m-1} + a_{m-2}x^{m-2} + \dots\dots + a_1 x + a_0 : a_i \in \{0,1\}\}$$

The following operations are defined in the elements of F_{2^m}:

- **Addition:** $a + b \equiv r \bmod 2$. This is equivalent to bitwise exclusive OR (XOR), where a, b, and r are bit strings.

- **Multiplication:** If $a, b \in F_{2^m}$, then $a * b \equiv r$. Multiplication is done using polynomials.

  Then,

  $$r = \{a_{m-1}x^{m-1} + a_{m-2}x^{m-2} + \dots + a_1 x + a_0\} * \{b_{m-1}x^{m-1} + b_{m-2}x^{m-2} + \dots + b_1 x + b_0$$

  $$r = \{r_{m-1}x^{m-1} + r_{m-2}x^{m-2} + \dots + r_1 x + r_0 \bmod f(x)$$

  For example, if $f(x) = x^4 + x + 1$, $a = x^3 + x^2 + 1$, and $b = x^3 + 1$,

  then, $r = a * b = (x^3 + x^2 + 1) * (x^3 + 1)$

  $r = x^6 + x^5 + x^2 + 1 \bmod (x^4 + x + 1) = x^3 + x^2 + x + 1$

- **Inversion:** If a is a nonzero bit stream element in F_{2^m}, the inverse of a, denoted as a^{-1}, is the unique integer $c \in F_{2^m}$ for which $a * b \equiv 1$.

Elliptic Curves and Points

There are several ways of defining equations for elliptic curves, but the most commonly used are the Weierstrass equations. The following elliptic curves over the field of rational numbers are nonsingular cubic curves in Weierstrass form with rational coefficients:

$y^2 + xy = x^3 + ax^2 + b$ and $y^2 = x^3 + ax + b$

In cryptography, the elliptic curves of interest are those defined over finite fields. That is, the coefficients of the defining equation $F(x, y) = 0$ are elements of F_q, and the points on the curve are of the form $P = (x, y)$, where x and y are elements of F_q.

An elliptic curve E defined over F_q is a set of points $P = (x_p, y_p)$, where x_p and y_p are elements of F_q that satisfy a certain equation, together with the point at infinity denoted by O. Elliptic curves are specified by two field elements, $a \in F_q$ and $b \in F_q$, called the *coefficients of E*. The field elements x_p and y_p are called the x-coordinate of P and the y-coordinate of P, respectively. F_q could be of the form F_p, which is the finite field containing $q = p$ elements, where p is a prime and m is a positive integer, or F_{2^m} which is the finite field containing $q = 2^m$ elements.

An elliptic curve is said to be nonsingular if at least one of the partial derivatives $\partial F / \partial x$, $\partial F / \partial y$ is nonzero at the point (Koblitz, 1994). The curve coefficients of each type of finite field must satisfy a side condition to guarantee the mathematical property of nonsingularity. The side condition is given below for each family of curves.

1. If p is an odd prime, then a and b shall satisfy $4a^3 + 27b^2 \neq 0$ in F_q, and every point $P = (x_p, y_p)$ on E (other than the point O) shall satisfy the following Weierstrass equation in F_p:

    $$y^2 = x^3 + ax + b$$

2. If p is a power of 2, then b shall be nonzero in F_q, and every point $P = (x_p, y_p)$ on E (other than the point O) shall satisfy the following Weierstrass equation in F_q:

    $$y^2 + xy = x^3 + ax^2 + b$$

Arithmetic in an Elliptic Curve Group over F_p

An elliptic curve $E(F_p)$ over F_p, where p is an odd prime defined by the parameters $a, b \in F_p$, consists of the set of solutions or points $P(x, y)$ for $x, y \in F_p$, for the equation $y^2 + xy = y^2 \equiv x^3 + ax + b \bmod p$.

Adding Distinct Points P and Q

The addition of two points is similar to the addition of two points in plane geometry. If $P(x_p, y_p)$ and $Q(x_Q, y_Q)$ are distinct points such that $P \neq \pm Q$, then:

$$P(x_P, y_P) + Q(x_Q, y_Q) = R(x_R, y_R)$$
$$\text{where, } x_R \equiv \lambda^2 - x_P - x_Q \bmod p$$
$$y_R \equiv \lambda(x_P - x_R) - y_P \bmod p$$

Figure 8-1. Addition of two points P and Q

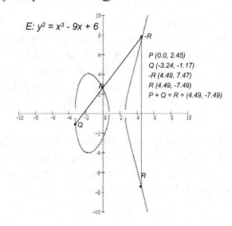

Copyright © 2008, IGI Global. Copying or distributing in print or electronic forms without written permission of IGI Global is prohibited.

and $\lambda \equiv \dfrac{(y_Q - y_P)}{(x_Q - x_P)} \bmod p$

λ is the slope of the line through $P\,(x_p, y_p)$ and $Q\,(x_Q, y_Q)$. (Koblitz, 1994, p 170).

Given two points on the curve P and Q, the line through them meets the curve at a third point, $-R$. The group law is defined by $P + Q - R = 0$; therefore, $P + Q = R$ where the negative of the point $R(x, y)$ is the point $R\,(x, -y)$.

The group $E(Fp)$ is abelian, which means that $P + Q = Q + P$ for all points P and Q in $E(Fp)$.

Subtracting Two Distinct Points P and Q

The subtraction of two points is similar to the addition of one point to a negative of the other point. If $P\,(x_p, y_p)$ and $Q\,(x_Q, y_Q)$, are distinct points such that $P \neq \pm Q$, then:

$$P\,(x_P, y_P) - Q\,(x_Q, y_Q) = P(x_p, y_p) + Q(x_Q, -y_Q) = R\,(x_R, y_R)$$

The negative of the point $Q\,(x_q, y_q)$ is the point $-Q\,(x_q, y_q) = Q\,(x_q, -y_q)$.

Doubling the Point P

Provided that $y_p \neq 0$,

then $P\,(x_P, y_P) + P\,(x_P, y_P) = R\,(x_R, y_R)$

where $x_R \equiv \lambda^2 - 2x_P \bmod p$

$y_R \equiv \lambda\,(x_P - x_R) - y_P \bmod p$

Figure 8-2. Doubling the point P

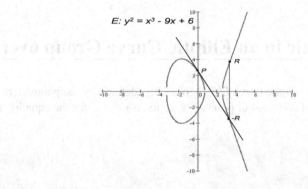

E: $y^2 = x^3 - 9x + 6$

Figure 8-3. Adding P to -P

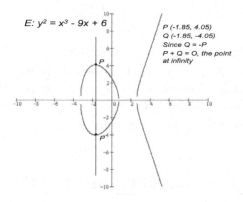

and $\lambda \equiv \dfrac{(3x_P^2 + a)}{(2y_P)}$ mod p

λ is the slope of the line through $P(x_P, y_P)$ and a is the coefficient of x in the elliptic curve, $y^2 = x^3 + ax + b$.

Adding P to - P

The negative of the point $P(x_P, y_P)$ is the point $P(x_P, -y_P)$, so,

$P(x_P, y_P) - P(x_P, -y_P) = P(x_P, y_P) - P(x_P, -y_P) = O$. *O* is the *point at infinity*.

Elliptic Scalar Multiplication

The elliptic scalar integer multiplication of an elliptic curve point, P, is defined as the process of adding P to itself k times. This operation is analogous to exponentiation in finite field cryptography.

Arithmetic in an Elliptic Curve Group over $F_2{}^m$

A nonsupersingular elliptic curve $E(F_{2m})$ over F_{2m}, defined by the parameters $a, b \in F_{2m}$, consists of the set of solutions or points $P(x, y)$ for $x, y \in F_{2m}$ for the equation $y^2 + xy = x^3 + ax^2 + b$.

Adding Distinct Points P and Q

The addition of two points is similar to the addition of two points in plane geometry. If P (x_P, y_P) and $Q (x_Q, y_Q)$, are distinct points such that $P \neq \pm Q$, then:

$$P (x_P, y_P) + Q (x_Q, y_Q) = R (x_R, y_R)$$

where $x_R \equiv \lambda^2 + \lambda + x_P + x_Q + a \quad in \ F_{2^m}$

$y_R \equiv \lambda (x_P + x_R) + x_P + y_P \quad in \ F_{2^m}$

and $\lambda \equiv \dfrac{(y_P + y_Q)}{(x_P + x_Q)} \ in \ F_{2^m}$

Subtracting Two Distinct Points P and Q

Subtracting two points is similar to the addition of one point to the negative of the other point. If $P (x_P, y_P)$ and $Q (x_Q, y_Q)$ are distinct points such that $P \neq \pm Q$, then:

$$P (x_P, y_P) - Q (x_Q, y_Q) = P(x_P, y_P) + Q(x_Q, x_Q + y_Q) = R (x_R, y_R)$$

The negative of the point $Q (x_Q, y_Q)$ is the point $- Q (x_Q, y_Q) = Q (x_Q, x_Q + y_q)$.

Doubling the Point P

Provided that $y_P \neq 0$, then $P (x_P, y_P) + P (x_P, y_P) = R (x_R, y_R)$,
where $x_R \equiv \lambda^2 + \lambda + a \quad in \ F_{2^m}$

$y_R \equiv \lambda(x_P + x_R) + x_R + y_P = x_P^2 + (\lambda + 1)x_R \quad in \ F_{2^m}$

and $\lambda \equiv x_P + \dfrac{y_P}{x_P} \ in \ F_{2^m}$

Lopez and Dahab (2000) proposed the following formula to double the point P when b is equal to 1 and a is 0 or 1 in the equation $y^2 + xy = x^3 + ax^2 + b$. For $P (x_P, y_P) + P (x_P, y_P) = R (x_R, y_R)$,

$$M = \frac{1}{x_P^2}$$

$$x_3 = x_P^2 + M \ and \ y_3 = M + ax_R + (y_P^2 + 1) * (1 + M^2)$$

Adding P to - P

The negative of the point P (x_P, y_P) is the point $-P$ $(x_P, x_P + y_P)$, so
$P(x_P, y_P) + P(x_P, x_P + y_P) = O$. O is the *point at infinity*.

The point at infinity, O, plays a role analogous to that of the number zero in ordinary addition. Thus $P + O = P$, $P + (-P) = O$ for all points P.

Order of a Point

The repeated addition of a point to itself, scalar multiplication, generates a new point, $Q = kP$; however, there is always a time when adding the point to itself results in $O = kP$, the point at infinity. The order of a point P is the smallest positive number k such that $kP = O$.

Table 8-1 shows all the points of E $F_{(23)}$: $y^2 = x^3 + x + 1$ and their *orders*. Figure 8-4 shows the graph when all the points of E $F_{(23)}$: $y^2 = x^3 + x + 1$ are plotted. Note that the points are

Table 8-1. Points of E $F_{(23)}$: $y^2 = x^3 + x + 1$

Point	Order	Point	Order	Point	Order	Point	Order
(0,1)	28	(9,16)	28	(7,11)	14	(13,16)	7
(0,22)	28	(18,3)	28	(7,12)	14	(17,3)	7
(1,7)	28	(18,20)	28	(12,4)	14	(17,20)	7
(1,16)	28	(19,5)	28	(12,19)	14	(11,3)	4
(3,10)	28	(19,18)	28	(5,4)	7	(11,20)	4
(3,13)	28	(6,4)	14	(5,19)	7	(4,0)	1 (infinity)
(9,7)	28	(6,19)	14	(13,7)	7		

Figure 8-4. Points in the E: $y^2 = x^3 + x + 1$ mod 23

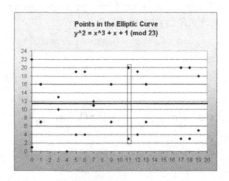

symmetric for this curve around $y = 11.5$ because in elliptic curves, for every x value there are two y values, that is, for every point P there must exist another point $-P$.

The point $P(0, 1)$, as well as all other points with an order of 28, are the generators of a maximal subgroup $E: y^2 = x^3 + x + 1$ (mod 23) because they generate the maximum number of points. The point $P(7, 11)$ is a generator of a different subgroup where 14 points are generated.

The generator point selected for encryption is the point that generates the highest prime factor of $\#E(F_q)$. In this example, that number is 7, so any of the points that has an order of 7 can be used; then, $\#E(F_q) = h * n = 4 * 7$, and h is the cofactor. In this example, $h = 4$.

Curve Order

When the point $P(0, 1)$ in $E\ F_{(23)}: y^2 = x^3 + x + 1$ is added to itself, the order of the point $P(0,1)$ is 28, which is the smallest positive number k such that $kP = O$. The generated points are 27, plus the point at infinity for a total of 28.

If the order of a point is the maximum, in this case 28, then it is the *curve order* and is denoted as $\#E(F_q)$. The order of any point is always a factor of the curve order, $\#E(F_p)$. In this example, the point orders 14, 7, and 4 are factors of 28.

Hasse's theorem states that the number of points in $E(F_q)$, is in the range $p + 1 - 2\sqrt{p} \le \#E(F_q) \le p + 1 + 2\sqrt{p}$. René Schoof (Koblitz, 1994, p183) developed an algorithm to calculate the number of points in $E(F_q)$; this algorithm has been improved by V. Miller, N. Elkies, J. Buchmann, V. Muller, A. Menezes, L. Charlap, R. Coley, and D. Robbins.

Selecting an Elliptic Curve and G, the Generator Point

There are several procedures to select an elliptic curve for cryptographic purposes. The following are some of the criteria:

1. Select a large prime number, p, to be used as the module.
2. Select the coefficients, a and b, randomly and define $E\ (F_p): y^2 = x^3 + ax + b$.
3. Calculate the curve order $\#E(F_p)$.
4. Check that $\#E(F_p)$ satisfies the MOV condition that does not divide $p^k - 1$ for all values of $k \le (\log p)^2$ because then the curve is supersingular; in practice, $k \le 20$ is sufficient. Also, check that $\#E(F_p) \ne p$ in order to resist a Smart-Satoh-Araki (SSA) attack (Vo, 2003).

5.   Check that $\#E(F_p)$ is divisible by a prime number n that is sufficiently large, $n > 2^{160}$, to be able to resist the parallelized Pollard-ρ and Pollard-λ attacks.

6.   Check that the largest prime divisor of $\#E(F_p)$ does not divide $p^k - 1$ for $k = 1, 2, 3, . . .$<large limit>.

Another way to select the elliptic curve is by selecting the curve order first:

1.   Select a large prime number, p, to be used as the module.

2.   Select the curve order, $\#E(F_p)$, such that:

$$p + 1 - 2\sqrt{p} \leq \#E(F_q) \leq p + 1 + 2\sqrt{p}.$$

3.   Check that $\#E(F_p)$ is divisible by a large prime number, r.

4.   Make sure that r does not divide $p^k - 1$ for $k = 1, 2, 3, . . . 10$.

5.   Use the Atkin-Morain algorithm to find parameters a and b in F_p such that the elliptic curve E has an order of $\#E(F_p)$.

Once an elliptic curve is selected, it is necessary to select the point G, the generator of a subgroup.

1.   Select a random point G on $E(F_q)$ and a large prime number n that divides $\#E(F_p)$.

2.   Check that $n G = O$, n being the point order.

NIST (Federal Information Processing Standards (FIPS), 2000) recommends a certain set of elliptic curves for government use. This set of curves can be divided into two classes: curves over a prime field F_p and curves over a binary field F_{2^m}. The curves over F_p are of the form $y^2 = x^3 - 3x + b$ with b random, while the curves over F_{2^m} are either of the form $y^2 + xy = x^3 + x^2 + b$ with b random or Koblitz curves. A Koblitz curve has the form $y^2 + xy = x^3 + ax^2 + 1$ with $a = 0$ or 1.

Elliptic Curve Domain Parameters

When two parties are going to use elliptic curve cryptography, there are several parameters on which they should agree, either because they were selected by them or by a third party, such as NIST (Federal Information Processing Standards (FIPS), 2000) or by Certicom (Standards for Efficient Cryptography Group (SECG), 2000b). Those parameters are called the *elliptic curve domain parameters*.

The elliptic curve domain parameters determine the arithmetic operations involved in the public-key cryptographic schemes, F_p and F_{2^m}. The domain consists of six parameters which are calculated differently for F_p and $F_2{}^m$, and which precisely specify an elliptic curve and base point.

The six domain parameters are the following:

$$T = (q; FR; a, b; G; n; h)$$

in which

- q: Defines the underlying finite field F_q. The field size is defined by the module, so, $q = p$ or $q = 2^m$; $p > 3$ should be a prime number.

- FR: Field representation of the method used for representing field elements in $\in F_q$, either $E(F_p)$ or $E(F_{2m})$.

- a, b: The coefficients defining the elliptic curve E, elements of F_q.

- G: A point, $G = (x_G, y_G)$, on an elliptic curve called the *base point* or *generating point*; it is defined by two field elements x_G and y_G in F_q.

- n: The order of the base point G, normally a large prime.

- h: Called the *cofactor*, $h = \#E(F_q) / n$, where n is the order of the base point G. h is normally a small number.

The domain parameters represent an elliptic curve E and a designated point G on E called the *base point*. The base point has order n, a large prime. The number of points on the curve is $\#E(F_q) = h * n$ for some integer h (the cofactor) not divisible by n. For efficiency reasons, it is desirable to make the cofactor as small as possible.

Elliptic curve domain parameters need to be shared by the entities using a particular crypto system. In all cases, the EC domain parameters may be public; the security of the system does not rely on these parameters being secret.

Elliptic Curve Domain Parameters Over F_p

The elliptic curve domain parameters over F_p are the sextuple:

$$T = (p; a; b; G; n; h), \text{ consisting of}$$

1. An integer p specifying the finite field $F(p)$ such that $t = \lceil \log_2 p = 2t \rceil$, if $t \neq 256$ or such that $t = \lceil \log_2 p = 521 \rceil$ if $t = 256$.

2. The integer $t \in (56, 64, 80, 96, 112, 128, 192, 256,)$ is the approximate security level in bits required from the elliptic curve domain parameters.

3.   Two elements $a, b \in F_p$ specifying an elliptic curve $E\,F_p$ defined by the equation: E : $y^2 \equiv x^3 + ax + b$ (mod p). a and b are integers in the interval $(0, p - 1)$ and $4a^3 + 27b^2$ $\neq 0$ (mod p).

4.   A base point $G = (x_G, y_G)$ on $E\,(F_p)$. x_G and y_G are integers in the interval $(0, p -1)$.

5.   A prime n, so $n\,.\,G = O$. Check that $p^B \neq 1$ (mod n) for any $1 \leq B < 20$.

6.   An integer h which is the cofactor $h = [\,\#E\,(F_p)\,]\,/n\,.\,h \leq 4$, and $n\,.\,h \neq p$

Elliptic Curve Domain Parameters over $F_2{}^m$

The elliptic curve domain parameters over GF (2^m) are the septuple:

$T = (m; f(x); a; b; G; n; h)$, consisting of

1.   An integer m specifying the finite field $F_2{}^m$. The "Standard for Efficient Cryptography" (Standards for Efficient Cryptography Group (SECG), 2000a) suggests using m as one of the integers in the set $\{113, 131, 163, 193, 233, 239, 283, 409, 571\}$ to facilitate interoperability.

2.   An irreducible binary polynomial $f(x)$ of degree m specifying the representation of $F_2{}^m$

3.   Two elements $a, b \in F_2{}^m$ specifying the elliptic curve $EF_2{}^m$ defined by the equation: E: $y^2 + xy = x^3 + ax^2 + b$ in $EF_2{}^m$. a and b are binary polynomials of degree $m - 1$ or less and $b \neq 0$.

4.   A base point $G = (x_G, y_G)$ on $EF_2{}^m$.

5.   A prime n, so $n\,.\,G = O$. $2^{mB} \neq 1$ (mod n) for any $1 \leq B < 20$.

6.   An integer h which is the cofactor $h = \#E\,F_2{}^m$, $h \leq 4$, $n\,.h \neq p$, and
$$h = \left\lfloor (\sqrt{2^m} + 1)^2\,/\,n \right\rfloor$$

Cryptography Using Elliptic Curves

There are two essential properties of group fields when they are used in elliptic curve cryptography:

1.   A group should have a finite number of points. An elliptic curve has an infinite number of points, but an elliptic curve over F_q has a finite number of elements.

2.   The operation that is used should be easy to compute but very difficult and time con-suming to reverse.

Public-key systems use large finite group properties. For Diffie-Hellman, ElGamal, DSS, and RSA, the security depends directly on the relative difficulty of performing two group operations: discrete logarithms and exponentiation.

In the multiplicative group $Zp*$ discrete logarithm (Diffie-Hellman, ElGamal, DSS), the following is the discrete logarithm problem: given elements y and x of the group, and a prime p, find a number k such that $y = x^k \bmod p$.

For example, if $y = 2$, $x = 8$, and $p = 341$, then find k such that $2 \equiv 8^k \bmod 341$. In the Diffie-Hellman discrete logarithm, y is the public key, g is a large random number, p is the modulo, and k is the private key that the cryptanalyst is trying to find out. If the modulo were not included, it would be easy to solve k by finding $log_x y$, but when the modulo is included, the logarithm has a different but analogous meaning. This type of logarithm is called *discrete* to distinguish it from the classical logarithm.

If k is an integer, and P is a point on an elliptic curve, then the operation kP is the addition of P to itself k times. This repeated addition of the point with itself, $Q = kP$, called the *scalar integer multiplication* of elliptic curve point P, is analogous to exponentiation in a discrete logarithm cryptosystem. It is an operation that is easy to compute but very difficult and time consuming to reverse.

For elliptic curve public-key cryptography, the relative difficulty of breaking an EC is based on the following elliptic curve discrete logarithmic problem (ECDLP): given an elliptic curve $E(F_q)$, a point $P \in E(F_q)$ of an order n, and a point $Q \in E(F_q)$, determine the integer k, $0 \leq k \geq n-1$, such that $Q = kP$, provided that such integer k exists.

Johnson and Menezes, (1999, pp 26-29) described 15 attack methods based on algorithms known for solving the elliptic curve discrete logarithmic problem. One of these methods is the Naive Exhaustive Search (brute force) in which all the multiple points of P: P, $2P$, $3P$, $4P$, . . . , are calculated until Q is found. Worst-case scenario, this method can take up to n steps.

Attacks on the Elliptic Curve Discrete Logarithm Problem (ECDLP)

NASA's Advanced Supercomputing (NAS) Division's technical report, *A Survey of Elliptic Curve Cryptosystems* (Vo, 2003), states that there is no known successful attack of subexponential time for the ECDLP and lists several of the exhaustive search (brute force) attacks. The most efficient general algorithms to resolve the ECDLP are Pollard-ρ and Pollard-λ. Pollard-ρ takes $\sqrt{\pi n / 2}$ steps; each step is an elliptic curve addition. According to Certicom SEC1, Pollard-λ takes $2\sqrt{n}$ steps; ANSI X.62, states that Pollard-λ takes $3.28\sqrt{n}$. Pollard-ρ has been improved to require only $\sqrt{\pi n / 4}$ steps. Both methods can be parallelized so that if r processors are used, then the expected number of steps is divided by r. In order to avoid an exhaustive search, n should be greater than 2^{160}.

Another type of attack is the MOV reduction attack (Menezes, Okamoto, & Vanstone, 1993, pp. 1639-1646), which is successful in attacking the ECDLP on supersingular elliptic curves. That is the reason why supersingular elliptic curves in applied cryptography should

Figure 8-5. Parameters for an elliptic curve with 161-bit module

be avoided. Menezes, Okamoto and Vanstone showed that for supersingular elliptic curves, the value of k when $p^K - 1$ is divided by $\#E(Fp)$ is always less than or equal to 6. If k is larger than 6, then the curve is nonsingular. This important result provides a good upper limit on the attack of supersingular elliptic curves. In practice, it is better to check for $K \leq 20$. The elliptic curve being used as an example is supersingular because $\#E(F23) = 28$ divides 23^6 - 1, $[(23^6 -1) / 28] = 5286996$.

An elliptic curve over a finite field F_q, where $q = p^m$, is supersingular if p divides t, where $\#E(F_q) = q + 1 - t$. If otherwise, it is a nonsupersingular elliptic curve. t is the *trace* of E and is denoted as $tr(E)$. However, ANSI X9.63 (page 59) states that a curve is said to be supersingular only if $\#E(F_p) = p + 1$.

Figure 8-5 shows the parameters of an elliptic curve with a 161-bit module generated at Cryptomathic's Web site (2003). The order of the curve n is equal to $1.73 * 10^{46}$, meaning that the base point (x, y) can be added to itself: $k = 1.73 * 10^{46}$ before $kP = O$. If the Pollard-ρ algorithm is used, it is necessary to check $\sqrt{\pi} * 1.73 * 10^{46} / 4 = 1.16 * 10^{23}$ additions to break the encryption.

Table 8-2 shows the years that it would take a system doing 100,000 additions per second ($3.15 * 10^{12}$ additions per year) to break the system. It is usually estimated (optimistically) that a machine rated at 1 MIPS (million instructions per second) can perform roughly 40,000 elliptic curve additions per second.

In 1997, Certicom challenged the crypto community to break the following:

Table 8-2. Years required to break the system with the Pollard- ρ Method

Field size (in bits)	Size of n (in bits)	$\sqrt{\pi\ n\ /\ 4}$ Additions	Years to Break
163	160	$1.07 * 10^{24}$	$3.39*10^{11}$
191	186	$8.77 * 10^{27}$	$2.78*10^{15}$
239	234	$1.47 * 10^{35}$	$4.66*10^{22}$
359	354	$1.69 * 10^{53}$	$5.36*10^{40}$
431	426	$1.16 * 10^{64}$	$3.68*10^{51}$

Figure 8-6. ECC vs. DL and exponentiation key-lengths comparisons

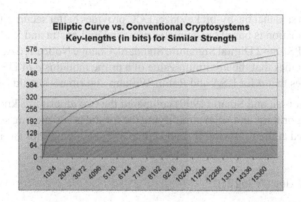

1. Randomly generated curves over F_p, where p is prime: ECCp-79, ECCp-89, ECCp-97, ECCp-109, ECCp-131, ECCp-163, ECCp-191, ECCp-239, and ECCp-359.

2. Randomly generated curves over F_{2m}, where m is prime: ECC2-79, ECC2-89, ECC2-97, ECC2-109, ECC2-131, ECC2-163, ECC2-191, ECC2-238, and ECC2- 353.

3. Koblitz curves over F_{2m}, where m is prime: ECC2K-95, ECC2-108, ECC2-130, ECC2-163, ECC2-238, and ECC2-358.

Certicom (2004) announced that Chris Monico, an assistant professor at Texas Tech University, and his team of mathematicians successfully solved Certicom Elliptic's Curve Cryptography (ECC)2 109-bit (field characteristic 2) challenge. The effort required 2,600 computers and took 17 months. Professor Monico also successfully solved, in 2002, Certicom ECCp-109 (prime field) challenge.

Table 8-3. Key length equivalent strengths

Security (Bits)	Symmetric Encryption Algorithm	Hash Algorithm	Diffie-Hellman and RSA Modulus Size		ECC
80	SKIPJACK	SHA-1	1024	1024	160
112	3DES	SHA-1	2048	2048	224
128	AES-128	SHA-256	3072	3072	256
192	AES-192	SHA-384	7680	7680	384
256	AES-256	SHA-512	15360	15360	512

Public Key Systems Public Key Size Comparisons

It has been said that bit-by-bit key size, ECC provides better security than DSA/DH or RSA. This information is based on estimates provided by Lenstra and Verheul (1999) and by the revised FIPS 186-2 Digital Signature Standard, Change Notice 1, dated October 5, 2001. The notice specifies that the minimum value of a prime modulus p of DSA should be 1024 bits. It also notes that n for RSA and Rabin-William algorithms should be at least 1024 bits.

Blake, Seroussi, and Smart (1999) compared the two algorithms known to break ECC and discrete algorithms and, after simplifying the formulas and making several approximations, they arrived at the following formula comparing key-length for similar levels of security:

$$n = \beta \ N^{1/3} \ (\log (N \log 2))^{2/3}$$

where $\beta \approx 4.91$. The parameters n and N are the "key sizes" of ECC and DL cryptosystems. The relationship is plotted in Figure 8-6.

The best know algorithm for integer factorization (RSA) is almost of the same complexity as finite field cryptography (FFC), so this comparison also applies to conventional public-key crypto systems based on factorization (Blake, Seroussi, & Smart, 1999).

The information on Table 8-3 is accepted as having good estimates and appears in many papers related to ECC.

The RSA public-key algorithm uses a nonprime large number, RSA modulo n, which is equal to the product of the two large prime factors p and q. In Table 8-3, the minimum RSA public-key size refers to the bit-length of the RSA modulo.

As mentioned before, in the multiplicative group $Zp*$ discrete logarithm (Diffie-Hellman, ElGamal, DSS), the discrete logarithm problem is based on the difficulty of given elements y and x of the group, and a prime p: find a number k such that $y = x^k \bmod p$. If k can be found, the system can be broken. In Table 8-3, the minimum finite field cryptography (FFC) public-key size refers to the bit-length of the modulo p.

The difficulty of the elliptic curve discrete logarithmic problem (ECDLP) depends on the size of the largest prime divisor of the curve order, which is close to p. According to Pollard, that difficulty is proportional to the square root of the largest prime factor of the curve order. For that reason, p, $\#E(F_p)$, and n are usually chosen such that p and n are close (Lenstra & Verheul, 1999). In Table 11- 3, the minimum elliptic curve cryptography key size refers to a bit-length of n. That is why when selecting an elliptic curve for cryptography purposes, $\#E(F_p)$ should be divisible by a prime number n that is sufficiently large, and h the cofactor should be small, $h = [\#E (F p)] / n$.

Software Implementations

In a finite field, raising an integer to the kth power can be accomplished by the repeating square method; for example, $3^{128} = ((((3^2)^2)^2)^2)^2)^2)^2)$ for a total of 7 operations. The same can be accomplished with an elliptic curve, finding $128 P = 2(2(2(2(2(2(2P))))))$, for a total of 7 operations. According to Koblitz (1994, p 178), the number of operations to calculate the above is the same. Therefore, from the point of view of number of operations, there is no difference between using exponentiation or point addition.

Using elliptic curve cryptography requires operations involving different types of data, such as integers, bit strings, octet strings, points on the EC, and field elements. For example, the plaintext needs to be encoded as points on the EC before it is enciphered. The letter m (plaintext) or the integer 5785 (the result of hash function) needs to be converted to a bit string and imbedded as points on an EC before any type of encryption function is done. Once encryption is done, the new EC points need to be converted back to letters or integers for transmission. The same procedure is done for deciphering. ANSI X.62-199X defines the different data types and conversions.

Key Pair Generation

The public and private keys of an entity A are associated with a particular set of elliptic curve domain parameters $(q; FR; a; b; G; n; h)$. To generate a key pair, entity Alice does the following (Barker, Johnson, & Smid, 2007):

1. Selects a random or pseudorandom integer d in the interval $(1, n-1)$
2. Computes $Q = d * G$
3. Makes Q the public key, Pub_A, and d the private key, $Priv_A$
4. Checks that x_G and y_G are elements of the elliptic curve equation by calculating
    $$y_Q^2 \equiv x_Q^3 + ax_Q + b \mod p \text{ or } y_Q^2 + x_Q y_Q = x_Q^3 + ax_Q + b \text{ in } F_{2^m}$$
5. Check that $nQ = O$

Table 8 -1 shows all the points on the curve $y^2 = x^3 + x + 1$ (mod 23) with their point orders. Since n should be a prime factor of $\#E(F_{23})$, a point with an order of 7 should be selected. The cofactor h is equal to 28 / 7 = 4.

The point G could be (5, 19), one of the several points with $n = 7$. The domain parameters, $T = (p; a; b; G; n; h)$, are $T = [23; 1; 1; (5, 19); 7, 4]$.

Select $d = 4$, so $Q = 4$ (5, 19). After adding the point (5, 19) to itself four times, the result is $Q = 4$ (5, 19) = (13, 16).

Alice's public key is $Pub_A = Q = (13, 16)$ and her private key is $Priv_A = 4$.

Check the public key:

1. $y_Q{}^2 \equiv x_Q{}^3 + ax_Q + b \mod p$

    $16^2 \mod 23 \equiv 13^3 + 13 + 1 \mod 23$

    $3 \mod 23 \equiv 12 \mod 23 + 14 \mod 23 \equiv 3 \mod 23$

2. $nQ = O; 7 (13, 16) = O$

Enciphering and Deciphering a Message Using ElGamal

The procedure to encipher a message is as shown in the exchange between Alice and Bob:

1. Alice generates her domain parameters $T = (p; a; b; G; n; h)$ and public key, $Pub_A \equiv Priv_A * G \mod p$, and sends them to Bob. For this example, Alice's domain

Figure 8-7. EC encryption using ElGamal

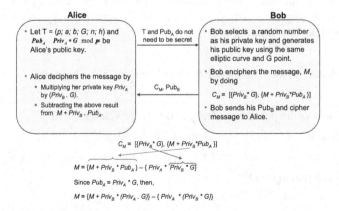

parameters are $T = [23; 1; 1; (5, 19); 7; 4]$, the private key is 6, and the public key is $Pub_A \equiv 6*(5, 19) \mod 23 \equiv (5, 4) \mod 23$.

2. Bob selects a random number, $Priv_B$, for example, 5.

3. Bob converts the message M, which is represented as an integer in binary into an octet string, and then into a field element point. The resulting point does not need to be one of the points of the curve, but it needs to be in the finite group F_{23}. In this example, the message $M = (8,20)$ is not one of the points in Table 8-1, but the x_m and y_m values of M are lower than 23, meaning that they are in the finite group of F_{23}.

4. Bob enciphers the message as follows:

$$C_M = [\{Priv_B * G\}, \{M + Priv_B * Pub_A\}]$$
$$C_M = [\{5*(5, 19)\}, \{(8, 20) + 5*(5, 4)\}]$$
$$C_M = [\{(17,20)\}, \{(8, 20) + (17, 3)\}] = [\{(17, 20)\}, \{(1, 0)\}]$$

Alice deciphers the message as follows:

1. Multiplies her private key $Priv_A$ by $(Priv_B . G)$

2. Subtracts the above result from $M + Priv_B . Pub_A$

$$M = \{M + Priv_B * Pub_A\} - \{Priv_A * Priv_B * G\}$$

Since $Pub_A = Priv_A * G$, then,

$$M = \{M + Priv_B * (Priv_A . G)\} - \{Priv_A * (Priv_B * G)\}.$$

For this example:

$$M = [\{(1, 0)\} - \{6*(17, 20)\}] = [\{(1, 0)\} - \{(17, 3)\}]$$
$$M = [\{(1, 0)\} + \{(17, -3)\}] = [8, 20]$$

Figure 8-8. EC key agreement using Diffie-Hellman

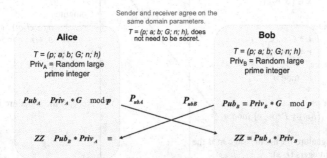

ECDH Key Agreement

In a key agreement scheme, each party combines thier own private key with the other party's public key to come up with a secret key, which will later be used in a symmetric cryptosystem. The IEEE P1363 (2007) calls this procedure DL/ECKAS-DH1, the *Discrete Logarithm and Elliptic Curve Key Agreement Scheme*, Diffie-Hellman, but it is also known as ECDH and ECDHE (Ephemeral).

The procedure to exchange a key using Diffie-Hellman is as follows:

1. Sender and receiver, Alice and Bob, agree on the elliptic curve domain parameters $T = (p; a; b; G; n; h)$, which do not need to be kept secret. For this example, the domain parameters are $T = [23; 1; 1; (5, 19); 7; 4]$.

2. When communication between Alice and Bob is established, they randomly generate secret numbers $Priv_A$ and $Priv_B$ and their corresponding public keys, as:

   $Pub_A \equiv Priv_A * G \mod p$ and $Pub_B \equiv Priv_B * G \mod p$.

   For this numerical example, $Pub_A \equiv 6 * (5, 19) \mod 23 \equiv (5, 4) \mod 23$

   and, $Pub_B \equiv 2 * (5, 19) \mod 23 \equiv (17, 23) \mod 23$

3. Alice and Bob exchange Pub_A and Pub_B over the nonsecure channel.

4. Alice computes ZZ, the shared secret value, by:

   $ZZ \equiv Pub_B * Priv_A \quad ZZ \equiv (17, 3) * 6 \mod 23 \equiv (17, 20) \mod 23$

5. Bob computes z, the shared secret value, by:

   $ZZ \equiv Pub_A * Priv_B \quad ZZ \equiv (5, 4) * 2 \mod 23 \equiv (17, 20) \mod 23$

Figure 8-9. ECCDSA signature generation and verification

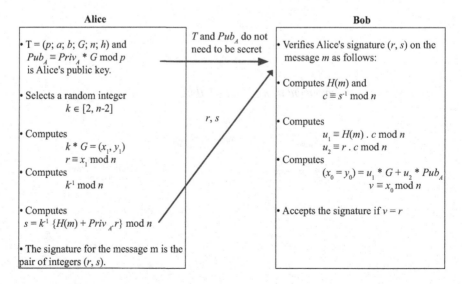

6.   Alice and Bob convert the shared secret value z to an octet string ZZ and use ZZ as the shared secret key for symmetric encryption algorithms to secure their communications.

ECDSA Signature Generation

Let E be the elliptic curve that satisfies the equation $y^2 + xy = x^3 + ax^2 + b$ or $y^2 = x^3 + ax + b$ with $T = (q; FR; a, b; G; n; h)$ as its domain parameters. Also, let Alice, the signer, create her private key such that $Pub_A = Priv_A . G \mod p$. Further, let Bob, the recipient, have authentic copies of the domain parameters and Alice's public key. For a numerical example, the same domain parameters $T = [23; 1; 1; (5, 19); 7; 4]$ will be used.

Alice signs the message m as follows:

1.   Selects a random integer $k \in [2, n-2]$. In this example, $k = 3$.

2.   Computes $k * G = (x_1, y_1)$ in the way that the Pub_A was calculated; converts x_1 to an integer, and then calculates $r \equiv x_1 \mod n$. If $r = 0$, Alice would go to step 1. For this numerical example, $(x_1, y_1) = k . G = 3 . (5, 19) = (13, 7); r \equiv 13 \mod 7 \equiv 6 \mod 7$

3.   Computes k^{-1}; $3^{-1} \mod 7 \equiv -2 \mod 7 \equiv 5 \mod 7$.

4.   Compute $s = k^{-1} \{H(m) + Priv_A.r\} \mod n$.

      H is the secure hash algorithm SHA. In this example, assume $H(m) = 10$.

      $Priv_A$ is Alice's private key, in this case, 5.

      $s \equiv 5(8 + 6.6) \mod 7 \equiv 220 \mod 7 \equiv 3 \mod 7$

      If $s = 0$, then Alice would go to step 1.

      The signature for the message m is the pair of integers (r, s), $(6, 3)$.

ECDSA Signature Verification

Bob verifies Alice's signature (r, s) in the message m as follows:

1.   Computes $c \equiv s^{-1} \mod n$ and $H(m)$.

      $c \equiv 3^{-1} \mod 7 \equiv -2 \mod 7 \equiv 5 \mod 7$

2.   Computes $u_1 \equiv H(m) . c \mod n$ and $u_2 \equiv r . c \mod n$

      $u_1 \equiv 8.5 \mod 7 \equiv 5 \mod 7$ and $u_2\, 6.5 \mod 7 \equiv 2 \mod 7$

3.   Computes $(x_0, y_o) = u_1 * G + u_2 * Pub_A$, convert x_0 to an integer, and calculate $v \equiv x_0 \mod n$

$(x_0, y_o) = 5 . (5, 19) + 2 . (5, 4) = (17, 20) + (17, 20) = (13, 7)$

$v \equiv x_0 \bmod p = 13 \bmod 7 \equiv 6 \bmod 7$

4.   Accepts the signature if $v = r$. In this numerical example, $v = 6 \bmod 7 = r$.

EC Cipher Suites

There are many algorithms that can be used for encryption, key exchange, message digest, and authentication; the level of security for each of these algorithms varies. Establishing a connection between two entities requires that they tell each other what crypto algorithms they understand. Normally one of the entities involved in the communication proposes a list of algorithms, and the other entity selects the algorithms supported by both. The selected algorithms may not have matching levels of security, reducing the overall security of the communication.

A cipher suite is a collection of cryptographic algorithms that matches the level of security of all the algorithms listed in the cipher suite. To enable secure communications between two entities, they exchange information about which cipher suites they have in common, and they then use the cipher suite that offers the highest level of security.

At the 2005 RSA conference, NSA introduced a common set of elliptic curve cryptographic algorithms for hashing, digital signatures, and key exchanges with the intention of protecting both classified and unclassified national security systems and information. NSA's goal in introducing Suite B EC Cryptographic Algorithms was to provide a common set of elliptic curves to developers of commercial products to design products that would be used both in government and commercially. NSA proposed that Suite B Cryptography include the following algorithms (NSA, n.d. a):

Encryption

Advanced Encryption Standard (AES) - FIPS 197 (with keys sizes of 128 and 256 bits)

Digital Signature

Elliptic Curve Digital Signature Algorithm - FIPS 186-2 (using the curves with 256 and 384-bit prime modulo)

Key Exchange

Elliptic Curve Diffie-Hellman or Elliptic Curve MQV Draft NIST Special Publication 800-56 (using the curves with 256 and 384-bit prime modulo)

Hashing

Secure Hash Algorithm - FIPS 180-2 (using SHA-256 and SHA-384)

A cipher suite may look like this:

CipherSuite TLS_ECDHE_ECDSA_WITH_AES_256_CBC_SHA384

This cipher suite means, "Use TLS protocol with Elliptic Curve Diffie-Hellman Ephemeral for key exchange, use Elliptic Curve Digital Signature Algorithm for digital signatures, use 256-bit AES for data encryption and use SHA384 for hashing (integrity).

The following is a list of some ECC Cipher Suites:

HMAC-Based Cipher Suites

The first group of four cipher suites uses AES in CBC mode with an HMAC-based MAC:

CipherSuite TLS_ECDHE_ECDSA_WITH_AES_128_CBC_SHA256

CipherSuite TLS_ECDHE_ECDSA_WITH_AES_256_CBC_SHA384

CipherSuite TLS_ECDH_ECDSA_WITH_AES_128_CBC_SHA256

CipherSuite TLS_ECDH_ECDSA_WITH_AES_256_CBC_SHA384

Galois Counter Mode-Based Cipher Suites

The second group of four cipher suites uses the new authenticated encryption modes defined in TLS 1.2 with AES in Galois Counter Mode (GCM):

CipherSuite TLS_ECDHE_ECDSA_WITH_AES_128_GCM_SHA256

CipherSuite TLS_ECDHE_ECDSA_WITH_AES_256_GCM_SHA384

CipherSuite TLS_ECDH_ECDSA_WITH_AES_128_GCM_SHA256

CipherSuite TLS_ECDH_ECDSA_WITH_AES_256_GCM_SHA384

The Elliptic Curve Digital Signature Algorithm (ECDSA) is the elliptic curve analogue of the DSA signature method as described in FIPS-186-3. Elliptic Curve Diffie-Hellman (ECDH) is a key agreement protocol variant of the Diffie-Hellman protocol using elliptic curve cryptography.

Summary

Today, public key systems such as RSA and Diffie Hellman use 1024-bit parameters; however, the US National Institute for Standards and Technology has recommended that these 1024-bit systems should not be used after the year 2010. Also, the National Institute of Standards and Technology recommends that when using AES 128, 192, or 256, the RSA and Diffie-Hellman key sizes should be of 3072, 7680, or 15360 bits in order to be able to provide equivalent security. For the same equivalent security, elliptic curve cryptosystems only require 256, 384, or 521 bits.

Because of their smaller key size, elliptic curve cryptosystems are more computationally efficient than RSA and Diffie-Hellman and require a much smaller number of bits transmitted to perform key exchanges.

The US government has already made the decision to move to elliptic curve crypto systems (National Security Agency (NSA), n.d. b). The National Institute of Standards and Technology (NIST) has standardized on 15 elliptic curves, ten of them for binary fields, and five for prime fields. In the next ten years, the US Department of Defense will replace all existing crypto equipment with elliptic curve crypto systems. To facilitate the transition to elliptic curve crypto systems, the National Security Agency purchased a license from Certicom that covers all intellectual properties for elliptic curve crypto systems using prime field curves with 256, 384, or 521 bits. It seems that commercial vendors of cryptosystems will not have to pay royalties to Certicom (2005) when they are selling equipment to the government that uses elliptic curve cryptosystems with 256, 384, or 521 bits; however, it is recommended that NSA be contacted directly to discuss patents and royalties on this issue.

Learning Objectives Review

1. What are the negatives of the following elliptic curve points over real numbers? $P(-3,-5)$, $R(3,7)$, $-P(-3,5)$, $-R(3,-7)$

2. Given two points P and Q, a line through them meets the curve at a third point R. (T/F)

3. The point $P(8, 5)$ is a point on the elliptic curve $y^2 = x^3 - 10x - 3$. (T/F)

4. Does the point $P(4, 5)$ lie on the elliptic curve $y^2 \equiv x^3 + x - 26 \pmod{13}$? (Yes/No)

5. In ECC, $Q = k * P$ is an operation that is easy to compute but very difficult and time consuming to reverse. (T/F)

6. The order of a point P is the largest positive number k such that $kP = O$. (T/F)

7. ECC provides better security than RSA. (T/F)

8. The point order of an elliptic curve used for encryption should be the largest prime number n that divides $\#E(F_p)$. (T/F)

9. The domain parameter $T = (q; FR; a, b; G; n; h)$ precisely specifies an elliptic curve and a base point. (T/F)

10. ECC can be used for digital signature, encryption, key agreement, and integrity. (T/F)

11. Name two essential properties of group fields when they are used in elliptic curve cryptography.

12. Elliptic curve domain parameters should not be made public because the security of the system relies on these parameters being secret. (T/F)

13. Elliptic curve cryptography requires a larger key size in order to offer the same level of security as the RSA algorithm. (T/F)

14. Which encryption algorithm is best suited for communication with handheld wireless devices?

   a. ECC

   b. RSA

   c. SHA

   d. RC4

15. Why or why not is the ECC encryption algorithm best suited for handheld wireless devices?

16. Define point order in elliptic curves.

17. Define curve order in elliptic curves.

18. In general, an ECC key bit-size of 160 is equivalent to:

   a. RSA 512 key-bit size

   b. RSA 1024 key-bit size

   c. Diffie-Hellman 768 key-bit size

19. In ECC, a public key is generated by adding the point G to itself d times and the result is a point $Q = d * G$. Then k is made public and Q is kept private. (T/F)

20. A field $F(2^7)$ consists of _____ elements.

References

Barker, E., Johnson, D., & Smid, M. (2007). *Recommendation for pair-wise key establishment schemes using discrete logarithm cryptography* (NIST SP 800-56A). National Institute of Standard and Technology (NIST). Retrieved June 28, 2007, from http://csrc.nist.gov/publications/nistpubs/800-56A/SP800-56A_Revision1_Mar08-2007.pdf

Blake, I., Seroussi, G., & Smart, N. (1999). *Elliptic curves in cryptography*. Cambridge, UK: Cambridge University Press.

Brown, M., Cheung, D., Hankerson, D., Lopez, J., Kirkup, M., & Menezes, A. (2000). PGP in constrained wireless devices. In *Proceedings of the 9th USENIX Security Symposium*.

Cryptomathic. (2003). *Elliptic curve online key generation*. Retrieved June 28, 2007, from http://www.cryptomathic.com/labs/ellipticcurvedemo.html#Key-Generation

Certicom. (n.d.). *Elliptic curve tutorial*. Retrieved June 28, 2007, from http://www.certicom.com/research/online.html

Certicom. (2004). *Elliptic curve cryptography challenge winner* (Press release). Retrieved June 28, 2007, from http://www.certicom.com/index.php?action=company,press_archive&view=307

Certicom. (2005). *FAQ: The National Security Agency's ECC License Agreement with Certicom Corp*. Retrieved June 28, 2007, from http://www.certicom.com/download/aid-501/FAQ-The%20NSA%20ECC%20License%20Agreement.pdf

Federal Information Processing Standards (FIPS). (2000). *Digital signature standard (DSS)* (FIPS PUB 186-2 (+Change Notice)). Retrieved June 28, 2007, from http://csrc.nist.gov/publications/fips/fips186-2/fips186-2-change1.pdf

Institute of Electrical and Electronic Engineers (IEEE). (2007). *Standard specifications for public key cryptography* (IEEE Standard P1363.1).

Johnson, D., & Menezes, A. (1999). *The Elliptic Curve Digital Signature Algorithm (ECDSA)*. Retrieved June 28, 2007, from http://citeseer.ist.psu.edu/johnson99elliptic.html

Koblitz, N. (1994). *A course in number theory and cryptography* (3rd ed.). New York: Springer-Verlag.

Lenstra, A., & Verheul, E. (1999). Selecting cryptographic key sizes. *The Journal of Cryptology*. Springer-Verlag. Retrieved June 28, 2007, from http://citeseer.ist.psu.edu/287428.html

Lopez, J., & Dahab, R. (2000). *An overview of elliptic curve cryptography*. Sao Paulo, Brazil: University of Campinas, Institute of Computing. Retrieved June 28, 2007, from http://citeseer.ist.psu.edu/333066.html

Menezes, A., Okamoto, T., & Vanstone, S. (1993). Reducing elliptic curve logarithms to logarithms in a finite field. *IEEE Transaction on Information Theory 39*(5), 1639-1646.

National Security Agency (NSA). (n.d. a) NSA Suite B cryptography. June 28, 2007, from http://www.nsa.gov/ia/industry/crypto_suite_b.cfm

National Security Agency (NSA). (n.d. b). *The case for elliptic curve cryptography*. Retrieved June 28, 2007, from http://www.nsa.gov/ia/industry/crypto_elliptic_curve.cfm?MenuID=10.2.7

Standards for Efficient Cryptography Group (SECG). (2000a). *Elliptic curve cryptograph (SEC1)*. Certicom Research. Retrieved June 28, 2007, from http://www.secg.org/collateral/sec1_final.pdf

Standards for Efficient Cryptography Group (SECG). (2000b). *Recommended elliptic curve domain parameters (SEC 2)*. Certicom Research. Retrieved June 28, 2007, from http://www.secg.org/collateral/sec2_final.pdf

Vo, S. (2003). *A survey of elliptic curve cryptosystems* (NAS-03-012). NASA's Advanced Supercomputing (NAS) Division. Retrieved on June 28, 2007, from http://www.nas.nasa.gov/News/Techreports/2003/PDF/nas-03-012.pdf

Chapter IX

Certificates and Public Key Infrastructure

Certificates and Public Key Infrestructure

In public-key encryption, the secrecy of the public key is not required, but the authenticity of the public key is necessary to guarantee its integrity and to avoid spoofing and playback attacks. A user's public key can be authenticated (signed) by a certificate authority that verifies that a public key belongs to a specific user. In this chapter, digital certificates, which are used to validate public keys, and certificate authorities are discussed.

When public-key is used, it is necessary to have a comprehensive system that provides public key encryption and digital signature services to ensure confidentiality, access control, data integrity, authentication, and non-repudiation. That system, *public-key infrastructure* or *PKI*, is also discussed in this chapter.

Objectives

- Be able to discuss the purpose and value of certificates and the process of certification
- Understand the certificate life cycles and how PKI manages the complete life cycle of certificates
- Be able to choose the appropriate trust model for a system

Introduction

The secrecy of a public key is not required, but its authenticity is necessary to guarantee its integrity and to avoid spoofing and playback attacks. If an attacker could replace an organization's public key with his own public key, then the secret information intended for an organization would be available to the attacker. The attacker could receive the information, decipher it, and send it on to the organization. A spoofer could, also, intercept the communications of two organizations and make them believe that they are talking to each other when, in reality, they are talking to the intruder.

The public key of each user can be authenticated (signed) by a certificate authority. The certificate authority only certifies one public key number for each user. When the network is established, when a user is added to the network, or when a user changes the user's public key, the public key is certified by a certificate authority. After the certification, the user can send the certified public-key number to any other user who can then verify its authenticity.

It is also possible to make the certificate a function not only of the user's public key, but, also, of an identification block. The block identifies, for example, the user's computer serial number, the user's telephone number, the network, the certificate number, the expiration date of the certificate, and certain authorizations. The certificate is created by linking the public key and the identification block. When two users establish communications, their certificates are exchanged, thereby validating their identification.

The public-key components and the identification block of a user could be written to a smart card. Using the smart card, the components could be physically (or electronically) transported to a certified authority where the certificate is generated and loaded back into the smart card. The certificate stored in the smart card would then be loaded into the user's computer.

Figure 9-1. Certification

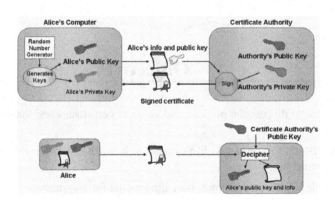

X.509 Basic Certificate Fields

X.509 is the most widely used certificate format for PKI. It is used in SSL, IPsec, S/MIME, SET, and now on PGP. RFC 4325 (Santesson & Housley, 2005) lists the following X.509 certificate basic fields:

- **Version:** This field gives the version of the encoded certificate.

- **Certificate serial number:** The serial number is a unique positive integer assigned by the CA to each certificate. Certificate users must be able to support serial number values up to 20 octets.

- **Signature algorithm identifier:** This field contains the algorithm identifier for the algorithm used by the CA to digitally sign the certificate. The algorithm could be RSA or DSA.

- **CA issuer name:** The issuer field identifies the certification authority that has signed and issued the certificate.

- **Validity period:** The validity period field is the time interval during which the CA certifies that it will maintain information about the status of the certificate. The field is represented as a sequence of two dates: the date on which the certificate validity period begins and the date on which the certificate validity period ends.

- **Subject name:** The subject field identifies the entity whose public key is authenticated.

- **Subject public-key information:** This field is used to carry the public key and public-key parameters, as well as the identifier of the public-key algorithm used (e.g., RSA, DSA, or Diffie-Hellman).

- **Issuer unique ID:** This is an optional field used to allow the reuse of issuer names over time.

- **Subject unique ID:** This is an optional field used to allow the reuse of subject names over time.

- **Extensions:** This field must appear only if the certificate version is 3. The extensions defined for X.509 v3 certificates provide methods for associating additional attributes with users or public keys and for managing a certification hierarchy, such as CA Key Identifier and Subject Key Identifier.

The information from the above fields is signed using the CA's private key. The CA's digital signature and the information from the above fields are (1) concatenated; (2) written using a syntax notation system called *Abstract Syntax One*; (3) converted into binary data using distinguish encoding rules (DER) encoding system; and then (4) converted to ASCII characters using base-64 encoding.

Figure 9-2. X.509 fields

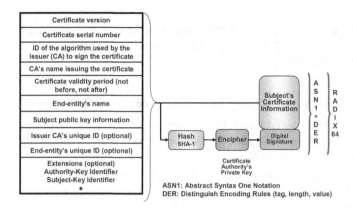

RSA Certification

In the RSA certification, the certificate authority generates its own secret prime numbers p_{ca} and q_{ca}, its own secret encryption exponent $Priv_{ca}$, and its corresponding public decryption exponent Pub^{ca}.

The certificate authority's public numbers Pub^{ca} and N_{ca} ($N_{ca} = p_{ca} \cdot q_{ca}$) are provided to all users in the network so everybody has these numbers available. The bit length of N_{ca} should be greater than all users' public numbers.

The CA certifies Alice's public key and identification number by computing the certificate public number of A:

$$C_{Alice} = (Ident_{Alice}\ Pub_{Alice})^{Priv_{ca}} \bmod N_{CA}$$

Equation 9-1

Upon receiving the certificate, Alice's computer verifies the certificate by checking:

$$(Ident_{Alice},\ Pub_{Alice}) = C_{Alice}{}^{Pub_{ca}} \bmod N_{CA}$$

Equation 9-2

When Alice wants to establish a secure communication with any computer, Alice will send her certificate C_A to the other computer and since all the computers have Pub_{ca} and N_{ca}, then Bob's computer, the receiving computer, can obtain $Ident_A$ and Pub_A by calculating:

$$(Ident_{Alice},\ Pub_{Alice}) = (C_{Alice})^{Pub_{CA}} \bmod N_{CA}$$

Equation 9-3

Cylink (Seek) Certification

For the Cylink (SEEK) certification (Newman, Omura, & Pickholtz, 1987), make a and p the same for all computers and for the certificate authority. The number a is a random number and p a strong prime, such as $p = 2q + 1$, with q being a prime.

The certificate authority generates its own Pub_{ca} and $Priv_{ca}$, according to Diffie-Hellman:

$$Pub_{ca} = a^{Priv_{ca}} \bmod p \qquad \text{Equation 9-4}$$

The CA certifies Alice's public key and identification number by computing the certificate public number of A:

$$M_A = Pub_A^{Ident_A} \bmod p \qquad \text{Equation 9-5}$$

and randomly generates a secret certification number R_A for Alice; then the CA computes its corresponding public number

$$C_{caA} = a^{R_A} \bmod p \qquad \text{Equation 9-6}$$

and, finally, computes a number V_A that can satisfy the following equation:

$$M_A = [\ Priv_{ca}\, C_{caA} + R_A V_A\ ] \bmod (p - 1). \qquad \text{Equation 9-7}$$

The certificate authority sends C_A and V_A back to Alice, who checks that the certification was done by a certificate authority by computing:

$$M_A = Pub_A^{Ident_A} \bmod p \qquad \text{Equation 9-8}$$

$$a^{M_A} \bmod p \qquad \text{Equation 9-9}$$

$$Pub_{ca} \bmod p \qquad \text{Equation 9-10}$$

$$C_{caA} \bmod p \qquad \text{Equation 9-11}$$

$$S_A = (\ Pub_{ca}^{C_{caA}} \bmod p\ )\ (\ C_{caA}^{V_A} \bmod p\ ) \bmod p \qquad \text{Equation 9-12}$$

and verifying the relationship

$$S_A = a^{M_A} \bmod p \qquad \text{Equation 9-13}$$

To prove that $a^{M_A} \bmod p = (\ Pub_{ca}^{C_{caA}} \bmod p\ )(\ C_{caA}^{V_A} \bmod p\ ) \bmod p$:

Equation 9-4 and 9-6 are replaced in Equation 9-12

$$S_A = [(\ a^{Priv_{ca}} \bmod p\ )^{C_{caA}} \bmod p\ ]\ [(\ a^{R_A \bmod p}\ )^{V_A} \bmod p\ ] \bmod p$$

$$S_A = (\ a^{Priv_{ca} C_{caA} + R_A V_A}\ ) \bmod p$$

and, since $a^{\ x \bmod (p-1)} = a^x \bmod p$ then,

$$[\ a^{(Priv_{ca} C_{caA} + R_A V_A) \bmod (p-1)}\ ] \bmod p = [\ a^{Priv_{ca} C_{caA} + R_A V_A}\ ] \bmod p$$

When Alice wants to establish a secure communication with Bob, she will send her certificate C_{caA}, her public key Pub_A, V_A and M_A to Bob. Since both computers have a, p, and Pub_{ca}, Bob can authenticate Alice's certificate by calculating:

$$S_B = (Pub_{ca}{}^{C_{caA}} \bmod p) \, (C_{caA}{}^{V_A} \bmod p) \bmod p$$

and verifying that

$$S_B = a^{M_A} \bmod p.$$

In this technique, the receiving computer cannot deduce, compute, or find Alice's identification.

Cylink Certification Based on ElGamal

Using Cylink certification based on ElGamal, a and p are the same for all computers and for the certificate authority. The number a is a random number and p a strong prime such as $p = 2q + 1$; q is a prime.

The certificate authority generates its own Pub^{ca} and $Priv^{ca}$; according to Diffie-Hellman:

$$Pub_{ca} = a^{Priv_{ca}} \bmod p.$$

Equation 9-14

At the moment of generating the certificate for Alice, the certificate authority generates a secret number R:

$$R_A$$

and the public number V:

$$V_{caA} = a^{R_{caA}} \bmod p.$$

Equation 9-15

The hash function is calculated by:

Equation 9-16

$$H_{caA} = Hash(M_A, V_{caA})$$

where M_A is Alice's signed message.

The certificate authority calculates the digital signature by:

$$S_{caA} = (R_{caA} + H_{caA} \, Priv_A) \bmod p.$$

Equation 9-17

The digital signature, S_{caA}, the hash function, H_{caA}, and the number V for Alice, V_{caA}, are loaded into Alice's computer. Alice verifies the certificate by verifying the relationship:

$$a^{S_{caA}} \bmod p = V_{caA} \, Pub_A^{H_{caA}} \bmod p.$$

Equation 9-18

This procedure is carried out for all computers.

The following information needs to be installed in Alice's and Bob's computers for them to work in public key with certification:

Alice	Bob
$Priv_A$	$Priv_B$
Pub_A	Pub_B
M_A	M_B
Sj_{caA}	S_{caB}
V_{caA}	V_{caB}
Pub_{ca}	
Pub_{ca}	

Both computers exchange the following information:

$$M_A, Pub_A, S_{caA}, V_{caA} \quad \rightarrow$$
$$\leftarrow \quad M_B, Pub_B, S_{caB}, V_{caB}$$

Each computer corroborates the authenticity of the other computer's certificate by calculating:

Alice	Bob
$H_{caB} = Hash(\, M_B, V_{caB}\,)$	$H_{caA} = Hash(\, M_A, V_{caA}\,)$
$a^{S_{caB}} \bmod p = V_{caB} \, Pub_B^{H_{caB}} \bmod p$	$a^{S_{caA}} \bmod p = V_{caA} \, Pub_A^{H_{caA}} \bmod p$

If both computers are able to corroborate the equality, then both computers know that the certificates come from the certificate authority and the authenticity of Alice and Bob are verified.

Variation of ElGamal Certification

This digital signature is a variation of the ElGamal digital signature. The differences between the two are the way in which the signature S is calculated, and how the authenticity of the signature is computed.

The certificate authority generates its Pub_{ca} and $Priv_{ca}$, according to Diffie-Hellman, with the condition that p is chosen such that $p-1$ has at least one large prime factor.

$$Pub_{ca} = g^{Priv_{ca}} \mod p$$

Equation 9-19

To install the certificate generated by the certificate authority in Alice's computer, first the identification of Alice's computer $Ident_A$ is generated. The identification may consist of the computer's serial number, telephone number, Alice's name, and so forth. At the moment of generating the certificate, the certificate authority generates a secret number R:

$$R_A$$

and the public number V:

$$V_{caA} = g^{R_{caA}} \mod p.$$

Equation 9-20

The hash function is calculated by:

$$H_A = Hash(\,Ident_A,\,Pub_A,\,V_{caA}\,).$$ Equation 9-21

The certificate authority calculates the digital signature by:

$$S_{caA} = (\,R_{caA} * H_{caA} + V_{caA} * Priv_{ca}\,) \mod q$$

Equation 9-22

where $q = p - 1$.

As can be seen, the private key $Priv_{ca}$ of the certificate authority is part of the digital signature. This verifies that the certificate authority has authenticated the digital signature.

The digital signature S_{caA} and the number V for Alice, V_{caA}, are loaded into Alice's computer. This procedure is carried out for all computers.

The following information needs to be installed into Alice's and Bob's computers for them to work in public key with certification:

Alice	Bob
$Priv_A$	$Priv_B$
Pub_A	Pub_B
$Ident_A$	$Ident_B$
S_{caA}	S_{caB}
V_{caA}	V_{caB}
Pub_{ca}	Pub_{ca}

Both computers exchange the following information:

$$Ident_A, Pub_A, S_{caA}, V_{caA} \quad \rightarrow$$

$$\leftarrow \quad Ident_B, Pub_B, S_{caB}, V_{caB}$$

Each computer corroborates the certificate's authenticity with the following equation:

Alice   **Bob**

$$g^{S_{caB}} \bmod p = (V_{caB}{}^{H_B} * Pub_{ca}{}^{V_{caB}}) \bmod p \quad \rightarrow \qquad \text{Equation 9-23}$$

$$\leftarrow g^{S_{caA}} \bmod p = (V_{caA}{}^{H_A} * Pub_{ca}{}^{V_{caA}}) \bmod p$$

If both computers are able to corroborate the equality, then both computers know that the certificate comes from the certificate authority, and the authenticity of Alice and Bob is verified.

Demonstration that $g^{S_{caA}} \bmod p = (V_{caA}{}^{H_A} * Pub_{ca}{}^{V_{caA}}) \bmod p$.

By replacing S_{caA} from Equation 9-22 in $a^{S_{caA}}$, it can be written that:

$$g^{S_{caA}} \bmod p = a^{(R_{caA} * H_A + V_{caA} * Priv_{ca}) \bmod q} \bmod p. \qquad \text{Equation 9-24}$$

Since $q = p - 1$ and, according to equation $g^{x \bmod p - 1} \bmod p = g^x \bmod p$,
Equation 9-24 can be written as follows:

$$g^{S_{caA}} \bmod p = a^{(R_{caA} * H_A + V_{caA} * Priv_{ca})} \bmod p$$

$$g^{S_{caA}} \bmod p = [a^{(R_{caA} * H_A)}] * [a^{V_{caA} * Priv_{ca})}] \bmod p$$

$$g^{S_{caA}} \bmod p = [a^{R_{caA} * H_A} \bmod p] * [a^{V_{caA} * Priv_{ca}} \bmod p] \bmod p$$

$$g^{S_{caA}} \bmod p = [a^{R_{caA} * H_A} \bmod p] * [a^{V_{caA} * Priv_{ca}} \bmod p] \bmod p$$

$$g^{S_{caA}} \bmod p = [(a^{R_{caA}} \bmod p)^{H_A}] * [(a^{Priv_A} \bmod p)^{V_{caA}}] \bmod p$$

From Equations 9-19 and 9-20, it can be stated:

$$g^{S_{caA}} \bmod p = (V_{caA}{}^{H_A} * Pub_{ca}{}^{V_{caA}}) \bmod p.$$

This variation of ElGamal's certificate algorithm is more robust than other ElGamal versions because in:

$$g^{S_{caA}} \bmod p = (V_{caA}^{H_A} * Pub_{ca}^{V_{caA}}) \bmod p,$$

the factor V is included not only in the base, but, also, in the exponent.

Public-Key Infrastructure (PKI)

There are many applications available to implement communications or network security. When public key is used, however, it is necessary to have a comprehensive system that efficiently delivers security services such as confidentiality, access control, data integrity, authentication, and non-repudiation in a cohesive manner. That system is *Public-Key Infrastructure* or *PKI*. PKI enables organizations to set up and define secure networks by authenticating the validity of each person involved in a secure transaction, in a consistent manner, across a wide variety of applications.

In the next chapters, secure mail, IPsec, and SSL protocols will be discussed. The protocols specify how a specific process is carried out, but they do not describe how to manage keys and certificates on behalf of users and applications in a way that is transparent. The term transparency means that the end-users do not need to know how the complex process to manage keys and certificates is done, and the process is virtually transparent to them.

VPNs are the standard used to provide privacy, authentication, integrity, and non-repudiation. It may seem that if a corporation uses VPNs then it does not need PKI, but the reality is that VPNs and PKI are complementary.

The following are some of functions carried out by a PKI:

- Manages the complete life cycle of keys and certificates
- Provides key backup and recovery
- Updates automatic key pairs and certificates
- Manages key histories
- Supports cross certification

According to RFC 3647 (Chokhani, Ford, Sabett, Merril, & Wu, 2003), "Internet X.509 Public Key Infrastructure Certificate Policy and Certification Practices Framework," the following are the required elements for a usable PKI:

- A certificate authority
- A certificate repository
- A certificate revocation system
- Key backup recovery

- Support for non-repudiation of digital signatures
- Automatic update of key pairs and certificates
- Management of key histories
- Support for cross certification
- Open standards and support for legacy applications

PKI Management Model

RFC 4210 (Adams, Farrell, Kause, & Mononen, 2005), "PKI Certificate Management Protocols," indicates that there are four entities involved in PKI management. Those entities are (1) the PKI user, also called the *end-entity* (i.e., the entity to be named in the subject field of a certificate); (2) the certification authority (i.e., the entity named in the issuer field of a certificate); (3) a registration authority, which is an optional component of PKI management; and (4) the repository site.

End-Entities (PKI Users)

An end-entity is a user of PKI certificates and/or an end-user system that is the subject of a certificate. End-entities include not only human users of applications, but, also, applications themselves (e.g., for IP security). All end-entities require secure local access to some information—at a minimum, their own name and private key, the name of a CA, which is trusted by this entity, and that CA's public key (or a fingerprint of the public key when a self-certified version is available elsewhere).

According to RFC 3647 (Chokhani, Ford, Sabett, Merril, & Wu, 2003), the following are an end-entity's obligations:

- Accuracy of representations in certificate application
- Protection of the entity's private key
- Restrictions on private-key and certificate use
- Notification upon private-key compromise

The registration and authentication process is as follows (see Figure 9-3):

1. Alice registers with the certificate authority and applies for a certificate.
2. The CA verifies Alice's identity and issues a certificate.
3. The CA publishes the certificate at a repository site.

Figure 9-3. PKI and certificates

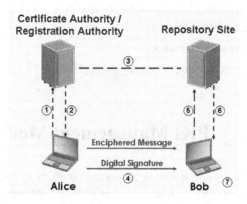

4.   Alice sends her enciphered message and certificate to Bob. The message was signed with Alice's private key to ensure authenticity, message integrity, and non-repudiation.

5.   After receiving the message, Bob goes to the repository site to check the authenticity of Alice's certificate.

6.   The repository site gives the status of Alice's certificate.

7.   Bob verifies the message's integrity using Alice's public key.

Certification Authority

As stated before, in public-key systems, the secrecy of the public key is not required, but the authenticity of the public key is necessary to guarantee its integrity and to avoid spoofing and playback attacks. The identity and public key of each PKI user can be authenticated (signed) by a certificate authority.

The term CA refers to the entity named in the issuer field of a certificate. A CA can issue several kinds of certificates including the following: user (end-entity) certificates, CA certificates (a certificate for itself or for another CA), and cross certificates (an authentication process across security domains). In general, an end-entity is certified by CA and that CA is certified by another CA. At some level, the chain should end, and it ends at the root CA that certifies itself. The term *root CA* is used to indicate a CA that is at the root of a structure similar to that of a tree.

The certification authority may or may not actually be a real "third party" from the end-entity's point of view. Quite often, the CA will actually belong to the same organization as the end-entities it supports. A security domain is the logical domain in which a CA issues and manages certificates, e.g., in a corporation it would be a department.

According to RFC 3647 (Chokhani, Ford, Sabett, Merril, & Wu, 2003), the following are the CA's and/or RA's obligations:

- Registering and accepting applications for certificates from end-users and other entities
- Issuing and notification of issuance of a certificate to the subscriber who is the subject of the certificate being issued
- Validating the entities' identities that are requesting certificates
- Notification of issuance of a certificate to others, other than the subject of the certificate
- Revoking, renewing, and suspension of a certificate and notification to the subscriber whose certificate is being revoked, renewed, or suspended
- Notification of revocation or suspension of a certificate to those other than the subject whose certificate is being revoked or suspended
- Publishing directories of valid and revoked certificates

Registration Authority (RA)

In addition to end-entities and CAs, many environments call for the existence of a registration authority separate from the certification authority. An RA is an optional system to which a CA delegates certain management functions. The functions will vary from case to case, but they may include end-entity verification process, personal authentication, token distribution, revocation reporting, name assignment, key generation, archival of key pairs, and so forth. The RA, however, does not issue certificates or CRLs.

Since the RA is an optional component, when it is not present, the CA is assumed to be able to carry out the RA's functions, so that the PKI management protocols are the same from the end-entity's point of view.

The RA is, in fact, another end-entity and all RAs are certified end-entities, meaning that they have private keys that are usable for signing. One RA may work with more than one CA. In some circumstances, end-entities will communicate directly with a CA even when an RA is present. For example, for initial registration and/or certification, the subject may use its RA, but communicate directly with the CA in order to refresh its certificate.

The RA's obligations are the same as the CA's.

Repository Site

The repository site is a system or collection of distributed systems that stores certificates and CRLs and serves as a means of distributing these certificates and CRLs to end-entities. CRLs are defined by the standard RFC 4325 (Santesson & Housley, 2005).

Certificates are stored at a repository site so that applications can retrieve them on behalf of a user. The term repository refers to a network service that stores and distributes information, in this case, certificates.

The certificate revocation list (CRL), which tracks expired certificates, is also stored in the repository site. As an option, in certain circumstances, a CA may delegate the publication of certificate revocation lists to a CRL Issuer.

According to RFC 3647 (Chokhani, Ford, Sabett, Merril, & Wu, 2003), the repository site obligation is the timely publication of certificates and revocation information.

PKI Management Requirements

The following are some of the PKI management requirements listed in RFC 4210 (Adams, Farrell, Kause, & Mononen, 2005) that should be implemented:

1. PKI management must conform to the ISO /IEC 9594 -8 / ITU – T X.509 standard.

2. It must be possible to update regularly any key pair without affecting any other key pair.

3. The use of confidentiality (encryption) in PKI management protocols could be kept at different levels in order to ease countries' regulatory problems.

4. PKI management protocols must allow the use of different industry-standard cryptographic algorithms, specifically including RSA, DSA, MD5, and SHA-1.

5. PKI management protocols must not preclude the generation of key pairs by the end-entity concerned, by an RA, or by a CA. Key generation may also occur elsewhere, but for the purpose of PKI management, it is assumed that key generation occurs whenever the key is first present at an end-entity, RA, or CA.

6. PKI management protocols must support the publication of certificates by the end-entity concerned, by an RA, or by a CA.

7. PKI management protocols must support the production of certificate revocation lists by allowing certified end-entities to make requests for the revocation of certificates.

8. PKI management protocols must be usable over a variety of "transport" mechanisms, including, specifically, mail, http, TCP/IP, and ftp.

9. The final authority for certification creation rests with the CA; no RA or end-entity equipment can assume that any certificate issued by a CA will contain what was requested. A CA may alter certificate field values or may add, delete or alter extensions according to its operating policy.

10. Whenever scheduled, noncompromised CA key updates should be supported.

11. The CA itself may, in some implementations or environments, carry out the functions of an RA.

12. When an end-entity requests a certificate containing a given public-key value, the end-entity must be ready to demonstrate possession of the corresponding private-key value.

Figure 9-4. Certificate life cycle

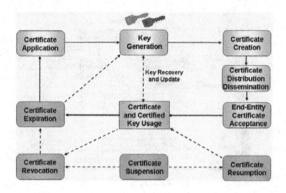

Certificate Life-Cycle

PKI is about managing certificates and keys during their complete life cycles and the entities involved (Adams & Lloyd, 2003). There are three phases in the life of a certificate and keys: initialization, issued, and cancellation.

Phase 1 Initialization	Phase 2 Issued	Phase 3 Cancellation
o **Key-pair generation** o **Registration** o **Certificate creation** o **Key & certificate distribution** o **Certificate dissemination** o **Key backup**	o **Certificate retrieval** o **Certificate validation** o **Key recovery** o **Key update** o **Certificate update**	o **Certificate suspension** o **Certificate expiration** o **Certificate revocation** o **Key history** o **Key archive**

PKI Management Operations

Figure 9-5 shows the relationships among PKI entities in terms of PKI management operations. The arrows in the diagram indicate protocols that take place in the different life cycle phases.

Processes Exchanged between End-Entity and CA

The processes exchanged between an end-entity and a CA are related to certification. These occur in two situations: at initialization, when a certificate is requested, and, after the certificate is issued.

Figure 9-5. PKI management operations

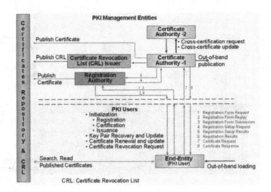

Initialization

Initialization refers to the process whereby an end-entity, which does not have a certificate from a CA contacts the CA or RA to get one. The end result of this process (when it is successful) is that a CA issues a certificate for an end-entity's public key, and then returns that certificate to the end-entity, and/or posts it in a public repository.

This process may, and typically will, involve multiple steps, possibly including an initialization of the end-entity's equipment. For example, the end-entity's equipment must be securely initialized with the public key of a CA to be able to be used in validating certificate paths. Furthermore, an end-entity typically needs to be initialized with its own key pair(s). The following are the initialization phase components:

1. **Registration:** Registration is the process in which the identity of the end-entity is established and verified, by either by the CA or the RA.

2. **Key pair generation:** Key pair generation is the process by which the public-key pair is generated by the end-entity, the RA, or by the CA. In some environments, a trusted party may generate the key pair. If the key pair is going to be used for non-repudiation, then it should be generated by the end-entity, the owner of the public-key pair.

3. **Certificate creation:** Certification creation is the process by which the CA creates the certificate. Only the CA can generate certificates.

4. **Certificate and key-pair distribution:** Certificate and key-pair distribution is the process of distributing the certificate to the end-entity. If the CA generated the key pair, then the key pair also needs to be sent to the end-entity.

5. **Certificate dissemination:** Certificate dissemination is the process by which the certificate is disseminated to the end-entity and to the repository site by the CA. The certificate can be sent to the end-entity using physical delivery; this is called *out-of-band distribution*. The certificate also can be sent to an end-entity application (S/MIME); this is called *in-band distribution*.

6. **Key backup (optional):** Key backup is the process of storing the key pair at a trusted third party's location.

Key-Pair Recovery and Update

Once the certificate has been generated and disseminated, an end-entity has an exchange process with a CA in two situations. Those situations are key recovery and key update. The key-pair recovery process allows end-entities to recover key material from a CA or RA when they lose key material or forget passwords, or when the devices where key material is stored get corrupted. This process implies that all key material is stored and available for backup.

There are two functions for public-key pairs. One pair is used to encipher and decipher data; this pair is called the *encryption pair*. The other pair is for digitally signing messages and verifying certificates and is called the *signing-key pair*. Key-pair backup and recovery refers to the encrypting-key pair; the organization can recover the end-entity private key if the key is lost or otherwise becomes inaccessible. Without back up and recovery, loss of a private key may mean loss of valuable data.

The backup and recovery of signing keys, however, should not be allowed because it destroys the basic requirement of non-repudiation. Non-repudiation is based on the requirement that the person who has access to the private key is under the sole control of the end-entity. When end-entities lose or corrupt their signing-key pair, it is acceptable to generate a new key pair.

The key-pair update process supports the regular update of every key pair. Key pairs need to be updated regularly (i.e., replaced with a new key pair), and a new certificate should be generated for the new key pair.

Certificate Renewal and Update

Certificates are assigned a valid time period. When a certificate expires, it can be renewed or updated. Renewal means that the public key and end-entity information remain the same and a new certificate is issued. Update means that a new public-key pair and end-entity information are generated and a new certificate is issued.

Certificate Revocation Request

When a certificate is issued, it is expected to be in use for its entire period of validity. However, various circumstances may cause a certificate to become invalid prior to its expiration date. The process of invalidating a certificate prior to its expiration date is called *certificate revocation*. The process is initiated by an authorized person who advises a CA of an abnormal situation requiring certificate revocation. It is not possible to detect by looking at a certificate whether it has been revoked or not, so it is a difficult process to keep up with all the revoked certificates.

Processes Exchanged Between CA and Repository

Two processes are exchanged between a CA and the repository site. These processes are called *certificate dissemination* and *revocation list.* Once the CA creates a certificate, or revokes a certificate, the CA needs to disseminate this information to the repository site for publication.

Certificate Dissemination

Certificate dissemination is the process by which a certificate is disseminated to the end-entity and to the repository site by the CA. Repository sites publishe certificates and CRL via Light Weight Directory Access Protocol LDAP (RFC 4510 – 19).

Revocation List

An end-entity or an authorized entity could request a key certificate revocation when the end-entity's private key has been compromised or when the end-entity is no longer part of the CA domain, for example, an employee who has left the organization.

After the certificate is revoked, the CA disseminates the revocation using certificate revocation lists. See the "CRL Basic Fields" section in this chapter for more information on CRLs.

Processes Exchanged Between CA and RA

As mentioned before in the *PKI* management model section, the functions of the RA vary, but, in general, include the end-entity verification process. Once the verification process is done, the RA submits to the CA registration setup request on behalf of the end-entity. The CA responds to the RA with a registration results. The RA sends registration results the end-entity, which submit a certificate request to the CA. The CA sends to the end-entity a certificate response. See Figure 9-5.

Another RA function is to publish the certificates issued, so this information must be passed from the CA to the RA.

Figure 9-6. Certificate path and validation

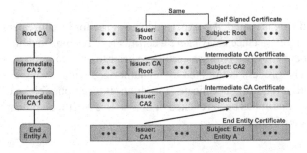

Processes Exchanged between End-Entity and Repository

There are two processes exchanged between an end-entity and a repository site. These processes are called *certification retrieval* and *certificate validation*.

Certification Retrieval

Certification retrieval is the process by which an end-entity retrieves an end-entity certificate to either (1) encrypt data destined for another end-entity using the public key included in the certificate, or (2) verify a digital signature received from another entity.

Certificate Validation

Once the certificate is retrieved, and before it is used, the end-entity needs to validate the certificate. The certificate validation includes the following assurance:

- The certificate was issued by a trusted CA. Validate the certificate.
- The certificate has not been changed. Check the integrity.
- The certificate has not expired. Check the validity time period as indicated by the parameters "Not Valid Before" and "Not Valid After."
- The certificate has not been revoked. Check the CRL.

Processes Exchanged Between CA1 and CA2

There are situations in which end-entity Alice has been certified by CA1 and end-entity Bob has been certified by CA2. Alice trusts only the certificates signed by CA1, and Bob trusts only the certificates signed by CA2. If Alice would like to certify Bob, it is not possible because Alice and Bob are in different domains. The mechanism of cross-certification, CA1 cross-certifies CA2, can be used to the extent that Alice trusts the end-entities certified by CA2, including Bob.

The processes exchanged between CA1 and CA2 are initiated when one CA requests issuance of a cross-certificate from the other CA. Specific types of cross certificates include the following: (1) inter-domain cross-certificate—when the subject and issuer CAs belong to different administrative domains; (2) intra-domain cross-certificate—when the CAs belong to the same domain.

When doing cross-certification, it is possible to set some controls. For example, the trust can be extended to certain groups within an organization within the other CA: a specific department, several groups, or to a limited number of end-entities. For example, organization "A" may set cross certification so that their customer account managers will only accept certificates from organization "B"s purchasing department.

CRL Basic Fields

The RFC 4325 (Santesson & Housley, 2005), "Internet X.509 Public Key Infrastructure Certificate and Certificate Revocation List (CRL) Profile," describes the format and semantics of certificates and certificate revocation lists (CRLs) for the Internet PKI.

X.509 defines one method of certificate revocation. This method involves every CA periodically issuing a signed data structure called a *certificate revocation list* (CRL). A CRL is a time-stamped list identifying revoked certificates; it is signed by a CA or CRL issuer and is made freely available in a public repository. Each revoked certificate is identified in a CRL by its certificate serial number. When a certificate-using system uses a certificate (e.g., for verifying a remote user's digital signature), that system not only checks the certificate's signature and validity, but also acquires a suitably-recent CRL and checks that the certificate serial number is not on that CRL.

In X.509, only the issuer of a certificate can revoke it. If the CA loses its private signing key, then it would not be able to produce CRLs nor perform normal key rollovers. CAs should maintain secure backup for signing keys. If the CA's private key is compromised by an attacker who obtains the private key unnoticed, the attacker might issue bogus certificates and CRLs, which would undermine confidence in the system. RFC 4325 recommends that if such a compromise is detected, all certificates issued by the compromised CA must be revoked, preventing services between its users and users of other CAs. Rebuilding after such a compromise will be problematic, so CAs are advised to implement a combination of strong technical measures (e.g., tamper-resistant cryptographic modules) and appropriate management procedures (e.g., separation of duties) to avoid such an incident.

RFC 4325 (Housley, Polk, Ford, & Solo, 2002; Santesson, & Housley, 2005) lists the following CRL basic fields:

- **Version**: This field describes the version of the encoded CRL. When the CRL is Version 2, this field must be present. For CRL Version 1, the field is not present.

- **Signature:** This field contains the algorithm identifier for the algorithm used to sign the CRL.

- **Issuer name:** The issuer name identifies the entity that signed and issued the CRL.

Figure 9-7. CRL fields

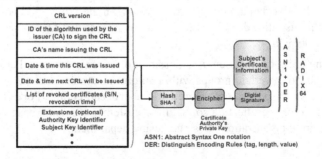

- **This update:** This field indicates the issue date of this CRL and may be encoded as "UTCTime" or "GeneralizedTime."

- **Next update:** This field indicates the date by which the next CRL will be issued. The next CRL could be issued before the indicated date, but it would not be issued any later than the indicated date.

- **Revoked certificates:** This field list all the certificates revoked during the time period between the previous CRL update and this update. When there are no revoked certificates, the revoked certificates list MUST be absent. Otherwise, revoked certificates are listed by their unique serial numbers. The date on which the revocation occurred is also specified.

- **Extensions:** This field may only appear if the version is 3. If present, this field is a sequence of one or more CRL extensions.

The information from the fields is signed using the CA's private key. The CA's digital signature and the information from above fields are (1) concatenated; (2) written using a syntax notation system, *Abstract Syntax One*, (3) converted into binary data using *distinguish encoding rules* (DER) encoding system, and then (4) converted to ASCII characters using base-64 encoding.

CA Trust Models

CAs act as agents of trust by validating PKI users' identity and public keys. All PKI users must have a registered identity. The concept is known as *third-party trust*; a PKI user can trust the certificate issued by a CA as long as the user trusts the CA. "Alice trusts Bob" means "Alice trusts the CA that signed Bob's certificate."

A security domain is the logical domain in which a CA issues and manages certificates, for example, in a corporation, a department. For example, if Alice and Bob work for the same corporation and are in the same department, they may have the same CA. If Alice and Bob are not in the same domain and work for different organizations, how can each of them establish trust?

Two end-entities can establish trust in each other by using one of several *trust models*. Those trust models are Hierarchy, Mesh, Web Model, and User Centric (Adams & Lloyd, 2003, pp. 131-149).

Hierarchical Trust Model

In a hierarchical trust model, the root CA is at the top, and below are several layers of intermediate CAs. The layer below the lowest layer of intermediate CAs consists of nonCAs, and end-entities or end users.

Each of the intermediate CAs is considered an entity. In this model, all entities in the hierarchy trust the root CA. The advantage of this model is that it is relatively simple to implement; the disadvantage is that it does not allow cross certification between CAs.

In Figure 9-8, entity A's certificate is signed by CA3 and entity F's certificate is signed by CA5. If A wants to communicate with F, but A and F do not trust each other, in order to establish trust, they need to find a CA that both trust, in this case, the Root CA. If end-entity H wants to certify end-entity F, it needs to go all the way to CA2 to do so.

Mesh Trust Model

In the section "Processes Exchanged between CAs," the concept of cross certification was explained. Cross-certification is the process of interconnecting Root CAs. In a mesh trust model, all root CAs are initially cross-certified with each other, or whenever their respective communities need to communicate with each other.

Trust List Model (Web Trust Model)

In terms of the number of users, the trust list, also called *Web model*, is the most widely used trust model. Firefox and Microsoft Explorer Web browsers are distributed with about 100 CA public keys pre-installed. Each browser user has a local file of trusted self-signed root certificates. The browsers normally are distributed with an initial set of root certificates, but users can add to this set or delete certificates from it. In addition, organizations may have provision for loading or managing the trust list from a central network management server. In the trust-list model, the Web browser acts as a virtual root CA because Web users trust the CA installed in their software.

The browsers can use the pre-installed certificates to sign, verify, encrypt and decrypt S/MIME e-mail messages and establish transport layer security (TLS) and secure socket layer (SSL) sessions. Browsers can also verify the signatures on signed codes.

For an end-user, managing the numerous trusted CA certificates installed in a browser is a very difficult task; besides, there is no practical way to prevent either users or others with

Figure 9-8. Hierarchical trust model

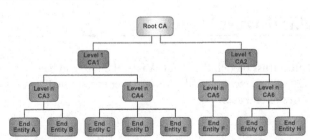

Figure 9-9. Mesh trust model

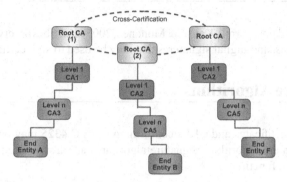

Figure 9-10. Web trust model

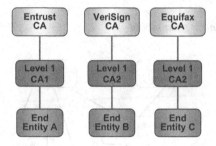

access to users' workstations from making unauthorized alterations to the list. The practice of distributing an initial file of such self-signed certificates with browser products, and the fact that there are only two leading browsers in the market, make the self-signed certificates included with the browsers the de facto CA accreditation.

In this model, there is no practical mechanism to revoke certificates. If Firefox or Microsoft make a mistake and install a "bad" CA, there is no way to revoke that certificate from the millions of Web browsers in use, unless MS and Firefox update the CA list.

User Centric Trust Model

Pretty good privacy (PGP) uses the user-centric trust model in a decentralized environment. In PGP, any user can act as a certifying authority and validate another PGP user's public-key certificate. However, a certificate generated by Alice, who is acting as CA, may not be valid to another user because he knows that Alice cannot be trusted as a CA. In the user-centric model, each user is directly responsible for deciding which certificates to accept and which ones to reject.

Encryption Algorithms Supported in PKI

RFC 4210 (Adams, Farrell, Kause, & Mononen, 2005) describes the cryptographic algorithms, hash functions, and digital signatures that may be used to sign certificates and CRLs.

Signature Algorithms

Function: Certificates and CRLs conforming to RFC 4325 may be signed with any public-key signature algorithm. Signature algorithms are always used in conjunction with a one-way hash function.

The data to be signed (e.g., the one-way hash function output value) is formatted for the signature algorithm to be used. Then, a private key operation (e.g., RSA encryption) is performed to generate the signature value. This signature value is then ASN.1 encoded as a

Figure 9-11. User-centric trust model

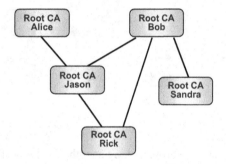

Table 9-1. Comparison of trust models

Characteristics	Hierarchical	Mesh	Trust List (Web)
Trusted key(s)	"Root" CA	CA that issued user's certificate	File of (usually) many trusted CA certificates in each browser
Trust paths	Chain of parent-child certificates	Mesh of bi-directional cross certificate pairs	Pre-ordered certificate list
Trust path finding	Directory based, comparatively simple	Directory based, complex	Minimal; find individual certificates in LDAP directory
Cross Certification	May be supported	Basis of PKI	No direct capability
Certificate Status	Certificate revocation list	Certificate revocation list	None.

bit string and included in the certificate in the signature field. According to RFC 4210, PKI messages are protected using digital signatures.

Mandatory Algorithm: DSA/SHA-1.

Other Algorithms: HMAC/SHA-1, RSA/MD5, and ECDSA/ECDH.

Defined:

- The Digital Signature Algorithm (DSA) is defined in the Digital Signature Standard (DSS) (FIPS-186-2). The U.S. Government developed DSA, and DSA is used in conjunction with the SHA-1 one-way hash function.

- The HMAC is defined in RFC 2104 (Krawczyk, Bellare, & Canetti, 1997) "HMAC: Keyed-Hashing for Message Authentication."

- The RSA signature algorithm is specified in PKCS #1 RFC 3447 (Jonsson & Kaliski, 2003).

- The Elliptic Curve Digital Signature Algorithm (ECDSA) is defined in X9.62-1998, "Public Key Cryptography for the Financial Services Industry: The Elliptic Curve Digital Signature Algorithm (ECDSA)". ECDSA is the elliptic curve mathematical analog of the Digital Signature Algorithm [FIPS 186-2].

Algorithm ID: {1 2 840 10040 4 3} for DSA/SHA-1

Public Modulo size: 1024 bits.

Public Key (Asymmetric) Algorithms

Function: Used for encryption of private keys transported in PKI messages.

Mandatory Algorithm: Diffie-Hellman.

Other Algorithms: RSA, ECDH.

Defined:

- The RSA is defined in RFC 3447, "Public-Key Cryptography Standards (PKCS) #1: RSA Cryptography Specifications Version 2.1."

- The Diffie-Hellman supported in X.509 PKI is defined in ANSI X9.42 (2003), "Public-Key Cryptography for The Financial Services Industry: Agreement of Symmetric Keys Using Discrete Logarithm Cryptography".

- The Elliptic Curve Diffie Hellman (ECDH) algorithm is a key agreement algorithm defined in ANSI X9.63-2001, "Public Key Cryptography for the Financial Services Industry: Key Agreement and Key Transport Using Elliptic Curve Cryptography". ECDH is the elliptic curve mathematical analog of the Diffie-Hellman key agreement algorithm as specified in X9.42.

Algorithm ID: {1 2 840 10046 2 1} for Diffie-Hellman.

Public Modulus Size: 1024 bits; prime integer: p; base integer: g.

Symmetric Algorithms

Function: Encryption of an end-entity's private key when the symmetric key is distributed in-band or out-of-band.

Mandatory Algorithm: 3DES, (3-key EDE, CBC mode).

Other Algorithms: RC5 and Cast 128.

Defined: The 3-DES is defined in FIPS 46-3.

Algorithm ID: {1 2 840 113549 3 7} for 3DES.

Private Key Proof of Possession (POP)

Certain attacks could allow an intruder to get a certificate for a specific public key without having possession of the private key. To prevent this type of attack, CAs and RAs check the binding between an end-entity and a key pair. RFC 4210 mandates that CAs/RAs must enforce POP by some means, either in-band or out-of-band. However, the private key of a key pair that is used for signing should not be sent to the CA/RA to prove possession because non-repudiation will be weakened.

Two Models for PKI Deployment

When an organization is going to deploy PKI, it could do so by in-sourcing or out-sourcing. In-sourcing gives an organization full control of the PKI implementation by utilizing its own resources, including personnel and hardware, and/or hiring external resources. Out-sourcing takes the PKI management burden from the organization, but gives control of the PKI operation to an external party.

According to Adams and Lloyd, (2003), when an organization is making a decision for PKI deployment, it should consider the following factors:

- Total cost of ownership, software, hardware, personnel, facilities, training, legal fees, and so forth
- Degree of control that the organization wants to maintain during the PKI operation
- The perceived sense of trust that customers might have from knowing that the PKI operation is out-sourced or in-sourced
- Response time associated with PKI related services

- Level of help desk support
- Flexibility and scalability
- Ability and willingness of the vendor to evolve to meet the future needs of the organization
- Disaster planning and recovery

Summary

If an attacker could replace an organization's public key with the attacker's own public key, then the secret information intended for an organization would be available to the attacker. Therefore, when using public-key crypto systems, it is necessary to be sure that the public key that is used really belongs to the named person or organization. One way of doing this is to use a service that authenticates the public key by verifying the identity of the entity who says it owns the public key. A certificate authority provides that service. The certificate authority also verifies whether or not the public key is still valid.

When an initiator submits the public key which belongs to the initiator, the initiator also provides a certificate that the responder submits to the certificate authority to validate the authenticity and validity of the initiator's public key. Therefore, a public-key certificate binds a subject's name to a public-key value.

When public key is used, however, it is necessary to have a comprehensive system that efficiently delivers security services such as confidentiality, access control, data integrity, authentication, and non-repudiation in a cohesive manner. That system is *public-key infrastructure* or PKI. PKI is about managing certificates and keys during their complete life cycles, as well as the entities involved. There are three phases in the life of a certificate and keys: initialization, issued, and cancellation.

Certificate authorities act as agents of trust by validating PKI users' identities and public keys. All PKI users must have a registered identity. The concept is known as third-party trust; a PKI user can trust the certificate issued by a CA as long as the user trusts the CA. Two end-entities can trust each other by using one of several trust models. Those trust models are hierarchy, mesh, Web model, and user centric.

Learning Objectives Review

1. Which of the following binds a subject name to a public-key value?

    a. A public-key certificate

    b. A public-key infrastructure

    c. A certificate authority

    d. A private key

2. In a root CA model, the CA is certified by _____.

3. Any application that provides confidentiality, access control, and data integrity requires a PKI implementation. (T/F)

4. In the trust-list model, also called Web model:

    a. The CA's public keys are pre-installed

    b. The user installs the CA's public keys

    c. Both

5. During registration, the identity of the end-entity is established and verified. (T/F)

6. Update means that a new public-key pair and information are generated and a new certificate is issued. (T/F)

7. The trust models by which two end-entities who are not in the same domain can establish trust in each other are called hierarchy, mesh, Web model, and user-centric. (T/F)

8. In a user-centric trust model, any user can act as a certifying authority and validate another user's public-key certificate. (T/F)

9. Certificate renewal means that the public key and its information remain the same. (T/F)

10. When a certificate expires, it can be:

    a. Renewed

    b. Updated

    c. Both

11. The field information for X.509 and CRL is sent in clear. (T/F)

12. The four entities involved in PKI management are: (1) _____; (2) _____ _____; (3) _____; (4) _____.

13. The three phases in the life of a certificate and keys are: _____, _____, _____.

14. What is the difference between in-sourcing and out-sourcing PKI deployment?

15. In public-key systems, secrecy of the public key is not required but the _____ of the public key is necessary to guarantee integrity.

16. What are the obligations of the repository site?

17. Certificates may be revoked before expiring because:

    a. The user's private key is assumed to be compromised

    b. The user is no longer certified by the particular CA

    c. The CA's certificate is assumed to be compromised

    d. a and b only

    e. All of the above

18. Registration authorities can issue certificates and CRLs. (T/F)

19. What is the difference between certificate renewal and certificate update?

20.   An organization decided to use digital signatures to sign documents for seven years. For how long should they keep records of the corresponding public and private keys?

References

Adams, C., Farrell, S., Kause, T., & Mononen, T. (2005). *Internet X.509 public key infrastructure certificate management protocols* (RFC 4210). Internet Engineering Task Force (IETF). Retrieved June 28, 2007, from http://www.ietf.org/rfc/rfc4210.txt?number=4210

Adams, C., & Lloyd, S. (2003). *Understanding PKI* (2nd ed.). Boston: Addison Wesley.

American National Standard Institute (ANSI). (2003). *Public Key Cryptography for the Financial Services Industry: Agreement of Symmetric Keys Using Discrete Logarithm Cryptography*. Retrieved June 28, 2007, from http://webstore.ansi.org/ansidocstore/product.asp?sku=ANSI+X9%2E42%3A2003

Chokhani, S., Ford, W., Sabett, R., Merril, C., & Wu, S. (2003). *Internet X.509 public key infrastructure certificate policy and certification practices framework* (RFC 3647). Internet Engineering Task Force (IETF). Retrieved June 28, 2007, from http://www.ietf.org/rfc/rfc3647.txt?number=3647

Jonsson, J., & Kaliski, B. (2003). *Public-key cryptography standards (PKCS) #1: RSA cryptography specifications version 2.1* (RFC 3447). Internet Engineering Task Force (IETF). Retrieved June 28, 2007, from http://www.ietf.org/rfc/rfc3447.txt?number=3447

Krawczyk, H., Bellare, M., & Canetti, R. (1997) *HMAC: Keyed-hashing for message authentication* (RFC 2104). Internet Engineering Task Force (IETF). Retrieved January 8, 2003, from http://www.ietf.org/rfc/rfc2104.txt?number=2104

National Institute of Standards and Technology (NIST). (n.d.). *Summary of ANSI X9.42 Agreement of Symmetric Keys Using Discrete Logarithm Cryptography*. Retrieved June 28, 2007, from http://csrc.nist.gov/CryptoToolkit/kms/summary-x9-42.pdf

Newman, D. B., Omura, J. K., & Pickholtz, R. L. (1987). Public key management for network security. *IEEE Network Magazine, 1*(2), 12-13.

Santesson, S., & Housley, R. (2005). *Internet X.509 public key infrastructure authority information access certificate revocation list (CRL) extension* (RFC 4325). Internet Engineering Task Force (IETF). Retrieved June 28, 2007, from http://www.ietf.org/rfc/rfc4325.txt?number=4325

Chapter X

Electronic Mail Security

Electronic Mail Security

In previous chapters of this book, crypto systems, security mechanisms, and security services have been discussed and reviewed as separate crypto modules. In Chapters 10 to 14, how these crypto modules are used to provide network security will be discussed.

Electronic mail enables users to exchange messages using computer communications facilities, but sending an e-mail message is like sending a postcard that anyone can read as it travels from post office to post office. When an e-mail message travels from one e-mail server to another, the e-mail is first stored in an e-mail server before it is sent to the next e-mail server.

A way to protect e-mail is by using writer-to-reader security in which the message is encrypted at the sender station and deciphered at the receiver station. There are several ways to make e-mail secure. Pretty Good Privacy (PGP) and Secure MIME (S/MIME) are presented in this chapter.

Objectives

- Be able to explain PGP security services work
- Know S/MIME Message Formats

Introduction

When a company sends a document using regular mail, employees may go to the extreme to safeguard the information by delivering the mail directly to the post office and using certified delivery, or by using courier companies. However, employees do not hesitate to send highly sensitive and confidential information, such as a business report or sales forecast, using e-mail. E-mail is the most used network-based application, but it is the least secure. Companies spend millions of dollars in hardware and security intrusion software, but very few encipher their e-mail communications.

To send and receive e-mails a user needs to be connected to an e-mail server. When a message is sent, the e-mail server receives and stores the message, and then sends it to another e-mail server that does the same. E-mails travel through many servers and each one keeps a copy of the message. Users cannot erase the e-mail on all those servers, so the copy of the e-mail stays in the server until the server owner decides to erase it. There are companies that have found a niche in developing specialized software that supposedly erases e-mail from all the servers where the e-mail has been archived.

A way to protect e-mail is by using writer-to-reader security in which the message is encrypted using privacy enhanced mail (PEM), MIME Object Security Services (MOSS), X.400, PGP, and S/MIME. PGP, which is a specification and a product, and S/MIME, which is a protocol, are compatible with Internet mail and work with Eudora e-mail, Netscape Messenger, and Microsoft Outlook.

Pretty Good Privacy (PGP)

PGP, developed by Phil Zimmermann, is a crypto system that uses data compression and symmetric and public-key cryptography. By compressing the data before it is encrypted, PGP strengthens cryptographic security because most cryptanalysis techniques use plaintext patterns to try to break the cipher.

The following steps describe the PGP encryption algorithm (Zimmermann, 2000):

1. The sender generates a session by entering a word or password in his/her computer using the keyboard or mouse. PGP uses the content and timing of user keystrokes and mouse movements to generate a random message encryption key. The message encryption key is a one-time secret key used to encipher the message by encrypting it with a symmetric encryption algorithm.

2. The message is hashed using SHA-1 and signed using DSA or RSA with the sender's private key creating a digital signature.

3. The cleartext message is concatenated with the digital signature, and the result is compressed using a compression package called *ZIP*.

4. The ZIP compressed cleartext message and digital signatures are enciphered with a symmetric algorithm (Cast-128, IDEA, or 3DES) using the one-time secret key generated previously by the sender.

Figure 10-1. PGP authentication and confidentiality

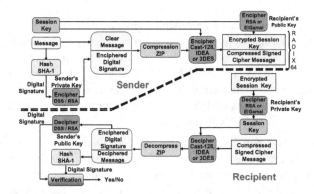

5.   The one-time message encryption key is enciphered with RSA or ElGamal using the recipient's public key.

6.   The enciphered message encryption key is concatenated with the compressed signed cipher message.

7.   The enciphered message concatenated with the enciphered one-time message encryption key is converted to an 8-bit ASCII format using an encoding technique called *RADIX-64* for compatibility with e-mail applications.

8.   To decipher and authenticate the message, the receiver reverses the above steps.

PGP E-Mail Compatibility

E-mail systems are designed with different formats and have limitations with regard to message size. To overcome these problems, PGP uses RADIX-64 to limit the encrypted message to ASCII characters and divides the message into blocks.

RADIX-64: E-Mail Format Compatibility

In secure digital communications, the ciphertext consist of bits, zeros and ones, without any format. Some encryption algorithms format the cipher text in blocks of 64-bits, in bytes (each byte is a sequence of eight bits treated as a single entity), or in words (each word is a group of 32 bits, with four bytes treated as single entity).

However, most e-mail systems only allow the transmission and reception of 8-bit ASCII codes. PGP converts 6 bits of ciphertext to 8-bit printable ASCII characters using an encod-

Table 10-1. Radix-64 conversion

Binary (6-bit)	Decimal	Radix-64	Binary (6-bit)	Decimal	Radix-64	Binary (6-bit)	Decimal	Radix-64
000000	0	A	010110	22	W	101100	44	s
000001	1	B	010111	23	X	101101	45	t
000010	2	C	011000	24	Y	101110	46	u
000011	3	D	011001	25	Z	101111	47	v
000100	4	E	011010	26	a	110000	48	w
000101	5	F	011011	27	b	110001	49	x
000110	6	G	011100	28	c	110010	50	y
000111	7	H	011101	29	d	110011	51	z
001000	8	I	011110	30	e	110100	52	0
001001	9	J	011111	31	f	110101	53	1
001010	10	K	100000	32	g	110110	54	2
001011	11	L	100001	33	h	110111	55	3
001100	12	M	100010	34	i	111000	56	4
001101	13	N	100011	35	j	111001	57	5
001110	14	O	100100	36	k	111010	58	6
001111	15	P	100101	37	l	111011	59	7
010000	16	Q	100110	38	m	111100	60	8
010001	17	R	100111	39	n	111101	61	9
010010	18	S	101000	40	o	111110	62	+
010011	19	T	101001	41	p	111111	63	/
010100	20	U	101010	42	q	(pad)		=
010101	21	V	101011	43	r			

Figure 10-2. PGP e-mail compatibility

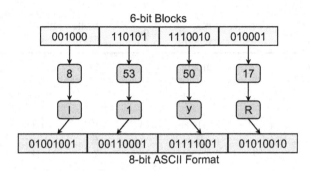

ing technique called RADIX-64 (Atkins, Stallings, & Zimmermann, 1996, p. 4). RADIX-64 is used in the Internet PEM format, as well as the Internet MIME format.

Figure 10-2 shows an example of ciphertext converted into 8-bit printable ASCII characters. The ciphertext is a group of blocks of 6-bits (8, 53, 50, and 7); using the Radix-64 conversion table, each 6-bit block is substituted by equivalent printable characters (I, 1, y, and R), and then converted to 8-bit ASCII codes.

E-Mail Size Compatibility

Most Internet e-mail facilities do not allow sending messages that are more than 50000 or 65000 bytes long. PGP overcomes this problem by breaking the message up into blocks that can be mailed separately. The blocks are put into files named with extensions, .as1, .as2, .as3, and so forth. The recipient's PGP software concatenates the files in their proper order before decrypting the message.

Key Rings

PGP uses public-key encryption to encipher the one-time message encryption key; to do so, it generates a key pair, the public key and the private key. Also, to be able to communicate with a recipient using public-key encryption, the PGP sender needs to have the recipient's public key. PGP stores the keys on the hard disk in two different folders, one named the *private key ring*, where the private keys are stored, and the other the *public key ring* where the public keys are stored (Network Associates, 2001). When senders add certified recipients to their certificates list, they will also add the recipients' public keys to their public key ring. If senders lose their private key ring, they will be unable to decrypt any previous information encrypted with the keys on that ring.

Figure 10-3. PGP private and public key rings

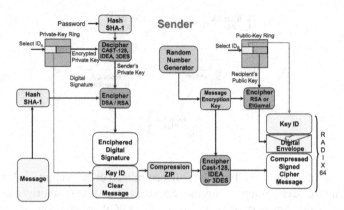

The keys in the private-key ring are stored in encrypted form (Oppliger, 2001). When the user generates a key pair, PGP performs the following procedure:

1. Asks the user to enter a password to bind it to the key pair

2. Uses SHA-1 to produce a 160-bit hash code of the password and then discards the password

3. Encrypts the private key with CAST-128, IDEA, or 3DES, using the 160 bits of the hash function as the key and then discarding the hash code

4. Stores the encrypted private key on the private-key ring

PGP Digital Certificates

PGP enciphers the one-time message encryption key with RSA or ElGamal using the recipient's public key. In a public-key environment, it is necessary to digitally certify that the recipient public key is not a forgery. Digital certificates include the following information: the end-user's name, ID, and public key, the hash value of the end-user's public key, the name of the certificate authority issuing the certificate, and a digital signature of the certificate authority. In essence, certificates identify (1) the owner of a particular public key and (2) the certificate authority issuing the certificate.

In any digital certificate model, the digital signature needs to be signed and certified by someone the user trusts. Alice trusts Bob's digital signature because Bob's digital signature has been certified by Trent; Alice is certain that Trent has done a good job verifying that the digital signature really belongs to Bob. In most public key systems, Trent is called a *certificate authority*.

Figure 10-4. User-centric trust model

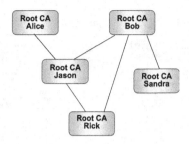

PGP can operate equally well in either a decentralized or in a centralized environment. In a PGP decentralized environment, any user can act as a certifying authority and validate another PGP user's public-key certificate. In a centralized PGP environment, users are certified by a specific certificate authority whom everyone trusts. Governments and some companies use trusted centralized certifying authorities, and no certificate is considered valid unless it has been attested to by that centralized CA.

In the PGP user-centric trust model, in a decentralized environment, any user can act as a certifying authority and validate another PGP user's public key certificate. In the user-centric model, each user is directly responsible for deciding which certificates to accept and which ones to reject.

In PGP, a trusted introducer is someone users trust to provide them with public-key certificates that are valid. For example, Jason asks Rick and Bob to be his introducers, and then sends them a copy of his public key with a request that they certify and return it. Jason can then include these certificates, the one from Rick and the one from Bob, on a public-key server. When a trusted introducer signs another person's public key, it means that the public key the introducer signed is valid, and other users do not need to verify the public key before using it.

A meta-introducer is a trusted introducer of trusted introducers. When Jason receives a certificate from Sandra, whom he does not know, Jason will see that Sandra's certificate is signed by Bob. Bob is a meta-introducer, and he introduced Sandra to Jason. A meta-introducer assumes the role of a root CA, and users explicitly trust a single meta-introducer's (root) certificate. Users also trust any certificates carrying the meta-introducer's signature. Jason may decide to reject or accept Sandra's certificate, depending on how much he trusts Bob being a good certificate authority.

However, a certificate generated by Rick's friend, who may act as a CA, may not be accepted by Jason because Jason knows that Rick's friend cannot be trusted as a CA. This illustrates that there are various levels of trusted authorities. Some people are good CAs, and others are not. So, when any user can act as a CA, whom do you trust?

In PGP, users have three convenient ways to determine levels of trust, and they are referred to as trust flag fields:

1. Do you trust the validity of the public key? This level of trust is computed by PGP, and it is called the *key legitimacy field*.

    a. **Complete:** The user is confident that the public key is valid.

    b. **Marginal:** The user does not completely trust the CA who issued the certificate.

    c. **Untrusted:** The user cannot say whether the public key is valid or not.

2. Do you trust the signer to certify public keys? This level of trust is calculated by PGP and is called the *signature trust field*.

3. Do you trust the owner of this public key to sign other public-key certificates? The user assigns this level of trust, and it is called the *owner trust field*.

    a. **Full:** The owner of this public key is fully trusted to introduce another public key.

    b. **Marginal:** The owner of this public key can be trusted to introduce another public key, but it is uncertain whether the owner is fully competent to do so.

    c. **Untrustworthy:** The owner of this public key should not be trusted to introduce another, therefore any occurrence of this key as a signature on another public key should be ignored.

    d. **Don't know:** There are no expressions of trust made about the owner of this public key.

Establishment of Trust

As mentioned before, in a PGP decentralized environment, any user can act as a certifying authority and validate another PGP user's public-key certificate.

Bob could get Alice's public key in any of the following ways:

- He can personally get Alice's public key from Alice.

- Alice can send her public key to Bob by e-mail and tell him her public-key fingerprint.

- Bob can get Alice's public key from a trusted person called an *introducer*.

- Alice can post her public key at a PGP Key Server and Bob can then download Alice's public key from the server. See Figure 10-5, steps 3-7.

- Once Bob downloads Alice's public key, he imports the public key to his key ring, signs it with his private key, and assigns a trust level.

- To download a public key from a server, the initiator goes to PGP Keys application, clicks on "Server" and then on Search. See Figure 10-6.

Figure 10-5. Downloading a public key from a PGP key server

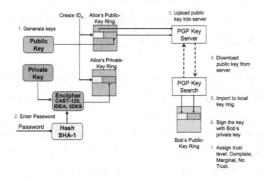

Figure 10-6. PGP key screen

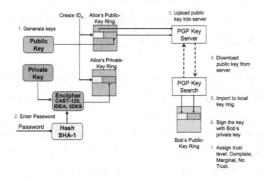

Figure 10-7. PGP keys with public key added

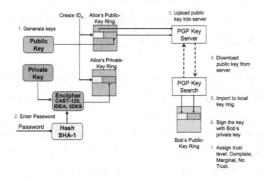

The PGP Key Search Window will open. Enter the name of the person to search for, right click the selected person's public key, and select "Import to Local Key Ring." The selected public-key will be added to the public key ring. See Figure 10-7.

Right click on the public key that was added to the public ring and select "Sign." The PGP Sign Key window will open, select the options to sign the public key and then click "OK."

PGP will open the "Enter Passphrase" window; enter the passphrase to sign the public key. See Figure 10-8.

Figure 10-8. PGP sign key window

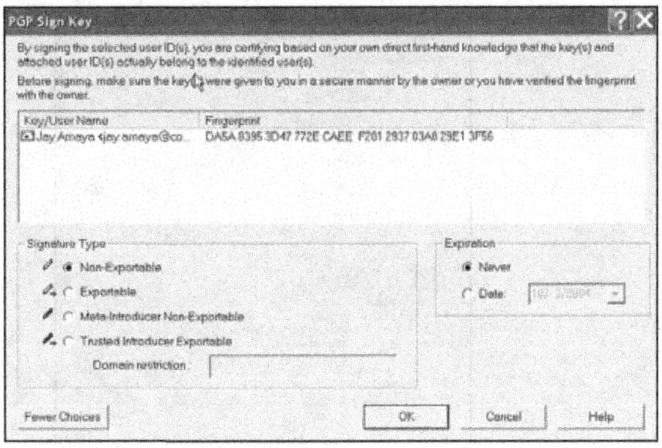

The options to sign the public key are the following:

- **Non-exportable:** The key is valid but the user does not want others to rely on the user's certification.

- **Exportable:** This is similar to a CA signing the public key. Others can rely on the signature and trust that the public key belongs to the person who claims to be the owner.

- **Meta-introducer non-exportable:** The owner of this public key is trusted, and any trusted introducers created by this key are also trusted. This signature is non-exportable.

- **Trusted introducer exportable:** The owner of this key is trusted and keys validated by the trusted introducer will appear valid to others. The trusted introducer signature is exportable.

Another window will open for the user to enter the passphrase, to sign the pubic key. See Figure 10-9.

Figure 10-9. PGP signing the public key

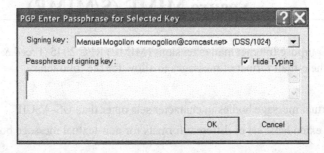

Figure 10-10. PGP public key properties

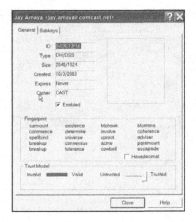

By Manuel Mogollon signing Jay Amaya's public key with his private key, Manuel is certifying that he is sure that the public key belongs to Jay Amaya. Now the public key is valid.

Once the public key is signed, then it is necessary to assign the level of trust to the owner of the public key so the owner can be trusted to sign other public-key certificates. In the PGP Key window, right click the public key and select "Properties."

A window with the properties will open. Move the bar "Untrusted/Trusted" either to the left (Untrusted), center (Marginal), or to the right (Trusted). See Figure 10-10. The different levels mean the following:

- **Untrusted:** The owner of this public key should not be trusted to introduce another; therefore, any occurrence of this key, such as a signature on another public key should be ignored.

- **Marginal:** The owner of this public key can be trusted to introduce another public key, but it is uncertain whether the owner is fully trustworthy to do so.

- **Trusted:** The owner of this public key is fully trusted to introduce another public key.

Secure MIME (S/MIME)

The multipurpose Internet mail extensions (MIME) RFC 2045 (Freed & Borenstein, 1996) redefine the e-mail format of messages to allow for the following:

1.   Textual message bodies in character sets other than US-ASCII

2.   An extendable set of different formats for non-textual message bodies

Table 10-2. Algorithms used in S/MIME

Function	Algorithm Used	Description
Digest Algorithm	Sending and receiving agents MUST support SHA-1. Receiving agents SHOULD support MD5 to provide backward compatibility with S/MIME v2.	A hash code of the message is created using SHA-1.
Signature Algorithms	Sending agents MUST support either DSA with SHA-1 or hash function with RSA. Receiving agents MUST support DSA with SHA-1 and hash function with RSA. A user agent should generate RSA key pairs at a minimum key size of 768 bits.	The message digest is encrypted to form the digital signature.
Key Encryption Algorithms	Sending and receiving agents must support RSA for key wrapping. A user agent should generate RSA key pairs at a minimum key size of 768 bits. Sending and receiving agents should support DH using the ephemeral-static mode.	The message encryption key is encrypted for transmission with message.
Message Encryption	Sending and receiving agents must support encryption and decryption with 3DES CBC, and should support encryption and decryption with AES at a key size of 128, 192, and 256 bits. Receiving agents SHOULD support encryption and decryption using the RC2 with a key size of 40 bits.	The message is encrypted using a one-time key.

3.   Multipart message bodies

4.   Textual header information in character sets other than US-ASCII

Secure MIME (S/MIME) refers to a specification (rather than to a product such as PGP) designed to add security to e-mail messages that use the MIME format. S/MIME is not restricted to e-mail, and it can be used with any transport mechanism that transports MIME data, for example: (1) HTTP; (2) automated message transfer agents that use cryptographic security services that do not require any human intervention.

S/MIME Version 3.1 is specified in RFC 3851 (Ramsdell, 2004b), "Secure/Multipurpose Internet Mail Extensions (S/MIME) Version 3.1 Message Specification." Table 10-2 shows the different algorithms used in S/MIME.

S/MIME uses digital signatures, data encryption, and hash functions to provide the following cryptographic security services for e-mail applications: authentication, message integrity, non-repudiation of origin and privacy, and data security.

The main difference between PGP and S/MIME is that PGP allows users to certify other users. Even thought PGP and S/MIME use X.509 certificates that are issued by certificate authorities and distributed by directory services, the two technologies do not interoperate because they used different protocols and message formats.

S/MIME supports multiple message digest, digital signature, key encryption, and data encryption algorithms.

S/MIME Message Formats

In order to create S/MIME messages, an S/MIME agent has to follow specifications listed in the Cryptographic Message Syntax (CMS), RFC 3852 (Housley, 2004). CMS defines six content types: data, signed-data, enveloped-data, digested-data, encrypted-data, and authenticated-data. Of these, only the data, signed-data, and enveloped-data content types are currently used for S/MIME. Data, SignedData, and EnvelopedData are used as identifiers for data, signed-data, and enveloped-data content:

- **Data content:** This content is intended for arbitrary data that may or may not have an internal structure.
- **SignedData content:** This content must be used by sending agents to apply a digital signature to a message or, in a case where there is no signature information, to determine a certificate. It should include all the required information such as algorithm identifier, certificates, certificate revocation lists, and other signer-related information.
- **EnvelopedData content:** This content type is used to apply privacy protection to a message. A sender needs to have access to a public key for each intended message recipient to use this service. This content type does not provide authentication.

Creating a Signed-Only Message

In S/MIME, there are two formats for digitally signed messages (Ramsdell, 2004a):

a.   **The application/pkcs7-mime with SignedData:** Messages signed using the Signed-Data format cannot be viewed by a recipient unless they have S/MIME facilities. However, if they have S/MIME facilities, these messages can always be verified for integrity, that is, that they were not changed in transit.

b.   **Multipart/Signing:** This format is a clear-signing format.

Multipart/Signing

Messages signed using the multipart/signed format can always be viewed by the receiver whether they have S/MIME software or not. In this context, "be viewed" means the ability to process the message essentially, as if it were not a signed message. The multipart/signed MIME type has two parts. The first part contains information about the MIME entity that is signed; the second part contains the "detached signature." In general, the multipart/signed form is preferred for sending, and receiving agents should be able to handle both.

Figure 10-11. SMIME multipart/signing

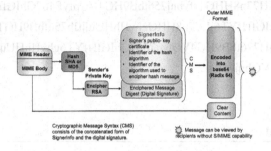

The procedure for a multipart/signing message is as follows:

1. Using a one-way hash function, SHA-1 or MD5, the sender generates a message digest.
2. The sender enciphers the message digest with his private key to create the digital signature.
3. The sender prepares a block of sender information known as SignerInfo that contains the sender's public-key certificate, an identifier of the hash algorithm, an identifier of the encrypting algorithm used to encipher the message digest.
4. The SignerInfo and the digital signature are concatenated to form a Cryptographic Message Syntax (CMS).
5. The CMS is encoded using Radix 64.
6. The resulting MIME entity, which consists of the CMS and the message in cleartext, is encapsulated into an e-mail and sent to the recipient.

The procedure to digitally sign a message in S/MIME is always the same, as indicated in steps 1 to 4. The file extension of the multipart/signing message is .p7s. The following is a sample message taken from RFC 3850 (Ramsdell, 2004a):

Content-Type: multipart/signed;

      protocol="application/pkcs7-signature";

      micalg=sha1; boundary=boundary42

--boundary42

Content-Type: text/plain

This is a clear-signed message.

--boundary42

Content-Type: application/pkcs7-signature; name=smime.p7s

Content-Transfer-Encoding: base64

Content-Disposition: attachment; filename=smime.p7s

ghyHhHUujhJhjH77n8HHGTrfvbnj756tbB9HG4VQpfyF467GhIGfHfYT6

4VQpfyF467GhIGfHfYT6jH77n8HHGghyHhHUujhJh756tbB9HGTrfvbnj

n8HHGTrfvhJhjH776tbB9HG4VQbnj7567GhIGfHfYT6ghyHhHUujpfyF4

7GhIGfHfYT64VQbnj756

--boundary42—

SignedData

In SignedData content, messages are signed and encoded using Radix-64; therefore, only users with S/MIME software are able to view the message.

The procedure for sending SignedData content is as follows (Ramsdell, 2004a):

1.   The sender uses the same procedure indicated in steps 1 to 4 in the multipart/signing to generate a CMS. CMS is the digital signature concatenated with the SignerInfo.

2.   The SignerInfo and the digital signature are concatenated to form a Cryptographic Message Syntax (CMS) of type signed-data.

3.   The CMS is concatenated with cleartext message and encoded using Radix 64.

4.   The resulting MIME entity is encapsulated into an e-mail and sent to the recipient.

The file extension of the multipart/signing message is .p7m. The following is a sample message taken from RFC 3850 (Ramsdell, 2004a):

Content-Type: application/pkcs7-mime; smime-type=signed-data;

name=smime.p7m

Content-Transfer-Encoding: base64

Content-Disposition: attachment; filename=smime.p7m

567GhIGfHfYT6ghyHhHUujpfyF4f8HHGTrfvhJhjH776tbB9HG4VQbnj777n8HHGT9-

Figure 10-12. SMIME signed data

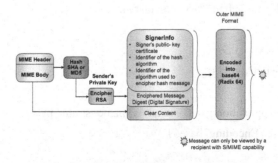

HG4VQpfyF467GhIGfHfYT6rfvbnj756tbBghyHhHUujhJhjHUujhJh4VQpfyF467GhIG-
fHfYGTrfvbnjT6jH7756tbB9H7n8HHGghyHh6YT64V0GhIGfHfQbnj75

Creating an Enveloped-Only Message

Enveloped-only MIME messages provide data integrity by enciphering the message without signing it. The procedure is as follows:

1. A pseudorandom one-time message encryption key is generated.

2. The MIME entity, the message, is enciphered with 3DES or RC/40, using the generated one-time message encryption key.

3. The generated one-time message encryption key is enciphered with RSA or DH, using the recipient's public key.

4. A block, RecipientInfo, is created, which contains the sender's public-key certificate, an identifier of the encryption algorithm used to encipher the one-time message encryption key, and the encrypted message encryption key.

5. The encrypted MIME entity, the message, and the RecipientInfo are concatenate to form a CMS object of type enveloped-data, which is encoded using Radix-64.

The file extension of the enveloped-data message is .p7m. The following is a sample message taken from RFC 3850 (Ramsdell, 2004a):

Content-Type: application/pkcs7-mime; smime-type=enveloped-data; name=smime.p7m

Content-Transfer-Encoding: base64

Content-Disposition: attachment; filename=smime.p7m

rfvbnj756tbBghyHhHUujhJhjH77n8HHGT9HG4VQpfyF467GhIGfHfYT-
67n8HHGghyHhHUujhJh4VQpfyF467GhIGfHfYGTrfvbnjT6jH7756tbB9Hf-
8HHGTrfvhJhjH776tbB9HG4VQbnj7567GhIGfHfYT6ghyHhHU-
ujpfyF40GhIGfHfQbnj756YT64V

Figure 10-13. SMIME envelope data

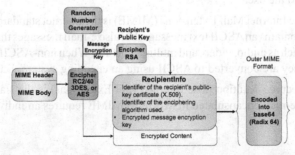

Signed and Enveloped MIME Entities

In S/MIME, it is possible to achieve signing and enveloping, as well as encryption, by using any of the signed-only and encrypted-only formats. This is possible because the input and output of S/MIME are always MIME entities. All S/MIME implementation must be able to receive and process arbitrarily nested S/MIME.

A message can be signed first and then enciphered, or vice versa. When a message is signed first and then enciphered, the digital signature is securely obscured by the encryption. In this case, a passive attacker would not be able to determine the sender because the information in the "From" field in a message may not be correct. It is possible to use anonymous e-mailers or gateways that strip off the originating e-mail address, and, in this way, the sender achieves anonymity.

When the message is encrypted first and then signed, the digital signature is exposed. This may be useful in those situations in which the receiver would like to verify the signature before decrypting the message.

Ramsdell (2004a) presents the security ramifications of choosing whether to sign first or encrypt first:

A recipient of a message that is encrypted and then signed can validate that the encrypted block was unaltered, but cannot determine any relationship between the signer and the un-encrypted contents of the message. A recipient of a message that is signed-then-encrypted can assume that the signed message itself has not been altered, but that a careful attacker may have changed the unauthenticated portions of the encrypted message.

Summary

When information is sent, even through regular mail, precaution is taken to ensure information confidentiality. The information is secured in an envelope, the correct address is verified, and a confirmation is sought that the information was received. However, when electronic e-mail is used, too often even simple precautions are not taken. For example, not too many companies encipher electronic mail, regardless of how easy and nonintrusive encryption is. PGP and S/MIME are two very easy ways to implement confidentiality and authentication. Several electronic mail systems have embedded S/MIME so well that it is transparent to the user.

Multipurpose Internet Mail Extensions (MIME) is the Internet standard for sending not only e-mail that contains an ASCII text message, but also e-mail messages that contain non-ASCII characters such as audio, video, and multimedia files. When non-ASCII characters are sent in an e-mail, they are converted to ASCII using an encoding system, Base-64 or RADIX-64.

S/MIME (Secure / Multipurpose Internet Mail Extensions) is the standard for encrypting and signing e-mail encapsulated in MIME. S/MIME requires an individual to install a certificate from a certificate authority to bind the user's public key to the individual's e-mail address.

Open PGP does not require a certificate authority to sign public keys because any user can certify and sign another user's public key. However, PGP now also supports X.509-based certificates, which allows it to work with S/MIME and use any certificate authority.

Learning Objectives Review

1. S/MIME provides confidentiality and integrity services. (T/F)

2. A _____ is a trusted introducer who can nominate and create other trusted introducers.

3. In PGP, why is the message compressed before it is encrypted?

4. S/MIME agents MUST use PKIX certificates to validate public keys as described in RFC 2459, "Internet X.509 Public Key Infrastructure (PKIX) Certificate and Certificate Revocation List (CRL) Profile." (T/F)

5. When users have S/MIME installed in Microsoft Outlook, they can only send e-mails to users who also have S/MIME installed. (T/F)

6. Security for e-mail is done at the _____ layer of the TCP/IP stack.

    a. Application

    b. Transport

    c. Network

    d. Data

7. In S/MIME, when a message is encrypted first and then signed:

    a. The identity of the sender is concealed

    b. It allows for authentication before decryption of the message

8. In PGP and S/MIME, the keys used to encipher the message are used:

    a. One time

    b. For a period of time determined by the user

9. Before using a public key to provide security services, the S/MIME agent MUST certify that the public key is valid. (T/F)

10. The PGP User Guide states that, "You should use a public key only after you are sure that it is a good public key that has not been tampered with, and that it actually belongs to the person with whom it is associated." You can verify that someone's public key is good by:

    a. Getting the public key from its owner

    b. Knowing that it is signed by someone you trust from whom you already have a good public key

    c. Both

11. A VeriSign Class 1 certificate binds the certificate to the:

    a. Owner's identification; the owner must appear in person or send notarized documents

    b. Owner's identification sent by mail to Verisign

    c. Owner's e-mail address

12. Which of the following S/MIME functions encrypts the cleartext message?

    a. Multipart/signing data

    b. Signed data

    c. Enveloped data

13. S/MIME provides the flexibility to encrypt and then sign a message, or sign and then encrypt a message. Possible uses of these features are to:

    a. Conceal the identity of the sender

    b. Allow authentication before decrypting the message

    c. Both

14. In Secure/MIME, when a message is signed first and then enciphered:

    a. The identity of the sender is concealed

    b. It allows authentication before decrypting the message

15. Radix-64 encoding is used in both PGP and S/MIME to:

    a. Encipher the cleartext message with a 64-bit key

    b. Create a 64-bit Key ID

    c. Provide e-mail system compatibility

    d. Convert EBCDIC to ASCII

16. The maximum size of an e-mail message that PGP can handle is dictated by the e-mail facility/system. (T/F)

17. S/MIME and PGP can interoperate when they both use X.509 digital certificates. (T/F)

18. RADIX-64 expands the enciphered message:

    a. 33%

    b. 25%

    c. 10%

19. PGP provides the following cryptographic security services for electronic messaging applications:

    a. Privacy and data security using encryption

    b. Authentication

    c. Message integrity and non-repudiation of origin using digital certificates

    d. All of the above

20. Which of the following crypto systems is used by PGP to encipher data?

    a.   An asymmetric crypto system

    b.   A symmetric crypto system

    c.   A symmetric key distribution system

    d.   An asymmetric key distribution system

References

Atkins, D., Stallings, W., & Zimmermann, P. (1996). *PGP message exchange formats* (RFC 1991). Internet Engineering Task Force (IETF). Retrieved February 1, 2003, from http://www.ietf.org/rfc/rfc1991.txt?number=1991

Freed, N., & Borenstein, N. (1996). *Multipurpose internet mail extensions (MIME) Part one: Format of Internet message bodies* (RFC 2045). Internet Engineering Task Force (IETF). Retrieved on February 15, 2003, from http://www.ietf.org/rfc/rfc2045.txt?number=2045

Housley, R. (2004). *Cryptographic message syntax (CMS)* (RFC 3852). Internet Engineering Task Force (IETF). Retrieved on February 2, 2003, from http://www.ietf.org/rfc/rfc3852.txt?number=3852

Network Associates (2001). *PGP 7.0 Windows 95/98/NT/2000 user's guide.* Retrieved February 2, 2003, from ftp://ftp.pgpi.org/pub/pgp/7.0/docs/english/PGPWinUsersGuide.pdf

Oppliger, R. (2001). *Secure messaging with PGP and S/MIME.* Norwood, MA: Artech House, Inc.

Ramsdell, B. (Ed). (2004a). *Secure/multipurpose internet mail extensions (S/MIME) Version 3.1 certificate handling* (RFC 3850). Internet Engineering Task Force (IETF). Retrieved on February 15, 2005, from http://www.ietf.org/rfc/rfc3850.txt?number=3850

Ramsdell, B. (Ed.). (2004b). *Secure/multipurpose internet mail extensions (S/MIME) version 3.1 message specification* (RFC 3851). Internet Engineering Task Force (IETF). Retrieved on February 5, 2005, from http://www.ietf.org/rfc/rfc3851.txt?number=3851

Zimmermann, P. (2000). *An introduction to cryptography.* Network Associates. Retrieved February 2, 2003, from http://www.pgpi.org/doc/guide/6.5/en/intro/

Chapter XI

VPNS and IPSEC

VPNS and IPSEC

Virtual private networks (VPN) and IPsec are discussed in this chapter. A VPN emulates a private wide area network (WAN) facility using IP networks, such as the public Internet or private IP backbones.

When VPNs are used, the Internet offers the appearance, functionality, and usefulness of a dedicated private network. One of the problems in using the Internet as a WAN is that the Internet is a public network and has relatively little security.

IPsec provides the following security services to VPNs: data origin authentication, access control, confidentiality (encryption), connectionless integrity, rejection of replayed packets (a form of partial sequence integrity), and limited traffic flow confidentiality.

Objectives

- Understand VPN concepts and advantages
- Learn how IPsec provides security services to IP Networks
- Become familiar with IPsec concepts of security associations, security protocols, and key management

Introduction

In RFC 2764 (Gleeson, Lin Heinanen, Armitage, & Malis, 2000), an IP based virtual private network is defined as an "emulation of a private wide area network (WAN) facility using IP facilities, including the public Internet, or private IP backbones." VPNs are used as the basic transport for connecting corporate data centers, remote offices, mobile employees, telecommuters, customers, suppliers, and business partners. The public network is used as a wide area communications network, and it offers the appearance, functionality, and usefulness of a dedicated private network.

Service providers sold T1 services to corporate clients as a way for the clients to create their own private networks for data traffic. Other technologies such as Frame Relay (FR) and asynchronous transfer mode (ATM) also allow the connection of different sites. The service provider maintains a "cloud" of frame relay connections, and the links are assigned only when needed. As a result, communication prices have gone down considerably.

A T1 leased line normally has a fixed price, with an additional mileage charge per month per mile. Even though frame relay fees do not include a charge for distance and are considerably less expensive than leased lines, monthly fees are still required for the permanent virtual circuits. T1 Internet connections have a monthly fixed price, so one of the main reasons to use the Internet as a corporate WAN is cost savings. There are other compelling arguments for replacing a private network, for example, scalability, responsiveness, and flexibility. Today, most corporations are using the Internet as their corporate WAN because of cost savings and reduced time to set up a connection.

There is a growing need to integrate more closely with partners, suppliers, and customers; there is also a corresponding need to "virtually" extend a company's geographic reach to include telecommuters and mobile personnel, remote offices and sites, and major vendors and contractors. Therefore, another reason to use the Internet as the corporate WAN network is the savings in long distance charges resulting from, for example, mobile employees not having to call an 800-number to access corporate modem banks. Instead, telecommuters and the mobile force place local calls to the ISP's POP to connect to the corporate network.

The following are some of the VPN benefits:

Figure 11-1. A corporate virtual private network over the Internet

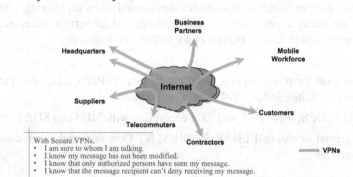

- Ease of use—facilitates electronic communications making corporations more efficient and productive.

- Lower communications cost

- Significant savings resulting from the elimination of long-haul leased lines, 800 numbers or long distance fees, modem banks, and multiple access connections

- Reduction of long distance phone call expenses with use of Voice over IP

- Savings of up to 65% on monthly circuit costs by moving from an FR and ATM environment to an IP VPN

- Lower teleworker connection costs, by as much as 20%-25% per month, over traditional dial-up & ISDN

- Use of standard protocols, IP and IPsec, which provide needed standardization

- Simplification of maintenance and support—reduces scalability issues and management complexity

In VPNs, "virtual" implies that the network is dynamic, with connections set up according to the organization's needs.

VPN Services

When corporations use the public Internet as a backbone for their communications, there are two alternatives for VPN use: either the service provider provides a secure, managed VPN service or the customer buys the equipment and installs it on his premises. In the first scenario, the service provider provides a service similar to the public switched frame relay or ATM service, and the customer trusts that packets will not be misdirected, modified in transit, or subjected to traffic analysis by unauthorized parties. In the second scenario, the customer does not trust the service provider and implements a VPN using CPE equipment that provides firewall functionality and security. In this case, the service provider is used solely for IP packet transport. In both scenarios, connecting the two VPN endpoints by a virtual tunnel creates security.

A VPN connection is established either by LAN to LAN or client to LAN connections. Gateway switches integrate all of the features needed (firewall, filtering, tunneling, security, bandwidth management and policy management) for high performance, reliable, and secure virtual private networking. Features may include the following:

- Support for point-to-point tunneling protocol (PPTP), L2F, and IPsec with Internet key exchange and X.509 Digital Certificates

- AES, DES, triple DES and RC4 encryption with MD5 and SHA hashing

- Internal or external LDAP, RADIUS, NT Domains, and token card authentication services

Figure 11-2. VPN applications

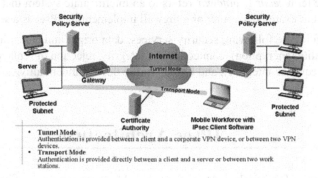

- **Tunnel Mode**
  Authentication is provided between a client and a corporate VPN device, or between two VPN devices.
- **Transport Mode**
  Authentication is provided directly between a client and a server or between two work stations.

The paths that the encapsulated packets follow in the Internet VPNs are called *tunnels*, not virtual circuits. Part of the encapsulation process performed by a tunnel endpoint includes adding a new address to the packet; this address is the one corresponding to the other endpoint of the tunnel.

IP Tunneling Mechanisms

There are several types of IP tunneling mechanisms and, depending on their form, they can provide some level of intrinsic data security. IP tunneling mechanisms include IP/IP, generic routing encapsulation (GRE) tunnels, layer 2 tunneling protocol (L2TP), IPsec, and multiprotocol label switching (MPLS). Some of these protocols are not often thought of as tunneling protocols, but they are and they do provide some type of protection.

IPsec is considered the best tunneling protocol for IP networks because it provides strong security services such as encryption, authentication, and key management.

L2TP is designed to transport point-to-point protocol (PPP) packets, and thus can be used to carry multiprotocol traffic, since PPP itself is multiprotocol. IP/IP and IPsec tunnels have no such protocol identification field, since the traffic being tunneled is assumed to be IP. L2TP, and PPP is used more in nonIP multiprotocol environments such as NETBEUI, IPX, and AppleTalk.

IPsec

IPsec provides security services at the IP layer by enabling a system to select required security protocols, determine the algorithm(s) to use for the service(s), and put in place any cryptographic keys required to provide the requested services.

IPsec can be used to protect one or more paths between a pair of communicating hosts, between a pair of communicating security gateways, or between a security gateway and a host. The term *security gateway* refers to an intermediate system that implements IPsec protocols. For example, a router or a firewall implementing IPsec is a security gateway.

IPsec provides the following security services: data origin authentication, access control, confidentiality (encryption), connectionless integrity, rejection of replayed packets (a form of partial sequence integrity), and limited traffic flow confidentiality.

IPsec Architecture

IPsec is a suite of protocols tied together to provide security services. Figure 11-3 shows the different architecture levels. Several documents address details of the IPsec architecture. RFC 4301 (Kent & Seo, 2005), for example, defines the basic architecture for IPsec-compliant systems, the conventions for naming payload formats, exchange types, and security-relevant information such as security policies or cryptographic algorithms and modes. The RFC 4301 also describes the interoperability of all of these elements.

IPsec Databases

There are three nominal databases in IPsec:

- **Security policy database (SPD):** Specifies the initiator and responder IP traffic policies.
- **Security association database (SAD):** Contains the parameters that are associated with each established security association. Each SA has an entry in SAD. The following data is included in SAD: security parameter index (SPI); encapsulated security payload

Figure 11-3. IPsec architecture

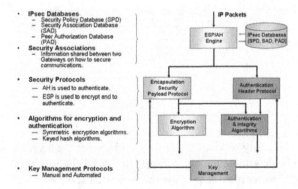

(ESP) encryption and integrity algorithms, key mode, IV, and so forth; authentication header (AH) authentication algorithm, MAC keys, and so forth.; SA lifetime; and IPsec protocol mode, tunnel or transport, applied to the SA.

- **Peer authorization database (PAD):** Provides the link between the SPD and a security management protocol (such as IKE) and the SPD.

Security Protocols

The security protocols consist of the IP Authentication Header (AH), RFC 4302 (Kent, 2005a), which is used to authenticate, and the IP Encapsulated Security Payload (ESP), RFC 4303 (Kent, 2005b), which is used to encrypt and to authenticate.

Security Associations (SA)

Security associations are created when information is shared between two gateways on how to secure a communication. SAs have three parameters:

- Security parameter index (SPI)
- IP destination address
- Security protocol ID, which identifies whether the SA is AH or ESP

Cryptographic Algorithms for Authentication and Encryption

RFC 4305 defines the mandatory, default algorithm for use with AH and ESP. RFC 4307 (Schiller, 2005) defines the mandatory algorithm for use with IKEv2. Each cryptographic algorithm has a separate RFC. AES, triple DES, and other symmetric encryption algorithms are used to encrypt the data. Keyed hash algorithms are used for authentication and integrity.

Key Management Protocols

The key management protocols are described in the Internet Key Exchange (IKEv2), RFC 4306 (Hoffman, 2005).

IPsec Protocols

Figure 11-4 shows the relationship of the IPsec protocols.

The following list defines some of the protocols:

1. Security architecture for IP, RFC 4301 (Kent & Seo, 2005)
2. Security protocols
    a. IP Authentication Header, RFC 4302 (Kent, 2005a)
    b. IP Encapsulating Security Payload (ESP), RFC 4303 (Kent, 2005b)
3. Algorithms for authentication and encryption—a separate RFC for each algorithm.
    a. Internet Key Exchange Version 2 (IKEv2), RFC 4306 (Hoffman, 2005)—A separate RFC for each algorithm

IPsec Negotiation

Refer to Figure 11- 5 for a description of IPsec negotiation.

Outbound Packet

1. The application calls the TCP/IP stack.
2. The TCP/IP packet is captured by the unprotect-protect engine.
3. After checking out the packet in the security policy database, the unprotect-protect engine determines whether it needs to be protected or allowed to bypass IPsec. In general, packets are selected for one of three processing modes based on IP address and transport layer header information matched against entries in the database (SPD). Each packet is either protected using IPsec services, discarded, or allowed to bypass IPsec protection.

Figure 11-4. IPsec protocol

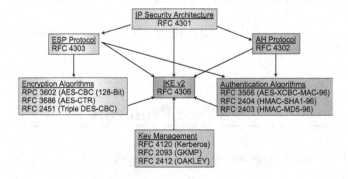

Figure 11-5. IPsec negotiation

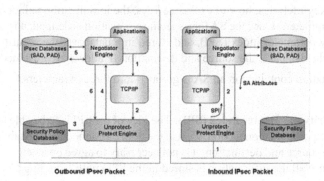

Outbound IPsec Packet   Inbound IPsec Packet

4.   If a packet needs to be protected, the unprotect-protect engine passes the address on to the negotiator engine that checks the address in the security association (SA) and the security parameter index (SPI).

5.   The negotiator engine looks up the SA and SPI in its internal database. If an SA has not been negotiated for that specific address, then the negotiator triggers the creation of an SA by initiating an IKE negotiation with the peer address.

6.   Once that negotiation is complete, the SPI and SA are passed on to the unprotect-protect engine. Now the unprotect-protect engine protects all packets sent to that address with keys negotiated by the negotiator.

Inbound Packet

1.   If an incoming packet comes in to the port reserved for the IKE negotiation (port 500 or 4500), and no SA has been negotiated with that incoming address, then the unprotect-protect engine will pass all of the IKE packets on to the negotiator.

2.   If the arriving packet has a security parameter index (SPI) associated with it, the SA associated with that SPI is retrieved from the IPsec databases. If the SPI is not in the database, then the packet can be rejected.

3.   If the arriving packet does not have an SPI embedded in it, the unprotect-protect engine can presume that the packet does not have an SA associated with it. Since there is no SA associated with the packet, it can be rejected.

Security Associations

An SA associates security parameters with the traffic to be protected. It can further be said that an SA describes the security parameters agreed upon between a sender and a receiver, such as a host or gateway, on how to secure a communication.

When a connection is established between a source and its destination, the two need to agree on, among other things, the encryption and authentication algorithms, the crypto keys, the key sizes, key lifetimes, how to exchange keys, the initialization values, and other related security parameters. Once the SA for a specific connection is defined, it is assigned an index, the security parameter index (SPI), and stored in a database, the security policy database (SPD). At the database, the source and destination IP addresses are added to the SA.

The information contained in an SA is grouped into three parameters:

- **Security parameter index (SPI):** The idea of the SPI is to be able to associate an SA with a particular connection, so, if in the future a connection is established between the same source and destination, it is not necessary to agree on a new security association because all the information is stored in the SPD with a binding SPI.

- **IP destination address:** This is the IP address of the end-user or a gateway such as a firewall or a router. In principle, the destination address may be a unicast address, an IP broadcast address, or a multicast group address. However, IPsec SA management mechanisms are defined currently only for unicast SAs.

- **Security protocol ID:** The security protocol ID indicates whether the security protocol is an Encapsulation Security Payload (ESP) or an Authentication Header (AH) protocol.

Security Protocols

IPsec provides mechanisms to provide security services to IP and upper layer protocols (e.g., UDP or TCP). IPsec protects IP datagrams by defining a security protocol in an SA. The SA associated with a connection could be an encapsulating security payload (ESP), or an authentication header (AH), but not both. If both AH and ESP protection are applied to a connection, then two (or more) SAs are created to provide protection to the connection. To secure typical, bidirectional communication between two hosts, or between two security gateways, two security associations (one in each direction) are required. Both ESP and AH security protocols support two modes of operation,i.e., transport or tunnel mode.

The AH protocol, RFC 4302 (Kent, 2005a), provides connectionless integrity, data origin authentication, and an optional anti-replay service. The ESP protocol, RFC 4303 (Kent, 2005b), may provide confidentiality (encryption), and limited traffic flow confidentiality. It also may provide connectionless integrity, data origin authentication, and an anti-replay service. Both AH and ESP are vehicles for access control, based on the distribution of cryptographic keys and the management of traffic flows relative to these security protocols.

Authentication Header

The AH protocol, RFC 4302 (Kent, 2005a), defines the format for IPsec packets that require data origin authentication, connectionless integrity, and anti-replay services only. The AH does not encrypt the data portion of the packet. AH may be applied alone, in combination with ESP, or in a nested fashion through the use of tunnel mode. Figure 11-6 shows the AH format. A description of each of the different fields is given below.

Next Header

The Next Header is an 8-bit field that identifies the type of header that the next payload after the Authentication Header has.

Payload Length

This 8-bit field specifies the length of the AH in 32-bit words (4-byte units), minus 2. In the AH, there are three 32-bit fixed words, so in the standard case of a 96-bit authentication, there are six words in the header, and the Payload field is 4.

Reserved

This 16-bit field is reserved for future use.

Figure 11-6. Authentication header

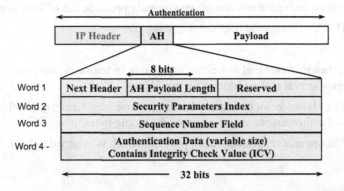

Security Parameters Index (SPI)

The security parameters index (SPI) tells which security protocols are being used and the algorithms and keys that are included in this field. The SPI is an arbitrary 32-bit value that, in combination with the destination IP address and security protocol (AH), uniquely identifies the security association for the datagram. The SPI value is selected by the destination system at the SA establishment. The Internet Assigned Numbers Authority (IANA), for future use, reserves the values in the range 1 through 255.

Sequence Number

The sequence number tells how many packets have been sent and provides anti-replay protection. This unassigned 32-bit field contains a monotonically increasing counter value (sequence number). It is mandatory and is always present even if the receiver does not elect to enable the anti-replay service for a specific SA. The sender's counter and the receiver's counter are initialized to 0 when an SA is established. The first packet sent using a given SA would have a sequence number of 1. If anti-replay is enabled (the default), the transmitted sequence number must never be allowed to cycle. The sender's counter and the receiver's counter must be reset (by establishing a new SA and, thus, a new key) prior to the transmission of the 2^{32}nd packet in an SA.

Integrity Check Value

This variable-length field contains the integrity check value (ICV) for the packet. The field must be an integral multiple of 32 bits in length and may include explicit padding. This padding is included to ensure that the length of the AH header is an integral multiple of 32 bits (IPv4) or 64 bits (IPv6). All implementations must support such padding.

The authentication algorithm employed for the ICV computation is specified by the SA. For point-to-point communication, suitable authentication algorithms include keyed message authentication codes (HMACs) based on symmetric encryption algorithms (e.g., AES) or on one-way hash functions (e.g., MD5 or SHA1). For multicast communication, one-way hash algorithms combined with asymmetric signature algorithms are appropriate, though performance and space considerations currently preclude use of such algorithms.

The AH ICV is computed over the following:

- IP header fields that are either immutable in transit or that are predictable in value upon arrival at the endpoint for the AH SA
- The AH header including next header, payload length, reserved, SPI, sequence number, and authentication data, and explicit padding bytes, if any
- The upper level protocol data, payload, which is assumed to be immutable in transit

The mandatory-to-implement authentication algorithms are:

- HMAC-SHA-1-96; must be supported
- AES-XCBC-MAC-96; should be supported
- HMAC-MD5-96; may be supported

Note: Some HMAC implementation truncates the output H to a given length t, so only part of the hash is outputted. The HMAC notation is as follows: HMAC – Hash algorithm – t. For example, HMAC - SHA1 - 96 is an HMAC that uses SHA1 for its hash function, and the resulting hash is truncated to 96 bits.

Encapsulating Security Protocol (ESP)

RFC 4303 (Kent, 2005b), "ESP protocol," provides the same security services that AH provides (data origin authentication, connectionless integrity, and anti-replay service); it also provides traffic flow confidentiality (encryption). The primary difference between the authentication provided by ESP and the authentication provided by AH is the extent of the coverage. Specifically, ESP does not protect any IP header fields unless those fields are encapsulated by ESP (tunnel mode). The set of services provided by ESP depends on options selected at the time that the security association is established and on the placement of the implementation.

Data origin authentication and connectionless integrity are joint services referred to as *integrity*. Either integrity or confidentiality can be used, but at least one of them must be selected. The anti-replay service may be selected only if integrity service is selected, and its election is solely at the discretion of the receiver. Traffic flow confidentiality requires selection of

Figure 11-7. ESP encapsulation

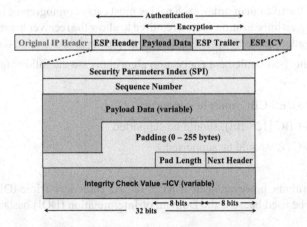

the tunnel mode and is most effective if implemented at a security gateway, where traffic aggregation may be able to mask true source-destination patterns.

The ESP handles encryption of IP at the packet level using symmetric key encryption. ESP is designed to use any number of encryption algorithms, the most common of which is the Advanced Encryption Standard (AES).

In Figure 11-7, notice the following:

- The ESP header is inserted between the IP header and the rest of the packet.
- The SPI and sequence number field provide the same functions as they do in the AH.
- The TCP portion, data (payload), and ESP trailer are all encrypted.
- ESP provides authentication in the same manner as the AH does.

The following is a description of the different fields:

Security Parameter Index (SPI)

Same as in the AH format.

Sequence Number

Same as in the AH format.

Payload Data

Payload Data is a mandatory, variable-length field containing data described by the Next Header field. ESP is designed for use with symmetric encryption algorithms and because IP packets may arrive out of order, each packet must carry cryptographic synchronization data, for example, an initialization vector, required to allow the receiver to establish cryptographic synchronization for decryption. The cryptographic synchronization data is in the payload.

The mandatory-to-implement encryption algorithms are the following:

- Triple DES-CBC; must be supported
- AES-CBC (128-Bit); should be supported
- AES-CTR; should be supported

Other algorithms, however, such as RC5, IDEA, Three-key Triple IDEA, Cast, and Blow-fish, could be used because the Domain of Interpretation (DOI) has assigned identifiers to them.

Padding

Padding is required for the following purposes:

- Some encryption algorithms require the length of the plaintext to be a multiple number of a block size. The padding is used to fill the plaintext to the size required by the algorithm. The plaintext consists of the payload data, the pad length, and the Next Header fields, as well as the padding.

- Padding is also added to the ciphertext to ensure that the resulting number of bits in the ciphertext is a multiple of 32 bits.

- Additional padding may be used to conceal the actual length of the payload, in support of (partial) traffic flow confidentiality.

The sender may add up to 255 bytes of padding.

Pad Length

The Pad Length field indicates the number of pad bytes. The range of valid values is 0-255, where a value of zero indicates that no padding bytes are present. The pad length field is mandatory.

Next Header

The Next Header is an 8-bit field that identifies the type of data contained in the Payload Data field as defined on the Web page of the IANA; for example, a value of 4 indicates IPv4, a value of 41 indicates IPv6. The Next Header field also could indicate an upper layer protocol identifier, for example, a value of 6 indicates TCP.

Integrity Check Value (ICV)

The integrity check value is the same for an ESP format as for an AH format except that for ESP, the ICV is computed over the ESP header, ESP trailer fields, and payload. If the encryption service is selected, the last two fields are in ciphertext form, as the encryption is applied before authentication.

AH and ESP Modes of Operation

IPsec may be implemented in two types of equipment, a host or a security gateway. A security gateway is an intermediate system between two networks; one side of the gateway is viewed as untrusted, the other side as trusted. The gateway implements IPsec on the untrusted interface in order to permit secure communications between hosts on the trusted side and hosts on the untrusted side.

Security services can be provided (1) between a pair of communicating hosts; (2) between a pair of communicating security gateways; or, (3) between a security gateway and a host.

AH and ESP support two modes of operation: the transport mode and the tunnel mode. A transport mode SA is a security association between two hosts. When a security gateway works in transport mode, it acts as a host: the traffic is destined for itself. A tunnel mode SA is a security association between a host and a gateway or between two gateways.

Transport mode is used to protect upper-layer protocols. Tunnel mode is used to protect entire IP packets, meaning that the entire IP packet is encapsulated in another IP packet, and a new IP header is inserted between the outer and inner IP headers.

In a transport mode, the security protocol header appears immediately after the original IP header and before payload data (i.e., any higher layer protocols, e.g., TCP or UDP and Data). In an ESP transport mode, SA provides security services only for the higher layer protocols, not for the original IP header or any extension headers preceding the ESP header. In the case of AH, the protection is extended to the original IP header.

For a tunnel mode SA, an outer header specifies the IPsec end-point and processing destination, plus an inner header that specifies the (apparently) ultimate destination for the packet. The security protocol header appears after the outer IP header, and before the inner IP header. If AH is employed in tunnel mode, portions of the outer IP header are afforded protection (as above), as well as all of the tunneled IP packets, that is, all of the inner IP header is protected, as well as higher layer protocols. If ESP is employed, the protection is afforded only to the tunneled packet, not to the outer header.

Figure 11-8. AH and ESP modes of operation

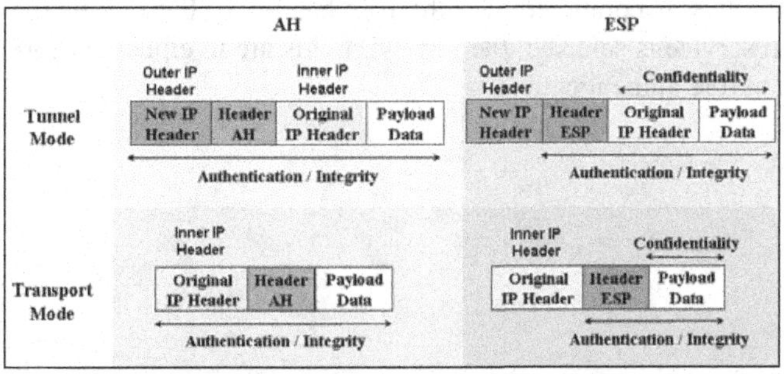

Algorithms for Encryption and Authentication in IPsec

IPsec allows users to determine which security services to use, the granularity at which a given security protection should be applied, and the encryption and authentication algorithms used. The following is a list of encryption and authentication protocols used in IPsec:

Authentication Header (AH) RFC 4302 (Kent, 2005a):

* HMAC (hash message authentication code)
* SHA1 (RFC 2841)
* MD5 (RFC-1828)

Encapsulation Security Payload (ESP) RFC 4303 (Kent, 2005b):

* Supports only symmetric encryption.
* DES, 3DES, RC5, IDEA, Three-key IDEA, CAST, Blowfish, AES.

Internet Key Exchange RFC 4306 (IKEv2) (Hoffman, 2005), RFC 2412 (Oakley) (Orman, 1998):

* Diffie-Hellman
* Public-key cryptography
* X.509 digital certificates

Internet Key Exchange (IKE v2)

Because IPsec security services use symmetric encryption, it is necessary for both hosts, source and destination, to agree to the mechanisms used to share the secret keys, as well as to the keys that are used for authentication/integrity and encryption services. IPsec supports both manual and automatic distribution of keys. Public key is used for automatic key management, but other automated key distribution techniques may be used.

RFC 4306, IKE v2 (Hoffman, 2005), combines the security concepts of authentication, key management, and security associations to establish the required security for government, commercial, and private communications on the Internet. It does so by defining procedures and packet formats to establish, negotiate, modify, and delete security associations (SA). IKE v2 defines payloads for exchanging key generation and authentication data, thus providing a consistent framework for transferring key and authentication data independent of the key generation technique, encryption algorithm, and authentication mechanism.

A security association (SA) payload indicates a proposal for a set of IPsec encryption algorithms, authentication mechanisms, and key establishment algorithms to be used in IKE, as well as for ESP and/or AH. IKE v2 is not bound to any specific cryptographic algorithm, key generation technique, or security mechanism; the independence from specific security mechanisms and algorithms provides a forward migration path to better mechanisms and algorithms. When improved security mechanisms are developed to counter new attacks against current encryption algorithms, authentication mechanisms and key exchanges would be created; in those situations, IKE v2 would allow the updating of the algorithms and mechanisms without having to develop a completely new IKE or to patch the current one.

A security association normally includes the parameters listed below, but might include additional parameters as well:

- Type of protection used, either ESP or AH
- Authentication algorithm used with AH
- Key(s) used with the authentication algorithm in AH
- Encryption algorithm and mode used with ESP
- Key(s) used with the encryption algorithm in ESP
- Initialization vector for the encryption algorithm used in ESP
- Authentication algorithm and mode used with the ESP transform
- Authentication key(s) used with the authentication algorithm in ESP
- Lifetime of the key used or time when key change should occur
- Hash algorithms to reduce data for signing used
- Information provided about a group over which to do a Diffie-Hellman exchange
- Lifetime of the security association established
- Source address(es) of the security association provided

IKEv2 Algorithm Selection

IKEv1 and IKEv2 provide mechanisms to negotiate which algorithms should be used to ensure interoperability between the initiator and the responder. For IKEv1, the algorithms were listed in RFC 2409, "The Internet Key Exchange (IKEv1)," but for IKE v2, the list was moved from RFC 4306 (Hoffman, 2005), "The Internet Key Exchange (IKEv1)" to RFC 4307 (Schiller, 2005), "IKEv2 Cryptographic Algorithms." If new algorithms are added, RFC 4306 will not need to be changed.

The following features are used by IKE and must be negotiated for the IPsec security association:

- Encryption algorithms to protect data
  o Must implement 3DES and should implement AES-CBC-128 and AES-CTR-128 modes
- Integrity protection algorithms to produce a fingerprint of the data
  o Must implement HMAC-SHA1-96, should implement AES-XCBC-96, and may implement HMAC-MD5-96

- Information about which Diffie-Hellman Modular Exponentiation Group (MODP) to use
  - o Must implement D-H MODP Group 2 (discrete log 1024 bits), should support D-H Group 14 (2048), and may support D-H elliptic curves over GF [2^{155}] and over GF [2^{185}]
- Pseudorandom function to use
  - o Must implement PRF-HMAC-SHA1 (RFC2104), should support PRF-AES-XCBC-PRF-128 (RFC 3664), and may implement PRF-HMAC-MD5 (RFC 2104)

IKE Message Exchanges

In IKE, an initiator proposes one or more cryptographic suites (sets of algorithms) that it is able to support, and the responder mixes-and-matches the suites to create an IKE_SA. The IKE_SA is then used to protect the negotiations for the protocol SA being requested. Two entities (e.g., IPsec servers) can negotiate (and have active) multiple IPsec SAs.

IKE communications consist of pairs of messages, a request followed by a response. The first IKE message exchange always begins with two requests/responses, IKE_SA_INIT (Figure 11-9), steps 1 and 2, and IKE_AUTH, steps 3 and 4. Two entities (e.g., IPsec servers) agree on how to protect further negotiated traffic between them. Subsequent IKE exchanges are CREATE_CHILD or INFORMATIONAL.

In IKE_SA_INIT, the initiator and responder negotiate the use of encryption algorithms by establishing an IKE_SA and, then, by exchanging information for key agreement by sending nonces and Diffie-Hellman values. The agreed keys are used to protect the IKE_AUTH exchange. At this point, the initiator and the responder have agreed on cryptographic key algorithms, but without authenticating each other.

In IKE_AUTH, the initiator and responder authenticate each other using authentication mechanisms such as digital signatures (exchanging certificates), Extensible Authentication Protocol (EAP), or pre-shared keys. In IKE_AUTH, the first IKE_SA and associated IPsec SA, called *child SA*, are created.

The subsequent IKE exchange consists of a single request/response, CREATE_CHILD_SA, that is used to negotiate additional child security associations, which are used to protect additional traffic between the initiator and the responder.

While the IKE_INIT and IKE_AUTH approaches have a higher start-up cost for most simple scenarios, there are several reasons why they would be beneficial for most other cases:

- It takes some time for entities (e.g., IPsec servers) to carry out IKE_INIT and IKE_AUTH, but then time is saved during the subsequent CREATE_CHILD_SAs. This allows multiple child SAs to be established among peers over time without having to start over for each communication.

Figure 11-9. IKE_INIT and IKE_AUTH

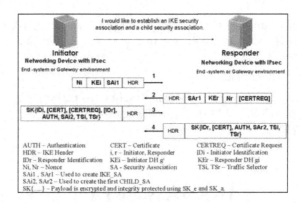

- IKE_INIT establishes an IKE-SA that includes shared secret information that is used to create CHILD_SAs.

- In IKEv2, the first child SA is created on the IKE_AUTH exchange.

- Subsequent CHILD_SAs require only one request/response message in the CREATE_CHILD_SA exchange, making it a very inexpensive operation.

Another IKE exchange is INFORMATIONAL; it is used by either party to convey control messages regarding errors or notifications during the operation of an IKE_SA. Informational exchanges may occur at any time after IKE_AUTH.

IKE_SA_INIT

In **Step 1**, Figure 11-9, the initiator sends an HDR that contains the Security Parameter Index (SPI), the IKE version number, and some message identifiers. These message identifiers include SAi1, which indicates the cryptographic algorithms the initiator supports for the IKE_SA, and the proposed Diffie-Hellman group. The other message identifiers are the KEi payload, which includes the initiator's Diffie-Hellman value, g^i, and the initiator's nonce (Ni), which is used to protect against replay attacks. The header (HDR) identifies the initiator's SPI (i.e., the initiator's reference for the IKE_SA to be established), the IKE version number, flags specific to the message, and a message identifier that is used for retransmissions and matching responses to requests. The SAi1 payload includes the supported cryptographic algorithms for the IKE_SA. The SAi1 payload identifies at least one proposal that contains algorithms for encryption, the pseudorandom function, integrity, and the proposed Diffie-Hellman group. The KEi payload includes the initiator's Diffie-Hellman value. The Ni payload contains the initiator's nonce, which is used to protect against replay attacks.

In **Step 2**, Figure 11-9, the responder sends an HDR, which contains the initiator's SPI, the IKE version number, and the same message identifiers used by the initiator. The responder chooses a cryptographic suite by mixing-and-matching the initiator's offered suites and expresses that choice to the initiator in SAr1. The responder also completes the Diffie-Hellman exchange with the KEr, g^r, and sends its nonce in *Nr*. The responder may also (optional) request a specific type of certificate, for example, X.509, by sending the request in [CERTREQ]. No identities are disclosed in the IKE_SA_INIT exchange, other than the IP addresses in the IP headers.

At this point, initiator and responder have negotiated a shared but unauthenticated IKE_SA (SAr1). Also, after the Diffie-Hellman key exchange, each party generates a shared but unauthenticated key, SKEYSEED, from which all keys are derived for that IKE_SA. The keys generated from SKEYSEED are known as the following: SK_e (encryption), and SK_a (message authentication, integrity); SK_d for deriving keys for child SAs; and SK_p for creating AUTH payload in the second request/response exchange. Note that separate SK_e and SK_a keys are generated for each direction. See "Generating Key Material in IKE" section in this chapter.

IKE_SA_AUTH

In **Step 3**, Figure 11-9, the header (HDR) includes the initiator's and the responder's SPI, the IKE version number, and the same message identifiers that were used in the IKE_SA_INIT. The notation SK {…}, also called *encrypted payload*, indicates that the payload is encrypted and integrity protected using SK_e and SK_a.

The following information is included in the initiator's encrypted payload:

- The initiator's identity IDi
- Optional: the initiator's certificate, [Cert], and a list of its trusted root CAs in [CER-TREQ]
- The identity of the responder to which the initiator wants to talk by sending [IDr]
- The SAi2 by which the initiator begins negotiation of the first non-IKE security association called *CHILD_SA*, as well as the protocol to be used, for example, Authentication Header (AH) or Encapsulating Security Payload (ESP)
- The traffic selectors TSi and TSr

The whole message is encrypted and its integrity protected using the initiator's SK_e and SK_a. The CHILD_SA is used for ESP and/or AH.

Traffic selectors, TS, allow end points to communicate each other's address and port range, as well as the IP protocol ID that they would like to use. For example, when the initiator sends {192.0.1.0 – 192.0.1.255} as TSi and {192.0.2.0 – 192.0.2.255} as TSr, it means that the initiator would like to tunnel all received information on its IP address range {192.0.1.0 – 192.0.1.255} and would like to tunnel all transmitted information to the responder's IP address range {192.0.2.0 – 192.0.2.255}.

In **Step 4**, Figure 11-9, the header (HDR) includes the initiator's and responder's SPIs, the IKE version number, and the message identifier sent by the initiator in step 3.

The following information is included in the responder's encrypted payload:

- The responder's identity IDr.
- Optional: the responder's certificate, [CERT], if it was requested.
- The AUTH field, which is used by the responder to authenticate itself to the initiator.
- SAr2 to complete the negotiation of CHILD_SA by accepting the proposed algorithms and identifying the negotiated protocol, that is, AH or ESP.
- The traffic selectors with TSi and TSr. If the responder agrees to the traffic selectors proposed by the initiator, the TSi and TSr that the responder sends should be the same as the TSi and TSr sent by the initiator.

All messages exchanged are encrypted and integrity protected with the responder's SK_e and SK_a. The agreed suite of cryptographic algorithms in SAr2 and the shared keys are used to protect the messages in a second message exchange.

CREATE_CHILD_SAs

The second message exchange consists of a single request/response, which may be initiated by either end, so, in this section, the term *Initiator*, refers to the end point initiating this exchange. The CREATE_CHILD_SA exchange is used to create new CHILD_SAs and to rekey IKE_SAs and CHILD_SAs. All messages are cryptographically protected using the encryption algorithms and keys negotiated in IKE_SA_INIT and IKE_SA_AUTH. However, to enable stronger guarantees of forward secrecy for the key generated for IKE_SA and for CHILD-SA, the CREATE_CHILD_SA request can use additional Diffie-Hellman exchanges to create new keys.

In **Step 5**, Figure 11-10, the initiator sends the header (HDR), which includes the initiator's and the responder's SPIs, the IKE version number, and the message identifiers. The notation SK {...} indicates that the payload is encrypted and its integrity protected using SK_e and SK_a. The initiator (1) sends notify, [N+], which contains additional details for the CHILD_SA (optional step); (2) proposes an SA; (3) sends a nonce in Ni payload; (4) sends a new Diffie-Hellman value, g^i, in Kei payload (optional step); and (5) sends the traffic selectors TSi and TSr. The whole message is encrypted and integrity protected using keys computed from SK_d.

In **Step 6**, Figure 11-10, the responder sends the header (HDR) which includes the initiator's and responder's SPIs, the IKE version number, and the message identifier. The responder (1) sends notify, [N+], which contains additional details for the CHILD_SA (optional step); (2) agrees to the proposed algorithms in an SA payload; (3) sends its nonce in Nr payload; (4) sends a new Diffie-Hellman value, g^r, in Kei payload (optional step); and (5) sends the

Figure 11-10. CREATE CHILD_SA exchange

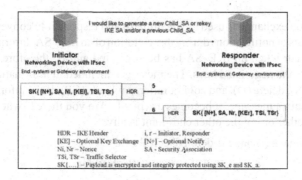

traffic selectors TSi and TSr. The whole message is encrypted and integrity protected using keys computed from SK_d.

IKE, ESP and AH security associations use secret keys that should be used only for a limited amount of time and to protect a limited amount of data. When an SA has expired, new security associations can be established by rekeying the IKE_SA or a CHILD_SA.

If CREATE_CHILD_SA is used to rekey IKE_SAs, then the following is exchanged:

Initiator	Responder
HDR, SK{ SA, Ni, [Kei]} →	
	← HDR, SK{ SA, Nr, [Ker]}

If CREATE_CHILD_SA is used to rekey CHILD_SAs, then the following is exchanged:

Initiator	Responder
HDR, SK{ N(REKEY_SA), [N+],	
SA, Ni, [Kei], TSi, TSr} →	
	← HDR, SK{ [N+], SA, Ni, [Kei], TSi, TSr}

Note that the initiator identifies the CHILD_SA being rekeyed in the leading notifying payload, N (REKEY_SA).

As stated in RFC 4718, IKE v2 Clarifications, section 5.2, rekeying the IKE_SA establishes new keys for the IKE_SA and resets the Message ID counters, but it does not authenticate the parties (no AUTH or payload is involved). IKEv2 does not have special provisions for reauthentication, so it is done by creating a new IKE_SA from scratch, using a new IKE_SA_INIT and IKE_SA_AUTH.

Informational Exchange in IKE

An information exchange is used by the initiator and responder to convey control messages regarding errors or notifications during the operation of an IKE_SA. Informational exchanges must only occur when an IKE_SA has been created and is, therefore, cryptographically protected with the negotiated keys. The messages included in informational exchanges are notification (N), delete (D), and configuration payloads (CP). If the informational exchange does not contain a message, it becomes a type of "Are you there?" where one end-point is verifying whether or not the other end-point is alive.

An informational exchange is defined as follows:

Initiator   **Responder**

HDR, SK { [N], [D], [CP], . . . }   →

                                        ←   HDR, SK{ [N], [D], [CP] . . .}

Generating Key Material in IKE

In IKE_SA, four cryptographic algorithms are negotiated: encryption algorithms, integrity protection algorithms, a Diffie-Hellman group, and a pseudorandom function (prf). Key material for all of the cryptographic algorithms used in both IKE_SA and CHILD_SA is always derived as the output of a prf algorithm. In IKEv2, Diffie-Hellman is the only key exchange algorithm used.

The Diffie-Hellman exchange has the following three components: a generator g, the modulo p, and a secret that in IKEv2 terminology is called i or r. During IKE_INIT, the initiator and responder exchange Diffie-Hellman information in KEi and KEr. That information includes g^i and g^r, as well as nonces Ni and Nr.

The shared key, SKEYSEED, is calculated by both the initiator and responder from the nonces exchanged and the generated Diffie-Hellman shared secret key, g^{ir}, according to the following formula:

Figure 11-11. Key exchange

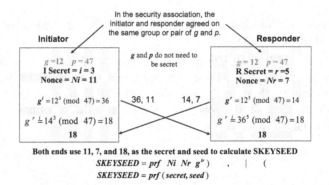

Both ends use 11, 7, and 18, as the secret and seed to calculate SKEYSEED
$$SKEYSEED = prf \ (Ni \ Nr \ g^{ir}) \quad , \quad | \quad ($$
$$SKEYSEED = prf \ (secret, seed)$$

$SKEYSEED = prf\,(\,Ni\,\|\,Nr\,,g^{ir}\,)$

Once SKEYSEED is generated by both ends, it is used to calculate seven other keys:

- SK_d for deriving new keys for the CHLD_SA
- SK_ai and SK_ar for integrity protection
- SK_ei and S_Ker for enciphering and deciphering all exchanges
- SK_pi and SK_pr for authentication

SKEYSEED's derivatives are calculated as follows:

{ SK_d ∥ SK_ai ∥ SK_ar ∥ SK_ei ∥ SK_er ∥ SK_pi ∥ SK_pr } = prf+ (SKEYSEED, Ni ∥ Nr ∥ SPIi ∥ SPIr). Note that prf+ is simple the prf of a prf.

The bits for SK_d, SK_ai, SK_ar, SK_ei, SK_er, SK_pi, and SK_pr are taken in order and from the generated bits of prf+.

prf+ (K, S) = T1 ∥ T2 ∥ T3 ∥ T4 ∥ … ∥ Tn

where

- T1 = prf (SKEYSEED, Ni ∥ Nr ∥ SPIi ∥ SPIr ∥ 0x01)
- T2 = prf (SKEYSEED, T1 ∥ Ni ∥ Nr ∥ SPIi ∥ SPIr ∥ 0x02)
- T3 = prf (SKEYSEED, T2 ∥ Ni ∥ Nr ∥ SPIi ∥ SPIr ∥ 0x03)
- T4 = prf (SKESEED, T3 | Ni ∥ Nr ∥ SPIi ∥ SPIr ∥ 0x04)
- Tn = prf (SKESEED, Tn-1 ∥ Ni ∥ Nr ∥ SPIi ∥ SPIr ∥ 0x0n)
- prf (key, seed) is a keyed pseudorandom function, for example, PRF-AES-XCBC-PRF-128 (RFC 3664).
- SPIi and SPIr are the security parameter indexes of the initiator and responder.

Note that each traffic direction uses different keys, so SK_ei and SK_ai are used to protect messages originating from the initiator, and SK_er and SK_ar are used to protect messages originating from the responder. Also, note that because Ni and Nr are used as the keys for the prf, then the nonces should be randomly selected and must be at least half the key size of the negotiated prf.

Generating Key Material for CHILD_SA

If additional CHILD_SAs are created in CREATE_CHILD_SA, the keying material is generated as follows:

KEYMAT = prf+ (SK_d, Ni || Nr), or KEYMAT = prf+ (SK_d, g^{ir} (new) || Ni || Nr)

In the first formula, the seed used in prf+ are the nonces from the CREATE_CHILD_SA exchange, Ni and Nr. In the second formula, the seed also includes a new-shared secret, g^{ir}, from the ephemeral Diffie-Hellman exchange of the CREATE_CHILD_SA exchange.

Integrity and Authentication in IKE

For authentication, IKEv2 uses digital signature algorithms, shared secrets, and EAP methods defined in RFC 3748. See Chapter VII, "Access Authentication," for more information about EAP.

The authentication payload, AUTH, has two types of information, the type of authentication method used and the authentication data. IKEv2 uses the following authentication methods: RSA digital signature, shared key message integrity code, and DSS digital signature. A description of authentication data can be derived by looking at IKE_INIT and IKE_AUTH exchanges.

Initiator		Responder
HDR, SAi, Kei, Ni	(Step 1)→	
	←(Step 2)	HDR, SAr, KEr Nr, [CERTREQ]
HDR, SK{ IDi, [CER],		
[CERTREQ], [IDr], AUTH,		
SAi2, TSi, TSr}	(Step 3)→	
		HDR, SK{ IDr, [CERT], AUTH,
	←(Step 4)	SAr2, TSi, TSr}

In **Step 3**, Figure 11-9, the authentication data that the initiator signs in AUTH includes the message sent in step 1, appended to Nr, and the value of prf (SK_pr, IDr'). Note the values of Nr and prf (SK_pr, IDr') are not sent, but included in the message that is signed. IDr' is the responder's ID payload without the header.

In **Step 4**, Figure 11-9, the authentication data that the responder signs in AUTH includes the message sent in step 2, appended to Nr, and the value of prf (SK_pr, IDi'). Note the values of Ni and prf (SK_pr, IDi') are not sent, but included in the message that is signed. IDi' is the initiator's ID payload without the header.

Steps 3 and 4 may include a certificate or certificate authority (CA) that provides evidence of the public-key ownership used to calculate digital signatures. IKEv2 allows an entity initiating communications to indicate which CAs it supports. After selection of a CA, the protocol provides the messages required to support the actual authentication exchange. The protocol provides a facility for identification of different certificate authorities, certificate types (e.g., X.509, PKCS #7, PGP, DNS SIG and KEY records), and the exchange of the certificates identified.

If the initiator would like to use extensible authentication, it does not include the AUTH payload in step 3, meaning that it has not proven its identity, IDi. The responder, then, includes an EAP payload in step 4 and defers sending SAr2, TSi, and TSr until authentication is completed. The initial SA will appear as follows:

Initiator		Responder
HDR, SAi, Kei, Ni	→	
	←	HDR, SAr, KEr Nr, [CERTREQ]
HDR, SK{ Idi, [CERTREQ], [IDr], SAi2, TSi, TSr}	→	
	←	HDR, SK{ IDr, [CERT], AUTH, EAP}
HDR, SK{ EAP }	→	
	←	HDR, SK{ EAP (success) }
HDR, SK{ AUTH }	→	
	←	HDR, SK{ AUTH SAr2, TSi, TSr }

Diffie-Hellman Group Descriptors

The ephemeral Diffie-Hellman key exchange is used in IKE to generate keying material, in this way supporting what is called *perfect forward secrecy*. Once a connection is closed, each end point forgets not only the exchanged keys, but also the secrets used in the Diffie-Hellman key calculation.

Three distinct group representations can be used with IKE. The three types are modular exponentiation groups (named MODP), elliptic curve groups over the field GF [2^n] (named EC2N), and elliptic curve groups over GF [P] (named ECP). For each representation, many distinct realizations are possible, depending on parameter selection.

RFC 2409, "The Internet Key Exchange (IKEv1)," and RFC 4307 (Schiller, 2005), "IKEv2 Cryptographic Algorithms," specify the following IKE groups:

- **Group 2:** A modular exponentiation group with a 1024-bit modulus
- **Group 14:** A modular exponentiation group with a 2048-bit modulus
- **Group 3:** An elliptic curve group over GF [2^{155}]
- **Group 4:** An elliptic curve group over GF [2^{185}]

RFC 3526 (Kivinen & Kojo, 2003), "More Modular Exponential (MODP) Diffie-Hellman Groups for IKE," specifies stronger Diffie-Hellman groups that are equivalent to AES strength. For example, the 128-bit AES requires a 3200-bit group, and the 192 and 256-bit keys would need groups that are about 8000 and 15400 bits respectively. The following are the new Diffie-Hellman groups proposed in RFC 3526:

- **Group 5:** A modular exponentiation group with a 1536-bit modulus
- **Group 15:** A modular exponentiation group with a 3072-bit modulus
- **Group 16:** A modular exponentiation group with a 4096-bit modulus
- **Group 17:** A modular exponentiation group with a 6144-bit modulus
- **Group 18:** A modular exponentiation group with an 8192-bit modulus

The following are examples of Diffie-Hellman groups:

Group 2: Modular Exponentiation with a 1024 Bit Prime

The generator $g = 2$

$p = 2^{1536} - 2^{1472} - 1 + 2^{64} * \{ [2^{1406} pi] + 741804 \}$.

Its hexadecimal value is:

FFFFFFFF FFFFFFFF C90FDAA2 2168C234 C4C6628B 80DC1CD1

29024E08 8A67CC74 020BBEA6 3B139B22 514A0879 8E3404DD

EF9519B3 CD3A431B 302B0A6D F25F1437 4FE1356D 6D51C245

E485B576 625E7EC6 F44C42E9 A637ED6B 0BFF5CB6 F406B7ED

EE386BFB 5A899FA5 AE9F2411 7C4B1FE6 49286651 ECE45B3D

C2007CB8 A163BF05 98DA4836 1C55D39A 69163FA8 FD24CF5F

83655D23 DCA3AD96 1C62F356 208552BB 9ED52907 7096966D

670C354E 4ABC9804 F1746C08 CA237327 FFFFFFFF FFFFFFFF

The primality of the number has been rigorously proven.

Group 3: An Elliptic Curve Group Definition

The elliptic curve is based on the Galois field $GF [2^{155}]$ with 2^{155} field elements. The irreducible polynomial for the field is $u^{155} + u^{62} + 1$. The equation for the elliptic curve is $y^2 + xy = x^3 + ax + b$, where x, y, a, b are elements of the field.

Elliptic curve parameters: $a = 0$ and $b = 471951$ in decimal and 7338F in hex.

Generator's points: $x = 123$ in decimal and 7B in hex; $y = 456$ in decimal and 1C8 in hex.

The group order (the number of curve points) is:

456719261665907161938655659143446351967692373316,

which is 12 times the prime

38059938472158930161554638261953862663974364443.

This prime has been rigorously proven. The generating point (x, y) has order 4 times the prime; the generator is the triple of some curve point.

IPsec and IKE v2 Identifiers

The way IPsec and IKEv2 define security-relevant information is by assigning specific protocol identifiers, and by describing how those protocols are used. Those identifiers are listed in the Internet Assigned Numbers Authority, (IANA). When negotiating security associations, the source and destination choose security protocols and cryptographic algorithms by using identifiers.

The following examples of IPsec and IKE v2 identifiers are presented to give an idea of how the identifiers are used, but it is not a substitute for reading the actual document specification:

IKEv2 Exchange Types, Part of the header (HDR)

Value	Type	Reference
34	IKE_SA_INIT	[RFC4306]
35	IKE_AUTH	[RFC4306]
36	CREATE_CHILD_SA	[RFC4306]
37	INFORMATIONAL	[RFC4306]

IKEv2 Security Protocol Identifiers

Protocol ID	Protocol	Reference
1	IKE	[RFC4306]
2	AH	[RFC4306]
3	ESP	[RFC4306]
4	FC_ESP_HEADER	[RFC4595]
5	FC_CT_AUTHENTICATION	[RFC4595]

Confidentiality Algorithm Identifiers

Number	Name	Reference
1	ENCR_DES_IV64	[RFC1827]
2	ENCR_DES	[RFC2405]
3	ENCR_3DES	[RFC2451]
4	ENCR_RC5	[RFC2451]
5	ENCR_IDEA	[RFC2451]
6	ENCR_CAST	[RFC2451]
7	ENCR_BLOWFISH	[RFC2451]
8	ENCR_3IDEA	[RFC2451]
9	ENCR_DES_IV32	[RFC4306]
11	ENCR_NULL	[RFC2410]
12	ENCR_AES_CBC	[RFC3602]
13	ENCR_AES_CTR	[RFC3686]
14	ENCR_AES-CCM_8	[RFC4309]
15	ENCR-AES-CCM_12	[RFC4309]
16	ENCR-AES-CCM_16	[RFC4309]
18	AES-GCM with a 8 octet ICV	[RFC4106]
19	AES-GCM with a 12 octet ICV	[RFC4106]
20	AES-GCM with a 16 octet ICV	[RFC4106]
21	ENCR_NULL_AUTH_AES_GMAC	[RFC4543]

Integrity Algorithm Identifiers

Number	Name	Reference
1	AUTH_HMAC_MD5_96	[RFC2403]
2	AUTH_HMAC_SHA1_96	[RFC2404]
3	AUTH_DES_MAC	[RFC4306]
4	AUTH_KPDK_MD5	[RFC1826]
5	AUTH_AES_XCBC_96	[RFC3566]
6	AUTH_HMAC_MD5_128	[RFC4595]
7	AUTH_HMAC_SHA1_160	[RFC4595]
8	AUTH_AES_CMAC_96	[RFC4494]
9	AUTH_AES_128_GMAC	[RFC4543]
10	AUTH_AES_192_GMAC	[RFC4543]
11	AUTH_AES_256_GMAC	[RFC4543]

IKEv2 Authentication Method

Value	Authentication Method	Reference
1	RSA Digital Signature	[RFC4306]
2	Shared Key Message Integrity Code	[RFC4306]
3	DSS Digital Signature	[RFC4306]
9	ECDSA with SHA-256 on the P-256 curve	
10	ECDSA with SHA-384 on the P-384 curve	
11	ECDSA with SHA-512 on the P-521 curve	

Pseudorandom Function

Number	Name	Reference
1	PRF_HMAC_MD5	[RFC2104]
2	PRF_HMAC_SHA1	[RFC2104]
3	PRF_HMAC_TIGER	[RFC2104]
4	PRF_AES128_CBC	[RFC4434]
8	PRF_AES128_CMAC	[RFC4615]

SA Life Type and SA Duration

The SA life type and SA duration specify the time-to-live for the overall security association. When the SA expires, all keys negotiated under the association (AH or ESP) must be renegotiated. The life type values are as follows:

Type	Value
Reserved	0
Seconds	1
Kilobytes	2

For a given life type, the value of the life duration attribute defines the actual length of the component lifetime—either a number of seconds, or a number of Kbytes that can be protected.

If unspecified, the default value shall be assumed to be 28,800 seconds (8 hours).

Encapsulation Mode

Type	Value
Reserved	0
Tunnel	1
Transport	2

Cryptographic Suites for IPsec

When IPsec is implemented in manual mode, there are many algorithms available, but two IPsec systems cannot interoperate unless they are using the same algorithms. The IPsec group proposed in RFC 4308 (Hoffman, 2005), "Cryptographic Suites for IPsec," uses two user interface suites (UI suites) that can cover typical configuration policies, and which can be used by system administrators to ease the burden of selecting among the many options in implementing IPsec systems. The suite concept is similar to TLS/SSL in which all parameters are listed and included in a single suite number/name. The initiator offers the responder one or more suites that it is able to support and lets the responder choose one of them. The two suites listed in RFC 4308 are for the use of IPsec in virtual private networks.

Suite VPN-A

IPsec:

- **Protocol:** Encapsulating Security Payload (ESP) [RFC2406]
- **ESP encryption:** TripleDES in CBC mode [RFC2451]
- **ESP integrity:** HMAC-SHA1-96 [RFC2404]

IKE and IKEv2:

- **Encryption:** TripleDES in CBC mode [RFC2451]
- **Pseudorandom function:** HMAC-SHA1 [RFC2104]
- **Integrity:** HMAC-SHA1-96 [RFC2404]
- **Diffie-Hellman group:** 1024-bit Modular Exponential (MODP) [RFC2409]

Suite VPN-B

IPsec:

- **Protocol:** ESP [RFC2406]
- **ESP encryption:** AES with 128-bit keys in CBC mode [AES-CBC]
- **ESP integrity:** AES-XCBC-MAC-96 [AES-XCBC-MAC]

IKE and IKEv2:

- **Encryption:** AES with 128-bit keys in CBC mode [AES-CBC]
- **Pseudorandom function:** AES-XCBC-PRF-128 [AES-XCBC-PRF-128]
- **Integrity:** AES-XCBC-MAC-96 [AES-XCBC-MAC]
- **Diffie-Hellman group:** 2048-bit MODP [RFC3526]

Summary

A virtual private network (VPN) creates a private network using the infrastructure of a public network such as the Internet. A VPN is able to establish a tunnel on layer 2 (data layer) and layer 3 (network layer) of the OSI model. At layer 2, VPNs establish tunneling protocols such as the layer 2 forwarding (L2F) protocol, the point-to-point tunneling protocol (PPTP), and the layer 2 tunneling protocol (L2TP). The only VPN protocol for layer 3 is the IPsec.

The L2F, PPTP, and L2TP protocols are strictly tunneling protocols. IPsec provides the encryption and authentication that the layer 2 tunneling protocols lack. IPsec actually provides all of the following security services: data origin authentication, access control, confidentiality (encryption), connectionless integrity, rejection of replayed packets (a form of partial sequence integrity), and limited traffic flow confidentiality.

One factor to consider when implementing IPsec is that it requires the installation of the client's software in each remote client machine. This is not a problem when a company has control of all of its networked computers, but when it wants to provide secure access to suppliers or vendors, then installing the client's software is not possible.

An important aspect of security is how to manage, exchange, transport, or wrap keys in a security association. In IPsec, it is necessary for hosts, source and destination, to agree to the mechanisms used to share the secret keys, as well as the keys that are used for authentication/integrity and encryption services. IKE v2, RFC 4306 (Hoffman, 2005) combines the security concepts of authentication and key management to provide a framework for transferring key and data authentication that is independent of the key generation technique, encryption algorithm, and authentication mechanism.

Learning Objectives Review

1. Encapsulation Security Payload (ESP) provides the same security services as the Authentication Header (AH), but in two modes instead of one. (T/F)

2. ESP and AH use the same authentication algorithms. (T/F)

3. IPsec is a network layer VPN technology, meaning it operates independently of the application(s) that may use it. (T/F)

4. Once an IPsec tunnel is negotiated via IKE, one-to-many connections of various types (Web, email, file transfer, VoIP) can flow over it, each destined for different servers behind the VPN gateway. (T/F)

5. A Security Protocol Identifier (SPI) indicates whether the security protocol is an Encapsulation Security Payload (ESP) or an Authentication Header Protocol (AH). (T/F)

6. In the tunnel mode, authentication is provided between a client and a corporate VPN device or between two VPN devices. (T/F)

7. A VPN provides security when corporate data is transmitted over a public network. (T/F)

8. Two security associations (one in each direction) are required to secure typical, bi-directional communication between two hosts, or between two security gateways. (T/F)

9. In VPN equipment, it is possible to specify that the lifetime of the negotiated key can be set up in seconds or in bits. Therefore:

   a. If the installer selects seconds, a new session key is exchanged after the default lifetime, 5 hours.

   b. If the installer selects bits, then every 5 megabytes a new session key is exchanged.

   c. A new key is generated after the customer-specified number of seconds, or bits, has passed by.

   d. A and B

10. IPsec is considered the best tunneling protocol for IP networks because it provides strong security services such as Encryption, Authentication, and Key management. (T/F)

11. An Encapsulated Security Payload (ESP) security mechanism provides:

    a. Integrity

    b. Authentication

    c. Confidentiality

    d. All of the above

12. An Authentication Header (AH) security mechanism does not provide:

    a. Integrity

    b. Authentication

    c. Confidentiality

    d. None of the above

13. Which of the following is not a component of IPsec?

    a. Authentication Header

    b. Internet Key Exchange

    c. Key Distribution Center

    d. Encapsulating Security Payload

14. Both ESP and AH security protocols support _____ and _____ modes of operation.

15. The Authentication Header provides support for _____ and for _____ _____.

16. L2F, PPP, L2TP, and IPSEC can be used for encryption and key management in IP environments. (T/F)

17. In IPsec, the SA associated with a connection could be AH, ESP, or both. (T/F)

18. In IPsec, which traffic security protocol(s) is (are) used to encipher and which one(s) is (are) used to authenticate?

19.   Are all VPNs secured? Explain.

20.   What are Diffie-Hellman groups?

References

Frankel, S., & Herbert, H. (2003). *The AES-XCBC-MAC-96 algorithm and its use with IPsec* (RFC 3566). Internet Engineering Task Force (IETF). Retrieved June 28, 2007, from http://www.ietf.org/rfc/rfc3566.txt?number=3566

Gleeson, B., Lin A., Heinanen, J., Armitage, G., & Malis, A. (2000). *A framework for IP based virtual private networks* (RFC 2764). Internet Engineering Task Force (IETF). Retrieved June 28, 2007, from http://www.ietf.org/rfc/rfc2764.txt?number=2764

Hoffman, P. (2004). *The AES-XCBC-PRF-128 algorithm fo the internet key exchange protocol (IKE)* (RFC 3664). Internet Engineering Task Force (IETF). Retrieved June 28, 2007, from http://www.ietf.org/rfc/rfc3664.txt?number=3664

Hoffman, P. (2005). *Cryptographic suites for IPsec* (RFC 4308). Internet Engineering Task Force (IETF). Retrieved June 28, 2007, from http://www.ietf.org/rfc/rfc4308.txt?number=4308

Kaufman, C. (Ed.). (2005). *Internet key exchange (IKEv2)* (RFC 4306). Internet Engineering Task Force (IETF). Retrieved June 28, 2007, from http://www.ietf.org/rfc/rfc4306.txt?number=4306

Kent, S. (2005a). *IP Authentication header* (RFC 4302). Internet Engineering Task Force (IETF). Retrieved June 28, 2007, from http://www.ietf.org/rfc/rfc4302.txt?number=4302

Kent, S. (2005b). *IP Encapsulating security payload (ESP)* (RFC 4303). Internet Engineering Task Force (IETF). Retrieved June 28, 2007, from http://www.ietf.org/rfc/rfc4303.txt?number=4303

Kent, S., & Seo, K. (2005). *Security architecture for the Internet protocol* (RFC 4301). Internet Engineering Task Force (IETF). Retrieved June 28, 2007, from http://www.ietf.org/rfc/rfc4301.txt?number=4301

Kivinen, T., & Kojo, M. (2003). *More modular exponential (MODP) Diffie-Hellman Groups for IKE* (RFC 3526). Internet Engineering Task Force (IETF). Retrieved June 28, 2007, from http://www.ietf.org/rfc/rfc3526.txt?number=3526

Orman, H. (1998). *The OAKLEY key determination protocol* (RFC 2412). Internet Engineering Task Force (IETF). Retrieved June 28, 2007, from http://www.ietf.org/rfc/rfc2412.txt?number=2412

Schiller, J. (2005). *Cryptographic algorithms for use in the Internet key exchange version 2 (IKEv2)* (RFC 4307). Internet Engineering Task Force (IETF). Retrieved June 28, 2007, from http://www.ietf.org/rfc/rfc4307.txt?number=4307

Chapter XII

TLS, SSL, and SET

TLS, SSL, and SET

In an Internet commercial transaction, the secure Web server and the buyer's computer authenticate each other and encipher the data transmitted using transport layer security (TLS) or secure socket layer (SSL) protocols.

When a purchase is made online using a credit card, does the customer's bank need to know what was purchased? Not really. Does the seller need to know the customer's credit card number? Actually, the answer is no. The responses to these questions were the main premises of the secure electronic transaction (SET). In the late 1990's, SET was approved as the credit card standard, but it failed to be accepted because of its cost and the problems regarding distribution of end-user certificates. However, SET is explained in this chapter as an ideal protocol, from the point of view of certificates, digital signatures, and cryptography for securing credit card transactions over the Internet.

Objectives

- Learn how TLS and SSL provide security services to IP Networks
- Fully understand the SET protocol and transactions

Introduction

Online commerce is growing at a substantial rate, partially because of the implementation of several protocols that secure Internet transactions. When people purchase an item over the telephone, they give their credit card information to a person who may then sell the information to someone else. In an Internet transaction, buyers enter their credit card information into their computers, and when they hit the "Submit" button, the Web browser secures the credit card transaction. In that secure transaction, the secure Web server and the buyer's computer authenticate each other and encipher the data transmitted.

Several protocols are used to secure an Internet transaction, but the most widely used are SSL from Netscape, and the Internet standard of SSL, known as transport layer security (TLS). TLS versions 1.1, 1.0 and SSL versions 3.1 and 3.0 are very similar, which makes supporting both TLS and SSL easy. SSL and TLS are built into all Web browsers.

Even though both Netscape and Internet Explorer implemented SSL in their Web browsers, they did it differently. This meant that companies had to deploy a separate application for each of the two browsers. SSL 3.0 and 3.1 outgrew being just a Netscape standard, and continued development of the protocol is now the responsibility of the Internet Engineering Task Force. As a result, SSL 3.0 and 3.1 developed into a proposed standard for Transport Layer Security 1.0, RFC 2246, and TLS 1.1, RFC 4346 (Dierks & Rescorla, 2006). In this chapter, the TLS 1.1 protocol is explained, but all explanations are also applicable to the SSL 3.1 protocol.

The TLS and SSL protocols are used to secure a client-server communication over the Internet, and they negotiate and provide the essential functions of a secure transaction: mutual authentication, data encryption, and data integrity. There are two SSL versions: SSL 2.0 supports server authentication only; SSL 3.1 supports both client and server authentication. TLS 1.0 and 1.1 support both client and server authentication.

TLS and SSL allow users to define the level of security that best meets their needs. Both are industry standards and are used in millions of Internet transactions. Users can select RC4, DES, 3DES, or AES for encryption and, for authentication, they can select RADIUS (username and password), RSA SecurID (username and token + pin), or X.509 digital certificates.

A secure client-server communication requires server and client authentication, a cryptographic key exchange where both parties agree on a pre-master secret key, and the enciphering of data using keys generated from the pre-master key. When a client and a server agree to communicate using the TLS or SSL protocol, they also need to agree on several other key points: (1) which protocol and version (TLS 1.0, 1.1, SSL2 or SSL3) to use, as well as which cryptographic algorithm; (2) whether or not to authenticate each other; (3) that certain public-key encryption techniques will be used to generate a pre-master secret key; and (4) that session keys will be created to encipher the message. These processes are performed in the TLS or SSL handshake protocol.

Digital certificates allow the client and the server to identify each other. In all TLS and SSL handshakes, the client will authenticate and verify the identity of the server using digital certificates. The server can also request that the client send its a client digital certificate (optional). Because digital certificates are issued by certificate authorities, the TLS or SSL client must trust the certificate authority that issued the server's certificate in order for the

SSL handshake to be successful. After the TLS or SSL handshake has been successfully completed, information exchanged between the client and server is enciphered using the negotiated keys. An important advantage of TLS and SSL is their ability to negotiate unique encryption keys.

The primary goal of the SSL and TLS protocols is to provide privacy and data integrity between two communicating applications. In any TLS or SSL session, a client and a server are able to negotiate unique enciphering keys even if they have not previously communicated with each other.

One advantage of SSL and TLS is that they are application protocol independent. Higher-level protocols can layer on top of the SSL and TLS protocols transparently. The SSL and TLS standards, however, do not specify how protocols add security when SSL and TLS are used. The decisions on how to initiate SSL and TLS handshaking and how to interpret the authentication certificates exchanged are left up to the judgment of the designers and implementers of protocols that run on top of SSL and TLS.

Transport Layer Security (TLS)

The TLS protocol is composed of two layers: the TLS record protocol and the TLS handshake protocol. The record protocol takes messages to be transmitted, fragments the data into manageable blocks, compresses the data (optional), applies a MAC, encrypts, and transmits the result. This protocol consists of four protocols: TLS handshake protocol, TLS change cipher spec protocol, TLS alert protocol, and application protocol.

The TLS handshake protocol allows the server and client to authenticate each other and to negotiate an encryption algorithm and cryptographic keys before the application protocol transmits or receives its first byte of data.

Figure 12-1. TLS protocol stack

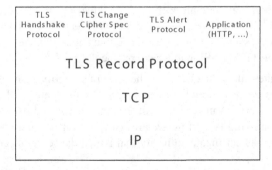

TLS Architecture

In TLS, a session is first established between a client and a server and, then, a connection is established. The TLS specification defines the terms used in the TLS architecture as follows:

- **Session:** A TLS session is an association between a client and a server. Sessions are created by the handshake protocol. Sessions define a set of cryptographic security parameters, which can be shared among multiple connections. Sessions are used to avoid the expensive negotiation of new security parameters for each connection.
- **Connection:** A connection is a transport (in the OSI layering model definition) that provides a suitable type of service. For TLS, such connections are peer-to- peer relationships. The connections are transient—every connection is associated with one session.

According to the TLS specification, the following are the session and connection parameters:

Session Parameters

- **Session identifier:** An arbitrary byte sequence chosen by the server to identify an active or resumable session state.
- **Peer certificate:** An X509.v3 certificate belonging to the peer. This element of the state may be null.
- **Compression method:** The algorithm used to compress data prior to encryption.
- **Cipher spec:** Specifies the data encryption algorithm (such as null, DES, etc.) and a MAC algorithm (such as MD5 or SHA). It also defines cryptographic attributes such as the hash size.
- **Master secret:** A 48-byte secret shared between the client and server.
- **Is Resumable:** A flag indicating whether the session can be used to initiate new connections.

Connection Parameters

- **Server and client random:** Byte sequences that are chosen by the server and client for each connection.
- **Server write MAC secret:** The secret key used in MAC operations on data written by the server.
- **Client write MAC secret:** The secret key used in MAC operations on data written by the client.

- **Server write key:** The symmetric cipher key used by the server to encipher data and by the client to decipher it.

- **Client write key:** The symmetric cipher key used by the client to encipher data and by the server to decipher it.

- **Initialization vectors:** When a block cipher in CBC mode is used, an initialization vector (IV) is maintained for each key. This field is first initialized by the SSL handshake protocol. Thereafter, the final ciphertext block from each record is preserved for use with the following record.

- **Sequence numbers:** Each party maintains separate sequence numbers for transmitted and received messages for each connection. When a party sends or receives a change cipher spec message, the appropriate sequence number is set to zero. Sequence numbers are of type unit64 and may not exceed $2^{64} - 1$.

TLS Record Protocol

The TLS Record Protocol provides connection security that has the following four basic properties:

1. The connection is private. Symmetric encryption (e.g., AES, DES, RC4, etc.) is used for data encryption, after an initial handshake in which a pre-master secret key is defined

2. The negotiation of a shared secret is secure. No attacker can modify the negotiation communication without being detected by the parties to the communication.

3. The peer's identity can be authenticated using asymmetric or public-key cryptography (e.g., RSA, DSS, etc.).

4. The connection is reliable. Message transport includes a message integrity check using a keyed MAC (HMAC). HMAC can be used with a variety of different hash algorithms, but TLS uses MD5 and SHA-1, denoting these as HMAC_MD5 (secret, data) and HMAC_SHA (secret, data). Additional hash algorithms can be defined by cipher suites.

Figure 12-2. Record protocol

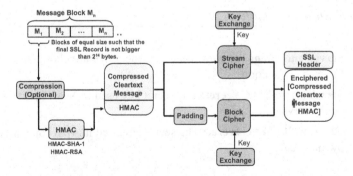

The record protocol is responsible for coordinating the client and server sessions. Figure 12-2 shows the record protocol.

First, the client message is divided into message blocks that have arbitrary length but no more than 2^{14} bytes, then compression is applied (optional), and, finally, a message authentication code (MAC) is computed. The compressed cleartext and the MAC are appended and enciphered using symmetric encryption, either stream ciphers or block ciphers. If a block cipher is used, some padding is required so the total data size, compressed message plus MAC plus padding, is a multiple of the cipher's block.

Enciphering the Data

TLS supports data encryption with one of the following symmetric encryption algorithms: RC4 using 128-bit, DES using 56-bit, 3DES using 168-bit, and AES using 128-bit and 256-bit. Most TLS solutions typically negotiate encryption strength downward to the level supported by the lowest end of the connection.

Public Key

Depending on the certificate authority, the key size of the public-key / private-key pair may be different. VeriSign uses either 512 bits or 1024 bits, depending on the server software. The VeriSign private key, used to sign certificates, is 1024 bits, and the session key used in the TLS transaction is the strongest permitted by US Government law (generally either 128 bit or 256 bits).

There are four record protocols: the handshake protocol, the alert protocol, the change cipher spec protocol, and the application data protocol.

Handshake Protocol

The cryptographic parameters of the session state are produced by the TLS handshake protocol, which operates on top of the TLS record layer. When a TLS client and server first start communicating, they agree on a protocol version, select cryptographic algorithms, authenticate each other (optional), and use public-key encryption techniques to generate shared secrets.

The handshake protocol can be divided into four phases.

Phase 1: Client_hello and Server_hello Messages

Client_hello and server_hello messages are used to establish security enhancement capabilities between client and server. The client_hello and server_hello establish the following attributes: protocol version, session_ID, cipher_suites, and compression_method. Addition-

Figure 12-3. Handshake protocol

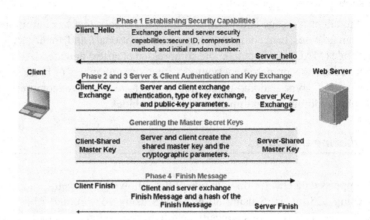

ally, two random values are generated and exchanged: ClientHello.random and ServerHello.random.

When a client first connects to a server, it is required to send the client_hello as its first message. The client can also send a client_hello in response to a server_hello request. The client_hello message to the server includes these elements:

*   **Client_version:** The version of the TLS or SSL protocol by which the client wishes to communicate during this session. This should be the most recent (highest valued) version supported by the client.

*   **Random:** A client-generated random structure that consists of (1) the current time and date in standard UNIX in a 32-bit format, according to the sender's internal clock; and (2) 28 bytes generated by a secure random number generator. These values serve as nonces and are used to detect replay attacks during key exchanges.

*   **Cipher_suites:** This is a list of cryptographic algorithm options supported by the client (in order of the client's preference, first choice first). Each cipher suite defines a key exchange algorithm, a symmetric encryption algorithm (including secret key length), and a MAC algorithm. The server will select a cipher suite or, if no acceptable choices are presented, return a handshake failure alert and close the connection. The cryptographic options supported by the client are sorted with the client's first preference first. The cipher_suites have two sections: (1) the type of key exchange supported; and (2) information about encryption algorithms and hash functions supported.

*   **Compression_methods:** This is a list of the compression methods supported by the client, sorted by client preference.

*   **Session_ID:** This is the ID of the session the client wishes to use for this connection. This field should be empty if no session_ID is available or if the client wishes to generate new security parameters.

The server will send a server_hello message in response to a client_hello message when the server is able to find an acceptable set of algorithms. If it cannot find such a match, it will respond with a handshake failure alert. The server_hello includes these elements:

- **Server_version:** This field will contain the lower of the TLS or SSL versions suggested by the client in the client_hello and the highest supported by the server.
- **Random:** The 28 bytes random number is generated by the server and must be different from the one sent by the client.
- **Cipher_suites:** This is the single cipher suite selected by the server from the list in ClientHello.cipher_suites. For resumed sessions, this field is the value from the state of the session being resumed.
- **Compression_methods:** The single compression algorithm selected by the server from the list in ClientHello.compression_methods.
- **Session_ID:** This is the identity of the session corresponding to the connection.

When the client sends a client_hello message, the server must respond with a server_hello message, or else a fatal error will occur and the connection will fail.

Phase 2 & 3: Authentication and Key Exchange

In Phase 2, immediately following the hello messages, the server sends (1) its authentication certificate, using an X.509.v3 certificate (or a modified X.509 certificate, in the case of Fortezza); (2) the server key exchange; (3) a message requesting a client certification (optional); and (4) a message indicating that the handshake of phase 2 is complete. The certificate type must be appropriate for the selected cipher suite's key exchange algorithm; it is generally an X.509.v3 certificate.

In TLS, the following key exchange methods are supported:

- **RSA:** The secret key is enciphered with the server's private key.
- **Fixed Diffie-Hellman:** The server's certificate has the Diffie-Hellman parameters, signed by a certificate authority (CA).
- **Ephemeral Diffie-Hellman:** The Diffie-Hellman parameters are signed using the server's RSA or DSS.
- **Anonymous Diffie-Hellman:** The Diffie-Hellman parameters are not signed.

Regardless of the key-exchange method, the server needs to specify the parameters for the key exchange. The server key-exchange message conveys cryptographic information to allow the client to communicate the pre-master secret: either an RSA public key to encrypt the pre-master secret with, or a Diffie-Hellman public key with which the client can complete a key exchange (with the result being the pre-master secret). The parameters vary, depending on the key exchange protocol that the server is proposing. For RSA or Diffie-Hellman, the parameters are as follows:

RSA

- The modulo of the server's temporary RSA key
- The public exponent of the server's temporary RSA key

Diffie-Hellman

- The prime modulus p used for the Diffie-Hellman operation
- The generator g used for the Diffie-Hellman operation
- The server's Diffie-Hellman public value y ($y = g^x \bmod p$)

The server key-exchange parameters are signed by creating a hash (MD5 or SHA) of the parameters and encrypting it with the server's private key. The hash includes not only the key-exchange parameters, but also the nonces from the initial hello messages.

Hash(ClientHello.random || ServerHello.random || ServerParams)

After sending the authentication certificate, the key exchange, and the certificate request (optional), the server sends a server_hello_done message indicating that the hello-message phase of the handshake is complete. The server then waits for a client response.

In Phase 3, the client determines whether or not the server's certificate is valid. If the certificate is valid, then the server's public key is authentic and the client is sure that the server is who it claims to be.

If the server has sent a certificate request message, the client must send either the certificate message or a no_certificate alert. This alert is only a warning; however, the server may respond with a fatal handshake failure alert if client authentication is required.

In the client key-exchange message, the client sets the pre-master key either though direct transmission of the RSA-encrypted secret, or by the transmission of the client Diffie-Hellman public key, which will allow each side to agree upon the same pre-master secret. When the key-exchange method is DH_RSA or DH_DSS, client certification has been requested, and the client is able to respond with a certificate. The Diffie-Hellman public-key parameters (group and generator) match those specified by the server in its certificate; otherwise, the client proposes its own Diffie-Hellman public-key parameters (group and generator).

The RSA or Diffie-Hellman parameters for the pre_master key are the following:

- **RSA:** A 48-byte pre_master_secret key, enciphered with the public key from the server's certificate or the temporary RSA key provided in a server key_exchange message. This pre_master_secret key is used to derive the master_secret key.

- **Diffie-Hellman:** The client's Diffie-Hellman public value ($g^x \bmod p$). If Diffie-Hellman is used, both client and server perform the Diffie-Hellman calculation to create a pre_master key.

Once the pre_master key has been created, either from RSA or from Diffie-Hellman, the master_secret key is computed as follows:

master_secret = PRF(pre_master_secret, "master secret," ClientHello.random + ServerHello.random)

The master_secret is used as an entropy source to generate random values for the export and non-export, MACS, secret keys, and initialization values (IV) required to encipher the data.

The pre_master_secret should be deleted from memory once the master_secret has been computed. The master_secret is always exactly 48 bytes in length. The length of the pre-master secret will vary depending on the key exchange method used. The PseudoRandom Function (PRF) is explained in the next section "Key Calculations."

Phase 4: Finish

In this phase, the client and server update the cipher_spec with the newly agreed-upon encryption algorithms, keys, and hash functions. Then, the client sends a finished message to verify that the key exchange and authentication processes were successful. The finished message is the first protected message with the just-negotiated encryption algorithms, hash functions, and symmetric encrypting keys. The finished message is hashed as follows:

MD5(master_secret || pad2 || MD5(handshake_messages || Sender || master_secret || pad1));

SHA(master_secret || pad2 || SHA(handshake_messages || Sender || master_secret || pad1));

Where pad1 and pad 2 are the values defined in the MAC, "handshake" refers to all handshake messages exchanged, and "sender" is a code that identifies whether the sender is a client (0x434C4E54) or a server (0x53525652).

No acknowledgment of the finished message is required and, at this point, client and server may begin sending confidential data immediately after sending the finished message.

Key Calculations

The record protocol requires an algorithm to generate keys and MAC secrets from the security parameters provided by the handshake protocol. As stated before, the master_secret generated during the Authentication and Key Exchange is used as an entropy source to generate keys and MAC secrets. The key material is generated as follows:

key_block = PRF (SecurityParameters.master_secret, "key expansion" SecurityParameters. server_random || SecurityParameters.client_random)

until enough key material is generated for the following four items: client_write_MAC_secret, server_write_MAC_secret, client_write_key, and server_write_key.

The master secret is a 48-byte secret shared between the two peers in the connection. The client random is a 32-byte value provided by the client, and the server random is a 32-byte value provided by the server.

The pseudorandom function (PRF) is used to expand secrets into blocks of data for the purposes of key generation or validation. The PRF takes as input a secret, a seed, and an identifying label and produces an output of arbitrary length. In the key_block formula above, the identifying label is "key expansion," which is the ASCII string of "key expansion". In order to make the PRF as secure as possible, it uses two hash algorithms in a way that should guarantee its security if at least one algorithm remains secure.

P_Hash Data Expansion Function

The data expansion function, P_hash(secret, data) uses a single hash function to expand a secret and seed into an arbitrary quantity of output. The P_hash(secret, data) is calculated as follows:

Figure 12-4. Key calculation: Key and MAC secrets

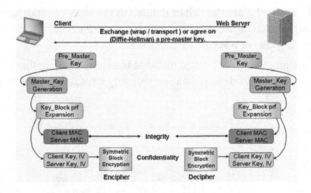

Figure 12-5. P_Hash

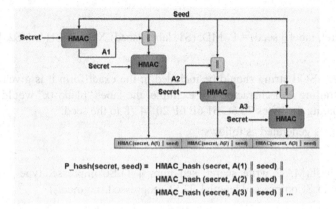

$$P\_hash(secret, seed) = HMAC\_hash(secret, A(1)\|seed) \| HMAC\_hash(secret, A(2) \|seed) \| HMAC\_hash(secret, A(3) \| seed) \| ...$$

A() is defined as

A(0) = seed

A(i) = HMAC_hash(secret, A(I - 1))

P_hash can be reiterated as many times as is necessary to produce the required quantity of data. For example, if P_SHA-1 were being used to create 64 bytes of data, it would have to be reiterated 4 times (through A(4)), creating 80 bytes of output data. The last 16 bytes of the final iteration would then be discarded, leaving 64 bytes of output data.

TLS's PRF using P_Hash Functions P-MD5 and P-SHA1

The P_hash data expansion function is used to create a pseudorandom function (PRF). TLS's PRF is created by splitting the secret in half and using one half to generate data with P_MD5 and the other half to generate data with P_SHA-1. Then, the outputs of these two expansion functions are XORed as follows:

PRF(secret, label || seed) = P_MD5(S1, label ||seed) XOR P_SHA-1(S2, label || seed);

The PRF is then defined as the result of mixing the two pseudorandom streams by XORing them together.

PRF(secret, label || seed) = P_MD5(S1, label ||seed) XOR P_SHA-1(S2, label || seed);

The label ASCII string should be included in the exact form it is given without a length byte or trailing null character. For example, the label "plano tx" would be processed by concatenating the bytes 70 6C 61 6E 6F 20 74 78 to the seed.

The MAC is generated as follows:

HMAC_hash(MAC_write_secret, seq_num || TLSCompressed.type || TLSCompressed. version || TLSCompressed.length || TLSCompressed.fragment))

Where "||" denotes concatenation, seq_num is the sequence number for this record and hash is the hashing algorithm specified by security parameters.

Alert Message Protocol

When an error is detected in the TLS handshake protocol, the detecting party sends an alert message to the other party. The TLS record layer supports alert messages that convey information about the status of the connection. There are two types of alerts: fatal and warning. A fatal alert message indicates that the connection is so bad that it needs to be terminated immediately. A warning alert message indicates that there are some problems in the connection. Like other messages, alert messages are enciphered and compressed, as specified by the current connection state.

The following are some of the error alerts defined in the TLS specification:

- **Unexpected_message:** An inappropriate message was received. This alert is always fatal and should never be seen in a communication properly implemented.
- **Bad_record_mac:** This alert is sent if a record is received with an incorrect MAC. This message is always fatal.
- **Decryption_failed:** This alert may be sent if a TLS ciphertext is decrypted in an invalid way: either it was not an even multiple of the block length, or its padding values, when checked, weren't correct. This message is always fatal.
- **Decrypt_error:** A handshake cryptographic operation failed, including being unable to correctly verify a signature, decrypt a key exchange, or validate a finished message.
- **Decompression_failure:** The decompression function received improper input (e.g., data that would expand to excessive length). This message is always fatal.

- **Handshake_failure:** Reception of a handshake_failure alert message indicates that the sender was unable to negotiate an acceptable set of security parameters given the options available. This is a fatal error.
- **No_certificate:** A no_certificate alert message may be sent in response to a certification request if no appropriate certificate is available.
- **Bad_certificate:** A certificate is corrupt. It contains signatures that do not verify correctly, etc.
- **Unsupported_certificate:** A certificate is of an unsupported type.
- **Certificate_revoked:** A certificate was revoked by its signer.
- **Certificate_expired:** A certificate expired or is not currently valid.
- **Certificate_unknown:** Some other (unspecified) issue arose in processing the certificate, rendering it unacceptable.
- **Illegal_parameter:** A field in the handshake was out of range or inconsistent with other fields. This is always fatal.

Change Cipher Spec Protocol

According to the TLS protocol, the Change Cipher Spec Protocol signals transitions in ciphering strategies. The protocol consists of a single byte message of value 1, which is encrypted and compressed under the current (not the pending) connection state. When the change_cipher_spec message is sent by either the client or the server, it notifies the receiving party that subsequent records will be protected under the newly negotiated CipherSpec and keys. The change_cipher_spec message is sent during the handshake, after the security parameters have been agreed upon, but before the verifying finished message is sent.

Application Protocol

An application protocol is a protocol that normally layers directly on top of the transport layer (e.g., TCP/IP). Examples include HTTP, TELNET, FTP, and SMTP. Application data messages are carried by the record layer and are fragmented, compressed, and encrypted based on the current connection state. The messages are treated as transparent data to the record layer. One advantage of TLS is that it is application protocol independent. Higher-level protocols can layer on top of the TLS protocol transparently.

SSL VPN

IPsec VPNs provide full use of network resources, including legacy applications, and are well suited for connecting branch offices, business intranets, remote employee access, and controlled/owned extranets. IPsec provides excellent secure access to all network resources and applications. However, IPsec's disadvantages are that it requires client-software, it is complex to manage, and user scalability is cumbersome.

SSL, on the other hand, does not need client-software, so the application can be accessed from any computer, in a kiosk, for example, but it is less secure than IPsec. SSL is a better fit for e-commerce, Web application portals, and multipartners extranets.

IPsec virtual private networks provide tunnels from external users' computers to internal networks. SSL is an easy way to connect external users' computers to internal application servers.

An SSL-based solution provides more flexibility than an IPsec VPN solution. Because there is no need for client-software, an employee could have secure access to the company networks from any browser devices such as PCs, handhelds, and PDAs.

An SSL VPN uses SSL and proxy technology to provide authorized and secure access for end-users to HTTP, client/server, and file sharing resources. SSL VPNs use SSL & TTL as the underlying transports to establish a secure session between any Web browser and the proxy server in the SSL VPN Gateway. It functions as a proxy for both client (Web browser) and server (Web server)—there is never a direct connection to the private network. The proxy technology in SSL VPNs gives a Web browser access to applications that SSL alone doesn't provide

In a SSL VPN (proxy server), two connections are established: one between the Web browser in the non-secure network and the SSL VPN proxy, and another connection between the SSL VPN proxy and the endpoint in the secure network. The proxy prevents users from making a direct connection into a secured network. A SSL VPN proxy acts as a server to the client and as a client to the server.

The SSL VPN ensures that authorized users have access only to specific resources, as allowed by the company security policy implemented by the SSL VPN proxy and integrated traffic management.

Proxy servers break the TCP/IP connection between client and server so the packet's IP address is not forwarded. They eliminate the exposure of internal IP addressing details to the

Figure 12-6. SSL VPN

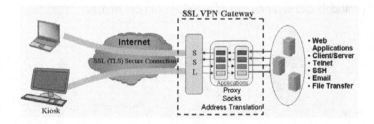

non-secure network by hiding the IP address of the endpoint on the secure network. Only the public IP address of the proxy server is visible from the non-secure network.

When an application client needs to connect to an application server, the client connects to a SOCKS proxy server. The proxy server connects to the application server on behalf of the client and relays data between the client and the application server. For the application server, the proxy server is the client.

The following are considered threats to an SSL VPN:

- Sensitive information may be left on computers at insecure locations.
- User passwords may remain on public-computers after users log off.
- User passwords are stored by the browser.
- Sensitive data, such as browser cache entries, URL entries, cookies, and any historical information created during the session, may remain on public computers after users complete their SSL VPN sessions.
- Downloaded files are stored in the public computer's temporary folder.
- Users forget to logout.
- Next public computer user may have access to applications.
- Worms and viruses may be transferred from the public computers to the corporate internal network.

Because SSL VPNs do not have the burden of configuring, installing, and supporting IPsec clients for each user, SSL VPNs are easier and less expensive to deploy and to support.

Secure Electronic Transaction Protocol (SET)

Through the Internet, consumers are able to pay for items purchased on line, pay bills, and do home banking. Consumers are using their payment cards to pay for transactions made over the Internet and to process their payments through the banks that issued their payment cards.

Whether consumers purchase products face-to-face or by mail order/telephone, there are existing procedures for authentication of the cardholder by the merchant. Because of the anonymous nature of the Internet, SET was developed to provide secure payment card transactions over the Internet.

Visa and MasterCard jointly developed the secure electronic transaction protocol as a method of securing payment card transactions over open networks. GTE, IBM, Microsoft, Netscape, RSA, Terisa, SAIC, and VeriSign provided assistance in the development of SET specifications.

SET uses cryptography to provide the following security services:

- Provide authentication that a cardholder is a legitimate user of a branded payment card account. RSA public-key encryption algorithm and X.509 V3 certificates are used to provide authentication.

- Provide authentication so that a merchant can accept branded payment card transactions through its relationship with an authenticated acquiring financial institution.

- Provide confidentiality of payment information. DES encryption algorithm is used to provide confidentiality.

- Preserve the integrity of payment data. SHA-1 hash function is used to provide integrity.

The SET specifications define the algorithms and protocols necessary for these security services.

SET Participants

There are five parties to every payment card transaction: cardholder, issuer, merchant, acquirer, and payment gateway.

The SET specification defines these five parties as follows:

- **Cardholder:** In the electronic commerce environment, consumers and corporate purchasers interact with merchants by means of personal computers. A cardholder uses a payment card that has been issued by an issuer. SET ensures that in the cardholder's interactions with the merchant, the payment card account information remains confidential.

- **Issuer:** An issuer is a financial institution that establishes an account for a cardholder and issues the payment card. The issuer guarantees payment for authorized transactions using the payment card in accordance with payment card brand regulations and local legislation.

Figure 12-7. SET participants

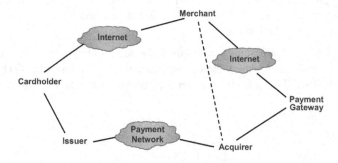

- **Merchant:** A merchant offers goods for sale or provides services in exchange for payment. With SET, the merchant can offer its cardholders secure electronic interactions. A merchant that accepts payment cards must have a relationship with an acquirer.

- **Acquirer:** An acquirer is the financial institution that establishes an account with a merchant and processes payment card authorizations and payments.

- **Payment gateway:** A payment gateway is a device operated by an acquirer or a designated third party that processes merchant payment messages, including payment instructions from cardholders. The payment gateway allows the acquirer to accept SET transactions over the Internet as well as to prepare them for submission to a payment network such MasterCard's Banknet® network.

SET Transaction Process

The following are the different steps in a SET electronic transaction:

1. The customer requests a digital wallet from an issuing bank and obtains a digital certificate from the issuer, a chip card, or other authentication vehicle.

2. The merchant obtains a digital certificate provided by his acquiring bank. Merchants wanting to sell online using SET must have two current certificates, one issued by their acquirer bank and one from the payment gateway.

3. The cardholder browses through an online catalog on the merchant's World Wide Web page, selects the items to be purchased, and fills an electronic order form. The cardholder uses a digital wallet to complete the order form.

4. The cardholder submits to the merchant a completed order, along with payment instructions. The order and the payment instructions are digitally signed by the cardholder. In the SET protocol, merchants cannot see the cardholder's credit card number – only the issuer bank is allowed to know the number. The cardholder does not send any critical information until the merchant is properly authenticated.

5. The merchant receives order information (OI) and payment information (PI), but the merchant cannot decipher the PI because the payment information is enciphered with the payment gateway's public key.

6. The cardholder's payment information, authentication data, and order information are sent by the merchant to the acquirer bank's payment gateway. The payment gateway translates a SET message into protocols recognized and used by the debit or credit card payment network. Payment gateways receive certificates through the SET Root CA, which is a CA at the top of the trust hierarchy.

7. The gateway authenticates the cardholder and merchant, deciphers the encrypted payment information, and then passes the information to the acquirer bank. The acquirer bank then launches an authorization request so that the issuer bank can approve or decline the cardholder's transaction. This request is sent through the payment network, the same network used for traditional transactions.

8. The issuer bank receives the authorization request as it would for any other physical transaction. Once the issuer checks the cardholder's line of credit, a response is sent back to the acquirer bank, either approving or denying the transaction.

9. The information again passes through the acquirer bank's gateway and is enciphered before the authorization is sent to the merchant. Provided the payment card is valid and has enough credit for the purchase, the merchant then receives authorization to fill the merchandise order.

SET Authentication and Confidentiality

SET relies on cryptography and digital certificates to ensure message confidentiality and authentication. Whenever cardholders, certificate authorities, merchants, acquirers, and issuers are exchanging information, either to get a certificate, to place orders, or to request payment authorization, the information is secured using digital signatures, digital envelopes, and encryption. Figure 12-8 shows this process.

The following steps are found in SET's process of authentication and confidentiality:

1. The sender generates a random session. The session key is a one-time secret key used to encipher the message by encrypting it with a symmetric encryption algorithm.

2. The message is hashed using SHA-1 and signed using RSA with the sender's private key creating a digital signature.

3. The cleartext message is concatenated with the digital signature and the sender's certificate.

4. The cleartext message, digital signatures, and certificate are enciphered with a symmetric algorithm (DES) using the one-time secret key generated previously by the sender.

Figure 12-8. SET authentication and confidentiality

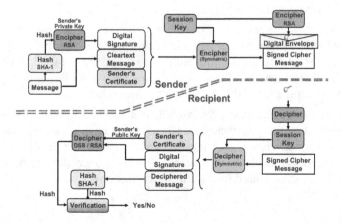

5.   The one-time session key is enciphered with RSA using the recipient's public key. The enciphered one-time session key is called a *digital envelope*.

6.   The enciphered session key is concatenated with the signed cipher message.

7.   To decipher and authenticate the message, the receiver performs the above steps in reverse.

As described in previous chapters, digital certificates are digital documents attesting to the binding of a public key to an individual or entity. In SET, the certificate authority provides certificates to cardholders, merchants, issuers, and acquirers to bind a public key to each individual or organization. When a CA grants these unique certificates, it is, in fact, certifying that those individuals and organizations are who they claim to be.

SET Hierarchy of Trust

In the SET environment, there exists a hierarchy of certificate authorities that is referred to as trust chaining. At the top of the hierarchy is the SET Root CA. The SET Root CA is owned and maintained by SET Secure Electronic Transaction LLC. Certificates include the owner's public-key.

- **Cardholder certificate:** A cardholder certificate functions as an electronic representation of the payment card and is approved by the issuer. A cardholder certificate does not contain the account number and expiration date. This certificate is transmitted to merchants with encrypted payment instructions. When the merchant receives the cardholder certificate, the merchant can be assured, even though the account number is hidden, that the payment card has been validated by the card-issuing financial institution or its agent.

- **Merchant certificates:** A merchant receives two certificates from the acquiring financial institution for each payment card brand that it accepts. One certificate is the merchant's certificate and the other is the payment gateway certificate. The merchant

Figure 12-9. SET hierarchy of trust

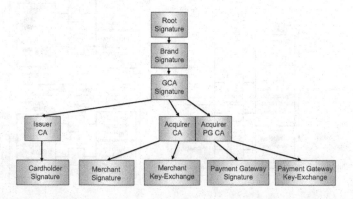

certificate functions as an electronic substitute for the payment brand decal that appears in the store window. The merchant certificate authenticates that the merchant has a relationship with a financial institution allowing him to accept the payment card brand. The merchant certificate is approved by the acquiring financial institution and provides assurance that the merchant holds a valid agreement with an acquirer.

- **Payment gateway certificate:** Payment gateway certificates are obtained by acquirers for their payment gateways. The certificates are issued to the acquirer by the Brand Certificate Authority. The gateway certificate includes the public key and encryption key that the cardholder uses to protect the cardholder's account information from the merchant.

- **Acquirer certificate:** An acquirer must be certified by the payment card brand in order to operate as a certificate authority so it can accept and process certificate requests directly from merchants.

- **Issuer certificate:** An issuer must be certified by the payment card brand in order to operate as a certificate authority so it can accept and process certificate requests directly from cardholders.

SET Transactions

In SET, there are three transactions that take place when a customer orders a product or service from a merchant: purchase request, payment authorization, and payment capture.

Purchase Request

Figure 12-10 shows the messages that are exchanged between a cardholder and a merchant in the purchase request. These messages include the following: initiate request, initiate response, purchase request, and purchase response.

Figure 12-10. SET transactions

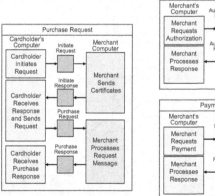

Figure 12-11. Merchant's initiate response

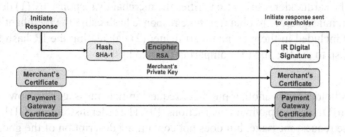

Purchase Initiate Request

The SET protocol is invoked when the cardholder is ready to place an order, i.e., after the cardholder has selected the articles that he is going to purchase, has completed the order form from the merchant, and has approved the merchant's terms & conditions. In the first exchange of messages, the cardholder's software sends the initiate request, which asks for the merchant to send his merchant certificate and his payment gateway certificate. The merchant needs to send his certificate and the certificate of the payment gateway he is affiliated with through his acquirer.

1. Merchant's software receives initiate request.
2. The merchant's software generates a response and digitally signs it by generating a message digest of the response. The message digest is then enciphered with the merchant's private signature key, producing a digital signature.
3. The merchant's software sends a response along with the merchant and payment gateway certificates to the cardholder.

The cardholder's software verifies the merchant's initiate response.

Figure 12-12. Cardholder verification of merchant's initiate response

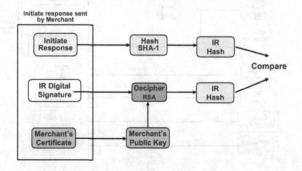

1.   The cardholder's software verifies the merchant and gateway certificates.

2.   The cardholder's software verifies the merchant's response by (1) deciphering the IR digital signature to obtain initiate response hash using the merchant's public key that is included in the merchant certificate; (2) calculating the IR hash by performing a hash to the IR; and (3) comparing the two hashes.

The cardholder sends another purchase request initiate message, but now with the order instruction (OI) and the payment instructions (PI). The order instruction (OI) has portions of the purchase request message, but does not contain the description of the goods purchased.

1.   The cardholder's software places the transaction identifier assigned by the merchant in the OI and the PI; this identifier will be used by the payment gateway to link the OI and the PI together when the merchant requests authorization.

2.   The cardholder's software generates a dual signature for the OI and the PI by computing the message digests of both, concatenating the two digests, computing the message digest of the result and encrypting that using the cardholder's private key. The message digests of the OI and the PI are sent along with the dual signature.

3.   The cardholder software generates a random symmetric encryption key, session key #1, and uses it to encipher the PI, the OI hash, and the dual signature. This key, along with

Figure 12-13. Dual signature

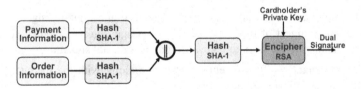

Figure 12-14. Cardholder purchasing and order instructions.

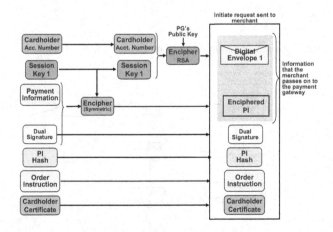

Figure 12-15. Merchant verification of purchase request

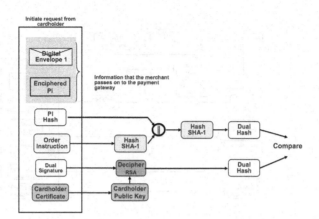

the cardholder's account information, is then enciphered with the payment gateway public key to create a digital envelope.

4. Finally, the cardholder's software transmits the purchase request to the merchant. The information in the digital envelope and the enciphered PI, which includes the PI information, the OI hash, and the dual signature, is not for the merchant, but for the payment gateway

Merchant Purchase Initiate Response

The merchant's software generates a response and digitally signs it by generating a message digest of the response and enciphering it with the merchant's private key. Along with the response, the merchant sends the merchant's certificate and the payment gateway's certificate.

1. The merchant's software verifies the cardholder certificate.

2. The merchant's software verifies the cardholder OI by (1) deciphering the dual signature to obtain the payment instructions hash (PI Hash) using the cardholder's public key that is included in the cardholder certificate; (2) calculating the PI hash by performing a hash to the OI, and using the PI hash that the cardholder sent; (3) comparing the results.

3. If the OI is authentic, the merchant processes the request (including forwarding the PI to the payment gateway for authorization).

4. The merchant's software creates a purchase response that is digitally signed by generating a message digest of the purchase response and enciphering it with the merchant's private signature key.

5. The signed purchase response and the merchant certificate are sent to the cardholder.

Figure 12-16. Merchant payment authorization request

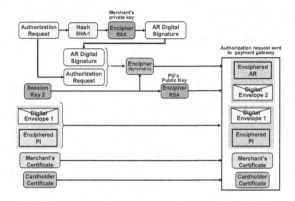

Payment Authorization

Payment authorization consists of two messages: authorization request, sent by the merchant, and authorization response, sent by the payment gateway. The gateway authenticates the merchant, deciphers the enciphered payment information, and then passes the information on to the acquiring bank. The acquiring bank then launches an authorization request so that the issuing bank can approve or deny the cardholder's transaction. This request is sent through the payment network, the same network used for traditional transactions.

The issuer receives the authorization request as it would for any other physical transaction. Once the issuer checks the consumer's line of credit, a response is sent back to the acquiring bank, either approving or denying the transaction.

The acquiring bank sends the information to the payment gateway, which, then, sends the authorization response to the merchant.

Merchant Payment Authorization Request

1. The merchant's software creates an authorization request message, which includes the amount to be authorized, the transaction identifier from the OI, and other information about the transaction.

2. The merchant's software digitally signs the authorization request by generating a message digest of the authorization request and enciphering it with the merchant's private signature key.

3. The authorization request is enciphered using a randomly generated session key #2. This key is placed in a digital envelope by enciphering it with the payment gateway's public key.

4. The merchant's software transmits the enciphered authorization request and enciphered PI from the cardholder purchase request to the payment gateway.

Figure 12-17. Gateway verification of merchant authorization request

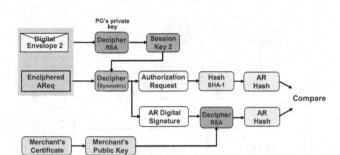

Gateway Payment Authorization Response

1.   Gateway verifies merchant certificate.

2.   Gateway verifies merchant's authorization request.

   a.   Gateway deciphers session key #2 with gateway's private key, then deciphers authorization request using session key #2.

   b.   Gateway verifies merchant's digital signature by deciphering it with the merchant's public key and comparing the result with a newly generated message digest of the authorization request.

3.   Gateway verifies cardholder's certificate.

4.   Gateway gets cardholder's payment information and order instructions and verifies the dual signature.

   a.   Gateway deciphers cardholder's enciphered PI and digital signature using the gateway's private key. Then, the gateway deciphers the digital envelope using the cardholder's public key to obtain session key #1, with which it deciphers the PI.

   b.   Gateway verifies cardholder's dual signature on the PI by deciphering it with the cardholder's public key and comparing the result with a newly generated

Figure 12-18. Gateway verification of cardholder PI and OI

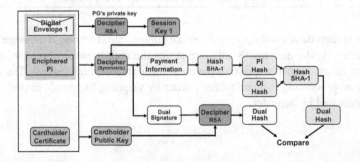

Figure 12-19. Gateway authorization response to merchant

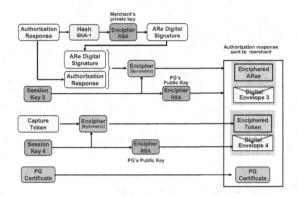

message digest of the concatenation of the message digests of the OI and the PI.

c.   Gateway ensures consistency between merchant's authorization request and cardholder's PI.

5.   Gateway sends authorization request through a financial network to cardholder's financial institution.

6.   Gateway sends authorization response to merchant.

a.   Gateway creates authorization response message and digitally signs it by generating a message digest of the authorization response and enciphering it with the gateway's private key.

b.   Gateway enciphers authorization response with a new randomly generated session key #3. This key is then enciphered with merchant's public key.

c.   Gateway creates a capture token and digitally signs it by generating a message digest of the capture token and enciphering it with the gateway's private key.

d.   Gateway enciphers capture token with a new randomly generated session key #4. This key and the cardholder's account information are then enciphered with the gateway's public key.

e.   Gateway transmits enciphered authorization response to merchant.

Merchant Verification of Payment Gateway Response

When the merchant's software receives the authorization response message from the payment gateway, the merchant's software stores the authorization response and the capture token to be used when requesting payment through a capture request. The merchant then completes processing the cardholder's order by shipping the goods or performing the services indicated in the order.

Figure 12-20. Merchant verification of PG authorization response

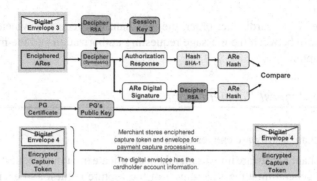

1. Merchant's software verifies gateway certificate.

2. Merchant's software deciphers session key #3 with merchant's private key, then deciphers authorization response using session key #3.

3. Merchant's software verifies gateway digital signature by deciphering it with the gateway public signature key and then comparing the result with a newly generated message digest of the authorization response.

4. Merchant's software stores enciphered capture token and envelope for later capture processing. Note that only the payment gateway is able to decipher the capture token because it has been enciphered with the payment gateway's public key.

5. Merchant completes processing of purchase request.

Figure 12-21. Merchant request payment capture

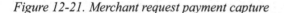
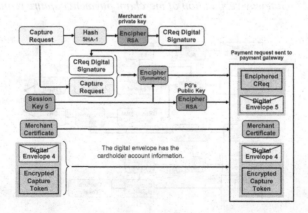

Payment Capture

After processing a cardholder order, the merchant will request payment. Normally, there is a time lapse between the message requesting authorization and the message requesting payment capture.

Merchant Request Payment Capture

1.   Merchant's software creates capture request.

2.   Merchant's software imbeds merchant certificate in capture request and digitally signs it by generating a message digest of the capture request and encrypting it with the merchant's private signature key.

3.   Merchant's software transmits encrypted capture request and encrypted capture token previously stored from the authorization response to the payment gateway.

4.   Merchant's software encrypts capture request with a randomly generated session key #5.

5.   This key is then encrypted with the payment gateway public key.

Payment Gateway: Payment Capture

When the payment gateway receives the payment capture request, it deciphers the information and uses the capture token information to format a clearing request, which it sends to the issuer via a payment card payment system. The payment gateway then generates a response and transmits it to the merchant. See Figures 12.22 and 12.23.

1.   Gateway verifies merchant certificates.

2.   Gateway verifies merchant payment capture.

Figure 12-22. Gateway verification of merchant payment capture request

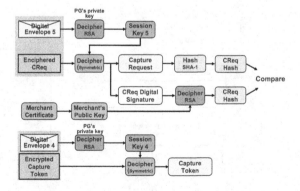

Figure 12-23. Gateway capture response

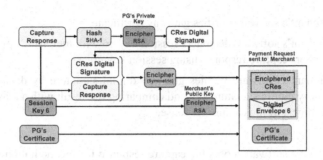

a. Gateway deciphers session key #5 with gateway's private key, then deciphers capture request using session key #5.

b. Gateway verifies merchant's digital signature by deciphering it with the merchant's public signature key and comparing the result with a newly generated message digest of the capture request.

c. Gateway deciphers session key #4 with gateway's private key, and then deciphers the capture token using session key #4.

d. Gateway ensures consistency between merchant's capture request and the capture token.

3. Gateway sends capture request through a financial network to cardholder's financial institution.

4. Gateway creates capture response message, (Figure 12.23), including gateway's signature certificate, and digitally signs it by generating a message digest of the capture response and encrypting it with the gateway's private signature key.

5. Gateway enciphers capture response with a new randomly generated session key #6. This key is then encrypted with the merchant's public key.

6. Gateway transmits encrypted capture response to merchant.

Figure 12-24. Merchant verification of gateway capture response

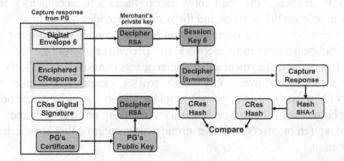

Merchant: Payment Capture Verification

1.   Merchant's software verifies gateway certificate.

2.   Merchant's software deciphers session key #6 with merchant's private key, and then deciphers capture response using session key #6.

3.   Merchant's software verifies gateway digital signature by deciphering it with the gateway public signature key and comparing the result with a newly generated message digest of the capture response.

The merchant's software stores the capture response for reconciliation when the Acquirer makes the payment.

Summary

The primary goal of the TLS/SSL protocols is to provide privacy, authentication, and data integrity between two communicating applications. A secure client-server communication requires server and client authentication, a cryptographic key exchange where both parties agree on a pre-master secret key, and the enciphering of data using keys generated from the pre-master secret key. An important advantage of TLS/SSL is its ability to negotiate unique encryption keys.

In all TLS and SSL handshakes, the client authenticates and verifies the identity of the server using digital certificates. The server can also request that the client send a client digital certificate (optional). The purpose of SSL certificates is to validate the identity of a site when a user connects to it. By authenticating the identity of a business, an SSL certificate protects online shoppers from fraud. The problem is that some certificate authorities do not do a good job of authenticating the identity of a company, nor that the Web site used a self-signed TLS/SSL certificate. The shopper has the illusion of security when, in reality, the shopper is open to possible phishing attacks. A new type of TLS/SSL certificate allows the shopper to see in the browser an additional window to the right of the address bar that shows information about the institution that owns the Web site, and the name of certificate authority that certified the institution. This new E-V TLS/SSL certificate thereby reduces the possibility that a phisher would be able to replicate the Web site.

When using an IPsec VPN, the remote user has access to a company's network; the user becomes a node on the network and the network provides access to all back-end applications. In situations where a company would like to provide only limited access to critical and specific applications in the network, the alternative to an IPsec VPN is an SSL VPN, which offers easier deployment and granular access controls. In SSL VPN, there is no need to install the client's software, only a Web browser is required. However, when evaluating an SSL VPN solution, it is important to make sure that it supports the application that is going to be secured. Connecting to the network using an SSL VPN requires the use of a password, so remote users must use strong access controls that have at least a two-factor authentication.

Learning Objectives Review

1. In general, public-key algorithms are used to encipher data and symmetric algorithms to exchange keys. (T/F)

2. The purpose of a(n) _____ is to link two messages that are intended for two different recipients.

3. Which of these statements is (are) correct?

   a. In SSL, the connection is private. Encryption is used after an initial handshake to define a secret key.

   b. In SSL, the peer's identity can be authenticated.

   c. In SSL, the connection is reliable.

   d. All of the above

4. In all TLS handshakes, the server requests that the client send a client digital certificate. (T/F)

5. Proxy servers break the TCP/IP connection between client and server so the packet's IP address is not forwarded. (T/F)

6. Which of the following statements pertaining to SSL is false?

   a. The SSL protocol was developed by Netscape to secure Internet client-server transactions.

   b. The SSL protocol's primary use is to authenticate the client to the server using public key cryptography and digital certificates.

   c. Web pages using the SSL protocol start with HTTPS.

   d. SSL can be used with applications such as Telnet, FTP, and email protocols.

7. Which of the following techniques is used to encipher data between a Web browser and a Web server?

   a. Kerberos

   b. IPsec

   c. PGP

   d. SSL

8. Which of these statements is correct?

   a. SSL VPNs are easier and less expensive to deploy and to support than SSL alone.

   b. SSL VPNs are easier and less expensive to deploy and to support than IPsec VPNs.

   c. Both are correct

9. In TLS, a session must first be established between a client and a server and, then, a connection can be established. (T/F)

10. TLS does not allow users to define the level of security that best meets their needs. (T/F)

11. In all TLS handshakes, the client authenticates and verifies the identity of the server by using digital certificates. (T/F)

12. In any SSL session, a client and a server are able to negotiate unique enciphering keys even if they have not previously communicated with each other. (T/F)

13. A digital signature is created by taking the hash function of a message and encrypting it with the sender's private key. (T/F)

14. TLS requires the installation of software and a Web browser on the client's equipment. (T/F)

15. Proxy technology in an SSL VPN allows a client to have direct access to the application. (T/F)

16. In TLS, a(n) _____ alert message indicates that the connection is so bad that it needs to be terminated immediately. A(n) _____ alert message indicates that there are some problems in the connection.

    a.   fatal; warning

    b.   warning; fatal

    c.   unexpected; expected

    d.   expected; unexpected

17. An SSL VPN protects internal server IP addresses from non-secure networks by:

    a.   Encapsulating them through ESP and tunneling

    b.   Encapsulating them through AH and tunneling

    c.   Exposing only the proxy server public IP address

    d.   None of the above

18. In TLS Handshake Protocol, what happens when a client sends a client_hello message, but the server fails to respond with server_hello message?

    a.   Fatal error occurs

    b.   Warning error occurs

    c.   Connection fails

    d.   a and c

19. TLS supports server authentication only. (T/F)

20. SSL VPNs are more secure than IPsec VPNs. (T/F)

References

Blake-Wilson, S., Nystrom, M., Hopwood, D., Mikkelsen, J., & Wright, T. (2006). *Transport layer security (TLS) extensions* (RFC 4366). Internet Engineering Task Force (IETF). Retrieved June 28, 2007, from http://www.ietf.org/rfc/rfc4366.txt?number=4366

Dierks, T., & Rescorla, E. (2006). *The transport layer security (TLS) protocol version 1.1* (RFC 4346). Internet Engineering Task Force (IETF). Retrieved June 28, 2007, from http://www.ietf.org/rfc/rfc4346.txt?number=4346

Freier, A., Karlton, P., & Kocher, P. (1996). *The SSL protocol version 3.0* (Internet-Draft). Internet Engineering Task Force (IETF). Retrieved June 28, 2007, from http://wp.netscape.com/eng/ssl3/3-SPEC.HTM#1

Santesson, S. (2006). *TLS handshake message for supplemental data* (RFC 4680). Internet Engineering Task Force (IETF). Retrieved June 28, 2007, from http://www.ietf.org/rfc/rfc4680.txt?number=4680

Santesson, S., Ball, J., & Medvinsky, A. (2006). *TLS user mapping extension* (RFC 4681). Internet Engineering Task Force (IETF). Retrieved June 28, 2007, from http://www.ietf.org/rfc/rfc4681.txt?number=4681

SET Secure Electronic Transaction Specification Book 1: Business Description. May 1997.

Chapter XIII

Web Services Security

Web Services Security

A service is an application offered by an organization that can be accessed through a programmable interface. Web services allow computers running on different operating platforms to access and share each other's databases by using open standards, such as extensible markup language (XML) and simple object access protocol (SOAP).

In this chapter, the following Web services mechanisms are discussed: (1) XML encryption, XML signature, and XML key management specification (XKMS); (2) security assertion markup language (SAML); and (3) Web services security (WS-security).

Objectives

- Understand how XML and Web Services are used
- Discuss how corporations could use Web Services
- Be able to explain the different types of security mechanisms in Web Services
- Understand, at a basic level, the point of implementation of XML encryption, XML digital signature, SAML, and WS-security
- Be able to demonstrate how assertions and security tokens are used in Web Services
- Understand the language syntax of XML, SOAP, and WS-Security.

Web Services

A service is an application offered by an organization that can be accessed through a programmable interface. It could be as simple as selling a movie ticket, allowing a passenger to select a seat on a flight, or letting suppliers access inventories to reduce inventory-related costs. Companies used point-to-point communications to integrate their applications by connecting business partners and customers; performance was improved by designing those applications as services that ran on centralized application servers. Travel agencies, for example, had software from different airlines installed in their systems so they were able to access the airlines reservation systems. Because the reservation systems were designed as object-oriented programming, which bonded data and processing together, if the travel agency wanted to sell airline tickets from several airlines, it needed different software for each airline.

Distributed computing protocols such as DCOM, CORBA, Distributed Smalltalk, and RMI were developed for services to agree on programming languages and shared context. Each of these protocols was constrained by vendor operability because they were built as silos. Further, none of these protocols operated effectively over the Web. With distributed computing protocols, software was developed for travel agencies to buy airline tickets from any airline, but it was still necessary to have another software to make hotel reservations or to rent a car.

Service oriented architecture (SOA) is also about distributed computing, but it provides a way to create sets of services and with such granularity that each service can be invoked, published, and discovered. With SOA, only one software is necessary to buy airline tickets or to rent a car, but SOA does not use standard Internet protocols.

Web services represent the convergence between service oriented architecture (SOA) and the Web; it takes all the best features of SOA and combines them with the Web. Unlike some software that is accessed via proprietary protocols, Web services are accessed via ubiquitous Web protocols. As a result, it is possible to go to a Web site and purchase a ticket, make hotel reservations, and rent a car.

The common aspect of all these services is that the information resides in databases, and all these databases are stored in specialized data servers, using proprietary formats that make them difficult to access or to connect to other databases. Even Web servers are only accessible through hyper-scripting languages.

Web services allow computers running on different operating platforms to access and share each other's databases by using open standards such as extensible markup language, XML, and simple object access protocol, SOAP. A Web service is an application, identified by a uniform resource identity, capable of being defined and located, as well as of interacting with other software applications.

By using common standards, Web services can make databases available across the Web; they unlock the databases and make their information available to other databases, workstations, or kiosks. The information can be used by other departments within a company, as well as by customers, vendors, suppliers, or the public in general. True application sharing requires a server-to-server (S2S) access.

Essentially, a Web service provider builds a typical Web service; then a description of the service is posted at a Web service registry. The registry is a searchable index which describes Web services and through which any of these services can be located and executed.

The following are some characteristics of Web services:

- Web services are accessible over the Web.
- Web services communicate using XML Web Protocol. XML is platform-independent and language-neutral, which allows for easy integration.
- Web services are designed with interfaces that can be called from other programs. This application-to-application programming interface can be invoked from any type of application client or service.
- Web services are registered at Web Service Registries, which allow the registry users to easily find the services that they need.
- Web services communicate by sending messages in plaintext to each other.
- Web services can be developed and deployed on any platform.
- All Web services applications use the same language, the extensible markup language (XML), to describe their interfaces and to encode their messages.

There are three essential developmental phases in creating a Web service: (1) the user interface (PC, cell phone, PDA, etc.), (2) the exchange of database information, and (3) the database interface, which varies from database to database. The development of phases 1 and 3 may be different, but the module written for phase 2 is always the same, so modules can be reused, thus reducing the cost of development.

When a user is looking for some specific Web pages on the Web, he uses search engines such as Google or Yahoo!. When a database is looking for specific information on another database, it uses a directory called *Universal Discovery, Description, and Integration (UDDI)*, to search for registries; UDDI is a type of directory in which companies list the Web services that they provide. IBM, Microsoft, and SAP are among the companies that maintain UDDI registries.

A search at one of the Web search engines produces many results, so the user has to select which one is the most appropriate. A search for "chips" at any Web search engine produces links to potato chips and to microchips. In XML, the Web services description language, WSDL, provides a description of what information is available at the Web service and the procedures for how to get the information needed from the database.

To be able to send XML over HTTP, it was necessary to create a new mechanism to wrap the information and send it over HTPP. That new mechanism is called *simple object access protocol (SOAP)*.

Independent of the Web browser used to visit a Web site, the information displayed on the monitor is the same. This is because Web sites are encoded using hypertext markup language (HTML), so the browser displays the same fonts, colors, and location on the screen as the graphical image at the Web server. HTML is a display language—not a data-representing language. XML was developed to recognize data in a field; as long as two databases have the same fields, for example, first name, last name, and telephone number, XML can extract the information needed from both databases.

Figure 13-1 and Table 13-1 show how these technologies relate to one another. The service provider who wants to make the service available to consumers registers the service in a UDDI registry using WSDL. The service provider describes its service and provides directions and pointers to find the service. The UDDI acts as directory that has descriptions of services and directions to find service providers.

When service consumers want to use a service, they query the UDDI registry to find a service that matches their needs. The UDDI finds the information, obtains the WSDL description of the service, as well as the access point of the service, and provides this information to the service consumer. Service consumers use the WSDL description to prepare a SOAP message in order to communicate with the service.

The XML text-based data has many advantages, but it is inefficient. Web services are slower than applications using binary data and, because data is sent in plaintext, there are some concerns about security.

In summary, Web service architecture consists of three primary functions:

- **Discovery:** Universal description, discovery and integration (UDDI)
- **Description:** Web services description language (WSDL)
- **Transport:** Simple object access protocol (SOAP)

Table 13-1. Web services technologies

Function	Web	Web Services
Locate a Web site	Search engine, Google, Yahoo, ...	UDDI
Web site description	Search engine description	WSDL
Transport protocol	HTTP	SOAP
Data format	HTML	XML

Figure 13-1. Web services interactions

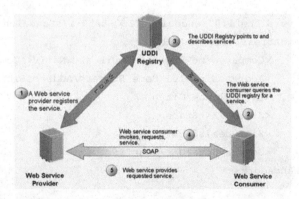

In the following sections, XML, SOAP, UDDI, WSDL, and XML security will be described in more detail.

Extensible Markup Language, XML

The World Wide Web Consortium (W3C) develops specifications, guidelines, software, and tools for the Web and is also a forum for information, commerce, communication, and collective understanding of the Web.

XML (Bray, Maler, Paoli, Sperberg-McQueen, & Yergeau, 2004) was developed by an XML working group (originally known as the SGML Editorial Review Board) formed under the auspices of the World Wide Web Consortium in 1996.

XML is used to exchange data. Unlike HTML, which was designed to display data and to focus on how data looks, XML was designed to describe data and to focus on what data is. XML was created to structure and store data, as well as to manage a large amount of simple or complex data in many forms without limitations. XML displays this data in a readable format.

When HTML is used to display data, the data is stored inside HTML. With XML, data can be stored in separate XML files outside the HTML, so changes in the data will not require any changes to the HTML code. If XML data is stored inside HTML pages, it is stored as data islands, so HTML only needs to be used for formatting and displaying the data.

XML functions similarly to Adobe PDF files. Adobe PDF files preserve the look and integrity of the original documents, and they can be read electronically by anyone, regardless of hardware and software platforms. XML functions in the same way; converting the data to XML allows incompatible database systems to exchange information. XML encodes information; therefore, many different types of applications using only a text editor can read it.

XML can be used not only to share data, but also to store data. Since XML data is stored in plaintext format, it is possible to store data in XML format so the stored data will be software and hardware independent, making it easier to retrieve the data.

XML syntax is very easy but very strict. The following is an example of an XML document:

```
        <?xml version="1.0" encoding="ISO-8859-1"standalone="no"?>
[1]    <NameAndAdress Role="Supplier">
[1a]           <CompanyName>Plano Hammers and Nails</CompanyName>
[1b]           <AddressLine>101 Some Street</AddressLine>
[1c]           <City>Plano</City>
[1d]           <State>TX</State>
[1e]           <ZipCode>75075</ZipCode>
[1f]           <CountryCode>US</Countrycode>
       </NameAndAddress>
```

```
[2]   <Catalog>
[2a]      <Hammer>
[2a1]        <Description>
                Five-inch hammer with rubber handle
          </Description>
[2a2]        <SKU>301245AB</SKU>
[2a3]        <Price>$2.45</Price>
          </Hammer>
[2b]      <Nail>
[2b1]        <Description>One-inch </Description>
[2b2]        <SKU>253648AA</SKU>
[2b3]        <Price>$2.45</Price>
          </Nail>
       </Catalog>
```

The first line in the document, the XML declaration, defines the XML version and the character encoding used in the document; it is expressed in Latin characters, for example, UTF-8, UTF-16, EUC-JP, and ISO-10646-UC-2. In this case, the document conforms to the 1.0 specification of XML and uses the ISO-8859-1 (Latin-1/West European) character set. The standalone declarations are "no" (parsing affected by external DTD subsets), or "yes" (parsing not affected by external DTD subset).

By definition, each XML document contains one or more root elements, the boundaries of which are delimited either by start-tags and end-tags, or, for empty elements, by an empty-element tag. The name in the start-tags and end-tags gives the element's type. In the example above, there are two root elements, the NameAndAddress [1] and the Catalog [2].

All XML documents must contain a single tag pair defining a root element, and all other elements must be within this root element. All root elements can have sub elements (child elements).

In the example above, the child elements, CompanyName, AddressLine, ZipCode, and CountryCode, are all nested inside the root element, NameAndAddress. Notice that each child element has its boundaries delimited by start-tags and end-tags.

Attributes are used to provide additional information about elements, and XML elements can have these attributes in the start-tag. Attribute values must always be enclosed in quotes, and either single or double quotes can be used. In the first line of the NameAndAddress tag, the role of the company, designated as "supplier," is presented as an attribute. The same attribute information could be presented as a child element, <role>Supplier<role>.

XML documents are self-describing, and the meaning of the data is obvious because it is just plain text enclosed in XML tags. The attribute name of the element is not abbreviated. The information contained in the element NameAndAddress has the name and address of Plano Hammers & Nails. This feature, the data being obvious, makes XML a good language for sharing data between programs, but it also makes it easy for anyone to read the document's content. Therefore, XML is particularly vulnerable to security compromises and, as a result, any XML message, including SOAP messages, must be enhanced with security features including encryption, digital signatures, authentication mechanisms, and privacy controls.

Versions, Namespaces, URIs, and Identifiers

A single XML document may contain markup vocabulary that is defined for and used by multiple software modules. Multiple markup vocabularies in a document could pose the problem of recognition and collision, so software modules may not be able to recognize the XML tags and attributes.

For example, the tag <Title> has different meanings, depending on whether it refers to a person or to an article. It is, therefore, necessary to create namespaces, xmlns:authr="authors. dtd" and xmlns:bk="book.dtd", to avoid confusion.

```
        <?xml version="1.0" encoding="ISO-8859-1"?>
        <library-entry xmlns:authr="authors.dtd" xmlns:bk="book.dtd">
[1]          <bk:book>
[1a]             <title>Economics</title>
[1b]             <price>$45</price>
[1c]             <isbn>1-234567-89-1</isbn>
[1d]             <authr:author>
[1d1]                <firstname>John</firstname>
[1d2]                <lastname>Doe</lastname>
[1d3]                <title>Mr</title>
                 </authr:author>
             </bk:book>
    </library-entry>
```

Now the tag <title> extends beyond the software modules book and author by using XML namespaces.

The XML namespace, W3C Recommendation (Bray, Hollander, & Layman, 1999), specifies a process for defining and using namespaces in XML. The recommendation defines an XML namespace as a collection of names, identified by a Uniform Resource Identifiers (URI) reference that is used in XML documents as element types and attribute names.

The following are some of the namespaces used in Web services:

Protocol	Prefix	Namespace
Web services description language	Wsdl	http://www.w3.org/2004/08/wsdl
SOAP messages	S12	http://www.w3.org/2003/05/soap-envelope
XML authentication	Ds	http://www.w3.org/2000/09/xmldsig#
XML encryption	Xenc	http://www.w3.org/2001/04/xmlenc#
XML key management	Xkms	http://www.xkms.org/schema/xkms-2001-01-20
Exclusive canonicalization	Ec	http://www.w3.org/2001/10/xml-exc-c14n#
WS-security utility	Wsu	http://docs.oasis-open.org/wss/2004/01/oasis-200401-wsswssecurity-utility-1.0.xsd
Web services security	Wsse	http://schemas.xmlsoap.org/ws/2002/04/secext

A namespace is used in XML to associate elements and attribute names to a URI, as well as to a mechanism to keep names separate and distinct. The combination of the universally managed URI namespace and the document's own namespace produces identifiers that are universally unique. The different namespaces mentioned in this chapter use URI to identify resources, algorithms, and semantics.

Namespaces have prefixes that associate a namespace with a URI reference. In Web services, the namespace has the following format:

xmlns:Prefix='http://www.w3.org/Year/Version/Name#.

For example, the XML digital signature has the following namespace:

xmlns:ds='http://www.w3.org/2000/09/xmldsig#'

Simple Object Access Protocol (SOAP)

SOAP (Mitra, 2003) is the standard communications protocol for Web services. In the same way that MIME (Multipurpose Internet Mail Extensions) defines the e-mail message format, SOAP defines the XML message format.

SOAP is supported by HTTP and is independent of any programming language or operating systems. As a transport mechanism for XML, SOAP provides a way for applications to communicate with one another over the Internet, independent of platform.

```
<SOAP:Envelope xmlns:SOAP=
    "http://schemas.xmlsoap.org/soap/envelope/">
```

```
[1]      <SOAP:Header>...content of header goes here...</SOAP:Header>
[2]      <SOAP:Body>...content of body goes here...</SOAP:Body>
       </SOAP:Envelope>
```

As with MIME, SOAP contains an envelope, the header, and the body. XML defines the format of the information and then SOAP adds the necessary HTTP headers to send it. The communication is peer-to-peer between an initial SOAP sender and an ultimate SOAP receiver and involves multiple message exchanges between these two nodes in request/response, solicit/response, and notification formats.

The original SOAP did not include security at all, but the Organization for the Advancement of Structured Information Standards (OASIS) has two security specifications to secure SOAP: the security assertion markup language (SAML) and Web services security (WS-Sec).

SAML addresses the issue of access authentication and authorization. WS-Sec addresses the issue of securing the content of Web services messages. SAML and WS-Sec can be used in a hierarchical trust model in which a certificate authority is required, and in a user-centric model in which a certificate authority is not required—similar to Pretty Good Privacy (PGP).

Universal Discovery, Description, and Integration, UDDI

Search engines are used to find information on the Internet, but a Web page is meaningless if a person or corporation cannot find it. It is the same with Web services; potential users go to a registry to find information about a specific service. Companies that want to publish their services on the Internet use a UDDI registry to register the information about the service they offer. Currently Microsoft and IBM in the US and SAP in Germany are among the companies that act as public UDDI operators. Information published in one public UDDI repository is replicated automatically in all other public repositories. Organizations can set up a private registry to support the requirements of a company or group of companies.

UDDI Version 3 (Clement, Hately, Von Riegen, & Rogers, 2003) specification defines a set of services that support the following: (1) the description and discovery of businesses, organizations, and other Web services providers, (2) the Web services they make available, and (3) the technical interfaces that may be used to access those services. UDDI provides a standard mechanism to register and discover Web services.

Conceptually, the business registration provided to an UDDI is organized as follows:

- **Business entity:** Describes a business or other organization that typically provides Web services. Includes name, short description, address, contact, and known business identifiers, including the Thomas Register identifier and a D-U-N-S number.
- **Business service:** Describes a collection of related Web services offered by an orga-nization, the business entity. Each business service entry contains a description of the

service, a list of categories that describe the service, and a list of binding templates that point to technical information about the service.

- **Binding template:** Describes the technical information for finding and using a particular Web service. The binding template represents the way the business service is accessed, for example, a telephone number, a Web site, or a Web service. Each business service can have multiple binding template entries.

- **tModel:** Describes a technical model representing a reusable concept, such as a Web service type, a protocol used by Web services, or a category system that is offered by multiple businesses, all supporting the same service interface. A tModel specifies information such as the tModel name, the name of the organization that published the tModel, a list of categories that describe the tModel, and pointers to technical specifications for the tModel. For example, there may be several companies offering weather reports, so all of them can use the same tModel.

- **Publisher assertion:** Describes, from the point of view of one business entity, the relationship that the business entity has with another business entity.

- Subscription: Describes a standing request to keep track of changes to the entities described by the subscription.

The UDDI standards process is managed by OASIS, with V3 being the latest version.

Web Services Description Language, WSDL

WSDL (Chinnici, Moreau, Ryman, & Weerawarana, 2004) is a document written in XML that describes the messages that must be exchanged to successfully interact with a Web service. It provides the name and location of the Web service, the type of data the Web service uses, how the request for a service should be sent, and how to put together and bind all the information.

The WSDL specification is divided into six major components:

- **Definitions:** The definitions element is the parent element in all WSDL documents. It gives the name of the Web service, lists multiple namespaces used throughout the remainder of the document, and contains all the service elements described below.

- **Message:** The message element defines and describes a one-way message, whether it is a single message request or a single message response.

- **Port type:** The port type defines multiple operations: a Web service, the intended recipient of a message, the messages themselves, and how the operations can be performed. An operation is a combination of messages labeled as input, output, or fault to indicate what part a particular message plays in the interaction. In the WSDL Version 2 specification, port types have been renamed as interfaces and ports as end-points.

- **Types:** The types element describes all the types of data used between the client and the Web service server. If the Web service uses only XML Schema built-in simple types, such as strings and integers, the types element is not required.

- **Binding:** The binding element defines the message format and protocol details for each port. WSDL-specific built-in extensions that define SOAP services and SOAP-specific information are included in the binding component.

- **Service:** The service element defines where the services are located and provides the address for invoking the specified service. Most commonly, this includes a URL for invoking the SOAP service.

The parent element of WSDL is Definitions and the child elements are Documentation, Types, Message, PortType, ServiceType, Binding, and Service.

```
        <wsdl:definitions name="nmtoken"? targetNamespace="uri">
        <import namespace="uri" location="uri"/> *
[1]             <wsdl:documentation> ... </wsdl:documentation>
[2]             <wsdl:types>...</wsdl:types>
[3]             <wsdl:message>...</wsdl:message>
[4]             <wsdl:porttype>...</wsdl:porttype>
[5]             <wsdl:serviceType>...</wsdl:serviceType>
[6]             <wsdl:binding>...</wsdl:binding>
[7]             <wsdl:service>...</wsdl:service>
        </wsdl:definitions>
```

Web Services Security

XML is a text-based, platform-independent standard used for Web services so that there can be a free exchange of information. Nevertheless, anyone who has access to an XML document can easily read the document, thus making XML and Web services more exposed to hackers. Businesses require that the exchange of high-value data such as business processes, e-commerce transactions, and the exchange of inventory information be protected. Government information, legal documents, financial data, and medical records have the same need for security.

Web services security provides the following security services: confidentiality, integrity, authentication, non-repudiation, and access control. Several mechanisms have been developed to provide those security services in Web services. They include XML encryption, XML signature, XML key management specification (XKMS), the security association markup language (SAML), and Web Services Security (ws-security).

XML Security

Point-to-point Web services connections can be secured using secure socket layer (SSL) or transport layer security (TLS). SSL is a session between a Web browser and a Web server, but if data needs to be relayed through several servers, a new SSL session needs to be created and data needs to be deciphered every time it reaches a server and encrypted before it is sent to another. In these multiple hops, each server will have access to the deciphered message—there is no end-to-end security in SSL. In addition, authentication with SSL is only established between the Web browser and the first Web server in the multiple hops.

When multiple hops are used, messages are stored, or more than one party has control over the authentication. In this case, it is necessary to move the security from the transport layer 3, SSL, to the application layer. XML security provides security at the application layer. XML security includes XML encryption and XML digital signature.

XML Encryption

The XML Encryption Syntax and Processing, W3C Recommendation (Imamura, Dillaway, & Simon, 2002) specifies a process for encrypting data and representing the result in XML. The data to be encrypted may be arbitrary data (including an XML document), an XML element, or an XML element content. The result of encrypting data is an XML encryption element, which contains or references the cipher data.

In a credit card transaction, certain information is relevant only to specific parties. The issuer, the financial institution that establishes an account for a cardholder and issues the payment card, does not need to know what product or service the cardholder is purchasing. The merchant, the company that offers goods or services for sale, does not need to know the credit card number. In XML, it is possible to encipher either a root or a child element of the transaction. XML encryption is not a new type of encryption algorithm, but a way to encipher XML elements.

In XML encryption, data is transformed into serialized octets for encryption and decryption operations. The application is responsible for transforming and marshalling the XML octets, so that they can be serialized into an octet sequence for enciphering and deciphering.

End-to-end XML security, where everything is encrypted, is not really possible when the information goes through firewalls, because firewalls need to look inside an XML document to determine whether or not to allow the packet to go through. XML messages are transferred over HTML, so port-based firewalls that block all ports with the exception of the ports used for Web protocols can not distinguish between an ordinary HTML message and an XML message. New firewalls are aware of the XML message and SOAP and, even though they are not able to decipher an XML message, they are able to look inside the XML message and determine whether or not it is safe to pass the XML message.

Encryption Granularity

The following is an example of XML credit card information:

```
        <?xml version="1.0" encoding="ISO-8859-1"?>
        <PaymentInfo>
[1]     <Name>John Doe</Name>
[2]         <CreditCard Limit='5,000' Currency='USD'>
[2a]            <Number>1234 5678 90123 4567</Number>
[2b]            <Issuer>My Bank</Issuer>
[2c]            <Expiration>04/06</Expiration>
        </CreditCard>
    /PaymentInfo>
```

In this example, number, issuer, and expiration are children of CreditCard. Name and CreditCard are children of the root element PaymentInfo.

XML encryption allows the following scenarios:

1. It is possible to encrypt the entire PaymentInfo root element without the eavesdropper knowing anything about the transaction - not even that the information is about a payment.

```
        <?xml version="1.0" encoding="ISO-8859-1"?>
        <EncryptedData
        Type='http://www.w3.org/2001/04/xmlenc#Element' xmlns='ht
        tp://www.w3.org/2001/04/xmlenc#'>
[1]             <CipherData>
[1a]                    <CipherValue>A23B45C56</CipherValue>
            </CipherData>
        </EncryptedData>
```

The CipherData element contains the ciphertext of the transaction.

2. An alternative scenario is to encipher only some of the child elements of the PaymentInfo and CreditCard elements. For example, only the card's number, issuer, and expiration date can be enciphered, but not the credit card holder's name and the limit child elements; in this way, intermediate agents will not know that "John" used a credit card with a particular limit. For this example, the content (character data or child elements) of the CreditCard element is encrypted as follows:

```
<?xml version="1.0" encoding="ISO-8859-1"?>

<PaymentInfo>
[1]      <Name>John Doe</Name>
[2]      <CreditCard Limit='5,000' Currency='USD'>
[3]      <EncryptedData
    xmlns='http://www.w3.org/2001/04/xmlenc#' Type='http://www.
    w3.org/2001/04/xmlenc#Content'>
[3a]                    <CipherData>
[3a1]                           <CipherValue>A23B45C56</CipherValue>
             </CipherData>
           </EncryptedData>
           </CreditCard>

</PaymentInfo>
```

3.   It is possible to encipher encrypted data. During super-encryption of an `Encrypted-Data` or `EncryptedKey` element, the entire element must be encrypted.

```
<?xml version="1.0" encoding="ISO-8859-1"?>

<EncryptedData
       xmlns='http://www.w3.org/2001/04/xmlenc#'  Type='http://
       www.w3.org/2001/04/xmlenc#Element'>
[1]      <CipherData>
[1a]<CipherValue>newEncryptedData</CipherValue>
          </CipherData>
       </EncryptedData>
```

The new `EncryptedData` is the enciphered data from scenario 2.

XML Encryption Syntax

The main role element in XML encryption is `EncryptedType` from which two role elements, `EncryptedData` and `EncryptedKey` are derived. While these two types of role elements are very similar with respect to their content models, they are used for different types of encryption. `EncryptedData` contains all the information needed to encipher XML data, and `EncryptedKey` contains the information to encipher keys. This section provides an overview and examples of XML encryption syntax. The following basic elements of XML encryption syntax are the same for `EncryptedData` or for `EncryptedKey`:

```
            <EncryptedData Id? Type? MimeType? Encoding?>
[1]             <EncryptionMethod/>?
[2]             <ds:KeyInfo>
[2a]                <EncryptedKey>?
[2b]                <AgreementMethod>?
[2c]                <ds:KeyName>?
[2d]                <ds:RetrievalMethod>?
[2e]                <ds:*>?
                </ds:KeyInfo>?
[3]             <CipherData>
[3a]                <CipherValue>?
[3b]                <CipherReference URI?>?
                </CipherData>
[4]             <EncryptionProperties>?
            </EncryptedData>
```

The following explains the meaning of some of the codes used:

- **ds:** Denotes a namespace from an XML Signature
- **?:** Indicates an optional element that could have a zero or one occurrence
- ***:** Denotes zero or more occurrences
- **[n]:** The numbers in brackets are used to show readers the beginning of an element. For example, XML encryption starts at [3].
- **Empty element tag:** Means that the element must be empty

For each data item to be enciphered as `EncryptedData` or `EncryptedKey` and then deciphered, there are certain steps that are required. The following are the XML encryption syntax steps:

1. Select an `EncryptedType` structure, either `EncryptedData` or `EncryptedKey`. An `EncryptedType` structure represents all of the information discussed below, including the type of encrypted data, encryption algorithm, parameters, key type, and so forth.

2. Select the algorithm (and parameters) to be used to encipher the data. This information is contained in the `EncryptionMethod` element.

3. Obtain and (optional) represent the key. This information is contained in the `ds:KeyInfo` element. As required, `ds:InfoKey` may have several child elements to identify the key (`ds:KeyName, ds:KeyValue, ds:RetrievalMethod,` etc.). If the key itself is to be encrypted for transport, then it is necessary to create an `EncryptedKey` element and apply an encryption process. `EncryptedKey`

Figure 13-2. Encrypted data element

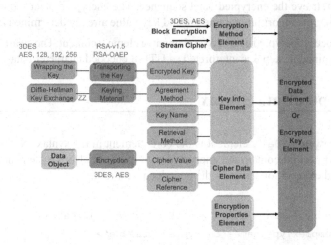

may be a child of ds:KeyInfo, or it may exist elsewhere and be identified in the RetrievalMethod.

4. Encipher the data. This information is contained in the CipherData element. The data needs to be converted to serial data in octets, UTF-8, and then the octets are enciphered using the algorithm and key from steps 2 and 3.

a. If the encrypted octet sequence is to be stored in the CipherData element within the EncryptedType, then the encrypted octet sequence is base64 encoded and inserted as the content of a CipherValue element.

b. If the encrypted octet sequence is to be stored outside the EncryptedType element, then it is necessary to provide information in a CipherReference element for the deciphering party to be able to retrieve the encrypted octet sequence.

5. Add additional information concerning the generation of the EncryptedData or EncryptedKey; this information could include the date/time stamp or the serial number of cryptographic hardware used during encryption. This information is placed in an EncryptionProperty element.

The party deciphering the XML enciphered data follows this procedure:

1. Process the EncryptedType element. This can be either EncryptedData or EncryptedKey to determine the algorithm, parameters and ds:KeyInfo element to be used to decipher the information.

2. Locate the data encryption key. This is done according to the ds:KeyInfo element, which may contain one or more child elements. If the data encryption key is encrypted, locate the corresponding key to decrypt it.

3. Decrypt the data contained in the CipherData element. If a CipherValue child element is present, then the associated text value is retrieved and base64 decoded to obtain the encrypted octet sequence.

a.   If a `CipherReference` child element is present, the URI and transforms are used to retrieve the encrypted octet sequence. The encrypted octet sequence is decrypted using the algorithm/parameters and key value already determined in step 2.

5.   Process decrypted data of type element or element content. The cleartext octet sequence obtained in step 3 is interpreted as UTF-8 encoded character data.

EncryptedData Syntax

The `EncryptedData` element is the core element in the syntax. Not only does its `CipherData` child contain the encrypted data, but it is also the element that replaces the encrypted element, or serves as the new document root.

```
        <EncryptedData Type='xenc:EncryptedDataType'/>
[1]     <complexType name='EncryptedDataType'>
[1a]            <complexContent>
[1a1]                   <extension base='xenc:EncryptedType'>
                        </extension>
                </complexContent>
        </complexType>
```

Example

```
<EncryptedData Id="eg1"
xmlns="http://www.w3.org/2001/04/xmlenc#"
xmlns:ds="http://www.w3.org/2000/09/xmldsig#"
xmlns:xsi="http://www.w3.org/2001/XMLSchema-instance"
xsi:schemaLocation="http://www.w3.org/2001/04/xmlenc#
xenc-schema.xsd">
.
.
.
</EncryptedData>
```

EncryptionMethod Syntax

`EncryptionMethod` is an optional element that describes the encryption algorithm used to encipher the data. If the element is absent, the encryption algorithm must be known by the recipient to be able to decipher the XML message. The permitted child elements of the `EncryptionMethod` are determined by the specific value of the algorithm attribute URI; the `KeySize` child element is always permitted. Depending on the encryption algorithms used, the syntax is one of the following:

```
[1]      <EncryptionMethod
         Algorithm='http://www.w3.org/2001/04/xmlenc#tripledes-cbc'/>
[1]      <EncryptionMethod
         Algorithm='http://www.w3.org/2001/04/xmlenc# aes128-cbc'/>
[1]      <EncryptionMethod
         Algorithm='http://www.w3.org/2001/04/xmlenc# aes256-cbc'/>
[1]      <EncryptionMethod
         Algorithm='http://www.w3.org/2001/04/xmlenc# aes192-cbc'/>
```

Block Encryption

3DES

In XML encryption, the 3DES encryption is used in three DES operations: encipher, decipher, and encipher in the Cipher Block Chaining (CBC) mode with 192 bits of key and a 64-bit initialization vector (IV). Of the key bits, the first 64 are used in the first DES operation, the second 64 bits in the middle DES operation, and the third 64 bits in the last DES operation. Each of these 64 bits of key contains 56 effective bits and 8 parity bits. Thus, there are only 168 operational bits out of the 192 being used in 3DES. The following is an example of 3DES EncryptionMethod syntax:

3DES: http://www.w3.org/2001/04/xmlenc#tripledes-cbc

AES

AES is used in the CBC mode with a 128-bit IV. If included in XML output, it is then base64 encoded. AES-128 and AES-256 are required in the implementation; AES-192 is optional.

AES-128: http://www.w3.org/2001/04/xmlenc#aes128-cbc

AES:256: http://www.w3.org/2001/04/xmlenc#aes256-cbc

AES-192: http://www.w3.org/2001/04/xmlenc#aes192-cbc

Stream Encryption

There are no required or optional stream cipher algorithms. Syntax and recommendations are given in the XML encryption standard to support user-specified algorithms.

KeyInfo Syntax

In XML, the data is enciphered using symmetric encryption algorithms; therefore, it is necessary for the recipient to get the secret key. The ds:KeyInfo in XML encryption and XML signature use the same syntax. The optional element `ds:KeyInfo` provides, in XML Encryption, information about the secret key used to encipher the data. All the `ds:KeyInfo`'s child elements yield a secret key.

There are four ways to send information about the secret key needed to decipher `Cipher-Data`:

1. If the parties have not exchanged secret keys previously, it is necessary to transport the secret key in a secure manner. This could be done by enciphering or wrapping the key for transport using a public key system. The element where this information is provided is called `EncryptedKey`.

2. If the parties have not exchanged secret keys previously, it is necessary to agree on a secret key. This could be done by using Diffie-Hellman for key agreement, and the element where the agreement information is provided is called `Agreement-Method`.

3. If the secret keys have already been loaded into both parties' systems, it is only necessary to define which of the secret keys was used to encipher the XML information. In general, every loaded secret key is associated with a name. The element where this information is provided is called `ds:KeyName`.

4. The information on how to find the key to decipher the XML document could be attached to the `KeyInfo` element or detached (not inside `ds:KeyInfo`). If the information on how to get the secret key is not attached to the `KeyInfo`, then the `RetrievalMethod` element is an alternative way to identify and locate the key by providing a link to the key information location.

EncryptedKey: Using Wrapping or Transport Algorithms

Symmetric key wrap algorithms are algorithms specifically created for wrapping, enciphering and deciphering symmetric keys. Both parties need to share a key-encrypting-key that is used to wrap (encipher) the key that is going to be used to encipher the information. In cryptanalysis, the more a key is used, the higher the probability that it could be broken. By using a key-encrypting-key to wrap keys, then the KEK will be used a fewer number of times that if it were used to encipher messages.

The W3C XML Encryption Recommendation specifies two types of key wrapping: one using 3DES and the other using AES.

Wrapping a Key Using 3DES

The following algorithm, as described in the XML recommendation, enciphers a key (the key to wrap) using 3DES and a key checksum:

1. Represent the key being wrapped as an octet sequence; for a 3DES key, it will be 24 octets (192 bits).

2. Compute the key checksum and call it CKS.

Figure 13-3. Key wrapping

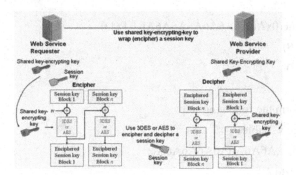

3.   Let *WKCKS* = *WK* || *CKS*, where || is concatenation.

4.   Generate 8 random octets and call this IV.

5.   Encrypt WKCKS in CBC mode using KEK as the key and IV as the initialization vector. Call the results TEMP1.

6.   Let *TEMP2* = *IV* || *TEMP1*.

7.   Reverse the order of the octets in TEMP2 and call the result TEMP3.

8.   Encrypt TEMP3 in CBC mode using the KEK and an initialization vector of 0x4ad-da22c79e82105. The resulting cipher text is the desired result. It is 40 octets long if a 168-bit key is being wrapped.

Identifiers and Requirements:

Algorithm="http://www.w3.org/2001/04/xmlenc#kw-tripledes"/>

Wrapping a Key Using AES

Assume that the key to be wrapped consists of N 64-bit data blocks denoted $P(1)$, $P(2)$, $P(3)$ ... $P(N)$. The result of wrapping will be $N+1$ 64-bit blocks denoted $C(0)$, $C(1)$, $C(2)$, ... , $C(N)$. The key-encrypting-key is represented by K. Assume integers i, j, and t and intermediate 64-bit register A, 128-bit register B, and an array of 64-bit quantities $R(1)$ through $R(N)$. AES(K)enc(x) is the operation of AES encrypting the 128-bit quantity x under the key K. MSB(x) and LSB(x) are, respectively, the most significant 64 bits and the least significant 64 bits of x.

The following algorithm, as described in the XML recommendation, enciphers a key (the wrapped key), using AES:

If N is 1, a single AES operation is performed for wrap or unwrap. If $N>1$, then $6 * N$ AES operations are performed for wrap or unwrap.

The key wrap algorithm is as follows:

If N is 1:

$B = \text{AES(K)enc}(0\text{xA6A6A6A6A6A6A6A6} \parallel P(1))$

$C(0) = \text{MSB}(B)$

$C(1) = \text{LSB}(B)$

If $N > 1$, perform the following steps:

1. Initialize variables:

    Set A to $0\text{xA6A6A6A6A6A6A6A6}$

    For $i = 1$ to N,

    $R(i) = P(i)$

2. Calculate intermediate values:

    For $j = 0$ to 5,

    For $i = 1$ to N,

    $t = i + j * N$

    $B = \text{AES(K)enc }(A \parallel R(i))$

    $A = t \text{ XOR MSB(B)})$

    $R(i) = \text{LSB}(B)$

3. Output the results:

    Set $C(0) = A$

    For $i = 1$ to N,

    $C(i) = R(i)$

Identifiers and Requirements:

AES-128 KeyWrap: http://www.w3.org/2001/04/xmlenc#kw-aes128 (Required)

AES-256 KeyWrap: http://www.w3.org/2001/04/xmlenc#kw-aes256 (Required)

AES-192 KeyWrap: http://www.w3.org/2001/04/xmlenc#kw-aes192(Optional)

Key Transport

Key transport algorithms are public key encryption algorithms specified for encrypting and decrypting keys. Their identifiers appear as algorithm attributes to EncryptionMethod elements that are child elements of EncryptedKey. EncryptedKey is in turn the child of a ds:KeyInfo element. The type of key being transported depends on the type of encryption algorithm that is going to be used as indicated in the EncryptionMethod.

Key transport algorithms may be used optionally to encrypt data in which they appear directly as the algorithm attribute of an EncryptionMethod. However, because public key algorithms are used, key transport algorithms are not efficient for the transport of any amounts of data significantly larger than symmetric keys.

Figure 13-4. Key transport

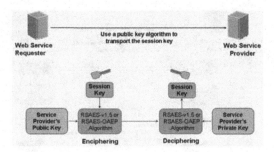

The XML encryption recommendation implements two required key transport algorithms: RSAES-PKCS1-v1.5 and RSAES-OAEP. Both transport algorithms are defined in RFC 3447, "PKCS #1: RSA Cryptography Specifications Version 2.1" (Jonsson & Kaliski 2003).

RFC 3447 recommends RSAES-OAEP for all new applications because it includes plaintext awareness. Optimal asymmetric encryption padding (OAEP) is a method for encoding messages developed by Mihir Bellare and Phil Rogaway. In RSAES-OAEP, the key is encoded first with OAEP and then encrypted with RSA.

Identifiers and Requirements:

RSA-v1.5: http://www.w3.org/2001/04/xmlenc#rsa-1_5

RSA-OAEP: http://www.w3.org/2001/04/xmlenc#rsa-oaep-mgf1p

Key Agreement

A key agreement algorithm allows a sender and a receiver to share a secret key computed from public-key algorithms. Normally, the shared secret key is not used as a key, but instead, is used to arrive at key material. In TLS/SSL (see Chapter XII, "Phase 2 & 3 Authentication and Key Exchange") the shared secret key is called the *pre-master key*, and from this pre-master key, the secret key is calculated.

RFC 2631 (Rescorla, 1999) describes the Diffie-Hellman key agreement method, in which, from a Diffie-Hellman shared secret, *ZZ*, key material is generated. The method described in RFC 2631 is used in XML encryption for `KeyAgreement`.

XML encryption does not provide an on-line key agreement negotiation protocol. The `AgreementMethod` element can be used by the originator to identify the keys and computational procedure that were used to obtain a shared encryption key.

As described in Chapter V, "The Diffie-Hellman Key Agreement Method," the DH key agreement consists of six parameters, two large primes p and q, a generator g, the public key, and optional validation parameters *seed* and *pgenCounter*. If it is necessary to exchange these parameters, the following syntax is used:

Figure 13-5. Key agreement

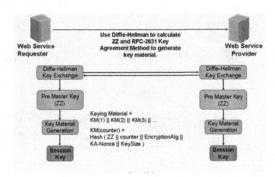

```
<element name="DHKeyValue" type="xenc:DHKeyValueType"/>
<complexType name="DHKeyValueType">
    <sequence>
        <sequence minOccurs="0">
        <element name="P" type="ds:CryptoBinary"/>
        <element name="Q" type="ds:CryptoBinary"/>
        <element name="Generator"type="ds:CryptoBinary"/>
    </sequence>
    <element name="Public" type="ds:CryptoBinary"/>
            <sequence minOccurs="0">
                <element name="seed" type="ds:CryptoBinary"/>
                <element name="pgenCounter" type="ds:CryptoBinary"/>
            </sequence>
    </sequence>
</complexType>
```

RFC-2631 describes how the Diffie-Hellman shared secret, *ZZ*, can be used to create key material.

Keying Material = KM(1) || KM(2) || KM(3) || ... where "||" is byte stream concatenation and KM(counter) = Hash (*ZZ* || other information).

In XML encryption, the key material is generated using the following formula for KM(counter):

KM(counter) = Hash (*ZZ* || counter || EncryptionAlg || KA-Nonce || KeySize) where:

- The counter is a one-byte counter starting at one and incrementing by one.
- The EncryptionAlg is the encryption algorithm attribute used in the Encryption-Method child of EncryptedData or EncryptedKey. Some of the encryption

algorithms are tripledes-cbc, aesES128-cbc, and aes256-cbc. See "EncryptionMethod Syntax" section in this chapter.

- The KA-Nonce is base64 decoding of the content of the KA-Nonce child of AgreementMethod, if present. If the KA-Nonce element is absent, it is null. The KA-Nonce element assures that different keying material is generated even for repeated agreements using the same sender and recipient public keys.

- The KeySize is the size in bits of the key to be derived from the shared secret.

Example

Shared secret key is *ZZ*.

Hash Algorithm is SHA-1.

Counter value is 1 and is represented by the two character UTF-8 sequence 01.

Encryption algorithm is aes256-cbc.

KA-Nonce = Zm9v and the base64 decoding of Zm9v is foo.

Key Size is 256.

Then, KM(1) = SHA-1 (ZZ01aes256-cbcfoo256).

For some algorithms, the key size is inherent in the URI. For others, such as for most stream ciphers, it must be explicitly provided. For each KM (counter), the only variable is the counter, but successive values of counter will produce an additional number of bytes of keying material. From the concatenated string of one or more KMs, enough leading bytes are produced to meet the need for an actual key; the remainder is discarded. For example, if the hash algorithm is SHA-1, which produces 20 octets (160 bits) of hash, then for 128-bit AES key, the first 16 bytes from KM(1) would be taken and the remaining 4 bytes discarded. For 256 bit AES, all of KM(1) suffixed with the first 12 bytes of KM(2) would be taken and the remaining 8 bytes of KM(2) discarded.

If the Diffie-Hellman shared secret, *ZZ*, is known to both parties, it is still necessary to let the receiving end know the KA-Nonce and the type of hash algorithm used to create key material.

The following is an example of a DH AgreementMethod element from the XML Encryption Recommendation:

```
[2b] <AgreementMethod
         Algorithm="http://www.w3.org/2001/04/xmlenc#dh"
         ds:xmlns="http://www.w3.org/2000/09/xmldsig#">
[2b1]          <KA-Nonce>Zm9v</KA-Nonce>
[2b3]          <ds:DigestMethod
         Algorithm="http://www.w3.org/2000/09/xmldsig#sha1"/>
[2b4]          <OriginatorKeyInfo>
         <ds:X509Data><ds:X509Certificate>
             . . .
```

```
        </ds:X509Certificate></ds:X509Data>
    </OriginatorKeyInfo>
[2b5]           <RecipientKeyInfo><ds:KeyValue>
        ...
    </ds:KeyValue></RecipientKeyInfo>
  </AgreementMethod>
```

KeyName

Assuming that in a symmetric encryption the secret key has been loaded into both parties, then only the name associated with the key needs to be sent.

In this example, the key is associated with the name John Smith:

```
[2]  <ds:KeyInfo xmlns:ds='http://www.w3.org/2000/09/xmldsig#'>
[2c]          <ds:KeyName>John Smith</ds:KeyName>
    </ds:KeyInfo>
```

In the example above, the information about the secret key is included in the `KeyInfo` element.

KeyRetrieval

The `ds:RetrievalMethod` provides an alternative method to identify and locate the keys. It does so by providing a link to an `EncryptedKey` element containing the key needed to decipher the `CipherData` associated with an `EncryptedData` or `EncryptedKey`

Figure 13-6. Key name

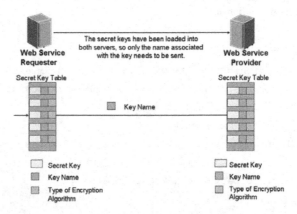

element. The ds:RetrievalMethod is always a child of the ds:KeyInfo element and may appear multiple times.

```
[2]   <ds:KeyInfo xmlns:ds='http://www.w3.org/2000/09/xmldsig#'>
[2d]    <ds:RetrievalMethod URI='#EK'
          Type="http://www.w3.org/2001/04/xmlenc#EncryptedKey"/>
      </ds:KeyInfo>
```

The URI could be any URI; for this example, it is called *#EK* and, in some place in the KeyInfo element, more information about #EK needs to be provided.

```
[2]     <ds:KeyInfo xmlns:ds='http://www.w3.org/2000/09/xmldsig#'>
[2d]      =<ds:RetrievalMethod URI='#EK'
            Type="http://www.w3.org/2001/04/xmlenc#EncryptedKey"/>
[2d1]           <EncryptedKey Id='EK'
                xmlns='http://www.w3.org/2001/04/xmlenc#'>
[2d1a]             <EncryptionMethod
                    Algorithm="http://www.w3.org/2001/04/xmlenc#rsa-
                    1_5"/>
[2d1b]             <ds:KeyInfo
                  xmlns:ds='http://www.w3.org/2000/09/xmldsig#'>
[2d1b1]             <ds:KeyName>John Smith</ds:KeyName>
                      </ds:KeyInfo>
[2d1c]             <CipherData>
[2d2c1]         <CipherValue>qZk+NkcGgW6PiVxeDbzQ2J0</CipherValue>
                        </CipherData>
                      </EncryptedKey>
                  </ds:KeyInfo>
```

In the above example, *#EK* points to EncryptedKey [2d1]. The EncryptedKey element is similar to the EncryptedData element and has the same child elements, but differs in that the data to be enciphered is always a key value. The child elements of EncryptedKey are shown in [2d1]. In the example above, the EncryptionMethod used to encipher the key is the rsa-1_5 public key algorithm, and the ds:KeyName of "John Smith" is a property of the key necessary for deciphering, using the CipherData. The CipherData's CipherValue is an octet sequence representing the enciphered *#EK* key.

CipherData Syntax

The CipherData is a mandatory element that provides the enciphered data. In the CipherData, either the enciphered data (as base64-encoded text of the CipherValue element) is included, or, a reference to an external location containing the encrypted data must be provided using the `CipherReference` element.

```
[3]     <element name='CipherData' type='xenc:CipherDataType'/>
            <complexType name='CipherDataType'>
                <choice>
[3a]            <element name='CipherValue' type='base64Binary'/>
[3b]            <element ref='xenc:CipherReference'/>
                </choice>
            </complexType>
```

CipherValue Syntax

The `CipherValue` is a mandatory element that provides the ciphertext. It could be included in the `CipherData` element or in an external reference.

```
[3]  <CipherData>
[3a]         <CipherValue>
qANQR1DBwU4DrsiJN1VVbfUQB/43s0AdSexsunBWAqBowywFLX8GM62pPlC7HzNqiP
uPi7UaCNRhUJ1pACbHa5TU+i8gd0z76KnKIgWQzMchPwKJoTRaBGqF91LPsOO7Tkn/
3eG9OCiKJsxA5PZV2ohmSCdtUScsJOXz+FXEMLUSF990yEmrgBrIaMgHJlBDbFpQuETt-
KUxPG1l6PipdcDNbTDf3iaubiPdIgcoReb7A/CMtf/xfSmfxmswTWZ/f/Us2bN++/
5hEB8rxKJqgxo8HRb4bEejPzQerCQ0oteT85w5TMz/96FDrPkKmwvWp2mCsgZRpY/8kcSp/
tpPMvB7San6/XTOfUhXKkxirP+2gLJ91bt+skp5E8c83rYoUofIvhLVIzChlirBF39WlJx
vikibzwcFOAzrvC+p4Kff6EAf/bC2KpNq0Jgti0xK3nw5sXceJPKMK9Cc5dypCKt7oJk/
+1aJ6
            </CipherValue>
    </CipherData>
```

CipherReference Syntax

If `CipherValue` is not supplied directly, the `CipherReference` URI contains an identifier, a reference, which, when processed, yields the ciphertext data.

```
[3b] <element name='CipherReference' type='xenc:CipherReferenceType'/>
            <complexType name='CipherReferenceType'>
            <sequence>
            <element name='Transforms' type='xenc:TransformsType'
                    minOccurs='0'/>
            </sequence>
            <attribute name='URI' type='anyURI' use='required'/>
```

```
        </complexType>
        <complexType name='TransformsType'>
            <sequence>
    <element ref='ds:Transform' maxOccurs='unbounded'/>
            </sequence>
        </complexType>
```

EncryptionProperties Syntax

Identifier: Type=http://www.w3.org/2001/04/xmlenc#EncryptionProperties.

Additional information concerning the generation of the EncryptedData or Encrypted-Key can be placed in an EncryptionProperty element, for example, the date/time stamp or the serial number of cryptographic hardware used during encryption can be added.

Message Digest Syntax

Message digest algorithms can be used in the AgreementMethod as part of the key derivation, with RSA-OAEP encryption as a hash function, and in connection with the HMAC message authentication code method in XML Signature.

The FIPS PUB 180-2 publication (Federal Information Processing Standards (FIPS), 1995), "Secure Hash Signature Standard" (SHS) defines, in addition to SHA-1, four new secure hash algorithms. Those new algorithms are SHA-224, SHA-256, SHA-384, and SHA-512.

The RIPEMD was developed in the framework of the EU project RIPE (Race Integrity Primitives Evaluation). Because of recent progress in cryptanalysis, a new version, RIPEMD-160 (Dobbertin, Bosselaers, & Preneel, 1996) was developed, with a 160-bit message digest.

The following are the identifiers and requirements for the XML encryption recommendation hash functions supported:

SHA1: http://www.w3.org/2000/09/xmldsig#sha1 (Required)

SHA256: http://www.w3.org/2001/04/xmlenc#sha256 (Recommended)

SHA512: http://www.w3.org/2001/04/xmlenc#sha512 (Optional)

RIPEMD-160: http://www.w3.org/2001/04/xmlenc#ripemd160 (Optional)

XML Signature

The XML-Signature (Eastlake, Reagle, & Solo, 2002) Syntax and Processing W3C Recommendation specifies a process for creating and representing digital signatures. XML signatures provide integrity, message authentication, and/or signer authentication services for data of any type, whether located within the XML that includes the signature or elsewhere.

XML signatures are applied to arbitrary digital content (data objects) in the same way as a digital signature is done. A hash function is applied to a data object, the resulting value is placed in an element (with other information), and that element is then cryptographically signed by enciphering with the sender's private key.

XML Signature Syntax

The Signature element is the root element of an XML signature, which has the following structure:

```
        <Signature ID?>
[1]        <SignedInfo>
[1a]           <CanonicalizationMethod/>
[1b]           <SignatureMethod/>
[1c]           <Reference URI? >
[1c1]              (<Transforms>)?
[1c2]              <DigestMethod>
[1c3]              <DigestValue>
               </Reference>)+
           </SignedInfo>
[2]        <SignatureValue>
[3]        <KeyInfo>)?
[3a]           <KeyName>
[3b]           <KeyValue>
[3c]           <RetrievalMethod>
[3d]           <X509Data>
[3e]           <PGPData>
[3f]           <SPKIData>
           </KeyInfo>
[4]        <Object ID?>)*
        </Signature>
```

Where ? denotes zero or one occurrence; + denotes one or more occurrences; and * denotes zero or more occurrences. The root element signature has the child elements SignedInfo, SignatureValue, KeyInfo, and ObjectID. SignedInfo, as a root element, has Canonicalization, SignatureMethod, and Reference as child elements.

The required SignedInfo element is the information that is actually signed. The SignedInfo root element has as child elements the CanonicalizationMethod, the SignatureMethod, and the Reference.

Core validation of `SignedInfo` consists of two mandatory processes: validation of the signature over `SignedInfo` and validation of each reference digest within `SignedInfo`.

The `CanonicalizationMethod` is the algorithm that is used to canonicalize the `SignedInfo` element before it is hashed as part of the signature operation.

The `SignatureMethod` is the algorithm that is used to convert the canonicalized `SignedInfo` into the `SignatureValue`. A data object is signed in the same way as is done for a digital signature. First, the message is hashed, and then it is signed with a secret key (symmetric encryption) or with a private key (assymmetric encryption).

Each `reference` element includes the digest method and resulting digest value calculated over the identified data object. It also may include transformations that produced the input to the digest operation.

`KeyInfo` indicates the key to be used to validate the signature. Possible forms for identification include certificates, key names, and key agreement algorithms, among others. `KeyInfo` is optional for two reasons. First, the signer may not wish to reveal key information to all document processing parties. Second, the information may be known within the application's context and need not be represented explicitly. Since `KeyInfo` is outside of `SignedInfo`, if the signer wishes to bind the keying information to the signature, a `reference` can easily identify and include the `KeyInfo` as part of the signature.

The following example, taken from the "XML Digital Signature Recommendation," shows the syntax in more detail:

```
      <Signature Id="MyFirstSignature"
      xmlns="http://www.w3.org/2000/09/xmldsig#">
[1]     <SignedInfo>
[1a]      <CanonicalizationMethod Algorithm="http://www.w3.org/TR/2001/
            REC-xml-c14n-20010315"/>
[1b]      <SignatureMethod Algorithm="http://www.w3.org/2000/09/
            xmldsig#dsa-sha1"/>
[1c]      <Reference URI="http://www.w3.org/TR/2000/
```

Figure 13-7. XML signature

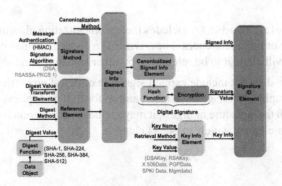

```
               REC-xhtml1-20000126/">
[1c1]                 <Transforms>
                <Transform Algorithm="http://www.w3.org/TR/2001/
                REC-xml-c14n-20010315"/>
             </Transforms>
[1c2]                  <DigestMethod Algorithm="http://www.w3.org/2000/09/
                xmldsig#sha1"/>
[1c3]                    <DigestValue>j6lwx3rvEPO0vKtMup4NbeVu8nk=</DigestValue>
           </Reference>
        </SignedInfo>
[2]     <SignatureValue>MC0CFFrVLtRlk=...</SignatureValue>
[3]     <KeyInfo>
[3b]     <KeyValue>
[3b1]                  <DSAKeyValue>
            <P>...</P><Q>...</Q><G>...</G><Y>...</Y><J>...</J>
           </DSAKeyValue>
          </KeyValue>
         </KeyInfo>
      </Signature>
```

In the above example:

- The `SignatureMethod` is DSA-SHA1 [1b].
- The hash method, `DigestMethod`, is SHA-1 [1c2] and the message digest result is shown in the `DigestValue` [1c3].
- The digital signature value is shown in the `SignatureValue` [2].
- `KeyInfo` [3] indicates that the key used to validate the signature was DSA [3b1], and its parameters, p, q, g, y, and j, are provided in the `KeyValue` element. See "KeyName and KeyValue Elements" section in this chapter.

SignedInfo Syntax

The structure of `SignedInfo` includes the canonicalization algorithm, a signature algorithm, and one or more references. The `SignedInfo` element may contain an optional ID attribute that will allow it to be referenced by other signatures and objects.

`SignedInfo` does not include explicit signature or digest properties, such as calculation time, cryptographic device serial number, and so forth. If an application needs to associate properties with the signature or digest, it may include such information in a `Signature-Properties` element within an object element.

```
[1]    <element name="SignedInfo" type="ds:SignedInfoType"/>
       <complexType name="SignedInfoType">
           <sequence>
[1a]           <element ref="ds:CanonicalizationMethod"/>
[1b]           <element ref="ds:SignatureMethod"/>
[1c]           <element ref="ds:Reference" maxOccurs="unbounded"/>
           </sequence>
           <attribute name="Id" type="ID" use="optional"/>
       </complexType>
```

SignatureMethod Syntax

The `SignatureMethod` is a required element that specifies the algorithm used for signature generation and validation. This algorithm identifies all cryptographic functions involved in the signature operation, for example, hashing, public key algorithms, MACs, padding, and so forth.

Message Authentication

For message authentication, an XML signature uses HMAC, which is a mechanism for message authentication that uses cryptographic hash functions. HMAC uses SHA-1 in combination with a secret shared key.

An HMAC algorithm takes two implicit parameters, the keying material determined from `KeyInfo` and the octet stream output from the `DigestValue`. HMACs and signature algorithms are syntactically identical but an HMAC implies a shared secret key.

Identifier: http://www.w3.org/2000/09/xmldsig#hmac-sha1

The HMAC algorithm (RFC2104) takes the truncation length in bits as a parameter; if the parameter is not specified then all the bits of the hash are output. The following is an example of a truncated 128-bit HMAC `SignatureMethod` element:

```
[1b] <SignatureMethod
        Algorithm="http://www.w3.org/2000/09/xmldsig#hmac-sha1">
[1b1]           <HMACOutputLength>128</HMACOutputLength>
     </SignatureMethod>
```

The output of the HMAC algorithm is ultimately the output (possibly truncated) of the chosen digest algorithm. In the example above, the HMAC output is truncated at 128 bits. This value is base64 encoded in the same straightforward fashion as the output of the digest algorithms.

Signature Algorithms

Signature algorithms take the same two implicit parameters that message authentication takes, the keying material determined from KeyInfo and the octet stream output from the DigestValue. Signature and HMAC algorithms are syntactically identical, but a signature implies public-key cryptography.

There are two signature algorithms used in an XML Signature: DSA and the RSASSA-PKCS1-v1_5 algorithm described in RFC 3447. The DSA algorithm takes no explicit parameters. An example of a DSA SignatureMethod element is the following:

```
[1b] <SignatureMethod Algorithm="http://www.w3.org/2000/09/xmldsig#dsa-
     sha1"/>
```

The output of the DSA algorithm consists of a pair of integers usually referred to by the pair (r, s). The signature value consists of the base64 encoding of the concatenation of the values r and s, in that order. An example of the SignatureValue element for a DSA signature (r, s) with values specified in hexadecimal would be the following:

r = 8BAC1AB6 6410435C B7181F95 B16AB97C 92B341C0

s = 41E2345F 1F56DF24 58F426D1 55B4BA2D B6DCD8C8

and

```
[2]     <SignatureValue>
           i6watmQQQ1y3GB+VsWq5fJKzQcBB4jRfH1bfJFj0JtFVtLotttzYyA==
        </SignatureValue>
```

The RSASSA-PKCS1-v1_5 algorithm described in RFC 3447 (RSA-SHA1) takes no explicit parameters. An example of an RSA SignatureMethod element is the following:

```
[1b]    <SignatureMethod Algorithm="http://www.w3.org/2000/09/xmldsig#rsa-
sha1"/>
```

The SignatureValue content for an RSA signature is the base64 encoding of the octet string computed as per RFC 3447. In RFC 3447, the message is hashed using SHA1 and then signed with RSA. The resulting base64 string is the value of the child text node of the SignatureValue element. An example is seen below.

```
[2] <SignatureValue>
    IWijxQjUrcXBYoCei4QxjWo9Kg8D3p9tlWoT4t0/gyTE96639InOFZFY2/rvP+/bM-
    J01EArmKZsR5VW3rwoPxw=
    </SignatureValue>
```

Reference URI Syntax

Reference URI is an element that may occur one or more times. Transforms, DigestMethod, the hash algorithm, and DigestValue, the result of the hash, are child elements of the Reference root element. Therefore, the Reference element specifies a digest algorithm, the digest value, the type of object to be signed, a list of transforms to be applied prior to digesting, and, optionally, an identifier to point at the data being signed.

```
[1c] <element name="Reference" type="ds:ReferenceType"/>
     <complexType name="ReferenceType">
               <sequence>
[1c1]                 <element ref="ds:Transforms" minOccurs="0"/>
[1c2]                 <element ref="ds:DigestMethod"/>
[1c3]                 <element ref="ds:DigestValue"/>
               </sequence>
               <attribute name="Id" type="ID" use="optional"/>
               <attribute name="URI" type="anyURI" use="optional"/>
               <attribute name="Type" type="anyURI" use="optional"/>
     </complexType>
```

In the following example, the Reference URI, M0, points to and identifies the data object that is signed. M0 points to dsig object and everything enclosed in dsig: Object will be signed.

```
[1c] <Reference URI = "M0">
[1c2]           <DigestMethod Algorithm="http://www.w3.org/2000/09/
                xmldsig#sha1"/>
                </DigestMethod>
[1c3]<DigestValue>qZk+NkcGgWq6PiVxeFDCbJzQ2J0=</DigestValue>
     </Reference>
         .
         .
         .
     <dsig:Object xmlns = "" xmlns:dsig=http://www.w3.org/2000/09/xmld-
     sig# ID="M0">
         .
         .
     </dsig:Object>
```

DigestMethod Syntax

`DigestMethod` is a required element that identifies the digest algorithm to be applied to the signed object.

Identifier: http://www.w3.org/2000/09/xmldsig#sha1

The SHA-1 algorithm takes no explicit parameters. An example of an SHA-1 element is the following:

```
[1c2]          <DigestMethod  Algorithm="http://www.w3.org/2000/09/
               xmldsig#sha1"/>
```

Only SHA-1 hash algorithm is defined in the XML signature. It is, however, possible to use the new digest algorithms, SHA-224, SHA-256, SHA-384, and SHA-512, which are defined in the FIPS PUB 180-2 publication, "Secure Hash Signature Standard (SHS)." Use of MD5 is not recommended because recent advances in cryptanalysis have cast doubt on its strength.

DigestValue Syntax

`DigestValue` is an element that contains the encoded value of the digest. The digest is always encoded using base64.

A SHA-1 digest is a 160-bit string. The content of the `DigestValue` element is the base64 encoding of the 160-bit string, viewed as a 20-octet stream. For example, if the message digest is A9993E36 4706816A BA3E2571 7850C26C 9CD0D89D, then the `DigestValue`, would be the following:

```
[1c3]          <DigestValue>qZk+NkcGgWq6PiVxeFDCbJzQ2J0=</DigestValue>

               QTk5OTNFMzY0NzA2ODE2QUJBM0UyNTcxNzg1MEMyNkM5Q0QwRDg5RA==
```

SignatureValue Syntax

The `SignatureValue` element contains the actual value of the digital signature, as seen below.

```
[2]   <element name="SignatureValue" type="ds:SignatureValueType"/>
      <complexType name="SignatureValueType">
        <simpleContent>
          <extension base="base64Binary">
            <attribute name="Id" type="ID" use="optional"/>
```

```
    </extension>
   </simpleContent>
 </complexType>
```

The `SignedInfo` element is canonicalized and then signed by hashing it and encrypting it to create a digital signature. The digital signature is always encoded using base64 and the result is the signature value.

KeyInfo Syntax

In Chapter VI, "Integrity and Authentication," several authentication methods were discussed, among them DSA, RSA, and X.509. In Chapter X, "Electronic E-mail Security," the way that PGP signs e-mails was discussed. XML signature supports all these digital signature mechanisms, so it is necessary to send the signing information used to validate the signature.

The XML signature recommendation defines `KeyInfo` as an optional element that enables the recipient(s) to obtain the key needed to validate the signature. `KeyInfo` may contain keys, names, certificates and other public-key management information, such as in-band key distribution or key agreement data. If `KeyInfo` is omitted, then the recipient will be able to identify the key used to sign the data.

The following list summarizes the `KeyInfo` types:

http://www.w3.org/2000/09/xmldsig#DSAKeyValue

http://www.w3.org/2000/09/xmldsig#RSAKeyValue

http://www.w3.org/2000/09/xmldsig#X509Data

http://www.w3.org/2000/09/xmldsig#PGPData

http://www.w3.org/2000/09/xmldsig#SPKIData

http://www.w3.org/2000/09/xmldsig#MgmtData

http://www.w3.org/2000/09/xmldsig#rawX509Certificate

The `KeyInfo` element has the following syntax:

```
[3]    <element name="KeyInfo" type="ds:KeyInfoType"/>
       <complexType name="KeyInfoType" mixed="true">
         <choice maxOccurs="unbounded">
[3a]       <element ref="ds:KeyName"/>
[3b]       <element ref="ds:KeyValue"/>
[3c]       <element ref="ds:RetrievalMethod"/>
[3d]       <element ref="ds:X509Data"/>
[3e]       <element ref="ds:PGPData"/>
```

```
[3f]      <element ref="ds:SPKIData"/>
          <any processContents="lax" namespace="##other"/>
          <!-- (1,1) elements from (0,unbounded) namespaces -->
        </choice>
        <attribute name="Id" type="ID" use="optional"/>
      </complexType>
```

KeyName and KeyValue Elements

The KeyName element is used by the signer to communicate a key identifier to the recipient. The key identifier identifies the key pair used to sign the message, but it may contain other protocol-related information that indirectly identifies a key pair.

The KeyValue element contains either a single public key that is used to validate the signature, or it may include externally defined public-key values.

```
[3a] <element name="KeyName" type="string"/>
[3b] <element name="KeyValue" type="ds:KeyValueType"/>
     <complexType name="KeyValueType" mixed="true">
      <choice>
[3b1]               <element ref="ds:DSAKeyValue"/>
[3b2]               <element ref="ds:RSAKeyValue"/>
            <any namespace="##other" processContents="lax"/>
      </choice>
     </complexType>
```

The DSAKeyValue and RSAKeyValue require that some parameters be shared by both parties for them to be able to sign the message and to verify the signed message. Those parameters are described below.

The DSAKeyValue Element

Identifier: Type="http://www.w3.org/2000/09/xmldsig#DSAKeyValue"

The DSA requires several parameters, some of them are shared and some of them are kept private. The following are the DSA parameters:

1. p is a prime modulus, where $2^{L-1} < p < 2^L$ for $512 \leq L \leq 1024$ and L a multiple of 64.

2. q is a prime divisor of p - 1, where $2^{159} < q < 2^{160}$.

3. $g = h^j = h^{(p-1)/q} \bmod p$, where h is any integer with $1 < h < p$ - 1 such that $h^{(p-1)/q} \bmod p > 1$ (g has order $q \bmod p$).

4. $j = (p - 1) / q$ (j is not a DSA parameter, but it is included in the DSAKeyValue element solely for efficiency).

5. x = a randomly or pseudo randomly generated integer with $0 < x < q$.

6. $y = g^x \bmod p$.

7. k = a randomly or pseudo randomly generated integer with $0 < k < q$.

The integers p, q, and g can be public and can be common to a group of users. The user's private and public keys are x and y, respectively. Parameters x and k are used for signature generation only, and must be kept secret. Parameter k must be changed for each signature. The parameters that are common or are public need to be sent as part of the DSAKeyValue element.

```
[3b1]<element name="DSAKeyValue" type="ds:DSAKeyValueType"/>
        <complexType name="DSAKeyValueType">
            <sequence>
                <sequence minOccurs="0">
[3b1a]          <element name="P" type="ds:CryptoBinary"/>
[3b1b]          <element name="Q" type="ds:CryptoBinary"/>
                </sequence>
[3b1c]          <element name="G" type="ds:CryptoBinary" minOccurs="0"/>
[3b1d]          <element name="Y" type="ds:CryptoBinary"/>
[3b1e]          <element name="J" type="ds:CryptoBinary" minOccurs="0"/>
                <sequence minOccurs="0">
[3b1f]              <element name="Seed" type="ds:CryptoBinary"/>
[3b1g]              <element name="PgenCounter" type="ds:CryptoBinary"/>
                </sequence>
            </sequence>
        </complexType>
```

The RSAKeyValue Element

Identifier: Type=»http://www.w3.org/2000/09/xmldsig#RSAKeyValue»

The RSA key values have two parameters: modulus and exponent. Those parameters need to be sent as part of the RSAKeyValue element.

```
[3b2]           <element name="RSAKeyValue" type="ds:RSAKeyValueType"/>
        <complexType name="RSAKeyValueType">
                <sequence>
[3b2a]              <element name="Modulus" type="ds:CryptoBinary"/>
```

```
[3b2b]                    <element name="Exponent" type="ds:CryptoBinary"/>
            </sequence>

    </complexType>
```

For example:

```
[3b2]<RSAKeyValue>

[3b2a]        <Modulus>xA7SEU+e0yQH5rm9kbCDN9o3aPIo7HbP7tX6WOocLZAtNfyx
    SZDU16ksL6WjubafOqNEpcwR3RdFsT7bCqnXPBe5ELh5u4VEy19MzxkXRgrMvavzyB-
    pVRgBUwU1V5foK5hhmbktQhyNdy/6LpQRhDUDsTv K+g9U cj47es9AQJ3U=
            </Modulus>

[3b2b]                    <Exponent>AQAB</Exponent>

    </RSAKeyValue>
```

The RetrievalMethod Element

A RetrievalMethod element within KeyInfo is used to convey a reference to Key-Info information that is stored outside the document. RetrievalMethod uses the same syntax as the URI reference except that there are no DigestMethod or DigestValue child elements, and the presence of the URI is mandatory.

```
[3c] <element name="RetrievalMethod" type="ds:RetrievalMethodType"/>
    <complexType name="RetrievalMethodType">
            <sequence>
                    <element ref="ds:Transforms" minOccurs="0"/>
            </sequence>
            <attribute name="URI" type="anyURI"/>
            <attribute name="Type" type="anyURI" use="optional"/>
    </complexType>
```

The X509Data Element

Chapter IX, "X.509 Basic Certificate Fields," describes the basic fields in an X.509 certificate. An X509Data element within KeyInfo contains one or more identifiers (fields) of the keys, the X509 certificates, or the revocation list. The content of X509Data is as follows:

- The X509IssuerSerial element, which contains the name of the entity that issued the X.509 certificate and the certificate serial number
- The X509SKI element, which contains the subject key identifier (SKI) in base64 encoded plain (Non-DER encoded). The subject, the end-entity, is the system or

person to whom the certificate is issued. The extension identifies the subject's public key being certified.

- The X509SubjectName element, which contains the subject's name
- The X509Certificate element is part of the content
- The X509CRL element, which contains a base64-encoded certificate revocation list (CRL)

Identifier: Type="http://www.w3.org/2000/09/xmldsig#X509Data"

The X.500 Directory uses distinctive names as entries in the directory and uses attributes followed by an equal sign to give a representation of and to further distinguish the names. The following X.500 distinctive name attributes (Sciberras, 2006) are used to clarify names in the XMLSig IssuerName and SubjectName elements:

Schema Definition

```
[3d]   <element name="X509Data" type="ds:X509DataType"/>
        <complexType name="X509DataType">
          <sequence maxOccurs="unbounded">
            <choice>
[3d1]         <element name="X509IssuerSerial" type="ds:X509IssuerSeri-
     alType"/>
[3d2]         <element name="X509SKI" type="base64Binary"/>
[3d3]         <element name="X509SubjectName" type="string"/>
[3d4]         <element name="X509Certificate" type="base64Binary"/>
[3d5]         <element name="X509CRL" type="base64Binary"/>
              <any namespace="##other" processContents="lax"/>
          </choice>
```

Table 13-1. X.500 distinctive name attributes

Attribute	Description
CN	Common Name
L	Locality Name
ST	State or Province Name
O	Organization Name
OU	Organizational Unit Name
C	Country Name
STREET	Street Address
DC	Domain Component
UID	User ID

```
        </sequence>

    </complexType>
```

Example

```
[3]   <KeyInfo>

[3d]     <X509Data>

[3d1]        <X509IssuerSerial>

[3d1a]          <X509IssuerName>CN=GoodCA, O=Certificates for All, L=Dallas,
     ST=Texas, C=US</X509IssuerName>

[3d1b]            <X509SerialNumber>12345678</X509SerialNumber>

[3d3]          <XML509SubjectName>CN=John  Doe,  O=PN&H,  L=Plano,  ST=
     Texas,C=US       </XML509SubjectName>

[3d4]          <X509Certificate>GjY1I6UtbINae45M. . . .</X509Certificate>

        </X509Data>d

    </KeyInfo>
```

The PGPData Element

Identifier: Type="http://www.w3.org/2000/09/xmldsig#PGPData"

The PGPData element within KeyInfo is used to convey information related to PGP public-key pairs and signatures on such keys. The PGP data values have two parameters:

- PGPKeyID, a base64Binary sequence containing a standard PGP public-key identifier as defined in Section 5.5 of RFC 2440, "OpenPGP Message Format" (Callas, Donnerhacke, Finney, & Thayer, 1998)

- PGPKeyPacket, a base64-encoded key material packet as defined in RFC 2440, "OpenPGP Message Format" section.

The above-named parameters need to be sent as part of the PGPData element. This can be done sending the parameters within a RetrievalMethod or using a Reference element.

```
[3e] <element name="PGPData" type="ds:PGPDataType"/>

    <complexType name="PGPDataType">

        <choice>

            <sequence>

[3e1]          <element name="PGPKeyID" type="base64Binary"/>

[3e2]          <element name="PGPKeyPacket" type="base64Binary" minOc-
```

```
curs="0"/>
        <any namespace="##other" processContents="lax" minOccurs
="0"maxOccurs="unbounded"/>
    </sequence>
    </choice>
</complexType>
```

The SPKIData Element

Identifier: Type="http://www.w3.org/2000/09/xmldsig#SPKIData"

The SPKIData element within KeyInfo is used to convey information related to RFC 2692, "Simple Public Key Infrastructure (SPKI)," (Ellison, 1999), public key pairs, certificates, and other SPKI data.

```
[3f] <element name="SPKIData" type="ds:SPKIDataType"/>
    <complexType name="SPKIDataType">
        <sequence maxOccurs="unbounded">
[3f1]       <element name="SPKISexp" type="base64Binary"/>
[3f2]       <any namespace="##other" processContents="lax" minOc-
    curs="0"/>
        </sequence>
    </complexType>
```

XML Key Management Specification

In general, key management is associated with the generation, distribution, negotiation, exchange, and destruction of crypto variables. However, the XML key management specification specifies protocols for distributing and registering public keys; these protocols are suitable for use in conjunction with the standard for XML signatures and XML encryption. This is mainly a public-key infrastructure issue.

The XML Key Management Specification (Hallam-Baker & Mysori, 2004) implements in XML the different phases of certificates and keys. Those specifications are the following:

- XML Key Information Service Specification (X-KISS), which defines the specifications to locate (retrieve) and validate certificates.
- XML Key Registration Service Specification (X-KRSS), which manages the life cycle of public keys and certificates.

Figure 13-8. XML key management

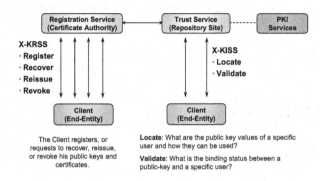

When discussing PKI and certificates, the public key of each user can be authenticated (signed) by a certificate authority. The certificate created by the CA binds the public key to the person or entity who owns the public key. In XKMS, the word "certificate" is not used; instead, "key binding" is used. Also, note that the word "service" in XML key information service and in XML key registration service does not refer to Web services, but only to the service provided by each of them.

There are two entities in communication protocol in XKMS: the client (requestor) and the service. The requestor presents a query request and the service responds with the result of the query. Therefore, XKMS has two syntaxes: one for the request and one for the response.

Key Information Service Message Set (X-KISS)

In XMLSig, signers may include information about their public signing key within the Key-Info element signature in order to send the public key to a verifier. However, KeyInfo may not contain information on where to locate the public key binding and nor how the public key is bound. The X-KISS Protocol supports these two services, locate and validate.

X-KISS Locate Service

The X-KISS locate service provides directory services, and it answers questions about the public-key values of a specific user and how the key can be used. The request element is QueryKeyBinding, a child element of LocateRequest, and because the service is not required to make an assertion concerning the validity of the binding, the response is UnverifiedKeyBinding, a child element of LocateResult.

Locate Request

The following is an example of a LocateRequest from the XKMS specification. The LocateRequest element has QueryKeyBinding as a child key element.

```
          <LocateRequest xmlns:ds="http://www.w3.org/2000/09/xmldsig#"
                  xmlns:xenc="http://www.w3.org/2001/04/xmlenc#"
                  Id="I8fc9f97052a34073312b22a69b3843b6"
                  Service="http://test.xmltrustcenter.org/XKMS"
                xmlns="http://www.w3.org/2002/03/xkms#">
            <RespondWith>KeyName</RespondWith>
            <RespondWith>KeyValue</RespondWith>
            <RespondWith>X509Cert</RespondWith>
            <RespondWith>X509Chain</RespondWith>
            <RespondWith>PGPWeb</RespondWith>
            <RespondWith>PGP</RespondWith>
[1]        <QueryKeyBinding>
[1a]          <KeyUsage>Encryption</KeyUsage>
[1b]            <UseKeyWith Application="urn:ietf:rfc:2440" Identifier="bob@
          bobcorp.test" />
[1c]            <UseKeyWith Application="urn:ietf:rfc:3851"
                       Identifier="bob@bobcorp.test" />
            </QueryKeyBinding>
          </LocateRequest>
```

In the `LocateRequest`, the client is querying about a key to encipher [1a] a message for the e-mail address bob@bobcorp.test [1b] using Open PGP (RFC 2440) [1b] according to the S/MIME Version 3 Message Specification (RFC 3851) [1c]. The client is querying the service to provide the results as indicated in `ResponseWith`.

The `UseKeyWith` element contains the following child elements:

- **Application:** A URI that specifies the application protocols with which the key may be used, such as S/MIME, SSL/TLS, TLS/HTTPS, TLS/SMTP, IPsec, and PKIX.
- **Identifier:** Specifies the subject to which the key corresponds within the specified application protocol, such as an e-mail address, a URI, DNS address, IP Address, and X509 Distinguish Name.

Locate Result

After locating the information, the service responses with `LocateResult`. The locate service uses the same ID for the `LocateRequest` as the `RequestID`.

The following is an example for a `LocateResult` from the XKMS specification.

```
          <LocateResult xmlns:ds="http://www.w3.org/2000/09/xmldsig#"
                  xmlns:xenc="http://www.w3.org/2001/04/xmlenc#"
                  Id="I8ce3809ab23500015cc27704b7eb0912"
```

```
                  Service=http://... ResultMajor="Success"
                   RequestId="I8fc9f97052a34073312b22a69b3843b6"
                   xmlns="http://www.w3.org/2002/03/xkms#">
[1]       <UnverifiedKeyBinding Id="I809ca03cf85b3cb466859694dbd0627d">
[1a]           <ds:KeyInfo>
[1a1]              <ds:KeyValue>
[1a1a]                 <ds:RSAKeyValue>
[1a1a1]                   <ds:Modulus>3FFtW...</ds:Modulus>
[1a1a2]                   <ds:Exponent>AQAB</ds:Exponent>
                       </ds:RSAKeyValue>
                   </ds:KeyValue>
[1a2]              <ds:X509Data>
[1a2a]<ds:X509Certificate>xlCb2IFr...</ds:X509Certificate>
[1a2b]<ds:X509Certificate>wdUZXNOI...</ds:X509Certificate>
                   </ds:X509Data>
               </ds:KeyInfo>
[1b]           <KeyUsage>Signature</KeyUsage>
               <KeyUsage>Encryption</KeyUsage>
               <KeyUsage>Exchange</KeyUsage>
[1c]           <UseKeyWith Application="urn:ietf:rfc:3851"
                   Identifier="bob@bobcorp.test" />
           </UnverifiedKeyBinding>
       </LocateResult>
```

The LocateResult element has UnverifiedKeyBinding [1] as a child key element, meaning that the key binding needs verification. The key values that the client was asking to locate are presented in [1a1a] as part of the KeyInfo [1a]. The public key belongs to bob@bobcorp, and it can be used to sign, encipher, and exchange messages and keys for S/MIME Version 3 Message Specification [1b]. It also provides the X.509 certificates in [1a2a] and [1a2b].

X-KISS Validation Service

A location service provides only information that is trustworthy but does not provide any assurance that it is valid. Therefore, the client should validate the information by forwarding the data to a validation service or by performing the necessary trust path verification. The validation service allows the client to obtain the status of the binding between the public key and the data elements. Furthermore, the status of each of the data elements returned is valid and all are bound to the same public key. A validation service only returns information that has been validated by the XKMS service and the client may rely on the information returned by the service without further validation.

The validation process is as follows: The client sends the XKMS service information containing some or all of the elements for which the status of the key binding is required. If the information is incomplete, the XKMS service may obtain the additional data required from a PKI service. Once the validity of the key binding has been determined, the XKMS service returns the status result to the client.

The validation service also provides all of the services provided by the XKISS locate service. See Figure 13-9.

Validate Request

The ValidateRequest element has QueryKeyBinding as a child key element. In the Validate Request, the client requests binding information for a particular public-key certificate whose X.509 certificate is indicated in [1a1a] and [1a1b]. The client is also asking about the validity of Alice's public key, and if Alice can use it to sign [1b] her e-mails with S/MIME Version 3 Message Specification [1c].

```
    <ValidateRequest xmlns:ds="http://www.w3.org/2000/09/xmldsig#"
        xmlns:xenc="http://www.w3.org/2001/04/xmlenc#"
        Id="Ie26380bfeb9d0c5bc526d5213a162d46"
        Service="http://test.xmltrustcenter.org/XKMS"
        xmlns="http://www.w3.org/2002/03/xkms#">
        <RespondWith>X509Cert</RespondWith>
[1]     <QueryKeyBinding>
[1a]        <ds:KeyInfo>
[1a1]           <ds:X509Data>
[1a1a]<ds:X509Certificate>xlCb2IFr...</ds:X509Certificate>
[1a1b]<ds:X509Certificate>wdUZXN0I...</ds:X509Certificate>
                </ds:X509Data>
            </ds:KeyInfo>
[1b]        <KeyUsage>Signature</KeyUsage>
[1c]        <UseKeyWith Application="urn:ietf:rfc:3851"  Identifier="alice@
    alicecorp.test" />
        </QueryKeyBinding>
    </ValidateRequest>
```

Validate Result

The validation service answers the request with a ValidateResult, indicating how the key can be used and for which application. It also provides information about the certificate, such as the validity interval and the key binding status.

The ValidateResult element has KeyBinding as a child key element. In the Validate Request, the client requests the following:

```
    <ValidateResult xmlns:ds="http://www.w3.org/2000/09/xmldsig#"
            xmlns:xenc="http://www.w3.org/2001/04/xmlenc#"
            Id="I34ef61b96f7db2250c229d37a17edfc0"
            Service=http://test.xmltrustcenter.org/XKMS
    ResultMajor="Success"
            RequestId="Ie26380bfeb9d0c5bc526d5213a162d46"
            xmlns="http://www.w3.org/2002/03/xkms#">
[1]   <KeyBinding Id="Icf608e9e8b07468fde1b7ee5449fe831">
[1a]    <ds:KeyInfo>
[1a1]      <ds:X509Data>
[1a1a]<ds:X509Certificate>xlCb2IFr...</ds:X509Certificate>
            </ds:X509Data>
        </ds:KeyInfo>
[1b]    <KeyUsage>Signature</KeyUsage>
        <KeyUsage>Encryption</KeyUsage>
        <KeyUsage>Exchange</KeyUsage>
[1c]    <UseKeyWith Application="urn:ietf:rfc:3851"
            Identifier="alice@alicecorp.test" />
[1d]    <Status StatusValue="Valid">
[1d1]          <ValidReason>Signature</ValidReason>
            <ValidReason>IssuerTrust</ValidReason>
            <ValidReason>RevocationStatus</ValidReason>
            <ValidReason>ValidityInterval</ValidReason>
        </Status>
      </KeyBinding>
    </ValidateResult>
```

Other StatusValue and StatusType elements are as follows:

```
[1d] <simpleType name="StatusValue">
      <restriction base="QName">
            <enumeration value="xkms:Valid"/>
            <enumeration value="xkms:Invalid"/>
            <enumeration value="xkms:Indeterminate"/>
      </restriction>
    </simpleType>
[1d1]<simpleType name="StatusType">
      <sequence>
            <element ref="xkms:ValidReason" minOccurs="0"
            maxOccurs="unbounded"/>
            <element ref="xkms:IndeterminateReason" minOccurs="0"
            maxOccurs="unbounded"/>
```

```
            <element ref="xkms:InvalidReason" minOccurs="0"
            maxOccurs="unbounded"/>
        </sequence>
    </simpleType>
```

Other `ValidityIntervals` are the following:

```
ValidityInterval
<UnverifiedKeyBinding>
    <element ref="xkms:ValidityInterval"/>
        <attribute name="NotBefore" type="dateTime"/>
            <attribute name="NotOnOrAfter" type="dateTime"/>
    <element ref="xkms:/ValidityInterval"/>
</UnverifiedKeyBinding>
```

Key Registration Service (X-KRSS)

As described in Chapter 9, "Certificates and Public Key Infrastructure," PKI is about managing certificates and keys during their complete life cycles. There are three phases in the life cycle of certificates and keys: initialization, issued, and cancellation.

The key registration service (X-KRSS) is more specific in the services that it supports. It only supports four services—register, recovery, reissue, and revoke.

Register

As in PKI, the first step in key binding is for the client or service to generate a key pair. If the client generates the key pair, then only the client knows the private key, and the private key can be used for non-repudiation. If the service generates the key pair, then the service acts as key escrow. It keeps a copy of the private key, so if the client loses it, it is possible for the service to decipher a data file.

Table 13-1. PKI phases

Phase 1 Initialization	Phase 2 Issued	Phase 3 Cancellation
o Key pair generation o Registration o Certificate creation o Key & certificate distribution o Certificate dissemination o Key backup	o Certificate retrieval o Certificate validation o Key recovery o Key update o Certificate update	o Certificate suspension o Certificate expiration o Certificate revocation o Key history o Key archive

Once the pair is generated, the registration service binds the public key to certain information through key binding.

Register Request

The `RegisterRequest` element has as child elements `PrototypeKeyBinding`, `Authentication`, `ProofofPossession`.

```
        <RegisterRequest xmlns:ds="http://..."
            xmlns:xenc="http://..."
            Id="I1494ac4351b7de5c174d455b7000e18f"
            Service="http://..."
            xmlns="http://...">
            <RespondWith>X509Cert</RespondWith>
            <RespondWith>X509Chain</RespondWith>
[1]     <PrototypeKeyBinding>
[1a]    <ds:KeyInfo>
[1a1]    <KeyValue> (RSAKEY, ECCKey,...) </Keyvalue>
[1a2]    <KeyUsage> (Signature, Encryption, Exchange)</KeyUsage>
[1a3]    <UseKeyWith> (Type of Application)</UseKeywith>
[2]     <Authentication>
[2a]     <KeyBindingAuthentication>
[2a1]         <Signature xmlns="http://...">
[2a1a]             <SignedInfo>
[2a1a1]            <CanonicalizationMethod Algorithm="http://..." />
[2a1a2]            <SignatureMethod Algorithm="http://..." />
[2a1a3]            <Reference URI="#...">
[2a1a3a]               <Transforms>
[2a1a3a1]                 <Transform Algorithm="http://..." />
                        </Transforms>
[2a1a3b]                <DigestMethod Algorithm="http://..." />
[2a1a3c]                <DigestValue>...</DigestValue>
                    </Reference>
                  </SignedInfo>
[2a1b]             <SignatureValue>...</SignatureValue>
              </Signature>
          </KeyBindingAuthentication>
        </Authentication>
[3]     <ProofOfPossession>
[3a]     <Signature xmlns="http://...">
[3a1]         <SignedInfo>
```

```
[3a1a]                    <CanonicalizationMethod Algorithm="http://..." />
[3a1b]                    <SignatureMethod Algorithm="http://..." />
[3a1c]                    <Reference URI="#...">
[3a1c1]                       <Transforms>
                                  <Transform Algorithm="http://..." />
                              </Transforms>
[3a1c2]                       <DigestMethod Algorithm="http://..." />
[3a1c3]                       <DigestValue>...</DigestValue>
                          </Reference>
                      </SignedInfo>
[3a2]                 <SignatureValue>...</SignatureValue>
                  </Signature>
          </ProofOfPossession>
      </RegisterRequest>
```

Register Response

The RegisterResponse element has as child elements KeyBinding and Pri-vateKey.

```
      <RegisterResult xmlns:ds="http://..."
          xmlns:xenc="http://..."
          Id="..."
          Service="http://..." ResultMajor="Success"
          RequestId="I1494ac4351b7de5c174d455b7000e18f"
          xmlns="http://...">
[1]     <KeyBinding Id="...">
[1a]       <ds:KeyInfo>
[1a1]        <ds:X509Data>
[1a1a]<ds:X509Certificate>xlCb2IFr...</ds:X509Certificate>
[1a1b]<ds:X509Certificate>wdUZXN0I...</ds:X509Certificate>
             </ds:X509Data>
           </ds:KeyInfo>
[1b]       <KeyUsage> (Signature, Encryption, Exchange) </KeyUsage>
[1c]       <UseKeyWith> (Type of Application) </UseKeywith>
[1d]       <Status StatusValue="Valid">
[1d1]         <ValidReason>Signature</ValidReason>
[1d2]         <ValidReason>IssuerTrust</ValidReason>
[1d3]         <ValidReason>RevocationStatus</ValidReason>
[1d4]         <ValidReason>ValidityInterval</ValidReason>
           </Status>
```

```
        </KeyBinding>
      </RegisterResult>
```

If the service generated the key pair, the private key is sent to the client encrypted.

```
      <PrivateKey>
          <xenc:EncryptedData>
              <xenc:EncryptionMethod Algorithm=(AES, tripledes-cbc,.) />
                  <xenc:CipherData>
<xenc:CipherValue>QrD5uLxDmXYV... </xenc:CipherValue>
                  </xenc:CipherData>
          </xenc:EncryptedData>
      </PrivateKey>
```

Recovery Service

When clients lose their private keys, they can ask the recovery service to send them a copy. In other words, the private key associated with a key binding is recovered. For key recovery to be possible, the recovery service must have escrowed the private key and, therefore, have a copy. If the registration service does not have a record of the key binding to be recovered, it will respond with NotFound.

The security policy of the issuer may consider it a breach of security when a client loses the private key and, as a result, the key and all of the associated key bindings would be revoked. This is especially true if the key recovery was requested by a third party such as the supervisor of the key holder.

Recover Request

A key recover request is similar to the initial registration of a key. The RecoverRequest element has as child elements RecoverKeyBinding and Authentication.

```
     <RecoverRequest xmlns:ds="http://..."
         xmlns:xenc="http://..."
         Id="I66f40510c322d281602ce76b9eb04d7d"
         Service="http://..."
         xmlns="http://...">
       <RespondWith>PrivateKey</RespondWith>
[1]   <RecoverKeyBinding Id="...">
[1a]     <ds:KeyInfo>
[1a1]       <ds:KeyValue>   (RSAKEY, ECCKey,...)</ds:KeyValue>
         </ds:KeyInfo>
```

```
[1a2]    <Status StatusValue="Indeterminate" />
      </RecoverKeyBinding>
[2]  <Authentication>
[2a]     <KeyBindingAuthentication>
[2a1]       <Signature xmlns="http://...">
[2a1a]         <SignedInfo>
[2a1a1]         <CanonicalizationMethod Algorithm="http://..." />
[2a1a2]         <SignatureMethod Algorithm="http://..." />
[2a1a3]         <Reference URI="#...">
[2a1a3a]            <Transforms>
[2a1a3a1]              <Transform Algorithm="http://...">
                            xmlns:ec="http://..." />
                       </Transform>
                    </Transforms>
[2a1a3b]            <DigestMethod Algorithm="http://..."/>
[2a1a3c]            <DigestValue>...</DigestValue>
            </Reference>
          </SignedInfo>
          <SignatureValue>...</SignatureValue>
        </Signature>
      </KeyBindingAuthentication>
     </Authentication>
    </RecoverRequest>
```

Recover Result

The `RecoverResult` element has as child elements `KeyBinding` and `PrivateKey`.

In the following example from the XKMS-2.0 Recommendation, the private key is revoked and new private-key parameters are created and sent to the subject. Note that the `RequestID` is the same ID as in the request.

```
    <RecoverResult xmlns:ds="http://www.w3.org/2000/09/xmldsig#"
        xmlns:xenc="http://www.w3.org/2001/04/xmlenc#"
        Id="Iacd24dbd4b3c79660f4d26aca7aaaea2"
        Service="http://test.xmltrustcenter.org/XKMS"
        ResultMajor="Success"
        RequestId="I66f40510c322d281602ce76b9eb04d7d"
        xmlns="http://www.w3.org/2002/03/xkms#">
[1]    <KeyBinding Id="I29cb8ac8a2ad878f7be44edfe53ea77a">
[1a]     <ds:KeyInfo>
[1a1]       <ds:KeyValue>
```

```
[1a1a]        <ds:RSAKeyValue>
[1a1a1]        <ds:Modulus>3FFtWUs...</ds:Modulus>
[1a1a2]        <ds:Exponent>AQAB</ds:Exponent>
              </ds:RSAKeyValue>
            </ds:KeyValue>
          </ds:KeyInfo>
[1b]      <Status StatusValue="Invalid">
            <InvalidReason>Signature</InvalidReason>
            <InvalidReason>IssuerTrust</InvalidReason>
            <InvalidReason>RevocationStatus</InvalidReason>
            <InvalidReason>ValidityInterval</InvalidReason>
          </Status>
        </KeyBinding>
[2]     <PrivateKey>
[2a]      <xenc:EncryptedData>
[2a1]       <xenc:EncryptionMethod Algorithm="http://www.w3.org/2001/04/
    xmlenc#tripledes-cbc"/>
[2a2]       <xenc:CipherData>
              <xenc:CipherValue>D5uLxDmXYV5I... </xenc:CipherValue>
            </xenc:CipherData>
            </xenc:EncryptedData>
          </PrivateKey>
        </RecoverResult>
```

Reissue Service

In the reissue service, a previously registered key binding is reissued.

Reissue Request

A reissue request is similar to the initial registration of a key. The ReissueRequest element has as child elements ReissueKeyBinding, Authentication, and ProofOfPossession.

```
<ReissueRequest xmlns:ds="http://www.w3.org/2000/09/xmldsig#"
    xmlns:xenc="http://www.w3.org/2001/04/xmlenc#"
    Id="I3a682dfb94cc8e9b3b648026783a8094"
    Service="http://test.xmltrustcenter.org/XKMS"
    xmlns="http://www.w3.org/2002/03/xkms#">
  <RespondWith>X509Cert</RespondWith>
  <RespondWith>X509Chain</RespondWith>
```

```
[1]     <ReissueKeyBinding Id=""""I518fc89b03369bccec3d1ee9d985c436">
[1a]       <ds:KeyInfo>
[1a1]          <ds:X509Data>
[1a1a]<ds:X509Certificate>xlCb2IFr... </ds:X509Certificate>
                 </ds:X509Data>
            </ds:KeyInfo>
[1b]       <Status StatusValue="Valid" />
         </ReissueKeyBinding>
[2]       <Authentication>
            <KeyBindingAuthentication>
            </KeyBindingAuthentication>
         </Authentication>
[3]       <ProofOfPossession>
            <SignedInfo>...    </SignedInfo>
               <SignatureValue>...</SignatureValue>
            </Signature>
         </ProofOfPossession>
      </ReissueRequest>
```

Reissue Result

The ReissueResult element has as a child element KeyBinding. The service accepts the registration and returns the following response:

```
      <ReissueResult xmlns:ds="http://..."
          xmlns:xenc="http://..."
          Id="..."
          Service="http://..." ResultMajor="Success"
          RequestId="..."
          xmlns="http://...">
[1]     <KeyBinding Id="...">
[1a]       <ds:KeyInfo>
                <ds:X509Data>
                   <ds:X509Certificate>xlCb2IFr.. </ds:X509Certificate>
                   <ds:X509Certificate>wdUZXN0I.. </ds:X509Certificate>
                </ds:X509Data>
            </ds:KeyInfo>
[1b]       <KeyUsage> (Signature, encryption, Exchange) </KeyUsage>
[1c]       <UseKeyWith (Type of Application) />
[1d]       <Status StatusValue="Valid">
                <ValidReason>Signature</ValidReason>
```

```
            <ValidReason>IssuerTrust</ValidReason>
            <ValidReason>RevocationStatus</ValidReason>
            <ValidReason>ValidityInterval</ValidReason>
        </Status>
      </KeyBinding>
    </ReissueResult>
```

Revoke Service

In the revoke service, a previously registered key binding is revoked. A revocation request needs only to contain sufficient information to identify the key binding and the authority requesting the revocation in order to revoke a key binding.

Revoke Request

The RevokeRequest element has as child elements RevokeKeyBinding, Authentication, and RevocationCode.

```
        <RevokeRequest xmlns:ds="http://..."
            xmlns:xenc="http://..."
            Id="I2aa2c2f37195c9c4364c55f15df68091"
            Service="http://..."
            xmlns="http://...">
[1]     <RevokeKeyBinding Id=" ="Ie91dfbf1c948d5cf142099676968caf1">
[1a]      <ds:KeyInfo>
[1a1]         <ds:X509Data>
[1a1a]            <ds:X509Certificate>x1Cb2IFr...</ds:X509Certificate>
            </ds:X509Data>
          </ds:KeyInfo>
[1a2]     <Status StatusValue="Indeterminate" />
        </RevokeKeyBinding>
[2]   <RevocationCode>PHx8li2SUhrJv2e1DyeWbGbD6rs=</RevocationCode>
      </RevokeRequest>
```

The RevocationCode element contains a MAC output value encoded as a base64 string of the pass phrase value. The default MAC algorithm used is HMAC-SHA1.

Upon initial registration, the RevocationCode value is obtained by first performing the MAC calculation on the pass phrase value, and then performing a second MAC calculation on the result.

Revoke Result

RevokeResult is the service response to the RevokeRequest.

```
<RevokeResult xmlns:ds="http://..."
    xmlns:xenc="http://..."
    Id="..."
    Service="http://..." ResultMajor="Success"
    RequestId="I2aa2c2f37195c9c4364c55f15df68091"
    xmlns="http://..." />
```

Security Assertion Markup Language (SAML)

SAML (Hughes & Maler, 2005) addresses issues involved with the use of authentication and authorization to Web services. Every time an end-user accesses a Web site on an Intranet or the Internet, it is required to enter a password. For this reason, end-users have many passwords to remember, and many store them in a personal device, such as a cellular phone or a PDA.

On an Intranet, it is possible to use a single sign-on (SSO) system as a solution to the problem. Users either use the same password to access all company Web sites, or they are only required to authenticate themselves one time, and then the system automatically assigns them their appropriate access privileges. SSO may solve the problem of multiple passwords inside one organization, but when access is required to other organizations or Web sites on the Internet, the problem still exists because each Web site requires the individuals or entities to identify and authenticate themselves.

Ideally, a subject's identity would be initially established and verified at a Web domain, and some type of credentials that assert the subject's identity would be given to the subject. When several Web domains are involved in a transaction, the subject should be able to show the asserted credentials, *assertions*, to other Web domains to prove his identity to complete the transaction. This requires making the assertion portable. Web services move SOAP messages with attached assertions, entity authentications. This is similar to an individual (message) traveling with a passport (assertion), visiting several countries (Web domains), and each country accepting as identification the same passport. Web domains can challenge an assertion, and there should be ways to prove the assertion. SAML solves the problem of Web single sign-on by allowing users to gain access to website resources in multiple domains without having to re-authenticate after initially logging on to the first domain.

In November 2002, SAML 1.0 became an OASIS standard; Version 1.1 was approved in September 2003 and SAML V2.0 was approved in March 2005. SAML is flexible, so it can be used with any XML file transferred within the enterprise or the Internet. It has been broadly implemented by all major Web access management vendors.

SAML Components

According to SAML V2.0 (Hughes & Maler, 2005), SAML has four components: assertions, protocol, bindings, and profiles. Figure 13-9 illustrates the relationships among the components.

The following is a description of SAML components and subcomponents:

1. **Assertions:** A package of information provided by an issuer that asserts the authentication, authorization, and attribute information of an entity. For example, an SAML assertion could state that the user is "John Doe", the user has "Gold" status, the user's e-mail address is john.doe@example.com, and the user is a member of the "engineering" group. SAML defines three kinds of statements that can be carried within an assertion.

a. **Authentication statement:** States that the specified subject was authenticated by a particular means at a particular time. Authentication statements are issued by the party that successfully authenticated the user. The party defines who issued the assertion, the authenticated subject, validity period, plus other authentication related information.

b. **Authorization statements:** States that a particular authentication authority has granted or denied permission to a subject to access the specified resource. It defines what the subject is entitled to do at a specific resource.

c. **Attribute statement:** Provides specific detail about the subject. It associates a subject with the supplied attributes.

2. **Protocol:** Defines a number of request/response protocols for obtaining assertions. The protocol is encoded in an XML schema as a set of request-response pairs.

3. **Binding:** Details exactly how the SAML protocol maps onto the messaging or communications transport protocols. For instance, the SAML specification provides a binding of how SAML request/responses are carried with SOAP exchange messages.

4. **Profile:** Defines how the SAML assertions, protocols, and bindings are combined to support a defined-use case.

Figure 13-9. SAML components

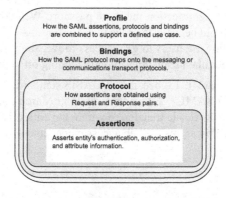

An example of the `Assertion` syntax is seen below.

```
      <saml:Assertion
      xmlns:saml="urn:oasis:names:tc:SAML:1.0:assertion"
      MajorVersion="1"
      MinorVersion="1"
      AssertionID="buGxcG4gILg5NlocyLccDz6iXrUa"
      Issuer="www.acompany.com"
      IssueInstant="2006-06-19T17:05:37.795Z">
[1]      <saml:Conditions>
             NotBefore="2006-06-19T17:00:37.795Z"
             NotOnOrAfter="2006-06-19T17:10:37.795Z"/>
[2]      <saml:AuthenticationStatement
             AuthenticationMethod="password"
             AuthenticationInstant="2006-06-19T17:05:17.706Z">
[2a]        <saml:Subject>
[2a1]         <saml:NameIdentifier
[2a1a]           NameQualifier=http://www.acompany.com
[2a1b]           Format="http://www.customformat.com/">
[2a1c]           uid=joe
             </saml:NameIdentifier>
[2b]         <saml:SubjectConfirmation>
[2b1]          <saml:ConfirmationMethod>
[2b1a]urn:oasis:names:tc:SAML:1.0:cm:artifact-01
               </saml:ConfirmationMethod>
               <ds:KeyInfo>
         <ds:KeyName>MyTourOperatorKey</ds:KeyName>
                      <ds:KeyValue> ... </ds:KeyValue>
                 </ds:KeyInfo>
             </saml:SubjectConfirmation>
             </saml:Subject>
           </saml:AuthenticationStatement>
[3]         <ds:Signature>...</ds:Signature>
      </saml:Assertion>
```

The `Conditions` element [1] specifies two conditions for this assertion. The `NotBefore` attribute tells the time before which the assertion is not valid, and the `NotOnOrAfter` attribute gives the time after which the assertion expires.

The `AuthenticationStatement` element [2] contains two attributes and one child element. The first attribute, `AuthenticationMethod`, indicates the authentication method used. The SAML specification defines identifiers for several authentication methods (See in this chapter, "SAML Components, Authentication Methods," for a list of authentication methods used in SAML). The second attribute, `AuthenticationInstant`, specifies the instant of time when the authentication took place. The only child element is `Subject`, which provides information on the subject that has been authenticated. The `Subject` element has two child elements, the `NameIdentifier` element, which specifies the subject's name, and the `SubjectConfirmation` element, which specifies the relationship between the subject of an assertion and the author of the assertion.

Authentication Method

The `AuthenticationMethod` defines which method was used to authenticate an assertion. Identifying the authentication method in the assertion allows the application to accept or reject the assertion because the subject did not go through an appropriate authentication. For example, some applications like e-mail only require passwords, but some others require stronger authentication methods. SAML can use passwords, Kerberos, secure remote passwords, hardware tokens, public keys (X.509, SPKI, XKMS, SSL/TLS certificates), and XML digital signatures.

An example of the `AuthenticationMethod` syntax is seen below.

```
[2]   <saml:AuthenticationStatement
                    AuthenticationMethod =
                    "Password"
                    "Kerberos"
                    "Secure Remote password"
                    "Hardware Token"
                    "SSL Client Certificate"
                    "X.509 Public Key"
                    "PGP Public Key"
                    "SKPI Public Key"
                    "XKMS Public Key"
                    "XML digital Signature"
      </saml1:AuthenticationStatement>
```

Confirmation Method

In the Assertion syntax example above, the `ConfirmationMethod` [2b1] is a child of the `SubjectConfirmation` element [2b]. There are two SSO profiles used for `SubjectConfirmation`: Browser/Artifact Profile and Browser/POST Profile.

Both profiles assume the following:

Figure 13-10. SAML profiles

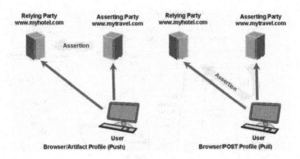

- A user has an authenticated session on the local source site (asserting party) using a standard commercial Web browser, using either HTTP or HTTPS.

- The user wants to access a resource on the destination Web site and is directed there.

- The destination Web site (relying party) needs to determine the identity and entitlements of the user.

- The destination site can then make whatever authentication and authorization decisions it needs to, based on the received assertion(s).

Browser/Artifact Profile

This profile is a pull model in which a credential artifact is sent to the user, so the user can present the credential artifact to the destination site. The destination site can use the credential artifact to obtain (or pull) the assertion from the asserting party.

The following steps describe the artifact confirmation method profile:

1. The user accesses the source Web site (mytravel.com).

2. The source Web site performs an access check and determines that the user does not have a current session and requires the user to be authenticated. As a result, the user is challenged to authenticate.

3. The user supplies back credentials, for instance, username and password.

4. If the authentication is successful, then a session is created for the user and the appropriate welcome screen of the portal application is displayed.

5. The user selects a menu option (or function) on the displayed screen that indicates that the user wants to access a resource or application on a destination Web site www.myhotel.com. This causes a HTTP request to be sent to the source site's inter-site transfer service. The request contains the target URL, in this case, myhotel.com.

6. The inter-site transfer service generates an assertion for the user while also creating an artifact that contains the source ID of the www.mytravel.com SAML responder,

Figure 13-11. Artifact confirmation method profile

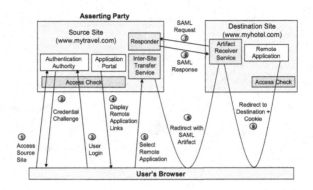

together with a reference to the assertion. The user's Web browser sends the artifact to the destination Web site, myhotel.com.

7. On receiving the HTTP message, the artifact receiver, on the destination Web site, www.myhotel.com, extracts the source-ID and determines which responder needs to be contacted. The artifact receiver will therefore know that it has to contact the www.mytravel.com SAML responder at the prescribed URL. The www.myhotel.com artifact receiver sends an SAML request to the www.mytravel.com SAML responder containing the artifact supplied by the inter-site transfer service of www.mytravel.com.

8. The www.mytravel.com SAML responder supplies an SAML response message containing the assertion generated during step 7.

9. The artifact receiver, on the destination Web site, www.myhotel.com, sends a redirection message containing a cookie back to the user browser. The user browser sends the cookie, which identifies the session, back to the myhotel.com application where an access check is done to establish whether the user has the correct authorization to access the www.myhotel.com Web site database.

Browser/POST Profile

This profile is a "push model" in which the assertion is sent back to the user so he can present it the destination site. The assertion is posted using HTTP.

The following steps describe the POST confirmation method profile:

1. Same as for artifact confirmation method profile
2. Same as for artifact confirmation method profile
3. Same as for artifact confirmation method profile
4. Same as for artifact confirmation method profile
5. Same as for artifact confirmation method profile

Figure 13-12. Post confirmation method profile

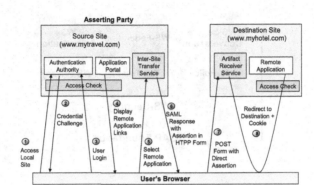

6.   The inter-site transfer service signs the user's assertion and sends back to the user's browser an SAML response that contains the user's SAML assertion.

7.   The user's browser issues an HTTP POST form containing the SAML response and sends it to the destination party's (www.myhotel.com) assertion consumer service.

8.   The destination party's assertion consumer service validates the digital signature on the SAML response. If the digital signature is valid, it sends a redirect to the user's browser causing it to access the destination application. An access check is made to establish whether the user has the correct authorization to access the www.myhotel.com Web site and its applications.

Web Services Security Language (WS-Security)

In the April 2002 white paper, "Security in a Web Service World, A Proposed Architecture and Roadmap," IBM and Microsoft (2002) proposed a security model and road map for developing a set of Web service security specifications to protect SOAP messages exchanged in a Web service environment. The security model developed brings together formerly incompatible security technologies such as public-key infrastructure, Kerberos, and others. It also provides a broad set of specifications that cover security technologies including authentication, authorization, privacy, trust, integrity, confidentiality, secure communications, and auditing across a wide spectrum of application and business topologies.

Figure 13-13 shows the Web services security stack that IBM and Microsoft are following. According to the whitepaper, this stack includes a message security model (WS-Security) that provides the basis for other security specifications. Layered on this, the policy layer includes a Web service endpoint policy (WS-Policy), a trust model (WS-Trust), and a privacy model (WS-Privacy). Follow-up specifications for federated security will include secure conversations (WS-SecureConversation), federated trust (WS-Federation), and authorization (WS-Authorization).

The whitepaper describes the different layers as follows:

Figure 13-13. Web services security model

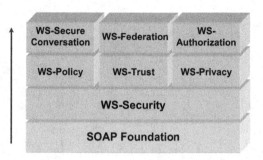

*   **WS-Security:** How to attach signature and encryption headers to SOAP messages. In addition, it describes how to attach security tokens, including binary security tokens such as X.509 certificates and Kerberos tickets, to messages.

*   **WS-Policy:** The capabilities and constraints of security (and other business) policies on intermediaries and endpoints (e.g., required security tokens, supported encryption algorithms, privacy rules).

*   **WS-Trust:** A framework for trust models that enables Web services to securely interoperate.

*   **WS-Privacy:** A model for how Web services and requesters state privacy preferences and organizational privacy practice statements.

*   **WS-SecureConversation:** How to manage and authenticate message exchanges between parties, including security context exchange and establishing and deriving session keys.

*   **WS-Federation:** How to manage and broker the trust relationships in a heterogeneous federated environment, including support for federated identities.

*   **WS-Authorization:** How to manage authorization data and authorization policies.

WS-Security Elements and Attributes

As stated in the security model whitepaper, WS-Security (Nadalin, Kaler, Monzillo, & Hallam-Baker, 2004) defines methods for embedding security in SOAP messages, for example, credential exchange, message integrity, and message confidentiality. WS-Security differs from SAML in that SAML defines how security assertions are expressed in XML format, and WS-Security defines how security is expressed in SOAP messages.

WS-Security states that security information should be contained in SOAP messages as follows:

- If XML signature is used, the header should contain the signature information that conveys how the message was signed, the key that was used, and the resulting signature value.

- If an element within the message is encrypted, the header should contain the encryption information that conveys the key that was used and how both parties arrived at the same secret key. Credentials, also called *access authentication*, *identification*, or *security tokens*, also should be within the headers. In wsse:Security, credentials are implemented in the header.

- The encrypted message element should be contained in the message body.

WS-Security Header

The security header parent element, `<wsse:Security>`, provides a mechanism for attaching security-related information targeted at a specific recipient; this may be either the ultimate recipient of the message or an intermediary.

The security header parent element has the following child elements: Security Token, XML Signature, and XML Encryption Reference.

An example of the `wsse:Security` syntax is seen below.

```
        <S:Envelope xmlns:S11="..." xmlns:wsse="...">
          <S:Header>
                <wsse:Security>
        <---Start Security Token Section--->
[1]                     <wsse:UsernameToken>
[1a]                        <wsse:Username>Zoe</wsse:Username>
                        </wsse:UsernameToken>
        <---End Security Token Section--->
        <---Start XML Signature Section--->
[2]                     <ds:Signature>
                            ......
[2a]                    <ds:Reference URI=#body">
                            ......
                        <ds:Signature>
        <---End XML Signature Section--->
        <---Start XML Encryption Reference List--->
[3]                     <xenc:ReferenceList>
[3a]                        <xenc:DataReference URI="body"/>
                        <xenc:ReferenceList>
        <---End XML Encryption Reference List--->
                </wsse:Security>
```

```
      </S:Header>

      <S:Body>
<---XML Encrypted Body--->
          <xenc:EncryptedData Id=body" Type="content">
               ......
          </xenc:EncryptedData>
      </S:Body>
   </S:Envelope>
```

SecurityTokens

Security tokens are defined in WS-Security as access mechanisms and methods used for authentication and authorization. Passwords are a type of unsigned security tokens. Signed security tokens are security tokens that are asserted and cryptographically signed by a specific authority, for example, an X.509 certificate or a Kerberos ticket. Security tokens in WS-Security are grouped as `UserNameToken`, `BinarySecurityToken`, or `XMLTokens`.

UserNameToken

The `<wsse:UsernameToken>` element defines how the user name and password information is enclosed in SOAP. The following illustrates the syntax of this element:

```
<wsse:UsernameToken wsu:Id="...">
        <wsse:Username>...</wsse:Username>
        <wsee:Password>...</wsse:Password>
</wsse:UsernameToken>
```

If the username and password are sent in clear, then SSL or some other transport mechanism should be used. An alternative is to concatenate and hash three items: the time stamp, a nonce, and the password. An example of a hashed password syntax is seen below.

```
<wsse:UsernameToken wsu:Id="...">
        <wsse:Username>...</wsse:Username>
        <wsee:PasswordType>"wsse:PassportDigest"
        LxYfQt6FlsF094hPi4wPU...
        </wsse:PasswordType>
        <wsse:nonce>.....</wsse:nonce>
        <wsu:Created> 2001-09-13T08:42:00Z</wsu:Created>
</wsse:UsernameToken>
```

BinarySecurityToken

X.509 certificates, Kerberos tickets, and other non-XML formats tokens are represented as binary strings. The `BinarySecurityToken` element describes the required special encoding format for inclusion in SOAP messages.

The `<wsse:BinarySecurityToken>` element defines two attributes that are used to interpret it. The `ValueType` attribute indicates what the security token is, for example, a Kerberos ticket. The `EncodingType` tells how the security token is encoded, for example, Base64Binary.

The following is an overview of the syntax for an X.509 with a Kerberos security token:

```
<wsse:BinarySecurityToken
    ValueType="...#X509v3"
        wsu:Id="X509Token"
    EncodingType="...#Base64Binary">
        MIIEZzCCA9CgAwIBAgIQEmtJZcOrqrKh5i...
</wsse:BinarySecurityToken>

<wsse:BinarySecurityToken
    ValueType="wsse:kerberosv5TGT"
        wsu:Id="myKerberosToken"
    EncodingType="...#Base64Binary">
        Qdtu4TYhds8Yhj5Na3g2...
</wsse:BinarySecurityToken>
```

XML Tokens

XML tokens, such as SAML assertions, can be embedded within the security header of a SOAP message.

Signature

A signature in WS-Security is simply the XML signature placed in the security header of a SOAP message. An XML signature in WS-Security can be used by the message recipient to authenticate or verify the security token, such as an X.509 certificate or an SAML assertion. The signature can also be used to verify that the message was not modified in transit, thus providing message integrity.

It is possible to sign a message before encryption or to encrypt it first and then sign it. The way in which it is done needs to be indicated in the syntax by placing either the encryption or the signing element first in the syntax.

If encryption is done first, then the syntax should be:

```
        <S:Envelope xmlns:S11="..." xmlns:wsse="...">
[1]         <S:Header>
[1a]            <wsse:Security>
[1a1]               [encryption element]
[1a2]               [signature element]
            </wsse:Security>
        </S:Header>
[2]         <S:Body>
            .....
        <</S:Body>
    </S:Envelope>
```

If signing is done first, then the syntax should be:

```
        <S:Envelope xmlns:S11="..." xmlns:wsse="...">
[1]         <S:Header>
[1a]            <wsse:Security>
[1a1]               [signature element]
[1a2]               [encryption element]
            </wsse:Security>
        </S:Header>
[2]         <S:Body>
            .....
        <</S:Body>
    </S:Envelope>
```

ReferenceList or EncryptedKey

The <xenc:ReferenceList> points out which part of the message body was encrypted. The <xenc:ReferenceList> child element is used when the sender and the receiver of the SAML message use a shared secret key to encipher the message body, and there is a need to provide information on how the key was sent.

In the example below, the pointer #bodyID in [1a1] points to [2a], indicating that the SOAP body was encrypted. Note that the shared key name is indicated in [2a1a].

The following illustrates the syntax of ReferenceList:

```
        <S:Envelope xmlns:S11="..." xmlns:wsse="..." xmlns:wsu="..."
        xmlns:ds="..." xmlns:xenc="...">
[1]     <S:Header>
[1a]        <wsse:Security>
```

```
[1a1]           <xenc:ReferenceList>
                    <xenc:DataReference URI="#bodyID"/>
                </xenc:ReferenceList>
          </wsse:Security>
       </S:Header>
[2]    <S:Body>
[2a]      <xenc:EncryptedData Id="bodyID">
[2a1]         <ds:KeyInfo>
[2a1a]            <ds:KeyName>CN=Hiroshi Maruyama, C=JP</ds:KeyName>
              </ds:KeyInfo>
[2a2]         <xenc:CipherData>
[2a2a]            <xenc:CipherValue>...</xenc:CipherValue>
              </xenc:CipherData>
          </xenc:EncryptedData>
       </S:Body>
    </S11:Envelope>
```

If the parties have not exchanged secret keys previously, it is necessary to transport the secret key in a secure manner. This can be done by enciphering or by wrapping the secret key for transport using a public-key system. The element where this information is provided is called <xenc:EncryptedKey>. Normally, a randomly generated symmetric key is encrypted using the recipient's public key.

The following example from the WS-Security standard illustrates the syntax of Encrypt-edKey:

```
    <S:Envelope xmlns:S11="..." xmlns:wsse="..." xmlns:wsu="..."
    xmlns:ds="..." xmlns:xenc="...">
[1]    <S:Header>
[1a]     <wsse:Security>
[1a1]        <xenc:EncryptedKey>
                ...
[1a1a]            <ds:KeyInfo>
[1a1a1]           <wsse:SecurityTokenReference>
[1a1a1a]              <ds:X509IssuerSerial>
                      <ds:X509IssuerName>
                        DC=ACMECorp, DC=com
                      </ds:X509IssuerName>
                      <ds:X509SerialNumber>
                        12345678
                      </ds:X509SerialNumber>
                      </ds:X509IssuerSerial>
```

```
                    </wsse:SecurityTokenReference>
                  </ds:KeyInfo>

                      ...

              </xenc:EncryptedKey>

          ...

          </wsse:Security>
      </S:Header>
[2]    <S:Body>
[2a]        <xenc:EncryptedData Id="bodyID">
[2a1]           <xenc:CipherData>
                   <xenc:CipherValue>...</xenc:CipherValue>
                </xenc:CipherData>
            </xenc:EncryptedData>
       </S:Body>
```

In the example above, the secret key is transported by encrypting it with the recipient's public key, which is within <wsse:SecurityTokenReference>. Also seen in the example, the X509 certificate has ACMECorp's name and serial number.

While XML encryption specifies that <xenc:EncryptedKey> elements be placed in <xenc:EncryptedData> elements, WS-Security strongly recommends that <xenc:EncryptedKey> elements be placed in the <wsse:Security> header.

Extended SOAP Message Example

The following sample message from WS-Security V 1.0 (Nadalin, Kaler, Monzillo, & Hallam-Baker, 2004), Section 11, illustrates the use of security tokens, signatures, and encryption. For this example, the timestamp and the message body are signed prior to encryption.

```
001  <?xml version="1.0" encoding="utf-8"?>
002  <S11:Envelope xmlns:S11="..." xmlns:wsse="..." xmlns:wsu="..." xmlns:
     xenc="..." xmlns:ds="...">
003    <S11:Header>
004      <wsse:Security>
005        <wsu:Timestamp wsu:Id="T0">
006          <wsu:Created>
007            2001-09-13T08:42:00Z</wsu:Created>
008          </wsu:Timestamp>
009
010          <wsse:BinarySecurityToken
                     ValueType="...#X509v3"
                     wsu:Id="X509Token"
```

```
                          EncodingType="...#Base64Binary">
011                       MIIEZzCCA9CgAwIBAgIQEmtJZcOrqrKh5i...
012              </wsse:BinarySecurityToken>
013              <xenc:EncryptedKey>
014                       <xenc:EncryptionMethod Algorithm=
                               "http://www.w3.org/2001/04/xmlenc#rsa-1_5"/>
015                       <ds:KeyInfo>
016                           <wsse:KeyIdentifier
                                   EncodingType="...#Base64Binary"
                                   ValueType="...#X509v3">MIGfMa0GCSq...
017                           </wsse:KeyIdentifier>
018                       </ds:KeyInfo>
019                       <xenc:CipherData>
020 <xenc:CipherValue>d2FpbmdvbGRfEOlm4byV0...
021                           </xenc:CipherValue>
022                       </xenc:CipherData>
023                       <xenc:ReferenceList>
024                           <xenc:DataReference URI="#enc1"/>
025                       </xenc:ReferenceList>
026               </xenc:EncryptedKey>
027               <ds:Signature>
028                   <ds:SignedInfo>
029                       <ds:CanonicalizationMethod Algorithm="http://
                               www.w3.org/2001/10/xml-exc-c14n#"/>
030                       <ds:SignatureMethod Algorithm="http://www.
                               w3.org/2000/09/xmldsig#rsa-sha1"/>
031                       <ds:Reference URI="#T0">
032                           <ds:Transforms>
033                           <ds:Transform Algorithm="http://www.
                               w3.org/2001/10/xml-exc-c14n#"/>
034                           </ds:Transforms>
035                           <ds:DigestMethod Algorithm="http://www.
                               w3.org /2000/09/ xmldsig#sha1"/>
036                           <ds:DigestValue>LyLsF094hPi4wPU...
037                           </ds:DigestValue>
038                       </ds:Reference>
039                       <ds:Reference URI="#body">
040                           <ds:Transforms>
041                               <ds:Transform Algorithm="http://www.
                               w3.org/ 2001/10/xml-exc-c14n#"/>
042                           </ds:Transforms>
043                           <ds:DigestMethod Algorithm="http://www.
```

```
                                    w3.org/ 2000/09/xmldsig#sha1"/>
044                                 <ds:DigestValue>LyLsF094hPi4wPU...
045                                 </ds:DigestValue>
046                             </ds:Reference>
047                         </ds:SignedInfo>
048                         <ds:SignatureValue>
049                             Hp1ZkmFZ/2kQLXDJbchm5gK...
050                         </ds:SignatureValue>
051                         <ds:KeyInfo>
052                             <wsse:SecurityTokenReference>
053                                 <wsse:Reference URI="#X509Token"/>
054                             </wsse:SecurityTokenReference>
055                         </ds:KeyInfo>
056                     </ds:Signature>
057                 </wsse:Security>
058             </S11:Header>
059             <S11:Body wsu:Id="body">
060                 <xenc:EncryptedData
        Type="http://www.w3.org/2001/04/xmlenc#Element"
                    wsu:Id="enc1">
061                 <xenc:EncryptionMethod Algorithm="http://www.w3.org/
                    2001/04/xmlenc#tripledes-cbc"/>
062                 <xenc:CipherData>
063                     <xenc:CipherValue>d2FpbmdvbGRfE0lm4byV0...
064                     </xenc:CipherValue>
065                 </xenc:CipherData>
066                 </xenc:EncryptedData>
067             </S11:Body>
068         </S11:Envelope>
```

Explanation of SOAP Message Example

Lines (003)-(058) contain the SOAP message headers.

- Lines (004)-(057) represent the `<wsse:Security>` header block. This contains the security-related information for the message.
- Lines (005)-(008) specify the timestamp information. In this case, it indicates the time the message was created.
- Lines (010)-(012) specify the binary security token that is associated with the message. In this case, it specifies an X.509 certificate that is encoded in Base64. Line (011) specifies the actual Base64 encoding of the certificate.

- Lines (013)-(026) show that EncryptedKey uses a public key to encrypt a shared key that is used to encrypt the body of the message. Key transport algorithms are public-key encryption algorithms particularly specified for encrypting and decrypting keys. Line (014) identifies RSAES-PKCS1-v1.5 as the key transport algorithm used to encrypt the key. Lines (015)-(018) indicate the identifier of the public key that was used to encrypt the shared key. Lines (019)-(022) specify the actual encrypted form of the symmetric key. Lines (023)-(025) identify the encryption block in the message that uses this symmetric key. In this case, it is only used to encrypt the body (Id="enc1"). Since this is a symmetric key, the key is sent in an encrypted form.

- Lines (027)-(056) specify the digital signature. This signature ensures the integrity of the signed elements. Lines (028)-(047) indicate what is being signed and the type of canonicalization being used. Line (029) specifies how to canonicalize (normalize) the data that is being signed. Line (030) specifies that the SignatureMethod used is the RSASSA-PKCS1-v1_5 algorithm described in RFC 3447 (RSA-SHA1). Line (035) indicates the DigestMethod algorithm used, SHA-1. Specifically, line (039) refers to the body of the message. The signature uses the XML signature specification identified by the ds namespace declaration in line (002).

- Lines (048)-(050) indicate the actual signature value—specified in line (043).

- Lines (051) to (055) provide information, partial or complete, as to where to find the security token associated with this signature. Specifically, lines (052) to (054) indicate that the security token can be found at (pulled from) the specified URL. Lines (052)-(054) indicate the key that was used for the signature. In this case, it is the X.509 certificate included in the message. Line (053) provides a URI link to lines (010)-(012).

- Lines (059) to (067) contain the body (payload) of the SOAP message.

- Lines (060)-(066) represent the encrypted metadata and form of the body using XML encryption.

- Line (060) indicates EncryptedData element, showing in line (061) the encryption algorithm used—Triple-DES in this case. Lines (063)-(064) contain the actual cipher text, that is, the result of the encryption. Note that there is no indication about key because the key used for encryption is referenced in line 24, URI = "#enc."

Summary

Web services standardize the mechanisms to describe, locate, and communicate online applications by allowing computers running on different operating platforms to access and share each other's databases. A Web service architecture consists of three primary functions: service discovery (universal discovery and integration), service description (Web services description language), and service transport (simple object access protocol). SOAP enables communication among Web services. WSDL provides a formal, computer-readable description of Web services through the use of XML. UDDI is a registry of Web services and descriptions of the services.

XML is text-based, so anyone who has access to an XML document can easily read the document, thus making XML and Web services more exposed to hackers. Web services security provides the following security services: confidentiality, integrity, authentication, non-repudiation, and access control. The discussion of how these mechanisms were developed includes XML encryption, XML signature, XML key management specification (XKMS), the security association markup language (SAML), and Web services security (WS-security).

Learning Objectives Review

1. For Web services, end-to-end security must be provided when intermediaries are not trusted by the communicating endpoints. (T/F)

2. Is information in XML sent in clear or it is enciphered?

3. What are Web services?

4. What is XML?

5. XML is particularly vulnerable to security compromises. As a result, any XML message, including SOAP messages, must be enhanced with security features including encryption, digital signatures, authentication mechanisms, and privacy controls. (T/F)

6. _____ is used to wrap XML information and send it over HTPP.

7. A problem with XML encryption is that it is not possible to encipher only part of a message. (T/F)

8. When data is relayed through several servers, only one SSL session is required to secure the session. (T/F)

9. Which encryption algorithms are used in XML encryption to encipher the message?

10. If communicating parties have not exchanged secret keys previously, how can they get the secret key to decipher an XML document?

11. What security services provide an XML signature?

12. SAML allows users to have portable identity on the Web. (T/F)

13. Name the different types of security tokens used in WS-Security.

14.   Which digest functions are used in XML signature?

15.   What is the difference between an assertion and a security token?

16.   SSL-encrypted messages have to be unencrypted at intermediary points, which opens a security hole. (T/F)

17.   Security tokens are attached to the body of a SOAP message. (T/F)

18.   Which encryption algorithm is used for key agreement in XML encryption?

19.   A SOAP message is an XML document information item that contains three elements: <Envelope>, <Header>, and <Body>. (T/F)

20.   What is a UDDI service registry server?

References

Bray, T., Hollander, D., & Layman, A. (1999). *Namespaces in XML*. World Wide Web Consortium (W3C). Retrieved June 28, 2007, from http://www.w3.org/TR/1999/REC-xml-names-19990114/

Bray, T., Maler, E., Paoli, J., Sperberg-McQueen, C. M., & Yergeau, F. (Eds.). (2004). *Extensible markup language (XML) 1.0* (3rd ed.). World Wide Web Consortium (W3C). Retrieved June 28, 2007, from http://www.w3.org/TR/2004/REC-xml-20040204/

Callas, J., Donnerhacke, L., Finney, H., & Thayer, R. (1998). *OpenPGP message format* (RFC 2440). Internet Engineering Task Force (IETF). Retrieved June 28, 2007, from http://www.ietf.org/rfc/rfc2440.txt?number=2440

Chinnici, R., Moreau, J., Ryman, A., & Weerawarana, S. (Eds.). (2004). *Web services description language (WSDL) version 2.0*. World Wide Web Consortium (W3C). Retrieved June 28, 2007, from http://www.w3.org/TR/wsdl20/

Clement, L., Hately, S., Von Riegen, C., & Rogers, T. (Eds.). (2003). *UDDI version 3.0.1 technical specification*. Organization for the Advancement of Structured Information Standards (OASIS). Retrieved June 28, 2007, from http://uddi.org/pubs/uddi_v3.htm

Dobbertin, H., Bosselaers, A., & Preneel, B. (1996). *RIPEMD-160: A strengthened version of RIPEMD*. German Information Security Agency

Eastlake, D., Reagle, J., & Solo, D. (2002). *XML-signature syntax and processing*. World Wide Web Consortium (W3C). Retrieved June 28, 2007, from http://www.w3.org/TR/xmldsig-core/

Ellison, C. (1999). *SPKI requirements* (RFC 2692). Internet Engineering Task Force (IETF). Retrieved June 28, 2007, from http://www.ietf.org/rfc/rfc2692.txt?number=2692

Federal Information Processing Standards (FIPS). (1995). *Secure hash standard* (FIPS PUB 180-2). Retrieved June 28, 2007, from http://csrc.nist.gov/publications/fips/fips180-2/fips180-2withchangenotice.pdf

Hallam-Baker, P., & Mysori, S. H. (Eds.). (2004). *XML key management specification (XKMS 2.0)*. World Wide Web Consortium (W3C). Retrieved June 28, 2007, from http://www.w3.org/TR/xkms2/

Hughes, J., & Maler, E. (Eds.). (2005). *Security assertion markup language (SAML) 2.0 technical overview, working draft 13*. Organization for the Advancement of Structured Information Standards (OASIS). Retrieved June 28, 2007, from http://www.oasis-open.org/committees/download.php/13786/sstc-saml-tech-overview-2.0.pdf

IBM Corporation & Microsoft Corporation (2002). *Security in a Web services world: A proposed architecture and roadmap, version 1.0*. Retrieved June 28, 2007, from http://www-128.ibm.com/developerworks/library/specification/ws-secmap/

IBM (2004). *Web services security (WS-security)*. Retrieved June 28, 2007, from http://www-106.ibm.com/developerworks/webservices/library/ws-secure/

Imamura, T., Dillaway, B., & Simon, E. (2002). *XML Encryption syntax and processing*. World Wide Web Consortium (W3C). Retrieved June 28, 2007, from http://www.w3.org/TR/xmlenc-core/

Jonsson, J., & Kaliski B. (2003). *Public-key cryptography standards (PKCS) #1: RSA cryptography specifications version 2.1* (RFC 3447). Internet Engineering Task Force (IETF). Retrieved on June 28, 2007, from http://www.ietf.org/rfc/rfc3447.txt?number=3447

Mitra, N. (Ed.). (2003). *SOAP version 1.2 part 0: Primer*. World Wide Web Consortium (W3C). Retrieved June 28, 2007, from http://www.w3.org/TR/2003/REC-soap12-part0-20030624/

Nadalin, A., Kaler, C., Monzillo, R., & Hallam-Baker, P. (Eds.). (2004). *Web services security: SOAP Message Security 1.0*. Organization for the Advancement of Structured Information Standards (OASIS). Retrieved June 28, 2007, from http://docs.oasis-open.org/wss/v1.1/wss-v1.1-spec-errata-os-SOAPMessageSecurity.pdf

Rescorla, E. (1999). *Diffie-Hellman key agreement method* (RFC 2631). Internet Engineering Task Force (IETF). Retrieved on June 28, 2007, from http://www.ietf.org/rfc/rfc2631.txt?number=2631

Sciberras, A. (Ed.). (2006). *Lightweight directory access protocol (LDAP): Schema for user applications* (RFC 4519). Internet Engineering Task Force (IETF). Retrieved June 28, 2007, from http://www.ietf.org/rfc/rfc4519.txt?number=4519

Wolter, R. (2001). *XML Web services basics*. Microsoft Corporation. Retrieved June 28, 2007, from http://msdn2.microsoft.com/en-us/webservices/aa740691.aspx

Chapter XIV

Wireless Security

Wireless Security

The nature of wireless is that of a physically open medium which makes authentication, access control, and confidentiality necessary in the implementation of a wireless LAN. There are three primary categories of networks: wireless local area network (WLAN), wireless metropolitan-area network (WMAN), and wireless personal area network (WPAN). The security for each of these types of wireless networks is discussed in this chapter.

Objectives

- Gain an overview of wireless security concepts and technology
- Fully understand and be able to recommend the appropriate technologies for the various wireless technologies

Introduction

When talking about wireless data communications, there are three primary categories of networks: wireless metropolitan-area network (WMAN), wireless local area network (WLAN), and wireless personal area network (WPAN). The terms WIMAX and Wi-Fi and are used instead of WMAN and WLAN respectively.

The Worldwide Interoperability for Microwave Access (WIMAX™) brand was created by the WiMAX Forum™, which is working to facilitate the deployment of broadband wireless networks based on the IEEE 802.16 standard. It achieves this by helping to ensure the compatibility and interoperability of broadband wireless access equipment. The organization is a global, nonprofit association formed in June of 2001 by equipment and component suppliers to promote IEEE 802.16 compliant equipment. WiMAX technology enables the delivery of last mile wireless broadband access as an alternative to cable and DSL.

WIMAX is similar to WI-FI in the sense that both create hot spots around a base station, but WIMAX has a wider range, up to 25 to 30 miles.

A WLAN or Wi-Fi can be used to connect computers to each other, to the Internet, and to wired networks. The Wi-Fi ™ (Wireless Fidelity) brand was created by the Wi-Fi Alliance. The organization is a global, nonprofit association formed in 1999 to certify the interoperability of IEEE 802.11 products, as well as to promote 802.11 standards as the global, wireless LAN standards across all market segments. The Wi-Fi Alliance has instituted a test suite to certify Wi-Fi products' interoperability. Wi-Fi networks use radio technologies based on the IEEE 802.11a, 802.11b, and 802.11g standards.

The Wi-Fi Alliance also created the brand Wi-Fi Protected Access (WPA) for the security enhancements in IEEE 802.11i, which address all known wired equivalent privacy (WEP) vulnerabilities in the original IEEE 802.11 security implementation. IEEE 802.11i proposes two enhancements: temporal key integrity protocol (TKIP), also known as WPA1, and CTR with CBC-MAC protocol (CCMP), also known as WPA2.

A wireless personal area network (WPAN) uses a low cost, short-range wireless specification called *Bluetooth* to connect mobile devices. The Bluetooth Special Interest Group (SIG), created in September 1998, is a trade association comprised of leaders in the telecommunications, computing, automotive, industrial automation, and network industries. The objective of SIG is to drive the development of Bluetooth wireless technology. The Bluetooth SIG name was inspired by Danish King Harald Bluetooth, known for unifying Denmark and Norway in the 10th century.

Figure 14-1. The wireless landscape

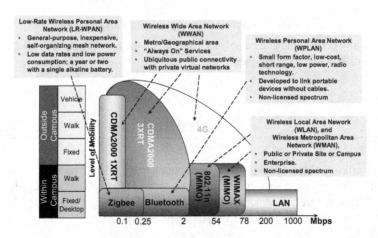

WIMAX

WIMAX is a fixed and mobile broadband wireless access system that can operate as a wireless metropolitan area network and deliver Internet access at distances across tens of miles and at a cost similar to IEEE 802.11 (Wi-Fi). The 802.16 standard on which WIMAX is based, was designed from the ground up to be truly broadband and packet-based. WIMAX provides a wireless alternative to cable and DSL for last mile (last km) broadband access.

A WIMAX network is very similar to a Wi-Fi network, but it operates at higher speeds, over greater distances, and for a greater number of users. From the point of view of the infrastructure, a WIMAX network is similar to a cellular network: it consists of a single WIMAX tower that covers a very large area called a *base station (BS)* and a *subscriber station (SS)*, which could be a small WIMAX receiver box, or mobile station. The receiver box can be installed inside or outside of a building or house.

The WIMAX tower node can simultaneously operate as a subscriber station and as a base station in a full mesh network using a line-of-sight link. Using this technology, there are currently several cities worldwide that are implementing WIMAX mesh networks using various base stations as backhauls to cover the whole city. These networks connect one or several of the base stations to an Internet backbone via a microwave link or by fiber optic cable.

The original WIMAX standard (2001) 802.16, "Fixed Wireless Broadband and Air Interface," used the spectrum in the 10 - 66 GHz. The 802.16-2004 standard, "Air Interface for Fixed Broadband Wireless Access Systems," consolidated 802.16, 802.16a, and 802.16c. The 802.16-2004 specifies two primary bands, the 10-66 GHz band to use where line-of-sight is necessary, and the licensed and unlicensed frequencies of 2 – 11 GHz for those physical environments where line-of-sight is not necessary.

In the line-of-sight service, a fixed dish antenna located on the roof or on a pole, points straight at the WiMAX tower. The higher frequencies in 10-66 GHz allow transmission with fewer errors, less interference, and more bandwidth. The target customers for these services are large carriers, as well as cities and enterprises. In the non-line-of-sight, 2 – 11 GHz spectrum, the subscriber station can be located inside a house or building and, because of the lower frequencies used, the transmission is not obstructed by physical locations.

Table 14-1. Wireless networks

Network	Standard	Range	Data Rate
WMAN (Wireless Metropolitan Area Network) – WIMAX	IEEE 802.16	Approximately 30 miles radius	78 Mbps
WLAN (Wireless Local Area Network) – Wi-Fi	IEEE 802.11	Approximately 300 feet radius	54 Mbps
WPAN (Wireless Personal Area Network) – Bluetooth	IEEE 802.15	Approximately 30 feet radius	1, 2, or 3 Mbps
LR-WPAN (Low-Rate Wireless Personal Area Networks) – Zigbee	IEEE 802.15.4	Approximately 150 feet radius	250 Kbps

The IEEE 802.16e (2005a) standard, also called *802.16-2005*, provides enhancements to 802.16-2004 to support subscriber stations moving at vehicular speeds. It also specifies a combined fixed and mobile broadband wireless access. The spectrum at 2.5 GHz and below (1.5GHz, 700MHz, etc.), which has better characteristics for full mobility deployment, is targeted at large carriers and spectrum owners. The WIMAX throughput is around 38 Mbit/sec when using orthogonal frequency division multiplexing (OFDM), and 78 Mbit/sec when OFDM is combined with multiple-input, multiple-output antenna processing technology.

In summary, WIMAX could expand the availability of broadband service to residences and businesses that are not served by carriers because of the high cost of wire deployment, especially in low-density rural locations in developed countries, as well as those locations in emerging markets where user connectivity is sporadic.

WIMAX (IEEE 802.16e) Security

WIMAX security provides subscribers with privacy, authentication, and confidentiality across the broadband wireless network. It does this by applying cryptographic transformations to the data carried between the BS and the SS, either fixed or mobile.

In addition, WIMAX security provides operators with strong protection from theft of service. The BS protects against unauthorized access to data transport services by securing the associated service flows across the network. For key management, WIMAX employs an authenticated client/server key management protocol in which the BS, the server, controls the distribution of keying material to an SS. Additionally, the basic security mechanisms are strengthened by adding digital-certificates to the key management protocol for device-authentication of the SS or mobile station.

In WIMAX and in Wi-Fi, the unit of data exchanged between two peer entities to implement the access control management protocol is called *medium access control management protocol data unit* (MPDU). The MPDU term is used in this chapter when describing the data exchanged between a base station and a subscriber station or mobile station, in the case of WIMAX, or between a client and the access point, in the case of Wi-Fi.

WIMAX security has three component protocols:

- Secure encapsulation of MPDU
- Authentication for the SS to obtain authorization and traffic keying material from the BS, and to support periodic reauthorization and key refresh. X.509 digital certificates issued by the subscriber station manufacturer (in the case of RSA with SHA-1) or an operator-specified credential (in the case of EAP) are used for authentication.
- A privacy key management protocol providing the secure distribution of keying data from the BS to the SS

WIMAX uses cryptographic suites to specify a set of supported data encryption authentication algorithms, and the rules for applying those algorithms.

WIMAX Key Management Protocol

The privacy key management (PKM) authentication protocol establishes a shared secret key called an *authorization key* (AK) between the SS and the BS. The shared AK is then used to secure subsequent PKM exchanges of traffic encryption keys (TEKs). This two-tiered mechanism for key distribution permits refreshing of TEKs without incurring the overhead of computation-intensive operations.

With the AK exchange, the BS authenticates the identity of a SS and the services the SS is authorized to access. By doing this, the BS associates an SS authenticated identity to a paying subscriber, and to the data services that the subscriber is authorized to access.

There are two privacy key management protocols supported in IEEE 802.16e (2005a) PKMv1 and PKMv2. PKMv2 has more enhanced features such as a new key hierarchy, AES-CMAC, AES-key-wraps, and multicast and broadcast services (MBS).

In PKMv2, there are two authentication schemes, one based on RSA and one based on EAP; therefore, there are two primary sources of keying material. The keys used to protect message integrity and transport the traffic encryption keys are derived from source key material generated by the authentication and authorization processes.

The traffic-key management portion of the PKM protocol adheres to a client/server model, where the SS (a PKM client) requests keying material, and the BS (a PKM server) responds to those requests, ensuring that individual SS clients receive only the keying material for which they are authorized.

Primary Authorization Key (PAK)

The RSA-based authorization process yields the pre-primary authorization key (pre-PAK), which is one of the possible roots of the key hierarchy. The pre-PAK is sent by the BS to the SS encrypted with the public key of the SS certificate. Pre-PAK is mainly used to generate the primary authorization key (PAK). The optional EAP integrity key (EIK) used to authenticate the EAP payload is also generated from pre-PAK.

Master Session Key (MSK)

If an RSA mutual authorization took place before the EAP exchange, the EAP messages may be protected using EIK-EAP Integrity Key derived from pre-PAK.

The result of the EAP exchange between the BS and SS is the master session key (MSK), which is the other possible root of the key hierarchy. After the exchange, MSK is known to the AAA server, to the authenticator (transferred from AAA server), and to the SS. The SS and the authenticator derive a pairwise master key (PMK) and optional EIK by truncating the MSK to 320 bits. MSK has a 512-bit length; PMK and EIK have a 160-bit length.

Figure 14-2. Authorization key generation

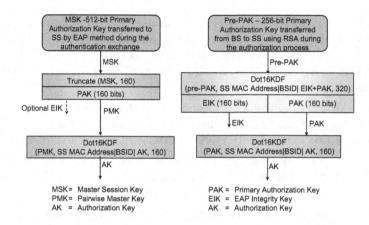

Authorization Key (AK)

Independent of whether RSA or EAP authentication is used, the AK is derived by the BS and the SS from the PMK (from EAP-based authorization procedure) and/or the PAK (from RSA-based authorization procedure). The AK has 160-bit length.

Message Authentication Keys (HMAC/CMAC)

MAC keys are used to sign messages in order to validate the authenticity of these messages. The message authentication keys used to generate the cipher-based MAC (CMAC) value (Dworkin, 2005) and the HMAC digest are derived from the AK. The HMAC has a 160-bit length and CMAC has a 128-bit length.

A CMAC is a message authentication code (MAC) algorithm that is based on a symmetric key block cipher. CMAC is specified in Special Publication 800-38B, "Recommendation for Block Cipher Modes of Operation: The CMAC Mode for Authentication" (Dworkin, 2005). The downlink authentication keys CMA_KEY_D and HMAC_KEY_D are used to authenticate messages in the downlink direction. The uplink authentication key CMA_KEY_U and HMAC_U are used to authenticate messages in the uplink direction.

Key Encrypting Key (160 bits) and Traffic Encryption Key

Another key, the key-encrypting key (KEK), is derived directly from the AK by both the BS and the SS. The KEK is used to encrypt keys for transport from the BS to the SS. In addition, the BS randomly generates the traffic encryption key (TEK), enciphers it using KEK, and sends it to the SS in the TEK exchange. KEK and TEK have a 128-bit length. The TEK-128 is encrypted with AES key wrap.

Figure 14-3. CMAC, HMAC, and KEK generation

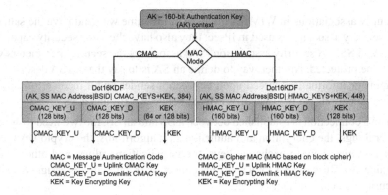

The BS and SS maintain two sets of TEKs and their associated initialization vectors (IVs) per security association identifier (SAID), corresponding to two successive generations of key materials. The two TEKs have overlapping lifetimes.

Group Key Encrypting Key and Group Traffic Encryption Key

The BS also randomly generates another key, the group key encrypting key (GKEK), which it enciphers using KEK and sends to all the subscriber stations in the group security association (GSA). GKEK is used to encrypt the group traffic encryption key (GTEK), which is sent in multicast messages by the BS to the subscriber stations in the same multicast group.

Figure 14-4. TEK and group keys generation

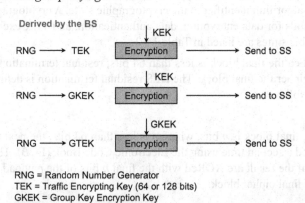

Security Associations

Security associations in WIMAX are used in the same way and have the same meaning as the security associations used in IPsec; they also have the same security capabilities used in TLS and SSL. A security association (SA) associates the security parameters with the traffic to be protected. Another way to define an SA is to say that an SA describes the security parameter information agreed upon between a sender and a receiver on how to secure a communication—in the case of WIMAX, between a BS and a SS.

When a connection is established between a BS and an SS, the two need to agree on, among other things, the encryption and authentication algorithms, the crypto keys, the key sizes, key lifetimes, how to exchange keys, the initialization values, and other related security parameters. Once the SA for a specific connection is defined, it is assigned an identifier, the security association ID (SAID).

There are three types of SAs in WIMAX: unicast connections, GSA for multicast groups, and MBSGSA for MBS services. The unicast SAs can be primary, static, and dynamic. In general, the following is the information contained in a SA:

- The SAID, a 16-bit identifier of the SA
- The KEK, a 128-bit key encryption key derived from the AK
- The TEK, 128-bit traffic encryption key, generated within the BS and transferred from the BS to the SS using a secure exchange
- The TEK's lifetime
- PNO and PN32, a 32-bit packet number for use by the link cipher
- RxPN0 and RxPN1, a 32-bit received sequence counter, for use by the link cipher

WIMAX Confidentiality: Encryption Algorithms

WIMAX uses two encryption algorithms to encipher data, DES in CBC mode and AES in CCM, CBC, or CTR modes. The type of encryption algorithm to use is designated in the data encryption algorithm identifier in the cryptographic suite. A cryptographic suite is the SA's set of methods for data encryption, data authentication, and TEK exchange. The WIMAX cryptographic suites are listed in Table 14-2.

In DES, when the final block is less than 64 bits, residual termination block processing is used to encipher the final block. The DES residual termination is defined in IEEE 802.16e (2005a) as follows:

- If the final block is n bits, where n is less than 64 bits, the next to last block is enciphered a second time using the Electronic Code Book (ECB). The most significant n bits of the result are XORed with the final n bits of the payload used to generate the short final cipher block.

Table 14-2. Allowed cryptographic suites

Value	Data Encryption	Data Authentication	TEK Exchange
0x000001	No data encryption	No data authentication	3-DES, 128
0x010001	CBC-Mode 56-bit DES	No data authentication	3-DES, 128
0x000002	No data encryption	No data authentication	RSA, 1024
0x010002	CBC-Mode 56-bit DES	No data authentication	RSA, 1024
0x020103	CCM-Mode 128-bit AES	CCM-Mode, 128-bit	ECB mode AES with 128-bit key
0x020104	CCM-Mode 128-bit AES	CCM-Mode	AES Key Wrap with 128-bit key
0x030003	CBC-Mode 128-bit AES	No data authentication	ECB mode AES with 128-bit key
0x800003	MBS CTR Mode 128-bit AES	No data authentication	AES ECB mode with 128-bit key
0x800004	MBS CTR mode 128-bit AES	No data authentication	AES key wrap with 128-bit key
All remaining values	Reserved		

- If the payload is less than 64 bits, the IV is DES encrypted and the most significant n bits of the resulting ciphertext are XORed with the n bits of the payload.

The AES CCM mode (Dworkin, 2004) is defined in NIST "Special Publication 800-38C, FIPS-197," and is explained in the WLAN Security Enhancement, "CTR with CBC-MAC Protocol" section. The AES CBC mode is defined in NIST Special Publication 800-38A, FIPS-197 (Dworkin, 2001), and is explained in Chapter III, "Cipher Block Chaining (CBC) Mode."

The AES-CBC residual termination is defined in 802.16-2005 as follows:

- If the final short plaintext block is a bits, where a is less than the cipher block size b, the next to last plaintext is enciphered and the ciphertext block is divided into two parts. One of the parts is a bits and the other part is $b - a$ bits. The $b - a$ part of the ciphertext is concatenated with the padding used in the short plaintext and is sent as the final block cipher. The short plaintext block is padded to complete a plaintext block, encrypted with AES in CBC mode, and sent as the next-to-last ciphertext.

- If the payload is less than the cipher block size, the most significant n bits of the generated CBC IV are XORed with the n bits of the payload to generate the short cipher block.

Figure 14-5. Residual termination block processing

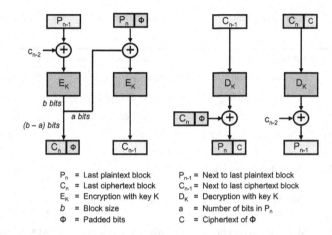

P_n = Last plaintext block	P_{n-1} = Next to last plaintext block	
C_n = Last ciphertext block	C_{n-1} = Next to last ciphertext block	
E_K = Encryption with key K	D_K = Decryption with key K	
b = Block size	a = Number of bits in P_n	
Φ = Padded bits	C = Ciphertext of Φ	

The AES CTR mode is defined in "NIST Special Publication 800-38A, FIPS-197" and is explained in Chapter III, "Counter (CTR) mode." In the CRT mode, input blocks are blocks of bits called *counters* that must have the property that each counter block in the sequence is different from every other counter block. There are several methods to generate the counters.

In WIMAX, a 32-bit nonce is made of an 8-bit rollover counter (ROC) and the 24-bit synchronization field or frame number. The nonce is repeated four times to construct the 128-bit counter block required by the AES-128 cipher: initial counter = nonce || nonce || nonce || nonce. The 8-bit ROC is sent in clear and concatenated with the AES-CTR ciphertext. Therefore, the encryption process yields a payload that is 8 bits longer than the plaintext payload.

The NIST AES key wrap algorithm is designed to wrap or encrypt key data. The key wrap operates on blocks of 64 bits. Before being wrapped, the key data is parsed into n blocks of 64 bits. The only restriction the key wrap algorithm places on n is that n be at least two. It is recognized that $n \leq 4$ will accommodate all supported AES key sizes.

WIMAX Integrity and Authentication

A BS authenticates a client SS during the initial authorization exchange. All SSs have factory-installed RSA private/public key pairs and X.509 certificates, or have an internal algorithm to generate such key pairs dynamically; they also have the means to create X.509 certificates. The digital certificate contains the SS's public key and MAC address. When requesting an authorization key an SS presents its digital certificate to the BS. The BS verifies that the digital certificate is authentic, and then uses the verified public key to encipher an AK, which the BS then transmits back to the requesting SS.

From the AK, the SS and the BS create the key for the CMAC, HMAC, and the key-encrypting key (KEK). When the service is ready to transmit and receive data, the SS requests a traffic encryption key (TEK) for the connection. Using a pseudorandom number generator,

Figure 14-6. WIMAX authorization and AK exchange

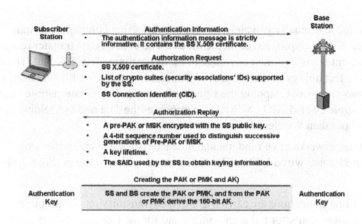

Figure 14-7. WIMAX re-authentication and TEK exchange

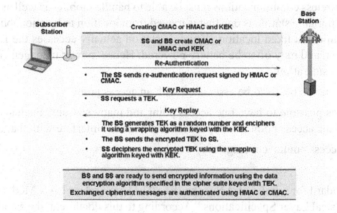

the BS generates a TEK. The TEK is encrypted using a wrapping algorithm keyed with the KEK and transmitted to the SS. The SS deciphers the encrypted TEK using the same wrapping algorithm keyed with KEK.

At this moment, the BS and the SS are ready to send encrypted information using the data encryption algorithm specified in the cipher suite keyed with TEK. Exchanged ciphertext messages are authenticated using HMAC or CMAC.

The AK and TEK have a limited lifetime and are periodically refreshed according to the authorized grace time and TEK grace time encoding.

Wi-Fi

WLANs are normally privately owned networks that companies or individuals set up for the use of their employees or their own use. The WLAN data transfer rate is currently up to 54 Mb, but it has a limited coverage of up to approximately 300 feet. The range of current 802.11g technology can be improved threefold by using multiple transmitter and receiver antennas and by overlapping the signals of two wireless-G compatible radios, the *Multiple In, Multiple Out* (MIMO). MIMO also improves the data rate by yielding up to 8 times more throughput than Wireless-G.

Wireless networks have fundamental characteristics that make them significantly different from traditional wired LANs. The following describes some of those differences:

- Communications are carried using radio transmission; some countries impose specific requirements for radio equipment and for the frequencies that can be used.

- Since communications are radio broadcast, they need to be protected.

- There are range limitations when using wireless networks that depend on the type of modulation, transmitting frequency, and type of antenna used.

- Wireless communications must be able to handle mobile, as well as portable stations. A portable station is one that is moved from location to location, but that is only used while at a fixed location. A mobile station actually accesses the LAN while in motion, and may often be battery powered. Hence, power management is an important consideration.

- A station needs to be associated with an access point.

- It is possible to have one access point and many stations. Each station's connection to the access point is independent and does not interfere with that of other stations.

- Access points' coverage may overlap.

The standard for wireless LAN is the IEE802.11, "Wireless LAN Medium Access Control and Physical Layer Specifications." According to this document, the standard given defines the protocol and compatible interconnection of data communication equipment via radio or infrared. The standard also specifies that local area networks (LANs) use the *carrier sense multiple access protocol* with the collision avoidance (CSMA/CA) medium sharing mechanism. The protocol includes authentication, association services, but confidentiality (encryption and decryption) is optional.

The medium access control is formatted as frames, and each frame consists of a header, a variable length frame body, and a frame check sum (FCS), which contains a cyclic redundancy code (CRC). The unit of data exchanged between two peer entities to implement the *access control management protocol*, as in WIMAX, is also called MPDU. The MPDU term is used when describing the data exchanged between a client and the access point.

The IEEE standards and task groups exist within the IEEE 802.11 working group (Table 14-2).

Table 14-2. IEEE 802.11 standards

IEEE 802.11	The original 1 Mbit/s and 2 Mbit/s, 2.4 GHz RF and IR standard (1999)
IEEE 802.11a	54 Mbit/s, 5 GHz standard (2001)
IEEE 802.11b	Enhancements to 802.11 to support 5.5 and 11 Mbit/s (1999)
IEEE 802.11c	Bridge operation procedures; included in the IEEE 802.1D standard (2001)
IEEE 802.11d	International (country-to-country) roaming extensions (2001)
IEEE 802.11e	Enhancements: QoS, including packet bursting (2005)
IEEE 802.11g	54 Mbit/s, 2.4 GHz standard (backwards compatible with b) (2003)
IEEE 802.11h	Spectrum managed 802.11a (5 GHz) for European compatibility (2004)
IEEE 802.11i	Enhanced security (2004)
IEEE 802.11n	802.11n builds upon previous 802.11 standards by adding MIMO (multiple-input, multiple-output) and orthogonal frequency-division multiplexing (OFDM). MIMO uses multiple transmitter and receiver antennas to allow for increased data throughput.
IEEE 802.11p	WAVE - Wireless Access for the Vehicular Environment (such as ambulances and passenger cars)
IEEE 802.11s	ESS mesh networking

The main objective of the 802.11 standard was connectivity, so several management features took priority over security protocol. The security in IEEE 802.11 was implemented using the optional wired equivalent privacy (WEP), which, according to the standard, was designed to protect authorized users of WLAN from casual eavesdropping. Wi-Fi protected access (WPA) replaced the WEP specification. WPA is a subset of the 802.11i. WPA uses RC4 temporal key integrity protocol (TKIP), which provides an increased number of initialization variables (IV) and stronger sequencing rules to prevent replay attacks. TKIP uses message integrity code (MIC) and provides synchronized key exchanges between clients and access points.

WPA runs in two modes, the pre-shared key (PSK) mode and the enterprise mode. In PSK, the key is statically configured in both the WLAN client and in the access point. In the enterprise mode, the existing 802.1X (port-based access control), and EAP and Radius protocols are used for authentication and distribution of a dynamically generated session key. The other 802.11i subset is WPA2, which includes all elements of the WPA standard while replacing RC4 TKIP (temporal key integrity protocol) with AES.

Concern about 802.11 security prevented many IT managers from deploying wireless LAN. Today, if WPA is implemented correctly using 802.1X and AES encryption, the wireless network is almost invulnerable to straight cracking techniques, and the intruder should not be able to read broadcast data.

In this section, the original 802.11 and 802.11i standards will be discussed, as these are the standards that relate to security, encryption, and authentication.

IEE802.11 Wireless LAN

In a wired LAN, a hacker needs to be connected physically to the network to be able to monitor the LAN traffic, so even though wired LANs are physically closed and controlled networks, authentication, access control, and confidentiality are required security services.

In a wireless shared medium, any IEEE 802.11-compliant station can receive all traffic that is within range of the access point and can transmit to any other 802.11 station within range. Thus, the connection of a single wireless link (without privacy) to an existing wired LAN may seriously degrade the security level of the wired LAN. The wireless physically open-medium nature of an IEEE 802.11 wireless LAN makes authentication, access control, and confidentiality a must in its implementation.

The following are the security services provided in IEEE 802.11:

1. Authentication
2. Confidentiality
3. Access control in conjunction with layer management
4. Secure roaming

Authentication

IEEE 802.11 defines two subtypes of authentication service: open system and shared key. Open system authentication is the simplest of the available authentication algorithms. Essentially, it is a null authentication algorithm. Any station that requests authentication with this algorithm may become authenticated. The type of authentication is set at the access point, and in some products, the open system authentication is the default authentication algorithm.

In a shared-key authentication, identity is demonstrated by knowledge of a shared secret. During the shared-key authentication exchange, both the challenge and the encrypted challenge are transmitted. The challenge is encrypted using the shared secret, so only those stations who know the shared secret key are authenticated. The shared secret key needs to be loaded, via a secure channel, into the access point and into all stations that request access. Shared-key authentication is only available if the WEP option is implemented.

Confidentiality: The Wired Equivalent Privacy Algorithm

IEEE 802.11 provides the ability to encrypt the contents of messages. This functionality is provided by the optional wired equivalent privacy (WEP), which, according to the standard, is not designed for ultimate security but rather to be at least as secure as wired networks.

The default privacy state for all IEEE 802.11 stations is in clear, and, if the privacy service is not invoked, all messages are sent unencrypted. Since many users didn't know about or didn't bother to change the setup, many WLAN were set to transmit in clear.

Figure 14-8. WEP encapsulation block diagram

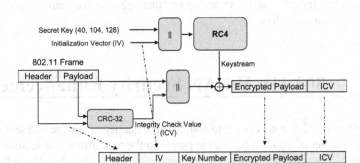

WEP Frame

The IEEE 802.11 WEP is a data confidentiality algorithm designated to protect authorized users of a wireless LAN from casual eavesdropping; WEP uses RC4, a symmetric encryption algorithm. Data confidentiality depends on an external key management service to distribute the key because the same key is used to encipher and to decipher.

The secret key is concatenated with an initialization variable (IV), and the resulting seed is input to RC4 to produce a key stream of k pseudorandom octets equal in length to the number of data octets that are to be transmitted. To protect against unauthorized data modification, an integrity algorithm operates on the plaintext to produce an integrity check value (ICV). The plaintext is concatenated with the ICV and the result is XORed with the RC4 pseudorandom keystream output. The ciphertext is then concatenated with the IV.

In WEP, each MPDU is considered a different message, so each MPDU is encrypted with a different key. However, in 802.11, there is no provision for key management, so there is no way for the access point and the client to exchange new keys to encipher each packet; nor can it be done in a situation, when packets are dropped, and it is necessary to resynchronize the RC4 symmetric encryption algorithm with a new key.

Since it was not possible to have a different key for each MPDU and to avoid the problem of starting at the same point every time re-synchronization was required, the designers of WEP added an IV that determines a different starting point in the RC4 keystream. The number of starting points was 2^{24} and the starting point was sent unencrypted. The secret key remained constant while the IV changed periodically; in this way, the IV extended the useful lifetime of the secret key. The fundamental problem, however, was that there was a finite number of starting positions, and WEP didn't specify an algorithm to generate the IVs. The result was that in most of the implementations, the IV started at zero and was incremented sequentially for each packet. With only 2^{24} number of possible IV starting positions and the IV selected at random, there was a 50% probability of using a previous IV after fewer than 4,792 MPDUs using birthday attack probability.

Another security problem with the 802.11 standard was that it selected 40-bits as the RC4 key size; this made it unable to resist brute-force attacks. Several papers were published describing the WEP weaknesses including one from Fluhrer, Mantin, and Shamir (2001) that outlined a completely passive attack that, when implemented, could defeat the WEP encryption key in as little as 15 minutes.

IEEE 802.11 didn't require that the same WEP key be used for all stations, but having a different key for each station created a key management problem when the number of stations was more than five.

802.11i: WLAN Security Enhancement

Initially, the 802.11e was going to address both quality of service and security, but as early as the summer of 2002, it became apparent to the task group that security needed special attention. The task group was then split into two task forces, 802.11e, which continued to work on quality of service and 802.11i, whose function was to provide security enhancement to 802.11. In June 2004, the IEEE Standards Association approved a security enhancement amendment to the original IEEE 802.11 specification. It was the IEEE 802.11i, "Wireless LAN Medium Access Control and Physical Layer Specifications: Medium Access Control Security Enhancement."

Several reports were written revealing 802.11's security weaknesses; among them were the following:

- Walker (2000) Report, "Unsafe at Any Key Size," which stated that WEP was flawed and increasing the key size wouldn't improved the security.

- Berkeley Report (Borisov, Goldberg, & Wagner, 2000), by a group of researchers at the University of California at Berkeley, "Security of the WEP Algorithm," which outlined several active and passive attacks on WEP.

- University of Maryland Report (Arbaugh, Shankar, & Wan, 2001), by a group of researchers at the University of Maryland, "Your 802.11 Wireless Network has No Cloths," which pointed out several flaws in the shared key and MAC addresses.

- Fluhrer, Mantin, and Shamir (2001) Report, by Scott Fluhrer from Cisco and Itshik Mantin and Adi Shamir from The Weizmann Institute, "Weaknesses in the Key Scheduling Algorithm of RC4,' which described a passive attack on WEP that defeated the WEP key in as little as 15 minutes.

- "Wireless network security, 802.11: Bluetooth and handheld devices (SP800-48)" (Karygiannis & Owens, 2002): discussed some known vulnerabilities in 802.11.

In order to fix WEP security flaws, an interim software solution was required that would not need hardware upgrades, and then, a final solution with different hardware not compatible with the previous version of WEP. The initial WEP hardware was based on a CPU with less power than an 80486 40 MHz processor, which did not have enough power and speed to implement the AES algorithm.

The IEEE 802.11i amendment added stronger encryption, authentication, and key management strategies for wireless data and system security. The amendment proposed two new data-confidentiality upgrades: (1) a software upgrade, temporal key integrity protocol (TKIP); (2) a hardware upgrade, counter mode with cipher block chaining message authentication code protocol (CCMP). In addition, IEEE 802.11i also uses IEEE 802.1X to control access to the network.

According to the standard, in addition to improving confidentiality, the 802.11i amendment also provides improvement for the following security issues:

- **Key management:** The enhanced confidentiality, data authentication, and replay protection mechanisms require fresh cryptographic keys. 802.11i provides new keys by means of protocols called the *4-way handshake* and *group key handshake*.

- **Data origin authenticity:** The data origin authenticity mechanism defines a means by which a station that receives a data frame can determine which station transmitted the MPDU. This feature is required to prevent one station from masquerading as another station. This mechanism is provided by using CCMP or TKIP.

- **Replay detection:** The replay detection mechanism defines a means by which a station that receives a data frame from another station can detect whether the data frame is an unauthorized retransmission. This mechanism is provided by using CCMP or TKIP.

Wi-Fi Protected Access (WPA or WPA1) and WPA2

WPA and WP2 are the WI-FI Alliance functionality certification versions of IEEE 802.11i. WPA and WPA2 use 802.1X and EAP for authentication. WPA and WPA2 continue the use of RC4 cipher with TKIP, but WPA2 also uses a stronger encryption mechanism with AES, using counter mode with cipher block chaining message authentication code protocol (AES-CCMP). Built into the CCMP algorithm is an integrity check.

Both WPA and WPA2 have personal and enterprise certified modes of operation that meet the needs for two different market segments. In the personal mode of operation, a pre-shared key (password) is used for authentication, while in the enterprise mode of operation; authentication is achieved via 802.1X and EAP. The personal mode requires only an access point and the client device, while the enterprise mode typically requires a RADIUS or other authentication server on the network.

The personal mode is designed for users who do not have authentication servers, such as RADIUS. For authentication, personal modes use a pre-shared key that is manually entered at the access point and at all user stations; consequently, a personal mode does not scale well in an enterprise network. The pre-shared key is used to generate the encryption key;

Table 14-3. WPA and WP2 mode types

	WPA	WPA2
Enterprise Mode (Business and Government)	Authentication: IEEE 802.1X/EAP Encryption: TKIP/MIC	Authentication: IEEE 802.1X/EAP Encryption: AES-CCMP
Personal (Small Office, Home)	Authentication: PSK Encryption: TKIP/MIC	Authentication: PSK Encryption: AES-CCMP

Figure 14-9. 802.11 security framework

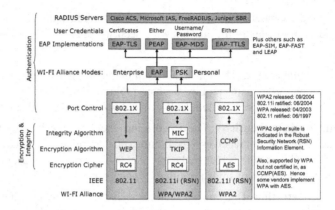

therefore, the PSK should be of sufficient strength by including a mix of letters, numbers, and non-alphanumeric characters. The personal mode uses the same encryption methods as enterprise mode. It supports per-user, per-session, and per-packet encryption via TKIP with WPA or AES with WPA2.

WPA and WPA2-enterprise use IEEE 802.1X authentication with EAP methods to provide mutual authentication and to ensure that only authorized users are granted access to the network and only to authorized areas within the network.

The enterprise mode is a certification given to products that are tested to be interoperable in both PSK and IEEE 802.1X/EAP modes of operation for authentication. In IEEE 802.1X an authentication, authorization, and accounting (AAA) server, a type of RADIUS, is required.

Temporal Key Integrity Protocol (TKIP)

As mentioned before, TKIP was designed in a way that the algorithm could be implemented within the hardware capabilities of most devices supporting only WEP. In this way, such devices could be field-upgradeable by the manufacturers.

Figure 14-10. TKIP encapsulation block diagram

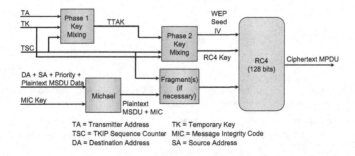

TKIP uses the RC4 stream cipher with 128-bit keys for encryption and 64-bit keys for authentication. The key selected by the user goes through two mixing functions, Phases 1 and 2. Phase 1 mixes the appropriate temporary key, TK, (pairwise or group) with the transmitter address, TA, with TKIP, and with sequence counter, TSC. Phase 2 mixes the output of Phase 1 with the TSC and TK to produce the WEP seed, also called the *per-frame key*. Both Phase 1 and Phase 2 rely on an S-box, the only difference being that the second S-box table is an octet-swapped replica of the first. The S-boxes substitute one 16-bit value with another 16-bit value.

To defend against active attacks, TKIP used a MIC called *Michael*. In the traditional way, the MIC was simply an authentication code, but the acronym MAC was already used in the 802.11 standard for another meaning. Similar to a MAC (see Chapter VI "Message Authentication Code"), the MIC was a key-dependent one-way hash function. The integrity provided by the MIC was based on the fact that it was not possible to generate a MIC without knowing the MIC key. An adversary without knowledge of the key would not be able to modify data and then generate an authentic MIC on the modified data. If the MIC key were known only by the source and the destination, this algorithm would provide both data origin authentication and data integrity for MPDUs sent between the two parties. In addition, only a station or access point with the identical MIC key could verify the hash.

Even though this MIC offered only weak defenses against message forgeries and other active attacks, it was the best that could be added to WEP due to constraints in the legacy hardware. MIC allowed devices to confirm that their packets were uncorrupted during the sending-and-receiving transmission process, thus preventing bit-flip attacks on encrypted packets. TKIP used different MIC keys depending on the direction of the data transfer.

Another improvement of TKIP over WEP was that the IV bit length was increased from 24 to 48 bits, so the 50% probability of a previous IV being used increased from fewer than 4,792 MPDUs to 19,629,343 MPDUs (calculated using the birthday attack).

CTR with CBC-MAC Protocol (CCMP)

AES-CCMP is the encryption protocol in the 802.11i standard data that provides data confidentiality. CCMP is based on the counter mode with CBC-MAC (CCM) using the AES encryption algorithm. The CCM protocol is defined in RFP 3610 and in NIST SP-800-38C.

According to the standard (Dworkin, 2004), the counter with CBC-MAC (CCM) is a generic authenticated encryption block cipher mode that is designated for use only with 128-bit block ciphers, such as AES. CCM can be considered a mode of operation of the block cipher algorithm. As with other modes of operation, a single key to the block cipher must be established beforehand among the parties to the data; thus, CCM is implemented within a well-designed key management structure. The key should be kept secret and should only be used with the CCM mode. The total number of invocations of the block cipher algorithm during the lifetime of the key should be limited to 2^{61}. The security properties of CCM depend, at the least, on the secrecy of the key.

The CCM specification essentially combines two cryptographic mechanisms that are based on the forward cipher function. One mechanism is the CTR mode for confidentiality; see Chapter III, "Counter (CTR) Mode." The CTR mode requires the generation of a sufficiently long sequence of blocks called the *counter blocks*. The counter blocks must be distinct within a single invocation and across all other invocations of the CTR mode under any given key, but they need not be secret. This requirement for the counter blocks extends to the CCM mode.

The other cryptographic mechanism within CCM is an adaptation of the cipher-block chaining technique to provide assurance of authenticity. Specifically, the CBC technique with an initialization vector of zero is applied to the data to be authenticated. The final block of the resulting CBC output, possibly truncated, serves as a MAC for the data. The algorithm for generating a MAC in this fashion is commonly called *CBC-MAC*. The same key, K, is used for both the CTR and CBC-MAC mechanisms within CCM. In IEEE 802.11i, CCMP uses a 128-bit key with a block size of 128 bits.

The nomenclature used in RFC 3610 and SP-800-38C are, in some instances, different. In the following section, the SP-800-38C nomenclature will be used.

The following are some of variables used in CCMP:

- a: The octet length of the associated data ($a = l(a)$ in RFC 3610)
- A: The associated data string
- $Alen$: The bit length of the associated data
- Bi: The ith block of the formatted input
- C: The ciphertext
- $Clen$: The bit length of the ciphertext
- $Ctri$: The ith counter block
- K: The block cipher key
- $Klen$: The bit length of the block cipher key
- m: The number of blocks in the formatted payload
- n: The octet length of the nonce
- N: The nonce
- $Nlen$: The bit length of the nonce
- P: The payload
- p: The octet length of the payload ($p = l(m)$ in RFC 3610)
- $Plen$: The bit length of the payload
- q: The octet length of the binary representation of the octet length of the payload ($q = L$ in RFC 3610)
- Q: A bit string representation of the octet length of P
- r: The number of blocks in the formatted input data (N, A, P)
- t: The octet length of the MAC ($t = M$ in RFC 3610)
- T: The MAC that is generated as an internal variable in the CCM processes
- $Tlen$: The bit length of the MAC

The bit length of each input string, that is, N, A, and P, is a multiple of 8 bits, so each input string is an octet string. The octet lengths of these strings are denoted n, a, and p, thus, n, a and p are integers. Similarly, the parameter t denotes the octet length of T. The octet length of P (i.e., the integer p) is represented within the first block of the formatted data as an octet string denoted Q. The octet length of Q, denoted q, is a parameter of the formatting function. The formatting in CCMP imposes the following length conditions:

1. t is an element of $\{4, 6, 8, 10, 12, 14, 16\}$ octets

2. q is an element of $\{2, 3, 4, 5, 6, 7, 8\}$ octets

3. n is an element of $\{7, 8, 9, 10, 11, 12, 13\}$ octets

4. $n + q = 15$

5. $a < 2^{64}$

The first length condition to select should be t, the size of the authentication field. The choice of the value for t involves a trade-off between message expansion and the probability that an attacker can undetectably modify a message.

The second choice is q, the size of the payload field. The maximum length of the payload is by definition, $p < 2^{8q}$, so P consists of fewer than 2^{8q} octets, that is, fewer than 2^{8q-4} 128-bit blocks. The fourth length condition above implies that either q determines the value of n or that n determines the value of q. The value of n, in turn, determines the maximum number of distinct nonces, namely, 2^{8n}. Thus, the fourth length condition amounts to a tradeoff between the maximum message size and the size of the nonce.

To authenticate and encrypt a message, the following information is required:

1.   An encryption key K suitable for the block cipher

2.   A nonce N of $15 - q$ octets; within the scope of any encryption key K, the nonce value must be unique. That is, the set of nonce values used with any given key must not contain any duplicate values. Using the same nonce for two different messages encrypted with the same key destroys the security properties of this mode.

3.   The message (payload) consisting of a string of p octets where $0 <= p < 2^{8q}$. The length restriction ensures that P can be encoded in a field of q octets.

4.   Additional authenticated data a consisting of a string of a octets. This additional data is authenticated, but not encrypted, and is not included in the output of this mode. It can be used to authenticate plaintext packet headers, or contextual information that affects the interpretation of the message. Users who do not wish to authenticate additional data can provide a string of length zero.

CBC-MAC Authentication

The following are the prerequisites for the authentication and encryption process of CCM: block cipher algorithm, key K, counter generation function, formatting function, and MAC

Figure 14-11. CBC-MAC

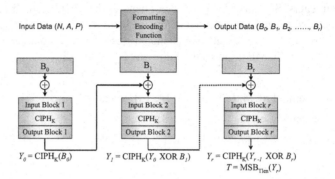

length *Tlen*. The following are the inputs: valid nonce *N*, valid payload *P* of length *Plen* bits, and a valid associated data *A*.

Steps:

1. Apply the formatting function to (N, A, P) to produce the blocks $B_0, B_1, ..., B_r$.
2. Set $Y_0 = CIPH_K(B_0)$
3. For $i = 1$ to r, do $Y_i = CIPH_K(B_i \oplus Y_{i-1})$
4. Set $T = MSBNT_{Tlen}(Y_r)$

where

- r = The number of blocks in the formatted input data (N, A, P)
- Y_r = The CBC-MAC result
- $MSBs(X)$ = The bit string consisting of the *s* left-most bits of the bit string X
- T = The MAC that is generated as an internal variable in the CCM processes
- $Tlen$ = The bit length of the MAC

Counter (CTR) Mode Encryption

1. Apply the counter generation function to generate the counter blocks $Ctr_0, Ctr_1, ..., Ctr_m$, where $m = \lceil Plen / 128 \rceil$
2. For $j = 0$ to m, do $S_j = CIPH_k(Ctr_j)$
3. Set $S = S1 \| S2 \| ... \| Sm$.
4. Return $C = (P \oplus MSB_{Plen}(S) \| T \oplus MSB_{Tlen}(S_0)$

Figure 14-12. Counter (CTR) mode encryption

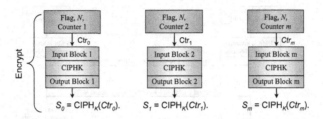

The first portion of *C* is the ciphertext of the payload and the second part is the authentication.

If the block cipher behaves as a pseudorandom permutation, by encrypting *T*, CBC-MAC collision attacks are avoided because the attacker doesn't get information about the CBC-MAC results.

CCM was designed for use in a packet network, and the authentication process requires the message length to be known at the beginning of the operation. This is not a problem because in almost all environments, message or packet lengths are known in advance. It is possible to compute the message authentication code and perform encryption in a single pass because authentication doesn't have to be completed before encryption can begin. The encryption key stream can be pre-computed, but authentication cannot.

Keys and Key Distribution in 802.11i

IEEE 802.11.i (2004) defines two key hierarchies: (1) pairwise key hierarchy, to protect unicast traffic and (2) group key hierarchy, consisting of a single key to protect multicast and broadcast traffic. The pairwise key can be used in TKIP or CCMP, so in a mixed environment, an AP may simultaneously communicate with some stations using TKIP or CCMP.

The client and access server (Radius) perform authentication using the EAP, via 802.1X, to agree on a 256-bit secret key called the *pairwise master key*.

The 4-way handshake protocol consists of the following steps:

- The authenticator sends message 1 to the supplicant at the end of a successful IEEE 802.1X PMK exchange, or when a station requests a new key. The message includes an ANonce, as well as a key description version (RC4 encryption with HMAC-MD5 or AES key wrap with HMAC-SHA1-128) and key data, the PMKID for the PMK being used during this exchange.
- On reception of message 1, the supplicant generates a new nonce, SNonce, and derives the PTK from ANonce and SNonce.
- The supplicant prepares and sends message 2. Message 2 includes the SNonce, the same key description selected by the authenticator, and key data information with the authentication and cipher suite enabled by the supplicant's policy. In other words, the

Figure 14-13. 4-way handshake protocol

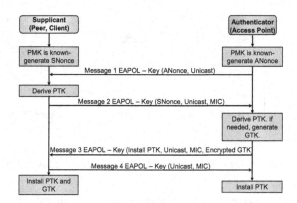

message contains the authentication and cipher suite that the station is proposing or supports. The message also includes the message integrity code.

- Upon reception of message 2, the authenticator derives the PTK, verifies message 2's integrity (MIC), and then, if needed, derives GTK. Finally, it prepares and sends message 3.

- The authenticator sends message 3, which includes the ANonce. In the key data field, the authentication and cipher suite selected by the authenticator are included, as well as the MIC, and an indication of whether or not to install the temporal keys, and the encapsulated GTK.

- When message 3 is received, the supplicant (1) verifies that the ANonce value in message 3 is the same as the ANonce value in message 1; (2) checks that the authentication and cipher suite sent by the access point are the same as the one sent in message 2; (3) verifies the MIC; (4) confirms that temporal keys are installed; and (5) prepares and sends message 4.

- Upon reception of message 4, the authenticator verifies the MIC.

Pairwise Hierarchy

The pairwise master key is used to generate a pairwise transient key (PTK) and the PTK is partitioned to create three types of keys.

The pairwise key hierarchy utilizes a pseudorandom function to expand the PMK to a 384-bit or a 512-bit PTK using a pseudorandom function. TKIP uses 512-bits and CCMP uses 384-bits. The PTK is partitioned into several keys:

- The key confirmation key (KCK) is used by IEEE 802.1X to provide data origin authenticity in the 4-way handshake and group key handshake messages; it consists of the first 128 bits (bits 0–127) of the PTK.

Figure 14-14. Pairwise hierarchy

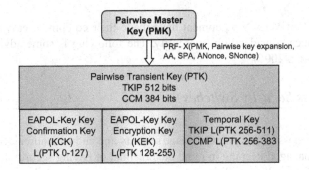

- The key encryption key (KEK) is used by the EAPOL-Key frames to provide confidentiality in the 4-way handshake and group key handshake messages; it consists of bits 128–255 of the PTK.

- Temporal keys are used by the station and consist of bits 256–383 (for CCMP) or bits 256–511 (for TKIP).

All these keys are used to protect unicast communications between the authenticator's and supplicant's respective stations. PTKs are used between a single supplicant and a single authenticator.

Group Hierarchy

The group key hierarchy utilizes a pseudorandom function to expand the GMK to a 128-bit or a 256-bit group temporary key (GTK). TKIP uses 256-bits and CCMP uses 128-bits. The GTK is partitioned into temporal keys to protect broadcast/multicast communication. The temporal key could have a length of 40, 104, 128, or 256 bits. GTKs are used between a single authenticator and all supplicants authenticated by that authenticator.

Figure 14-15. Group hierarchy

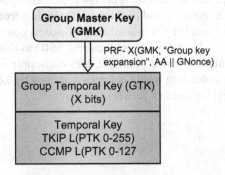

Securing WLAN

Manufacturers of WLAN equipment have made their equipment easy to set up without giving too much consideration to security. The following is some advice for securing a WLAN (Shinder, 2005).

Use Wireless Security Switches

Intelligent wireless access points manage security and authentication locally, and each one needs to be managed keeping in mind the potential of having security holes. It is not that complicated for small or medium business IT managers to set up three to ten access points. However, when companies install, for example 50 access points, IT managers need central-ized AP-management tools.

Wireless security switches remove the authentication and confidentiality management from the access points and place them in the switch. Wireless security switches use technologies such as WPA, access port control (802.1X), RADIUS servers, and Kerberos to effectively provide reliable security to a wireless network and to manage all WLAN air-based traffic. Access points become like simple radios that connect to the WLAN switch at layer 2 or layer 3.

Use Strong Encryption

WLAN equipment that supports the IEEE802.1i Enterprise mode and that uses AES encryption should be chosen for strong encryption. Equipment that supports this mode is labeled WPA2.

Turn Off SSID Broadcasting

The service set identifier is a 32-character unique identifier attached to the header of packets that identify one WLAN from another. A station should not be permitted to connect to the access point unless it can provide its unique SSID. The problem is that, by default, most WAPs broadcast the SSID, making it easy for users to find the network since it shows up on their wireless client computers. If the SSID were not broadcasted, users would have to discover the SSID to be able to connect, and then the SSID would become a type of password. The SSID is different from one WLAN to another, so all access points and all devices attempting to connect to a specific WLAN must use the same SSID as that WLAN. Because an SSID can be sniffed in plaintext from a packet, it does not supply any security to the network. Turning off SSID broadcasting would not deter a serious hacker, but it would deter casual users who try to piggyback onto a network.

Change the Default Administrative Password and SSID

With wireless equipment, as well as with routers and switches, most manufacturers use the same administrative password for all equipment in the same family. Those default passwords are well known, and hackers can use those passwords to have access-to-access points, routers, or switches, and to change the device settings. It is the same with SSID; manufacturers use the same SSID name for all wireless equipment. Therefore, the first things that should be changed after purchasing said equipment are the administrative passwords and the SSID name.

Turn Off the System

One of the advantages of a broadband connection is the all-time-connection. It is not necessary to dial up a connection every time a connection to the network is required. However, security advisors emphasize that to improve security, computers should be turned off when not in use. The same applies to a wireless network. If possible, the access point or wireless switch should be turned off when not in use, for example, at night or during the weekend, when there is no need for anyone to connect to the network.

Use MAC Filtering

With some access points, it is possible to use MAC address filtering. Therefore, it is possible to set up a list of computer MAC addresses that can have access to the access point. It is possible for a hacker to spoof a MAC address, but then there is an access control that stops the piggybacker.

Control the Wireless Signal Output

Manufacturers sell special high-gain antennas to extend the range of an access point. A typical 802.11b/g WAP has a range of 300 feet and now, 802.11n MIMO technology may double or triple that range. However, extending the range of an access point exposes the wireless networks to hackers. If possible, a directional antenna should be used instead of an omnidirectional, and the signal strength should be adjusted to reduce the range.

Use VPN

VPNs should be used to provide end-to-end security instead of securing only the air portion of the wireless connection. Connecting to the corporate network using VPN ensures that the session between the PC and the server is encrypted.

Use WLAN Audits

Unauthorized rogue access points can present a significant security threat. NetStumbler is a tool that can be used to find out if there are rogue access points connected to the network. Some wireless switches identify, classify and map the location of rogue APs, and then send an alarm to the administrator. They may even be designed to initiate attacks to contain the threat from rogue access points. Similarly, they may identify jamming flooding, as well as an RF-based DOS type of attack, and then map the location of the originating source.

Bluetooth

Bluetooth™ is an open standard conceived as a low-cost, low-profile, low-power, short-range radio technology. It was designed to create small wireless networks to replace cables for interconnecting devices such as wireless headsets, printers, and keyboards. Bluetooth can be used to enhance wireless connectivity by connecting almost any device to any other device; it could ultimately eliminate wires and cables between both stationary and mobile devices and between personal devices.

According to the Bluetooth Specification, an ad hoc network is a network typically created in a spontaneous manner. An ad hoc network requires no formal infrastructure and is limited in temporal and spatial extent. Devices in an ad hoc networks move in an unpredictable fashion; they are configured on the fly and maintain random dynamic network topology. They also control the network configuration, maintain and share resources, and rely on a master-slave system. When combined with other technologies, ad hoc networks can have access to a network or to the Internet. An example would be a computer using a mobile phone to access the Internet. Bluetooth networks are ad hoc networks.

Bluetooth ad hoc networks are established on a temporary and random basis. A Bluetooth network, called a *piconet*, consists of up to eight Bluetooth devices; it sets up a master-slave relationship with one device designated as master and the rest as slaves. Although only one device may perform as the master for each network, a slave in one network can act as the master for other networks, thus creating a chain of piconets referred to as a *scatter-net*.

In a Bluetooth network, the master of the piconet controls the changing network topologies. It also controls the flow of data between devices that are capable of supporting direct links to each other. As devices move about in an unpredictable fashion, these networks must be

Table 14-3. Power classes

Power Class	Maximum Output Power	Minimum Output Power	Range
1	100 mW	1 mW	Up to 300 feet
2	2.5 mW	1 mW	Up to 30 feet
3	1 mW	N/A	Less than 30 feet

reconfigured on the fly to handle the dynamic topology. The routing protocol that Bluetooth employs allows the master to establish and maintain these shifting networks.

Bluetooth operates in the 2.4 GHz industrial, scientific, and medical (ISM) nonlicense spectrum. The system uses frequency-hopping spread spectrum (FHSS) transmission. Devices in a piconet use a specific hopping pattern of 79 frequencies in the ISM band that changes frequency about 1,600 times per second. The master device controls and sets up the network's pseudorandom frequency hopping sequence, and the slaves synchronize to the master.

The original architect of Bluetooth was Ericsson Mobile Communications, but in 1998, IBM, Intel, Nokia, and Toshiba formed the Bluetooth SIG, which serves as the governing body for the specification. The latest version of the specification is Bluetooth (2004) Specification Version 2.0. The IEEE formed the 802.15 working group to define standards for wireless PANs. The 802.15.1 standard for WPAN™s is modeled after the Bluetooth specification. Part H of the Bluetooth Specification and Part 3, Section 13 of IEEE 802.15.1 (2005b) describe the encryption, authentication, and key generation schemes used in Bluetooth. Their content is almost the same.

Bluetooth provides three different power levels at the antenna connector of the device. See Table 14-3.

Security in Bluetooth

Bluetooth provides confidentiality and authentication for peer-to-peer communications over short distances. There are four variables used for security: a Bluetooth device address, two secret keys, and a pseudorandom number that is regenerated for each new transaction. The four variables and their bit lengths are shown in Table 14-4.

For authentication, the private user key, also referred to as the *link key*, is derived during initialization, and the private user key for encryption is derived during the authentication process. The random numbers are generated from a pseudorandom number generator and are nonrepeating. Even though the authentication key is used to generate the encrypting key, each is different. Every time encryption is activated, a new encrypting key is generated. The size of the encrypting key is configurable, 8 – 128 bits, to conform to export regulations and the policies of various countries about privacy. The authentication key is more static, so the particular application running in the device decides when to change the key.

Table 14-4. Variables used in authentication and encryption procedures

Variable	Bit Length
Bluetooth device address	48 bits
Private user key (Link Key), Authentication	128 bits
Private user key, encryption configurable length (byte-wise)	8 – 128 bits
Random number	128 bits

Figure 14-16. Key generation

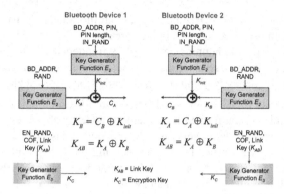

Bluetooth Key Generation

The first generated key is the link key, which must be generated and distributed among the devices during the initialization phase. The initialization, as well as the secret link-key generation, are carried out for each of the two devices that are using authentication and encryption. Several steps are carried out to generate the link key. Those are explained below.

1. Both Bluetooth devices create a 128-bit initialization key, K_{init}, to be used for key exchange during the generation of a link key. K_{init} is generated using Key Generator E_2, Mode 2, and by using as inputs BD_ADDR (Bluetooth device address), a PIN code, the length of the PIN code, and an initialization random number (IN_RAND). The BD_ADDR is the address of the device that receives IN_RAND.

2. Each Bluetooth device creates a 128-bit unit key, K_A and K_B, using key generator E_2, Mode 2. For each, its own BD_ADDR (Bluetooth Device Address) and a random number (RAND) are used as inputs.

3. Each device enciphers its unit key as follows: $C_A = K_A \oplus K_{init}$ and $C_B = K_B \oplus K_{init}$. Then, the devices exchange the enciphered keys (C_A and C_B). After receiving the cipher key, each unit deciphers the other device's unit key as follows: $K_B = C_B \oplus K_{init}$ and $K_A = C_A \oplus K_{init}$. The link key is $K_{AB} = K_A \oplus K_B$. If the devices have memory restrictions, then $K_{AB} = K_A$.

4. Each device creates the ciphering K_c using a Key Generator E_3 and by using as inputs an encryption random number (EN_RAND), the ciphering offset (COF), and the link key, K_{AB}, calculated above.

5. COF is determined in two ways. If the current link is a master key, it is derived from the master address (COF = BD_ADDR || BD_ADDR). Otherwise, COF is equal to the authenticated ciphering offset (ACO), which is calculated during the authentication process. The master generates and distributes EN_RAND to all slaves.

Figure 14-17. Bluetooth authentication

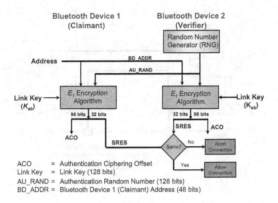

Bluetooth Authentication

The two Bluetooth devices in the authentication process are referred to as the "verifier" and the "claimant." The claimant is the device trying to prove its identity by knowledge of a secret key, the link key, and the verifier is the device that challenges the claimant to authenticate a random input in a challenge-response scheme. The verifier is not required to be the master.

The authentication function E_l uses the encryption function SAFER+ (Massey et al, 1998). The algorithm is an enhanced version of an existing 64-bit block cipher SAFER-SK 128.

The following describes the Bluetooth authentication process:

1. The claimant transmits its 48-bit address (BD_ADDR) to the verifier.

2. The verifier transmits a 128-bit random challenge (AU_RAND) to the claimant.

3. The claimant uses the E_l encryption algorithm to encipher BD_ADDR and AU_RAND, using the link key, K_{ab}, as the key. The verifier carries out the same encryption operation.

4. The claimant returns part of the encryption result, SRES, to the verifier.

5. The verifier compares the SRES from the claimant with its own generated SRES.

6. If both SRESs are the same, then the verifier allows the connection.

The ACO is used as a ciphering offset (COF) to generate the encrypting key K_c. See previous section, "Key Generation."

Figure 14-18. Bluetooth encryption

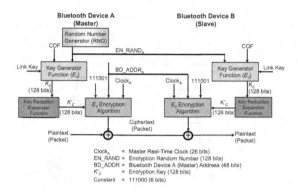

Bluetooth Encryption

In Bluetooth, user information can be protected by enciphering the packets' payload exchanged between two devices, using an encryption algorithm called E_0. The access code and the packet header are not encrypted.

There are three possible modes of confidentiality:

1. No encryption is performed on broadcast or point-to-point traffic.
2. Point-to-point only encryption
3. Point-to-point and broadcast encryption; all messages are encrypted.

The effective length of the encryption key may vary between 8 and 128 bits. The actual key length, K_C, as obtained from E_3, is 128 bits. Therefore, the key length must be reduced to the required length; after reduction, the result is expanded again to 128 bits in order to distribute the starting states more uniformly. The resulting encryption key is called K'_C.

Figure 14-19. Bluetooth encryption engine

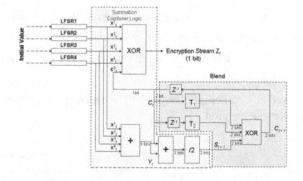

Table 14-5. LFSRs information

L	No. of Registers	Maximum Length	Prime Factorization Numbers	Feedback Taps	Output from Stage
1	25	3.35×10^7	31 • 601 • 1,801	0, 8, 12, 20, 25	24
2	31	2.4×10^9	2,147,483,647	0, 12, 16, 24, 31	24
3	33	8.58×10^9	7 • 23 • 89 • 599,479	0, 4, 24, 28, 33	32
4	39	5.49×10^{11}	7 • 8,191 • 79 • 121,369	0, 4, 28, 36, 39	32

The initial inputs to the encryption algorithm E_0 are the following: the encryption key, K'_c; a 48-bit address (BD_ADDR); the 26 bits of the master real time clock, $CLK_{26\text{-}1}$; a 128-bit random number EN_RAND; and a constant 111001, for a total of 208 bits. Since the $CLK_{26\text{-}1}$ changes with each packet, and even though the other variables remain the same, the encryption algorithms are reinitialized with each packet. A single bit change in any of the inputs produces an independent key stream, thus achieving orthogonality.

Bluetooth Crypto Engine

The Bluetooth encryption algorithm is based on an encryption method proposed by Massey and Rueppel. Massey's method consists of a classic key generator, using several LFSRs with some nonlinear functions operating on the N output sequence to produce the cipher stream. Rueppel's method consists of combining the N output of the LFRS by integer addition, which produces a carry-bit memory; then the output of the LFSR is combined with the carry-bit memory. The combination of both methods is known as the Massey and Rueppel method.

The E_0 Bluetooth crypto engine consists of four linear feedback shift registers of lengths $L_1 = 25$, $L_2 = 31$, $L_3 = 33$, and $L_4 = 39$, with feedback taps on $L_1 = 25$, 20, 12, 8 and 0; $L_2 =$

Figure 14-20. Bluetooth encryption engine initialization

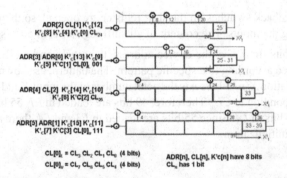

Table 14-6. LFSRs Initialization

L	Number of Stages	Bits Loaded During Initialization	Total Number of Clocks	Clocks with Feedback Closed
1	25	49	55	30
2	31	55	55	24
3	33	49	55	22
4	39	55	55	16

31, 24, 16, 12 and 0; L_3 = 33, 28, 24, 4, and 0; and L_4 = 39, 36, 28, 4, and 0. The output of the LFSRs is taken from positions 24, 24, 32, and 32 for L_1, L_2, L_3, and L_4 respectively. The crypto engine uses the XOR function to mix the output of the LFSRs, integer additions, and table mappings to blend the carry bit. See Figure 14-19.

The output of the encryption stream is obtained from the following equations:

$$S_{t+1} = (S^1_{t+1}, S^0_{t+1}) = \left\lfloor \frac{y_t + c_t}{2} \right\rfloor$$

$$c_{t+1} = (c^1_{t+1}, c^0_{t+1}) = S_{t+1} \oplus T_1 [c_t] \oplus T_2 [c_{t+1}]$$

$$z_t = x^1_t \oplus x^2_t \oplus x^3_t \oplus x^4_t \oplus c^0_t$$

Initialization Process

The initialization process is shown in Table 14-6 and Figure 14-20.

The crypto engine's initialization process is as follows:

1. All feedback switches on the shift register are opened, so there is no feedback when loading the inputs. The content of all shift register elements is set to zero.

2. Input bits from $K'c$, the device address, the clock, and a 6-bit constant 111001 are arranged according to a specific pattern. The pattern, as shown in Figure 14-20, uses the notation $X[n]$ where n is the octet number of the input X and the clock signal CLK_1, corresponding to CL_0. Therefore, 49 bits are loaded in $L1$, 55 bits in $L2$, 49 bits in $L3$, and 55 bits in $L4$. Since 55 bits are loaded in $L3$ and $L4$, there are a total of 55 clocks in the initialization.

Figure 14-21. Bluetooth crypto engine run-up

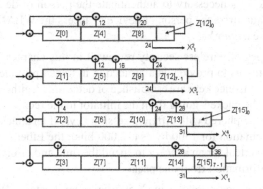

3. Both blend registers, c_{39} and c_{39-1}, are reset to zero, when the LSFR_4 switch is closed at $t = 39$.

Run-Up Process

After the key generator initialization process ends, the crypto engine is run-up to add confusion as follows:

1. The blend register is kept operating and the carry bit C_T is used during run-up.
2. The LFSRs are clocked 200 more times with all switches closed (t = 239).
3. The 200 stream cipher bits that were created are collected.
4. The last 128 of the 200 generated bits are loaded into the LFSRs according to Figure 14-21 at $t = 240$.

From this point on, when clocked, the crypto engine produces a keystream sequence that is bitwise XORed with the transmitted payload data for encryption to create the cipher text. At the receiving end, the same sequence is XORed with the ciphertext to decipher the payload.

The first bit to use for encryption is the one produced at $t = 240$. The crypto engine runs for the entire length of the current payload. Then, before the reverse direction is started, receiving the encrypted payload from the slave, the entire initialization process is repeated with updated values on the input parameters.

Summary

When designing security for any type of network, including wireless, the most important services are the ones already discussed throughout this book, that is, data protection, integrity, network authentication and authorization, and non-repudiation. To effectively secure a wireless network, it is necessary to authenticate the person or device connecting to the wireless network, authorize the person or device to access the WLAN, and protect the data transmitted over the network.

In the different types of wireless security reviewed in this chapter, Wi-Fi, WIMAX, and Bluetooth, the protocols to provide data protection in transit provide an excellent level of security. In all of them, once keys are established or determined, either by pre-shared keys or by key exchanges, the packets going from the initiator to the receiver and from the receiver to the initiator are enciphered with different session keys. If an attacker is able to break the packet, it gets information for 1500 bytes (12,000 bits), the Ethernet's largest packet size. This makes it impractical for an attacker to spend the time and effort that would be needed to break and get information from one packet.

In WIMAX, identity is demonstrated using X.509 digital certificates, in Wi-Fi by knowledge of a shared secret key, and in Bluetooth by the use of a secret key derived during initialization.

Learning Objectives Review

1.   Name four types of wireless technologies.

2.   Which wireless LAN technology offers the longest range?

3.   For better security, purchase WLAN equipment that supports the IEEE802.1i with Temporal Key Integrity Protocol (TKIP), also known as WPA1. (T/F)

4.   MIMO, multiple-input, multiple-output, as used by the 802.11n standard, offers up to 3 times the coverage, and up to eight times the speed, of current 802.11g networks. (T/F)

5.   For better range, purchase IEEE 802.n wireless equipment. (T/F)

6.   The security services offered in IEEE 802.11 are authentication, confidentiality, access control, and secure roaming. (T/F)

7.   TKIP was a temporary software solution to Wired Equivalent Privacy (WEP) flaws. (T/F)

8.   Wi-Fi Protected Access (WPA) replaced the WEP specification. (T/F)

9.   WPA2, 802.11i subset, includes all elements of the WPA standard while replacing RC4 TKIP with AES. (T/F)

10.   In WIMAX, when a connection is established between a subscriber station and a base station, the two need to agree on _____, _____, and _____.

11.   What is a good use for WIMAX technology?

12.   IEEE 802.1x, port-based access control, AEP, AES, and Radius are used in Wi-Fi. (T/F)

13.   In WI-FI, turning off the Service Set Identifier (SSID) broadcast will deter serious hackers. (T/F)

14.   Where is Bluetooth wireless technology used?

15.   What is an ad-hoc network?

16.   What is the range of a Bluetooth device?

17.   The Bluetooth E_0 encryption algorithm used to provide confidentiality is based on the classic key generator using linear feedback shift registers. (T/F)

18.   The SAFER block encryption algorithm is used in Bluetooth as the E_1 encryption function authentication. (T/F)

19.   What are WPA1 and WPA2?

20.   There are two different implementation options to choose from when moving to WPA/WPA2, Personal and Enterprise. What is the difference between them?

References

Arbaugh, W., Shankar, N., & Wan, Y. C. (2001). *Your 802.11 wireless network has no clothes.* College Park, MD: University of Maryland, Department of Computer Science. Retrieved of June 28, 2007, from http://www.drizzle.com/~aboba/IEEE/wireless.pdf

Bluetooth Special Interest Group (SIG). (2004). *Specification of the Bluetooth system V2.1.* Retrieved on June 28, 2007, from https://www.bluetooth.org/spec/

Borisov, N., Goldberg, I., & Wagner, D. (2000). *Security of the WEP algorithm,* (Berkeley report). Berkeley, CA: University of California. Retrieved June 28, 2007, from http://www.isaac.cs.berkeley.edu/isaac/wep-faq.html

Dworkin, M. (2001). *Recommendation for block cipher modes of operation methods and techniques* (NIST Special Publication 800-38A). National Institute of Standard and Technology (NIST). Retrieved June 28, 2007, from http://csrc.nist.gov/publications/nistpubs/800-38a/sp800-38a.pdf

Dworkin, M. (2004). *Recommendation for block cipher modes of operation: The CCM mode for authentication* and confidentiality (NIST Special Publication 800-38C). National Institute of Standard and Technology (NIST). Retrieved June 28, 2007, from http://csrc.nist.gov/publications/nistpubs/800-38C/SP800-38C.pdf

Dworkin, M. (2005). *Recommendation for block cipher modes of operation: The CMAC mode for authentication* (NIST Special Publication 800-38B). National Institute of Standard and Technology (NIST). Retrieved June 28, 2007, from http://csrc.nist.gov/publications/nistpubs/800-38B/SP_800-38B.pdf

Fluhrer, S., Mantin, I., & Shamir, A. (2001, August). *Weaknesses in the key scheduling algorithm of RC4.* Presented at the 8th Annual Workshop Selected areas in Cryptography. Cisco Systems and The Weizmann Institute, Department Computer Science. Retrieved June 28, 2007, from http://www.drizzle.com/~aboba/IEEE/rc4_ksaproc.pdf

Institute of Electrical and Electronic Engineers (IEEE). (2004). *Part 11: Wireless LAN medium access control (MAC) and physical layer (PHY) specifications amendment 6: Medium access control (MAC) security enhancements* (IEEE Standard 802.11i).

Institute of Electrical and Electronic Engineers (IEEE). (2005a). *Part 16: Air interface for fixed and mobile broadband wireless access systems* (IEEE Standard 802.16e).

Institute of Electrical and Electronic Engineers (IEEE). (2005b). *Part 15.1: wireless medium access control (MAC) and physical layer (PHY) specifications for wireless personal area networks (WPANs)* (IEEE Standard 802.15.1).

Karygiannis, T., & Owens, L. (2002). *Wireless network security, 802.11. Bluetooth and handheld devices* (SP800- 48). National Institute of Standard and Technology (NIST). Retrieved June 28, 2007, from http://csrc.nist.gov/publications/nistpubs/800-48/NIST_SP_800-48.pdf

Shinder, D. (2005, September 30). 10 ways to wireless security. *ZDNet*. Retrieved June 28, 2007, from http://news.zdnet.co.uk/security/0,1000000189,39223889,00.htm

Walker, J. (2000). *Unsafe at any key size; An analysis of the WEP encapsulation* (Intel Corporation). Retrieved June 28, 2007, from http://www.dis.org/wl/pdf/unsafe.pdf

Glossary of Terms

A

Access Control: The process of limiting access to the resources of a system only to authorized personnel. Access control provides protection against the unauthorized use of resources. It includes the prevention of the use of a resource in an unauthorized manner by identifying or verifying the eligibility of a station, originator or individual, to access specific categories of information.

Access Control Mechanism: Hardware or software features, operating procedures, management procedures, and various combinations of these designed to detect and prevent unauthorized access to system resources and to permit authorized access in an automated system.

Access Authentication: The act of identifying or verifying the eligibility of a station, originator, or individual to access specific categories of information.

AddRoundKey: In AES, subkey bytes are XORed into each byte of the array.

Advanced Encryption Standard (AES): A block encryption algorithm approved by the National Institute of Standards and Technology (NIST) for use by U.S. government organizations to protect secret and top secret (classified) information. AES itself is unclassified, with publicly disclosed encryption algorithm(s), and is available royalty-free, worldwide. AES could be implemented to support block sizes of 128-bits and key sizes of 128, 192, and 256 bits.

AJ (Antijamming): ECCM techniques such as frequency hopping and spread spectrum transmission.

Algorithm: Sequence of well-defined rules describing the solution to a problem in a finite number of steps.

Asymmetric Encryption: A crypto system that uses a pair of keys, mathematically related but different, to encipher and decipher messages. Messages encoded with either one of the keys can be decoded by the other. It is possible to make one of the keys public; however, the other one must be kept secret (private key). Pohlig Hellman, Schnorr, RSA, ElGamal, and elliptic curve cryptography (ECC) are popular asymmetric crypto systems.

Attack: The act of trying to bypass the security control of a system. An attack may be active, resulting in the alteration of data, or passive, resulting in the release of data. The fact that an attack is made does not necessarily mean that it will succeed. The degree of success depends on the vulnerability of the system or activity and the effectiveness of the existing counter measurements.

Authentication: (1) The security service that verifies the identity of a user, device, or other entity in a computer system or restricted area as a prerequisite for allowing access to resources in a system. Also, it ensures that a message is genuine, and that it came from a specific source. (2) The ability of one entity to determine the identity of another entity.

Authentication Header (AH): Defines the format for IPsec packets that require data origin authentication, connectionless integrity, and anti-replay service only. The AH does not encrypt the data portion of the packet. AH may be applied alone, in combination with the IP Encapsulating Security Payload (ESP), or in a nested fashion through the use of tunnel mode.

Authenticator: In EAP, the entity at one end of a point-to-point LAN segment that enables authentication of the entity attached to the other end of that link, the supplicant.

Authorization: Defines user's privileges once access is granted. It controls or restricts what the user is allowed to do on a network.

Automated Security Monitoring: The use of automated procedures to ensure that security controls are not circumvented.

B

Basic Key: The name of the main crypto variable changed by the user. The time elapsed between changes defines the crypto period. Other names for the Basic Key are the following: crypto variable, primary key, and key variable (AES/DES).

Binding: Process to associate two or more information elements. A certificate binds a public key to its owner. A public key is bound to its private key; they are mathematically related.

Bit: An abbreviation for "binary digit." A bit is the smallest information unit that can be used in an element of electronic storage.

Block Cipher: An encryption algorithm that, in conjunction with cryptographic variables, transforms a plaintext block of x bits into a ciphertext block of x bits. The positive integer x is called the block size. A block cipher cryptosystem can be configured as a block cipher or as a block stream cipher.

Block Cipher Modes of Operation: NIST Special Publication 800-38A recommendation regarding modes of operation to be used with symmetric key block cipher algorithms. Block ciphers can be configured to work in different modes of operation such as electronic code book (ECB), block cipher chaining (CBC), cipher feedback (CFB), output feedback (OFB), and counter (CTR) mode.

Brute Force: A cryptanalysis technique or other kind of attack method involving an exhaustive procedure that tries all possibilities, one-by-one. Brute force cracking programs will attempt to crack the encryption using every key combination no matter how long it takes.

Byte: A sequence of eight bits acting as a unit. A byte represents one of 256 characters.

C

Call Back: A procedure for identifying a remote terminal. In a call back, the host system disconnects the caller and then dials the authorized telephone number of the remote terminal to reestablish the connection.

Certificate: Information provided by an issuing organization, a trusted certificate authority, that identifies the owner of a particular public key. The certificate has a copy of the end-user's public key signed by the certificate authority, the hash value of the end-user's public key, the name of the key's owner, and a digital signature of the certificate authority. X.509 is the most widely used certificate format for PKI.

Certificate Authority: The entity that certifies the owner of a public key by issuing a digital certificate. When a digital certificate is presented to a CA, the CA certifies that the public key in the digital certificate belongs to the entity noted in the digital certificate.

Certificate Revocation List (CRL): List of all certificates that have been revoked by the certificate authority.

Chosen Ciphertext: Cryptanalytical attack where the analyst has a machine with the basic key and can enter any ciphertext he wishes and observe the plaintext or vice versa.

Chosen Plaintext: Cryptanalytical attack where the analyst has the ciphertext and the matching plaintext. Usually the keystream can be deduced.

Cipher: A method of transforming information in order to conceal its meaning. The information to be protected is broken down to the smallest possible element (usually the bit) or into a block and each element or block is enciphered independently.

Cipher Key Expansion: A key expansion routine that generates a key schedule with a total number of sub-keys equal to the required number of rounds. The AES algorithm takes the cipher key, K (128, 192, or 256 bits), and generates 10, 12, or 14 sub-keys for use in each of the rounds.

Cipher Suite: A combination of cipher protocols such as key exchange, symmetric and asymmetric encryption, and message integrity used in a specific protocol or RFC.

Ciphertext: Plaintext that has been enciphered.

Ciphertext Only: Cryptanalytical attack where the analyst has only the ciphertext.

Cipher-Text-Auto-Key (CTAK): A generation technique that uses previously generated cipher as part of an algorithm. It propagates errors and is self-synchronizing.

Cipher System: A cryptographic system in which cryptography is applied to information to transform it in such a way that unauthorized persons cannot understand it.

Cleartext: Information that is transmitted in clear—it is not enciphered.

Code: A cipher method that uses an arbitrary table (code book) to convert, and encode, letters, numbers, or words into different letters, numbers or words.

Code Book: Book that shows code word equivalents. It is similar to a dual language dictionary.

COMSEC (1960s): Communications security which provided protection against disclosure to unauthorized parties when information was transmitted or broadcasted from point-to-point. Security was accomplished by building secure "black boxes" using high-level encryption to protect the information.

COMPUSEC (Late 1970s): Computer security which provided not only protection against unauthorized disclosure of information, but also against new, additional threats, such as the injection of malicious code or the theft of data on magnetic media.

Compromise: The action of inadvertently providing information about secure equipment that would allow a cryptanalyst to partially or fully break a code.

Confidentiality: (1) A security service that protects against unauthorized individuals reading information that is supposed to be kept private. (2) Assurance that information is not made available or disclosed to unauthorized individuals, entities, or processes. Confidentiality is achieved by enciphering the information using encryption algorithms.

Confusion: The process of increasing the strength of a cipher system by making the relationship between the key and the ciphertext as complex as possible.

Congruence Arithmetic: A form of arithmetic in which only the remainder after division by a specific integer is used. If a is divided by p with a remainder b, $a = (k \cdot p) + b$, it is possible to say that a is congruent to b, modulo p.

Cost-Risk Analysis: The assessment of the cost of providing information security (protection) for an organization or a system versus the cost of losing or compromising information.

Cryptanalysis: The science of reading secret writing (cipher) without the benefit of a key.

Crypto Algorithm: A well-defined procedure or sequence of rules or steps used to produce a key stream or ciphertext from plaintext and vice versa.

Cryptography: The techniques of concealing a message by means of various transformations using either a code or a cipher.

Cryptology: The scientific study of all aspects of cryptography and cryptanalysis.

Cryptogram: Clear information that has been enciphered. Same as ciphertext.

Crypto Security: The security or protection resulting from the proper use of technically sound cryptosystems.

Cryptographic Variables: Any of the randomly generated variables that the user can frequently change to control the operation of the cipher algorithm that enciphers or deciphers information. The crypto variables are loaded into the crypto system to change its output. The size of a crypto variable is measured in bits. See also Key.

Crypto Period: Time period between changing the key.

Cryptography: The science of secret writing or the design of encryption devices.

Cryptology: The science of secret or hidden writing. Encompasses cryptography and cryptanalysis.

D

Data: (1) Information in the widest possible sense. (2) Generic name for information that is entered into a computer or information that is coming from a computer.

Data Encryption Standard (DES): An encryption algorithm approved in 1977 by the National Institute of Standards and Technology. It enciphers a 64-bit block of plaintext into a 64-bit block of ciphertext, under the control of a 64-bit crypto variable, where 56 bits make up the key and 8 bits are used for parity. It uses transposition and substitution and has 16 separate rounds of encipherment. Each round involves operations with a different 48-bit key developed from the original 64-bit cryptographic key. DES is no longer considered a strong encryption algorithm due to advances in large-scale attacks. 3DES and AES are generally preferred.

Data Security: The protection of data from unauthorized (accidental or intentional) modification, destruction, or disclosure.

Decipher: The process of translating the ciphertext back to intelligible information by means of a cipher system. Also, decrypt.

Diffusion: Transformations that increase the strength of a cipher system by dissipating the statistical properties of the plaintext across the ciphertext. Patterns in the plaintext do not appear in the ciphertext.

Digital Signature: The electronic equivalent of a signature on a message. A digital signature is created by taking the message's hash and encrypting it with the sender's private key. The ElGamal digital signature signs the message and not the message's hash as RSA and the Digital Signature Algorithm do. A digital signature must be a function of the documents it signs. Digital signatures provide authentication, non-repudiation, and integrity.

Digital Signature Standard (DSS): A standard for digital signing approved by the National Institute of Standards and Technology. It includes the Digital Signature Algorithm (DSA), RSA algorithm (MD5 and RSA public key), and Elliptic Curve DSA.

Diffie-Hellman: A key agreement algorithm based on the finite field discrete logarithm problem that is used by two entities that want to establish secure communications by exchanging only non-secret numbers using a non-secure channel like the Internet.

Double Domain: Logical and physical division of a machine into two parts: (1) "Red" domain where the sensitive plaintext and the crypto variables are located and (2) "Black" domain where the cipher (secure) is located.

Downline Indexing: A technique where the index of a key setting is transmitted downline to a receiving crypto unit and then used to select the operational key.

E

Electromagnetic Interference (EMI): Includes electromagnetic conduction, radiation, and RF susceptibility. Examples are MIL-STD-461 and MIL- STD-462 test EMI.

Elliptic Curve Cryptography (ECC): (1) An encryption system that uses the properties of elliptic curves and provides the same functionality of other public key cryptosystems such as encryption, key agreement, and digital signature; (2) A public key crypto system that provides bit-by-bit key size, the highest strength of any cryptosystem known today.

Elliptic Curve Domain Parameters: The parameters that two parties who are going to use elliptic curve cryptography need to share. The elliptic curve domain parameters determine the arithmetic operations involved in the public-key cryptographic schemes, F_p and F_2^m. The domain consists of six parameters which are calculated differently for F_p and F_2^m, and which precisely specify an elliptic curve and base point. The six domain parameters are the following: $T = (q; FR; a, b; G; n; h)$. The EC domain parameters may be public; the security of the system does not rely on these parameters being secret.

Emission Security: The protection resulting from all measures taken to deny unauthorized persons information of value that might be derived from interception and from an analysis of compromising emanations from systems.

Encapsulation Security Protocol (EAP): In IPsec, ESP provides the same security services that AH provides (data origin authentication, connectionless integrity, and anti-replay service), plus it also provides traffic flow confidentiality (encryption).

Encipher: The transformation of data from an intelligible form (plaintext) into an unintelligible form (ciphertext) to provide confidentiality by means of a cipher system. Also called Encryption.

Encryption Algorithm: Set of rules implemented in software or hardware and used in conjunction with the cryptographic variables to encipher plaintext and decipher ciphertext.

End-to-End Encryption: The protection of information passed in a telecommunications system by cryptographic means, from point of origin to point of destination.

Enemy: A convention used to refer to any individual or organization that tries to obtain confidential information from another individual or organization.

Entropy: In cryptography the measure of the key space. It is calculated using an approximation of the Shannon Information Entropy Formula. The entropy of a crypto system is equal to base two logarithm of the number of keys. AES key is 128 bits, the key space is 2128, and the entropy is 128. It is harder to break AES with an entropy of 128 than to break DES, which has an entropy of 56.

Error Propagation: Noise in the communication link that may produce errors in the ciphertext which, when deciphered, results in errors in the plaintext.

Euler's Theorem: If p is prime and a is not divisible by p (a and p are relatively prime, they have no common factor other than 1 and -1), then, $a^{\varphi(p)} = 1 \bmod p$, where $\varphi(p)$ is the Euler totien function, which is equal to the number of integers relatively prime to p in the range $1 \ldots (p - 1)$.

Exhaustive Search: Finding the key used to encipher a message by trying all the possible keys. Also called brute force attack.

Extended Key: Internal variable chosen by the user to adapt a key generator to the customer's needs. This variable is usually a permuting plug or program change. Other names for the extended key are the following: family key, ignition key, and secondary key.

Extensible Authentication Protocol (EAP): Originally created for use with PPP, it has since been adopted for use with IEEE 802.1X "Port-Based Network Access Control." EAP supports authentication mechanisms such as smart cards, Kerberos, digital certificates, one-time-passwords, and others. Authentication mechanisms are implemented in a number of ways called EAP methods, for example, EAP-TLS, EAP-TTLS, EAP-PEAP, and so forth. EAP is extensible because any authentication mechanism can be encapsulated within EAP messages. EAP allows the deployment of new protocols between the supplicant and the authentication server. The encapsulation technique used to carry EAP packets between peer and authenticator in a LAN environment is known as EAP over LANs, or EAPOL.

F

Fermat's Theorem: If p is prime and a is not divisible by p (a and p are relatively prime, they have no common factor other than 1 and -1), then, $a^{(p-1)} = 1 \bmod p$.

File Security: The means by which access to computer files is limited to authorized users only.

Finite Fields: A setting in which the usual mathematical operations (addition, subtraction, multiplication, and division by nonzero quantities) are possible; these operations also follow the usual commutative, associative, and distributive laws. Real numbers, rational numbers (fractions), and complex numbers are elements of infinite fields. Finite fields are fields that are finite. Discrete logarithm cryptography (DLC), which includes finite field cryptography (FFC) and elliptic curve cryptography (ECC), requires that the public and private key pairs be generated within a finite field.

Front-end Security: A security filter, which could be implemented in hardware or software, that is logically separated from the remainder of the system to protect the system's integrity.

H

Hash Function: Used to prove that the transmitted or stored data was not altered. A hash function H takes an input message m and transforms it to produce a hash value h that is a function of the message: $h = H(m)$. The input is a variable string and the output is a fixed-size string. The hash value is also called a message digest or a "fingerprint" of the message because there is a very low probability that two messages will produce the same hash value. Hash functions are hard to invert. Given the hash value, it is computationally infeasible to find the initial value m.

I

IEEE 802.1X: A data link layer transport protocol that defines port-access control standards for wireless and physical networks. Port access refers to "user port" access controlled by a wireless access point or wired switch. Users do not get IP-connectivity until they have successfully authenticated.

Information Assurance (IA Late 1990s): Deals with providing protection against unauthorized disclosure of information (confidentiality), modification of information (integrity), denial of service (availability), authenticity, and non-repudiation. Because the term "security" has been so closely associated with providing confidentiality for information, NSA and the Department of Defense adopted the term "Information Assurance" to encompass the five security services of confidentiality, integrity, availability, authenticity, and non-repudiation.

INFOSEC (Early 1980s): Information security was the result of the convergence of COMSEC and COMPUSEC.

Initialization Vector: An additional key that changes with every message, block, or IP packet. The initialization vector doesn't need to be secret, but it should not be used twice with the same key. In block ciphers, the initialization vector could be XORed with the first plaintext block, as is done in the cipher block chaining (CBC) mode, or used as a dummy plaintext in the cipher feedback (CFB) mode, output feedback (OFB) mode, and counter (CTR) mode.

Integrity: (1) The security service that ensures that data is not altered when transmitted from source to destination, or when it is stored. Assurance that data was not accidentally or deliberately modified in transit by replacement, insertion, or deletion. (2) The process of preventing undetected alteration of data. Message Digest 5 (MD5), Secure Hash Standard (SHA-1, SHA-256, SHA-384, and SHA-512), Message Authentication Codes (MACs), and the Keyed-Hash Message Authentication Code (HMAC) are mechanisms that check the integrity of a message.

Internal Security Controls: Hardware, firmware, and software features within a system that restrict access to resources (hardware, software, and data) to authorized subjects only (persons, programs, or devices).

Internet Key Exchange (IKE): Defines payloads for exchanging key generation and authentication data, thus providing a consistent framework for transferring key and authentication data independent of the key generation technique, encryption algorithm, or authentication mechanism used in IPsec.

IPsec: (1) A suite of security protocols standardized by the Internet Engineering Task Force (IETF) that addresses data privacy, integrity, authentication, and key management, as well as tunneling to TCP/IP networks. (2) A secure architecture that supports several applications that encrypt and/or authenticate all traffic at the IP level.

K

Key-Auto-Key (KAK): A key generation technique that uses the previously generated key as part of the algorithm. It does not usually propagate errors and is not self-synchronizing.

Kerberos: An Internet security standard protocol, RFC 4120, based on a trusted third-party authentication to offer authentication services to users and servers in an open distributed environment. Kerberos relies on secret-key symmetric ciphers for encryption and authentication and does not use public-key encryption; therefore, it does not produce digital signatures or authentication of authorship of documents. The authentication requires trust in a third party (the Kerberos server), so if the server is compromised, the integrity of the whole system is lost. Kerberos Version 4 uses DES and Version 5 uses any encryption algorithm; in Version 5, DES has to be used in the CBC mode. The Kerberos Authentication Server (KAS) keeps a database with the names of all the users and their secret keys.

Key: A parameter that controls the encryption and decryption operation of an encrypting algorithm, making the encryption and decryption processes completely defined and usable only to those having that key. Keys should be random or pseudorandom and they are measured in bits.

Key Agreement: In key management, a public-key protocol used by two parties to agree on a shared secret key. Normally, the shared secret key is not used as a key, but instead, is used to arrive at key material. Diffie-Hellman is used for key agreement.

Key-Encrypting-Key: In key management, a key used to encipher encrypting and decrypting keys. See Key-Transport.

Keyed-Hash Message Authentication Code (HMAC): Mechanism for message authentication using cryptographic hash functions in combination with a shared secret key.

Keystream: Pseudorandom stream of bits used by the ciphering algorithm to combine with the plaintext to form the ciphertext.

Keystream Generator: Device that produces the keystream. See Key Generator.

Key Diversity: The total number of bits of all key variables.

Key Generator: Device that generates an extremely long pseudorandom key-stream. The keystream bits are used by the ciphering algorithm to produce a ciphertext from a cleartext. Also called keystream generator.

Key Index: A system used to inform the receiving crypto unit which key variable was used to encipher a message or a communication session rather than transmitting the key variable itself.

Key Injector: An electronic device used to store key variables for distribution and loading into cryptographic equipment. Also called keyfill or keygun.

Key List Generator: Device that uses a random source to generate and create the list of keys.

Key Management: (1) The control and management of cryptographic resources such as equipment, manuals and personnel. (2) The system and equipment used to generate, distribute, load, and destroy crypto variables.

Key Transport: The process of encrypting a key variable with a key-encrypting-key and transmitting it to another cipher unit. In this case, the key variable itself rather than the index is transmitted.

Key Space: The number of different keys available, normally described in terms of bits. For example, AES key is 128 bits. For the same plaintext, a cipher algorithm is able to produce n different ciphertexts, one for each different key.

L

Linear Feedback Shift Register (LFSR): A shift register with a modulo-2 adder (XOR) and a feedback line. The Shift Register Sequence refers to the output, which is normally from the last stage, but it can be from any stage. GSM and Bluetooth encryption use non-linear feedback shift registers.

Linear Recursion: A theoretical register with a linear feedback equivalent that exactly simulates a key generator.

Logic Bomb: A resident computer program that triggers the perpetration of an unauthorized act when particular states of the system are realized.

M

MD5: A secure hashing function from RSA that converts an arbitrarily long data stream into a digest-fixed size of 128 bits.

Message Authentication Code (MAC): (1) A security mechanism that provides integrity checks based on a secret key. Typically, message authentication codes are used between two parties who share a secret key in order to authenticate information transmitted between those parties. (2) A key-dependent one-way hash function. One popular way to construct a MAC algorithm is to use a block cipher in the cipher-block-chaining (CBC) mode of operation with the IV =0.

Message Key: Automatically generated key variable for each message or transmission. Other names for the message key are the following: message indicator, modifier key, and initialization vector.

MixColumn: In AES, every column in the State Array is transformed using a matrix multiplication for inter-byte diffusion within columns (linear mixing). In the last round, the column mixing is omitted.

Modular Arithmetic: Part of the arithmetic in which mathematical operations are within the range of numbers specified by the module.

Monoalphabetic Substitution: One alphabetic character is substituted for another. The number of possible substitutions is 26! or 4.0329 x 1026.

N

Need-to-Know: The necessity for access to, knowledge of, or possession of specific information required to carry out official duties.

Non-Repudiation: Repudiation means denial by one of the entities involved in a communication of having participated in all or part of the communication. Non-repudiation refers to protection against an individual denying sending or receiving a message.

O

One-time Tape or Pad: A tape of random numbers used to encipher one and only one message. The tape needs to be sent to the receiver for him to be able to decipher the message.

One-time Password: Any type of authentication system that uses a secret pass-phrase to generate a sequence of one-time (single use) passwords by (1) hashing the secret pass-phrase a number of times equal to a challenge random number chosen by the authentication server; (2) adding to the password the information from a time-synchronization token; (3) generating a new password based on the previous password using a mathematical algorithm. In a one-time password system, the user's secret pass-phrase is never transmitted during authentication or during pass-phrase changes, thus, preventing replay attacks.

One-Way Function: Mathematical process easy to calculate in one direction but extremely difficult to calculate in the opposite way.

Order of a Point: In elliptic curve cryptography the repeated addition of a point to itself, scalar multiplication, generates a new point, $Q = kP$; however, there will always be a time when adding the point to itself results in $O = kP$, the point at infinity. The order of a point P is the smallest positive number k such that $kP = O$. If the order of a point is the maximum, then it is called the curve order.

P

Password: A prearranged identifier that the user possesses, such as words, special coded phrases, personal identification numbers (PINs), etc., that is used to authenticate an identity. When writing a password policy, organizations should consider the following: (1) How the password will be selected; (2) How often the password will be changed; (3) How long the password will be used; and, (4) How the system will handle (transmit) the password

Perfect Crypto System: From the theoretical point of view, the only system that is unbreakable is the one in which the keystream is totally random, infinitely long, and used only one time. A perfect crypto system is achieved only with Vernam's cipher, the one-time pad, in which the keystream is random, is as long as the message, and is used only one time.

Penetration: The successful act of bypassing the security mechanisms of a system.

Permutation: The different arrangement of a group of things, bits, and so forth.

Permuting Plug: Internal plug of the encryption unit that can be connected in different ways to modify the key generation algorithm.

Polynomial Check Sequence (PCS): Mathematical function calculated as a function of the basic key and annexed to it. The PCS is checked every time a basic key is introduced or transferred from the memory to the crypto system.

Physical Penetration: Access to a sensitive area by a hostile individual resulting in the loss of classified material.

Physical Security: The applications of physical barriers and control procedures as preventive measures or countermeasures against threats to resources and sensitive information.

Plaintext: Information to be enciphered, or ciphertext that has been deciphered to intelligible information (it can be read).

Polyalphabetic: Character substitution for each of the characters according to a key word, phrase, or stream.

Pre-Shared Secret Keys: In key management, a way to send information about the secret key needed to decipher a message. The secret keys are loaded into both parties' crypto systems beforehand, and it is only necessary to verify which of the secret keys was used to encipher the message. In general, every loaded secret key is associated with a name; therefore, only the name associated with the key needs to be sent to the recipient.

Pretty Good Privacy (PGP): A crypto system developed by Phil Zimmermann that uses data compression and symmetric and public key cryptography. PGP is used to encipher and authenticate email and for disk encryption, data at rest, and instant messaging.

Private Key: One of the two mathematically related keys that is kept secret.

Prime Numbers: A prime number is a natural number that is only divisible by ± 1 and $\pm$ the integer itself. Prime numbers are the basis of public key crypto systems such as RSA and key exchange algorithms such as Diffie-Hellman. Primes of the form $2^n - 1$ are known as Mersenne primes. If $2^n - 1$ is prime, then n is prime, but the converse, if n is a prime, then $2^n - 1$ is not always a prime number.

Pseudorandom Sequence of Digits: A sequence of digits produced from a key generator that appears to be random and passes all the statistical tests for randomness. There is no obvious connection between digits but, in fact, it is possible to reproduce the sequence using the same key variable.

Public-Key Cryptography: An asymmetric encryption method that uses a pair of mathematically related keys, one public and one private. Messages encoded with either one can be decoded by the other. Algorithms are used to prove the authenticity of the message originator and to exchange keys. Discrete logarithm systems such as exponentiation ciphers (RSA), ElGamal public-key encryption, digital signature algorithm (DSA), Diffie-Hellman key agreement, and elliptic curve cryptography are examples of public-key cryptography.

Public Key: One of the two mathematically related keys that is made public.

Public-Key Infrastructure (PKI): A mechanism for (1) establishing trust according to a defined trust model; (2) making entities uniquely identifiable within a domain; (3) distributing information regarding the validity of the binding between a particular key pair and an entity. PKI is about managing certificates and keys during their complete life cycles.

R

RADIX-64: An encoding technique used to convert 6 bits of ciphertext to 8-bit printable ASCII characters for e-mail format compatibility. RADIX-64 is used in PGP, the Internet Privacy-Enhanced Mail (PEM) format, and in the Internet MIME format.

Residual Risk: The portion of risk that remains after security measures have been applied.

Risk: The probability that a particular threat will exploit a particular vulnerability of a system or organization.

Risk Analysis: The process of identifying security risks, determining their magnitude, and identifying areas needing safeguards. Risk analysis is a part of risk management.

Risk Management: The total process of identifying, controlling, and eliminating or minimizing uncertain events that may affect system resources. It includes risk analysis, cost benefit analysis, selection, implementation and testing, security evaluation of safeguards, and overall security review.

S

S-Box: A bit substitution operation using a table of equivalences.

Secret Key: The keys or crypto variables used in a symmetric encryption algorithm.

Secure Hash Signature Standard (SHS): Hash algorithms approved by the National Institute of Standards (NIST). It consists of SHA-1, SHA-256, SHA-384, and SHA-512. The SHA is required for use with the Digital Signature Algorithm (DSA), as specified in the Digital Signature Standard (DSS), and, also, whenever a secure hash algorithm is required for federal applications. FIPS PUB 180-2 specifies four secure hash algorithms: SHA-1, SHA-256, SHA-384, and SHA-512. The message digests range in length from 160 to 512 bits, depending on the algorithm.

Secure Socket Layer (SSL): SSL protocol used to secure a client-server communication over the Internet, and they negotiate and provide the essential functions of a secure transaction: mutual authentication, data encryption, and data integrity. See Transport Layer Security (TLS).

Security Association (SA): In IPsec, the security parameters agreed upon between a sender and a receiver, and hosts or gateways on how to secure a communication. When a connection is established between a source and its destination, the two need to agree on, among other things, the encryption and authentication algorithms, the crypto keys, the key sizes, key lifetimes, how to exchange keys, the initialization values, and other related security parameters. The security parameters for that specific connection are stored in an SA and a Security Parameter Index is assigned to and stored in a database, the Security Policy Database. At the database, the source and destination IP addresses are added to the SA.

Security Council: A senior body established to provide top-level policy guidance for telecommunications security and the automated information system security activities of an organization. It provides initial objectives, policies, and organizational structures to guide the conduct of activities toward safeguarding sensitive information. It also establishes mechanisms for policy development and assigns implementation responsibilities. In private organizations, the IT Security Department or hired security consultants establish the security objectives and policies of the company.

Security Features: The security-relevant functions, mechanisms, and characteristics of system hardware and software. Security features are a subset of system safeguards.

Security Flaw: An error of commission or omission in a system that may allow protection mechanisms to be bypassed.

Security Label: The combination of a hierarchical classification and a set of nonhierarchical categories that represent the security of the information.

Security Officer: The person responsible for ensuring that security is provided for and implemented throughout the life cycle of a crypto network from the beginning of the concept's development plan through its design, operation, maintenance, and secure disposal.

Security Policy: The set of laws, rules, and practices that regulates how an organization manages, protects, and distributes sensitive information.

Sensitive Information: Any information for which the loss, misuse, modification of, or unauthorized access to, could affect the interest or the conduct of a government or organization.

Sensitivity Label: A piece of information that represents the sensitivity level of an object. Sensitivity labels are used as the basis for mandatory access control decisions.

Services Description Language (WSDL): Provides a description of what information is available at the Web service, and the procedures for how to get the information needed from the database.

Session Key: A crypto variable (key) used only for a relatively limited time, for example, during a telephone conversation. The session key is enciphered before it is sent to the receiver. See Key Transport.

ShiftRow: In AES, m bits of the State Array row are moved from the left to the right for inter-column diffusion (linear mixing)

Signal Intelligence (SIGINT): Intelligence gained through electronic eavesdropping.

Simple Object Access Protocol (SOAP): A mechanism used to wrap XML information and send it over HTTP.

Single-Failure: Design that avoids the failure of a single protection component of hardware or software that could cause an unnoticed exposure of sensitive information.

Spoofing: (1) An attempt to gain access to a system by posing as an authorized user. (2) The action of imitating the traffic and inserting oneself into the communications link.

Steganography: The art of completely concealing a message; e.g., using invisible ink and microdots.

Stream Cipher: An encryption algorithm that converts a key (crypto variable) into a cryptographically strong keystream, which is then exclusive-ORed, bit-by-bit, with the plaintext.

SubByte: In AES, a non-linear byte substitution using a substitution table S-box, 8 x 8.

Symmetric Encryption: The type of crypto system in which the enciphering and deciphering keys are the same. Stream ciphers and block ciphers (DES, AES) are types of symmetric encryption algorithms.

Substitution Table: Changing a group of bits for another group of bits from a look-up table or S-box.

Super-encipherment: Encryption of an already encrypted message, i.e., double, triple encryption. 3DES-EDC enciphers, deciphers, and enciphers the message using three different keys.

Supplicant: In EAP, it is the entity at one end of a point-to-point LAN segment that is being authenticated by an authenticator attached to the other end of that link.

T

Tampering: An unauthorized modification that alters the proper functioning of equipment or a system in a manner that degrades the security or functionality of the equipment or system.

TEMPEST: The study and control of compromising, spurious electronic signals emitted by electrical equipment.

Threat: Any circumstance or event with the potential to cause harm to a system in the form of destruction, disclosure, modification of information, and/or denial of service.

Threat Analysis: The examination of all actions and events that might adversely affect a system or operation.

Transmissions Security (TRANSEC): Hiding the real transmission of voice or data through techniques such as frequency hopping, spread spectrum, and transmission through information pulses.

Transposition: A cipher that permutes a set of bits or characters. Because it changes the order in which the bits or characters appear, it adds confusion.

Transport and Wrapping Keys: In key management, used to send the secret key needed to decipher a message. The secret key could be transported using public key algorithms or by wrapping the key using symmetric key algorithms. Key transport algorithms are public-key encryption algorithms specifically for encrypting and decrypting keys. Symmetric key wrap algorithms are algorithms specifically for wrapping, enciphering and deciphering symmetric keys. Both parties in a communication need to share a key-encrypting-key that is used to wrap (encipher) the key that is going to be used to encipher the information.

Transport Layer Security (TLS): TLS and SSL (Secure Socket Layer) protocols are used to secure the communication between a client (Web browser) and a server (Web server) over the Internet. TLS and TLS provides the essential functions of a secure transaction: mutual authentication (digital signature), confidentiality (data encryption), and data integrity (hash algorithms). TLS and SSL clients are embedded in Web browsers. TLS is based on SSL 3.0.

Trap Door: A hidden software or hardware mechanism that can be triggered to allow system protection mechanisms to be circumvented. Software developers may introduce trap doors into their codes to enable them to reenter the system and perform certain functions. Synonymous with back door.

Trojan Horse: A computer program with an apparent or actual useful function that contains additional (hidden) functions that surreptitiously exploit the legitimate authorizations of the invoking process to the detriment of security or integrity.

Tunneling: Tunneling allows the encapsulation of one protocol within the packets of a second protocol. IPsec, MPLS, L2TP, and PPP are examples of tunneling protocols.

Two-Factor Authentication: The act of identifying a user by using something the user knows, a PIN or password, and something unique the user possesses, a token.

U

Universal Discovery, Description, and Integration (UDDI): A type of directory in which companies list the Web services that they provide. IBM, Microsoft, and SAP are among the companies that maintain UDDI registries.

User Authentication: Usually based on one or more of the following: (1) What the user knows, something secret only the user knows such as a memorized personal identification number (PIN) or password; (2) What the user has, something unique the user possesses, such as a SecureID card (token generating a one-time password), a smartcard that can perform cryptographic operations on behalf of a user, or a digital certificate; (3) What unique feature (characteristic) the user has such as Biometrics (fingerprints, voiceprint).

V

Vernam Cipher: Cipher based on the one-time mixing of a plaintext with a random keystream using modulo 2 adder, XOR. If the keystreams are different for each message, and if each keystream is used only one time to encipher one message, then the cipher is considered perfect and unbreakable. This cipher system is also called the one-time system.

Vigenere Cipher: Cipher of polyalphabetic substitution in which the key is based on the plaintext or ciphertext.

Virtual Private Network (VPN): Private data communication channels that use a public IP network, i.e., the Internet, as the basic transport for connecting corporate data centers, remote offices, mobile employees, telecommuters, customers, suppliers, and business partners. The public network is used as a wide area communications network, and it offers the appearance, functionality, and usefulness of a dedicated private network.

Virus: A self-propagating Trojan horse composed of a mission component, a trigger component, and a self-propagating component.

Vulnerability: A weakness in a system's security procedures, system design, implementation, internal control, etc., that could be exploited to violate system security policy.

W

Web Services: Allow computers running on different operating platforms to access and share each other's databases by using open standards. They unlock databases and make their information available to other databases, workstations, or kiosks across the Web. Web services provide true application sharing required for server-to-server (S2S) access.

Word: A group of 32 bits that is treated either as a single entity or as an array of four bytes.

Work Factor: An estimate of the effort or time needed by a potential penetrator with specific expertise and resources to overcome a protective measure.

X

X.509: ITU-T recommendation X.509 is part of the X.500 series of recommendations that define a directory service. X.509 is the primary standard for certificates. It specifies not only the format of the certificate, but also the conditions under which certificates are created and used. Two types of authentication are used: simple authentication using passwords and strong authentication using public-key crypto systems. Public key infrastructure (PKI) is based on X.509, Version 3. X.509 is used in S/MIME, IP Security, TLS/SSL and SET.

References

Longley, D., & Shain, M. (1989). *Data & computer security: Dictionary of standard concepts and terms.* Boca Ration, FL: CRC Press, Inc.

Shirey, R. (2000). Internet security glossary (RFC 2828). Internet Engineering Task Force (IETF). Retrieved June 28, 2007, from http://www.ietf.org/rfc/rfc2828.txt?number=2828

Barker, E., Johnson, D., & Smid, M. (2007). Recommendation for pair-wise key establishment schemes using discrete logarithm cryptography (NIST SP 800-56A). National Institute of Standard and Technology (NIST). Retrieved June 28, 2007, from http://csrc.nist.gov/publications/nistpubs/800-56A/SP800-56A_Revision1_Mar08-2007.pdf

Committee on National Security Systems (CNSS) (2003). National information assurance (IA) glossary (CNSS Instruction No. 4009). Retrieved June 28, 2007, from http://www.cnss.gov/Assets/pdf/cnssi_4009.pdf

Cryptomathic. (n.d.). E-Security dictionary. Retrieved June 28, 2007, from http://www.cryptomathic.com/labs/techdict.html

About the Author

Manuel Mogollon has been involved in the field of cryptography since 1981, principally in the areas of encryption algorithms, product development, and academia. At AT&T Datotek, he collaborated with Datotek's chief cryptographer in the development of encryption algorithms based on linear feedback shift registers and public key for several encryptor units.

Mr. Mogollon is co-author of the manuscript, "Statistical Methods for Key Generator Evaluation," a paper written to provide the theoretical background for a series of randomness tests that were implemented in a crypto algorithm diagnostic tool software.

Mr. Mogollon has traveled extensively to many countries around the world, demonstrating from the mathematical point of view, the level of security of the different encryption algorithms used in AT&T Datotek products. He has given crypto seminars in Chile, Colombia, Egypt, Mexico, Spain, and Saudi Arabia.

Currently, Mr. Mogollon is a Nortel Senior Manager and adjunct professor in the Graduate School of Management, Information Assurance, at the University of Dallas, Center of Academic Excellence in Information Assurance Education, where he teaches Cryptography and Network Security.

Education and Training Seminars

- MBA in E-Commerce, University of Dallas, TX
- Bachelor of Science, Electrical Engineering, U.S. Naval Postgraduate School, Monterey, CA.
- Bachelor of Science, Naval Engineering, Colombian Naval Academy, Cartagena, Colombia.
- Six Sigma Green Belt.
- Courses on foundations of information assurance, information security risk mitigation, managing information security, and digital forensics.
- LAN - WAN Internetworking Course.
- Frame relay and ATM technologies course
- Network engineering fundamentals course

Index